Classroom Companion: Business

The Classroom Companion series in Business features foundational and introductory books aimed at students to learn the core concepts, fundamental methods, theories and tools of the subject. The books offer a firm foundation for students preparing to move towards advanced learning. Each book follows a clear didactic structure and presents easy adoption opportunities for lecturers.

Daniel Dan
Thomas Reutterer

Text Analytics in Marketing

A Practical Guide for Students and Researchers

Springer

Daniel Dan
School of Applied Data Science
MODUL University Vienna
Vienna, Austria

Thomas Reutterer
Department of Marketing
Vienna University of Economics
and Business
Vienna, Austria

ISSN 2662-2866 ISSN 2662-2874 (electronic)
Classroom Companion: Business
ISBN 978-3-032-08085-1 ISBN 978-3-032-08086-8 (eBook)
https://doi.org/10.1007/978-3-032-08086-8

This Springer imprint is published by the registered company Springer Nature Switzerland AG
The registered company address is: Gewerbestrasse 11, 6330 Cham, Switzerland

Foreword

Having spent more than ten years studying "the math of talking", as my wife puts it, it is wonderful to see a book with relevant, contemporary computational linguistic examples and concise, clear explanations of code. In fact, it brings many concepts to life, particularly for the R community, which could be argued was left behind in the excitement of TensorFlow and the hype of neural networks in large language models (LLMs). Professors Daniel Dan and Thomas Reutterer are exceptional scholars, bringing applied data science, business and marketing research acumen to bear on the field. Their backgrounds help expand typically dry computer science into meaningful and practical coding workflows which are both intellectually stimulating yet approachable, since each chunk of code has robust explanations.

This book covers many of the foundational natural-language processing methodologies needed to help practitioners stay grounded and understand that other techniques remain relevant and useful even with advances in LLMs. The book takes readers on a stewarded journey, starting with string manipulation and growing the readers' expertise so they can tackle more complex code, including clustering and classification tasks. Professors Dan and Reutterer not only teach many of the core components of language analysis, but also help contextualize them within an evolving and fast-moving environment. I find the book's topics helpful for all who are looking to explore the landscape of unstructured data, students, researchers, and practitioners alike. Each reader, in their own way, will be empowered to add NLP tasks to their skillset at a time in which these methods are in great demand. I fondly remember the first time I was able to apply sentiment analysis, dividing a corpus into positive and negative documents and then building visualizations based on single-token frequency. Despite being a relatively simple task, the output was invigorating and helped me embark on a long learning journey that continues to this day. Likewise, I suspect this book will set many practitioners on a path to growing and applying sophisticated NLP analysis to their respective fields. Overall, this work equips future machine-learning engineers with tools, examples from the field of marketing analytics, and a keen eye for what methods to apply in which context. Thus, it serves as a great instructional guide and also a sound reference work.

I have two "hot takes" for the field of NLP which are addressed in this book. Firstly, despite the excitement and continued expansion of generative AI, particularly LLMs, it is paramount that practitioners understand that frontier models don't solve all NLP tasks. The significant computational overhead, coupled with a lack of explainability, makes LLMs less than ideally suited for some analyses. Admittedly, these models are extremely helpful for a broad range of tasks, but using them can often be overkill. This book serves as a helpful reminder of the many other methods which can be applied, offering improved auditability and repeatability. Secondly, a basic understanding of vector embedding will serve the reader well as they grow their expertise. Embedding represents a technological breakthrough, powering the underlying technology of LLMs and retrieval augmented generation (RAG) workflows, and even shaping interactions in agentic AI systems. The final chapter should not be ignored by the reader! Without this fundamental understanding, practitioners may overestimate the capabilities of LLMs or fall short in leveraging their full potential.

May all readers have an adventurous learning journey following Professor Dan and Professor Reutterer's expertise in this book. I hope each of you experiences your own invigorating NLP moment through the many examples in this book, just as I did.

Ted Kwartler
Harvard Extension School
Faculty of Arts and Sciences
Cambridge, MA, USA
July 22, 2025

Acknowledgements

Thanks to a fruitful and mutually supportive collaboration—sometimes intellectually, sometimes psychologically—this manuscript has finally crossed the finish line.

There are far too many people to thank by name, but a few stood out for their helpful advice, patience, and insightful suggestions. Listed in strictly alphabetical order: Michael Barrowman, Ruggero Bellio, Astrid Dickinger, Sebastian Ferrari, Verena Foppa, Oscar Kjell, Maria Lord, Julian Nobis, Sabine Sedlacek, and Filipe Sengo-Furtado.

To everyone who, during our busiest and most stressful periods, reminded us—gently, or not-so-gently—to finish this book: thank you for your persistence. And to those who insisted we would never finish and should just let the project go: your doubts were oddly motivating. We are grateful to you all.

Any remaining flaws are ours alone.

■■ Competing Interest

The authors have no competing interests to declare that are relevant to the content of this manuscript.

Contents

About the Authors

Daniel Dan
is an Assistant Professor at Modul University Vienna (MU). He is the main founder of the School of Applied Data Science at MU. He has a degree in Computer Science and earned his PhD in Managerial and Actuarial Sciences (curriculum: Statistics and Actuarial Sciences) from the University of Udine, in Italy. He has a keen interest in text-mining methods and sentiment analysis of large text corpora through large language models. His expertise extends to a range of statistical modeling techniques, integrating machine-learning and deep-learning algorithms to address complex problems across different fields. His interests are not confined to these areas alone. He is deeply engaged with the cutting-edge realms of neural networks, transfer learning, and reinforcement learning.

Thomas Reutterer
is Professor of Marketing at the Vienna University of Economics and Business (WU Vienna), where he currently serves as Head of the Institute for Marketing and Customer Analytics, and currently holds the position of Academic Director of WU's PhD Program. His expertise focuses on analyzing, modeling and forecasting customer behavior in data-rich environments. His primary research, teaching and business-consulting interests focus on areas of retail and digital services, customer value and relationship management, and marketing models for customer-base analysis and decision support. In his research projects, Thomas works in interdisciplinary teams and employs advanced statistical, machine-learning methods and AI-enabled tools to provide decision support for various business applications. Ongoing projects include applying generative AI models to content marketing, dynamics in evolving customer-firm relationships, models for customer valuation and target marketing.

Introduction to Text Analytics in Marketing: A Practical Guide for Students and Researchers

D. Dan, T. Reutterer, *Text Analytics in Marketing*, Classroom Companion: Business,
https://doi.org/10.1007/978-3-032-08086-8_1

1

Keywords
Text analytics · Marketing analytics · R · NLP · UGC · Workflows · Reproducibility

This book is intended for a broad audience, ranging from novices to experts in data science and marketing. It serves as a bridge between the two fields, introducing foundational concepts and guiding readers through hands-on examples in R and RStudio, with a focus on applying text analytics to marketing contexts. At its heart is language, and language matters; it is a flow of data: When you take public transportation and hear people chattering, this overlapping of sounds creates an almost indistinct noise, but within it, information is being exchanged between travelers; however, if we focus, it is possible to cut through the "noise" and decipher these messages. Language, however, is especially durable when it is written down and leaves traces. When users express their opinions in writing on the Internet, they generate a huge stream of unstructured data in the form of text, known as user-generated content (UGC). This mass of data is both rich and overwhelming. Selecting, collecting, and analyzing UGC is daunting and requires specific tools. In this book, we will show you how to do this by combining conceptual insights with practical instruction, beginning with the basic terminology using R programming techniques before progressing to real-world text analysis. The goal is to equip readers with the skills needed to tackle similar challenges when dealing with real data.

Obviously, the process of carrying out text analytics requires certain qualities which are universal for anyone who learns: curiosity, patience, and determination. The goal is to extract meaningful insights from several textual sources. This book focuses on practical applications such as analyzing online reviews, extracting key trends, and using text data to inform marketing decisions. But given the right data set, the principles described here can be applied to any scientific field which uses huge volumes of text. The text analysts' work is similar to that of a detective: finding enough evidence to capture insightful information. This work is also a bridge (another one) between disciplines such as linguistics, computer science, mathematics, and statistics.

Marketing is a field in a constant state of change, and in recent years, it has been revolutionized by the ability to analyze text data on a large scale. Textual data can be represented by customer reviews, social media posts, opinions on forums, chats, or survey responses. Understanding these data points can reveal crucial information regarding the relationships between companies or brands and customers, through customer sentiment, preferences, and emerging trends. In this book, the focus on the methods of text analytics is tailored to marketing needs, providing examples and insights drawn from real-world scenarios.

Text mining is important in marketing for several reasons. First, it helps us understand customer feedback, and marketers can use it to analyze customer reviews, feedback, and social media mentions to discern customers' sentiments and preferences. This information can then be used to inform product development, marketing campaigns, and customer service strategies. Second, an important point is to identify trends and insights. Marketers can analyze large amounts of unstructured data to identify emerging trends, pain points, and areas of opportunity. The insights which emerge can inform marketing strategies and help companies stay ahead of their competition. Third, personalization is another crucial element that can help marketers segment customers and personalize marketing messages based on their preferences and behavior. And, last but not least, text mining can automate tasks like sentiment analysis, keyword extraction, and topic modeling, saving marketers time and resources.

In contemporary society and the digital economy, textual data have emerged as an important source of information for marketers, complementing traditional metrics in both richness and contextual relevance. As consumers increasingly engage with brands through digital platforms by writing online reviews, posting on social media, chatting with customer-service bots, or composing emails, the volume and variety of textual content have expanded at an unprecedented scale. This proliferation of unstructured language-based data presents both a challenge and an opportunity for marketing analysts: It is a challenge in terms of methodological complexity and an opportunity to gain more nuanced context-sensitive insights into consumer-firm interactions, brand perceptions, and market dynamics.

Unlike structured numerical data, text captures the subtleties of human expression. Emotions, intentions, and nuanced preferences are often inaccessible through standard surveys or transactional records. Advances in natural language processing (NLP) and machine learning (ML) allow for scalable analyses of such text, enabling marketers to use a systematic, data-driven interpretation of language to support their decision-making. Consequently, textual analysis is becoming central to applications ranging from sentiment analysis and brand positioning to customer segmentation and content marketing development.

A growing body of literature has explored the role of text analytics in marketing, and this book is closely aligned with several other contributions in this field. For example, Berger et al. (2020) provide a broad overview of how automated textual analysis can generate insights across various marketing domains, such as analyzing word of mouth, predicting brand crises, understanding consumer-firm interactions, and business-to-business communication. Similarly, Humphreys (2021) explores the use of automated text analysis in the context of consumer research and its potential for generating insights into marketing. There are several books which are oriented toward practice and use R for quantitative text analysis applications. An example is Ledolter and VanderVelde (2021) who provide an accessible introduction to the quantitative analysis of textual data. Yildirim and Kübler (2023) target more advanced marketing students and practitioners, while Ashlee (2016) covers core market topics in social media.

Our book is located in the same space but aims to provide a more applied treatment of the automated text analysis techniques introduced by Humphreys and Wang (2018). While their work presents an excellent overview of approaches such as dictionary-based methods, sentiment analysis, and topic modeling, we provide extensive R code and practical examples to implement these techniques. Like Ledolter and VanderVelde (2021), we adopt a practical, hands-on approach to textual analysis, but with a clear focus on marketing-specific applications. It also complements the work of Ashlee (2016) on social media by diving deeper into quantitative text analysis methodologies for marketing applications.

1.1 The Tools and Packages Used

This book uses the programming language R and the RStudio integrated development environment (IDE) extensively as tools for text analytics, and whether you are new to R or a more experienced user, this book offers helpful practical guidance. R provides a rich ecosystem of packages for manipulating, analyzing, and visualizing textual data. In the first few chapters, we cover essential built-in commands, but as we proceed, we will introduce libraries like `tidyverse` and `ggplot2` to conduct our analyses. Before we start, however, we need to install these tools on our computers, and at a conceptual level, this is a universal task, independent of your operating system. Very briefly, R can be installed from https://cran.r-project.org for all the main OS, either in precompiled binary form (the best choice for the vast majority of people) or from source code (for the bold and daring). The next step is to install RStudio from https://posit.co; this is the graphical interface that uses R to enhance its potential. Although initially developed to support only R, it now also supports Python and is designed to accommodate other programming languages. We suggest that you use the open-source edition from the Posit website. Be aware that the installation operation must be done in a specific sequence: first R and then RStudio.

Packages are a system of extensions that allow us to extend the basic capabilities of R by enhancing data analysis, graphical representation, or the ease of use. Once installed inside the R environment on your computer, the functions existing in the packages can be employed by simply using the package's name in the function `library(packageName)`. The difference between a package and a library is like getting a book from a bookstore: You buy some books, and they are wrapped by the clerk in a package, you bring them home, unwrap them, and put the books in your home library. This means you do not need to go and fetch the books (the functions of a package) all the time from the bookstore (the Internet) and bring them home (download them); you can simply read them at home (load the library from your computer).

Depending on whether you use the command line or the RStudio interface, there are different ways to install packages in R. Using the command line, you have three ways to install them:

- From the CRAN network (R Core Team 2025; the recommended procedure)
  - `install.packages("packagename")`
- From GitHub (git clone or `install_github()`) as a repository (some packages are not present on the CRAN network but are still useful)
  - `install.packages("devtools")`
  - `install_github("username/packagename")`
- From a file downloaded from the Internet

- install.packages("path_and_source", repos = NULL, type="source")
- install.packages("~/Downloads/packagex.zip", repos= NULL, type="source")
- install.packages(file.choose(), repos=NULL) # on Windows

If you employ packages in your code that have not been installed, RStudio will alert you whenever it sees that the library corresponding to a package is present, but not the package itself.

R does not automatically check for newer versions of the packages installed, so check from time to time that you are up-to-date, especially if you installed the packages a while ago. Be aware that elements might not operate better after an update. Some procedures or functions might be modified or even removed, so we advise exercising caution when updating packages. Here are some simple functions that are useful when dealing with the packages already installed on your computer.

```
# Check for the installed packages
installed.packages()

# List all packages, it checks if an update is available
old.packages()

# Update all (available) packages
update.packages()

# Update, without prompts for permission/clarification
update.packages(ask = FALSE)

# Updating only one package is like overwriting on top of the old
↪  one, it uses the same command
install.packages("package")
```

Two of the packages which give R users a lot more power to deal with and combine functions in R are `magrittr` and `tidyverse`. The former uses a set of "pipes" represented by the `%>%` operator to use the output of one function as the input of the next. In this small example, we introduce you to the difference this package can make in writing cleaner and more compact code. If the task is to take a vector of numbers, perform the square root of them, round the results to two decimal places, and keep the numbers greater than 2; using a traditional approach, you would write:

```
numbers <- c(1, 4, 9, 16, 25)

# Square root
```

1

```
sqrt_numbers <- sqrt(numbers)

# Round to two decimals
rounded_numbers <- round(sqrt_numbers, 2)

# Filter numbers greater than 2
filtered_numbers <- rounded_numbers[rounded_numbers > 2]

print(filtered_numbers)
```

```
[1] 3 4 5
```

The same result can be achieved with `magrittr` like this, using fewer variables and so less code:

```
library(magrittr)

numbers <- c(1, 4, 9, 16, 25)

filtered_numbers <- numbers %>%
  sqrt() %>%                # Step 1: Take the square root
  round(2) %>%              # Step 2: Round to two decimals
  .[. > 2]                  # Step 3: Filter numbers greater than 2

print(filtered_numbers)
```

```
[1] 3 4 5
```

In contrast, `tidyverse` relies on `magrittr` and is a collection of packages to be used in data manipulation, exploration, and visualization. For example, some of its key packages (among many others) are `dplyr`, which is used to filter, summarize, or join data; `ggplot2`, to visualize data; `tidyr`, to reshape data sets; and `readr`, to import comma-separated values (CSV) files.

Now that you have some knowledge of how to install R and packages, let us focus on how to obtain the accompanying data for this book.

1.2 Data Set Overview and Companion Website

Collecting data is a time-consuming activity because data are unstructured and ubiquitous on the Internet. But these data must be funneled into a structured data set so that our lives as analysts become much easier. ◘ Figure 1.1 shows how data has to be transformed into a more manageable format before it can be analyzed, such as CSV, JavaScript object notation (JSON), a tabular format, or any other structured form.

For the data set in this book, we decided to use one single source, an older collection of Amazon user reviews of tablets (Wang et al., 2014). This will serve as

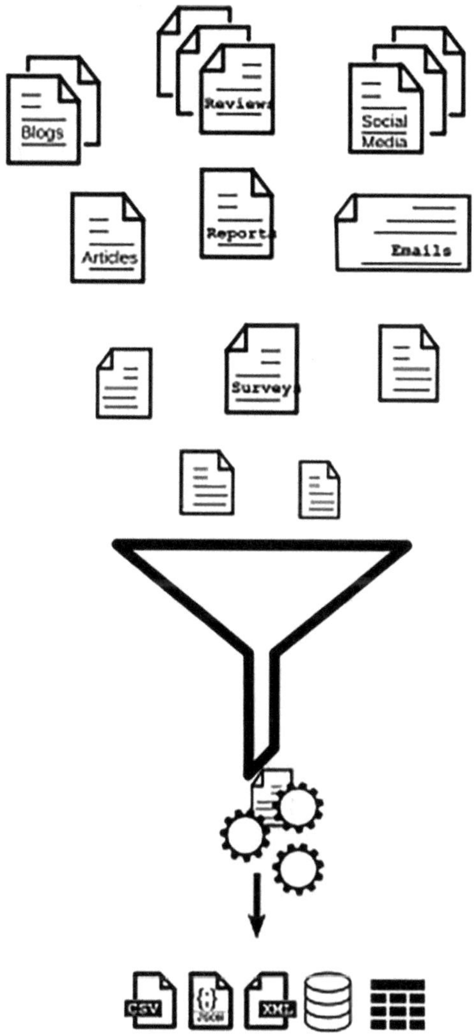

Fig. 1.1 Data from several sources, unstructured to structured. Authors' own figure

the context for applying the text analytics techniques presented here. A companion website—https://danieldanlab.github.io—was added as an essential resource for anyone interested in using this book as an instruction manual. It hosts the data set and other related files, additional examples of code and scripts, exercises for hands-on practice, and updates and supplementary material to extend your learning. Readers are encouraged to visit the website frequently to access these materials and enhance their understanding of the concepts discussed in the book. The goal is to equip the reader with constantly updated information, keeping the book as the foundation for learning and the website for updates, a problem-solving environment, suggestions for code, and any other helpful information which may arise.

1.3 Structure of the Book

The remainder of this book is structured to guide the reader through the fundamentals and advanced techniques of text analytics in the following way:

▶ Chapter 2 (*Textual Data*) deals with the basics of working with text in R, including commands, structures, and preprocessing. Basic R commands and regular expressions are presented with examples. Novice users learn how to clean text, deal with common problems in UGC, and prepare data for analysis. This chapter is the foundation for dealing with text data and prepares the ground for advanced analytical techniques.

▶ Chapter 3 (*Obtaining Textual Data*) tackles strategies for obtaining data for analysis, from simply importing text files and web scraping to working with application programming interfaces (APIs) and other commonly used methods. By the end of the chapter, readers will understand where to look for relevant data and how to bring them into R for preprocessing and analysis.

▶ Chapter 4 (*Basic Text Analysis*) starts with introducing techniques for text representation (e.g., bag-of-words, tf-idf) and visualization. Basic operations such as word frequencies, how to normalize text, and how to perform basic statistical analysis are introduced here. This chapter serves as an intermediary step between data preparation and more advanced analytical procedures, giving readers the first idea of the potential of information extraction from text processing.

▶ Chapter 5 (*Clustering*) analyzes methods for grouping text or documents, including hierarchical and k-means clustering, as well as density-based approaches. Meaningful patterns can be found by understanding how to group similar documents or words. Using these algorithms, we demonstrate how clustering reveals structures within preprocessed documents. The chapter also introduces a more direct link between text analytics and marketing applications.

▶ Chapter 6 (*Classification*) deals with supervised learning models for categorizing text data. Regular machine learning procedures, such as k-nearest neighbors, support vector machines, ensemble learning, as well as simple neural network models that are used in other fields, can also be applied to text. The chapter underlines how these methods help categorize data and connect classification to marketing applications.

▶ Chapter 7 (*Topic Modeling*) explores an essential element in many marketing applications, helping the reader to identify latent themes in text data using methods such as latent Dirichlet allocation. Readers can learn how to extract latent topics in data and understand their importance for marketing strategies. Visualization techniques are also discussed.

▶ Chapter 8 (*Sentiment Analysis*) deals with analyzing sentiment over time and understanding customer emotions, extracting sentiment polarization. It also introduces aspect-based sentiment analysis concepts, how to build sentiment word networks, and how to detect negative customer feedback. By the end of the chapter, the reader will have grasped the value of sentiment analysis for understanding customer perceptions.

► Chapter 9 (*Named Entity Recognition and Summarization*) deals with extracting key pieces of information, such as names, brands, and locations. Summarizing text is also tackled. The examples show how these methods are used in text analytics to enhance efficiency and understanding, without the need to explore the entire data set.

The last chapter (*Advanced Techniques*) introduces the concept of word embeddings, explores cosine similarity as a metric for comparing textual data, and discusses transformer models. Methods such as these, which bring artificial intelligence (AI) into analytics, allow readers to explore semantic relationships in documents. This chapter is the link that connects traditional natural language processing (NLP) methods with advances in AI through neural networks and text vectorization.

1.4 Key Features, Tools, and Challenges in Text Analytics

The book offers a practical, hands-on approach to text analytics. Key highlights include real-world examples using marketing data, code snippets, step-by-step tutorials, the integration of basic and advanced R packages, as well as free access to a dedicated website for extended learning. NLP is a vast and fast-changing domain; it includes subsections such as natural language understanding (NLU) and natural language generation (NLG), both of which are integral to analyzing and producing text. This book focuses on practical NLP applications, particularly in marketing contexts, but the techniques can be transferred to other domains, such as psychology or journalism.

Analyzing text data presents unique challenges, which we discuss in the book: for example, dealing with unstructured and inconsistent data formats and addressing encoding issues across operating systems (Windows, Linux, or macOS) and different languages. Managing linguistic variations, such as British vs. American English, is another key challenge. The book offers strategies and tools for navigating these complexities effectively.

This book is positioned at the intersection between computer science and marketing analytics, placing textual data at the core of insight generation and decision-making. The target audiences are data and computer scientists with an interest in marketing applications, as well as marketing analysts seeking to improve their computational abilities and gain access to a robust set of tools for processing textual data. The objective is to equip researchers and practitioners with the techniques and frameworks needed to extract value from text data systematically. Throughout the book, we illustrate the applications primarily using a data set containing customer feedback provided in online reviews. No prior programming experience is required; the book starts with fundamental concepts and progresses to advanced topics. Readers are encouraged to explore the exercises and access the companion website to maximize their learning experience. For the novice user, a good free resource to learn R is "An Introduction to R," which can be found here: https://intro2r.com.

1

References

Ashlee, H. (2016). *Social media. Enduring principle*. Oxford University Press.

Berger, J., Humphreys, A., Ludwig, S., Moe, W. W., Netzer, O., & Schweidel, D. A. (2020). Uniting the tribes: Using text for marketing insight. *Journal of Marketing*, *84*(1), 1–25. https://doi.org/10.1177/0022242919873106

Humphreys, A. (2021). Automated text analysis. In *Handbook of market research* (pp. 633–664). Springer. https://doi.org/10.1007/978--3-319-57413-4_26

Humphreys, A., & Wang, R. J.-H. (2018). Automated text analysis for consumer research. *Journal of Consumer Research*, *44*(6), 1274–1306. https://doi.org/10.1093/jcr/ucx104

Ledolter, J., & VanderVelde, L. S. (2021). *Analyzing textual information: From words to meanings through numbers*. https://doi.org/10.4135/9781071878828

Wang, X., Mai, F., & Chiang, R. H. (2014). Database submission-market dynamics and user-generated content about tablet computers. *Marketing Science*, *33*(3), 449–458. https://doi.org/10.1287/mksc.2013.0821

Yildirim, G., & Kübler, R. (2023). *Applied marketing analytics using r*. SAGE Publications Limited.

Textual Data, String Handling, Regular Expressions, and Data Structures

D. Dan, T. Reutterer, *Text Analytics in Marketing*, Classroom Companion: Business,
https://doi.org/10.1007/978-3-032-08086-8_2

Keywords
Textual data · Text manipulation · Normalization · UGC · Character vector · Vector · List · Data frame · Regular expressions · String operations

2

This chapter includes procedures for representing and manipulating text in R for marketing analytics. It begins with the rationale for text cleaning and provides examples of the difficulties presented by user-generated text—misspellings, alternative spellings, abbreviations, emojis, and mixed formats—and how these affect some practical examples. The chapter then introduces the primitive R data structures, how text is stored and accessed, and how to vectorize it. The practice sections provide examples for creating and indexing character vectors; concatenating character strings; measuring and summarizing string lengths; and exploring a product reviews data set with simple exploratory graphics. The gentle but thorough introduction to regular expressions covers many of the basic elements to consider when working with them. Practical issues and tips, including spell-checking and harmonizing language variants, will also be explored, including the pitfalls of automatic correction. Along the way, the short, reproducible code snippets and exercises will help convert new concepts into applied skills to create a robust preprocessing pipeline.

Learning Objectives

- Understanding the fundamental concepts of representing, manipulating, and working with text, such as data structures (vectors, arrays, and data frames), text strings, and characters
- Learning how to import a text data set and display its strings, handling common issues in UGC, such as misspelling, typos, and nonstandard formats
- Acquiring the skills to obtain and analyze information about strings within a data set
- Developing an understanding of regular expressions in R and their practical utility
- Practicing using regular expression tools including quantifiers, boundaries, operators, character classes, and sequences

2.1 Text Manipulation

2.1.1 Challenges Posed by User-Generated Content

It is rare for a marketing analyst to work with perfectly crafted texts. Since the focus of this book is on analyzing user-generated content (UGC), such as online reviews of products or services, blog entries, or social media posts, from a marketing perspective, we cannot expect any of these texts to be free from linguistic errors, typos, or misspellings. Unless they are revised or edited by professionals, these texts are likely to be imperfect (Moens et al., 2014).

Such linguistic errors in UGC can impact the analyses of these texts and, in turn, the marketing implications derived from them negatively. For instance, typos in reviews can shift the overall sentiment. Mistakes can lead to the misinterpretation of texts and potentially omit essential product information. Different spellings of the product name or features can make product comparisons inconsistent. Incorrectly spelled keywords might make it challenging for companies to track conversations and analyze customer sentiment (Berger et al., 2020). In some contexts, misspelling can even be used as an additional measure to reveal information about the communicator (Netzer et al., 2019). These are not the only problems found in UGC. There are also punctuation errors, incorrect capitalization, nonstandard abbreviations and acronyms, misused emojis, homophones, slang, jargon, incomplete sentences, and many more elements which can be misinterpreted. All in all, there are countless ways to write a text which present problems for textual analysis.

Thus, we often encounter situations when we need to search for, select, and partly modify or transform words, numbers, or whole phrases. This process, known as text manipulation, requires specific skills. It is necessary when aggregating text from different sources, such as from online product reviews with authors from different backgrounds, cultures, or with varying styles. The main goal of altering text in reviews is to create documents that are error-free, uniform, and ready to be analyzed. This is important because humans can correct misspelled words mentally but are slow, computers cannot make such a distinction but are fast. If the text is not polished, the resulting statistics will be flawed: For example, different spellings of the same word will be treated as separate words by the computer.

2.1.2 Spell-Checking and Harmonizing Variants

To catch common spelling errors, most of us use a spell checker of some form when we compose a text document, or at least we should have it activated. A spell checker is a function built into common text writing programs that detect misspellings by comparing the words in a drafted document with a database containing standard spellings. Among others, a popular text-mining package that includes prepackaged spellers to correct mistakes is the Enchant speller (AbiWord Project, 2024). Modern applications use artificial intelligence algorithms to do this, but although using such automatic tools for large-scale correction may seem convenient, it comes with risks. The main challenge is that these tools may not always determine context. This can lead to incorrect changes and generate unwanted errors. With advancements in AI, though, contextual understanding is becoming more accurate, thereby reducing such risks (Hu et al., 2020).

The discrepancy between English language variants that have a disparity in standardization, such as British English (GB) or American English (US) spelling, is another problem (Hitchings, 2008). When dealing with aggregated data, the probability of encountering both in the same corpus is high. Thus, a method to make them uniform is desirable. We can create ad hoc functions or procedures to manipulate text to overcome these difficulties. The operations we employ to achieve this take three forms: additive, subtractive, and substitutive. In the first case, we can add characters, strings, or numbers to a specific string anywhere, such as at the beginning, in the middle or at the end of a word, and before or after a specific character. In the same way, we can subtract or substitute them to obtain the desired result. In essence, *text is your data*, and managing it effectively is essential for accurate analysis.

> *Text normalization* is the systematic transformation of a corpus (e.g., unifying spelling, controlling replacements, casing, and punctuation) to make it as consistent as possible for analysis while preserving its meaning.

Now we will briefly introduce some basic concepts of how (textual) data are stored inside R. Readers who are merely interested in applications can skip this section. Later, we will delve into more advanced techniques and functions to help us manipulate textual data effectively.

2.2 Some Basics on Measurement Representation in R

Data are more than knowledge (Tuomi, 1999). The Oxford Dictionary defines *data* (Coombs, 1964) as: "The quantities, characters, or symbols on which operations are performed by a computer, which may be stored and transmitted in the form of electrical signals and recorded on magnetic, optical, or mechanical recording media." It is easy to see the *quantities* as numbers, the *characters* as letters, and the *symbols* as images and consider all these as *types of data*. In computer programming, we deal with two fundamental entities for accessing stored data: *variables* and *constants* (Ihaka & Gentleman, 1996). Variables in programming are used to point to stored data by assigning them an understandable, meaningful, and concise name. For example, we could use the variable name `temperature` to refer to a sequence of temperature values that you have measured. Then, the variable can be referenced and modified as needed by other computer routines. The *constant* represents a fixed value that cannot be altered but can be used in other functions. A classic example is *pi*, the ratio of the circumference of a circle to its diameter, commonly rounded down to *3.14*. Data need to be structured (Arasu & Garcia-Molina, 2003) to facilitate easy manipulation. For the sake of precision, you need to understand that a *variable* merely refers to a structure in which data have been stored; it does not store the data, it just gives them a name.

2.2.1 Vectors

A *vector* is the simplest form of data structure in R, commonly used alongside lists, matrices, arrays, and data frames. A vector can be *atomic*, meaning that it contains elements that are all of the same data type, for example, logical, integer, double, or character data. It can contain a single value, or it can hold multiple values. In ◘ Fig. 2.1, we can make an analogy between a vector, which contains values of a single data type, and a single-column chest of drawers filled with shirts. Each drawer represents an element in the vector, and we have named this vector `drawers`.

> *An atomic vector* is a one-dimensional ordered collection of values of the same type (e.g., logical, integer, double, character).

To populate our vector, we assign values to it using the variable name (`drawers`) and a discrete number of differently colored shirts: *23 red*, *32 blue*, *15 green*, *41 yellow*, and *12 white*. We use the function, `c()`, which stands for *combine*, to group these "shirts" together. The assignment is done using the `<-` operator: `drawers <- c(23, 32, 15, 41, 12)`.

To access the content of any drawer, we simply use the variable name and specify the desired element(s) using *square brackets*. For instance, `drawers[3]` retrieves the content of the third element of the vector variable, which is *15 green shirts*. Remember, what appears in the R console are numbers, not actual shirts. If we want to know the contents of the second and fifth drawers, we type: `drawers[c(2, 5)]`, which will return the number of shirts in both the second and fifth elements of the vector. As you can see, our vector contains *only shirts*, not t-shirts or pairs of pants. This shows that a vector can contain only elements of the same type (e.g., all numbers, all integers, or all characters). On top of that, it is *one dimensional*, because it is flat and linear.

2.2.2 Arrays

Let us introduce another piece of terminology: the *array*. In R, an *array* is like a vector but can have more than one dimension. An example of a two-dimensional array is a *matrix*. Technically, they are the same thing, but R likes to keep these two concepts separate due to the significant role matrices play in statistical computation. Obviously, we can have arrays with more than two dimensions, but visualizing these higher-dimensional structures can be challenging—if not impossible.

> *An array* is a vector whose shape has been defined in one or more dimensions. A 2-D array is a matrix, while arrays greater than 2-D follow the same principle.

2

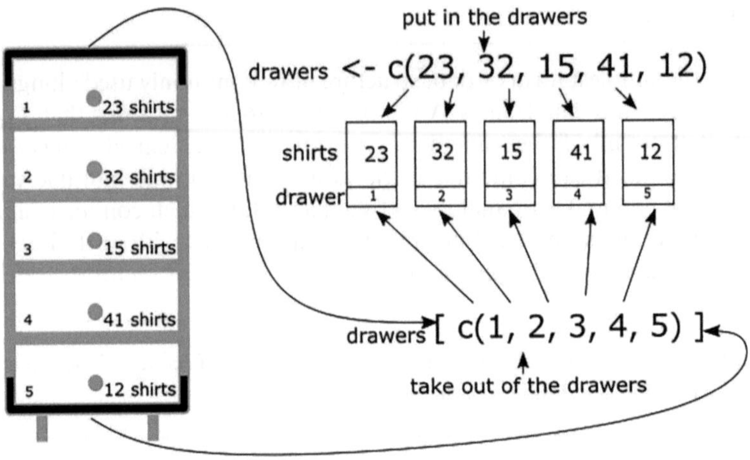

Fig. 2.1 An array in a chest of drawers. Authors' own figure

2.2.3 Lists

In R, a *list* is a data structure that can store different elements, such as numbers, strings, *vectors*, or even other lists. The key difference between a *list* and a *vector* lies in the types of data they can contain. While a *vector* must consist of elements of the *same data type*, a list can hold *heterogeneous data types*, including vectors, other lists, and even lists of lists. This flexibility makes lists a versatile data structure in R.

> *A list* is a flexible container that can hold elements of different types and lengths, such as vectors, other lists, or nested structures.

2.2.4 Vector Types in R

R language categorizes data into six basic atomic vector types: three numerical types (integer, numeric, complex), a logical type (TRUE or FALSE), a character type, and a raw type. For a more comprehensive understanding of these types, refer to the works of Kabacoff (2022) and Wickham (2019), which provide detailed explanations and examples.

These types are named intuitively to reflect the kind of data they hold. For instance, *integer vectors* store whole numbers, *numeric vectors* can hold decimal numbers, *complex vectors* are for complex numbers, *logical vectors* contain Boolean values (TRUE or FALSE), *character vectors* store text, and *raw vectors* are used for raw bytes. As an analogy, think of the data type as the material from which each chest of drawers is made. For instance, some might be made of wood (representing integers), others of plastic (representing characters), and some others of metal (representing logical values like TRUE or FALSE).

2.2.5 Data Frames

A *data frame* in R is structured like a table and is similar to a table in many standard spreadsheet programs such as Microsoft Excel, Google Sheets, Apple Numbers, or LibreOffice Calc.

Just as a table in these programs is composed of rows and columns, an R *data frame* is structured in the same way. Each *column* in a data frame can be considered to be a vector, holding data of the same type, much like a spreadsheet column containing numbers, text, or dates. The *rows* in a data frame correspond to individual records or observations, similar to how each row in a spreadsheet represents a specific item, person, or event.

> *A data frame* is a table where each column contains one type of vector (columns may differ in type, but they must have equal lengths) and each row is an observation/record.

To continue with our analogy between a data frame in R and a chest of drawers in the physical world, let us consider each row in the data frame to represent a person, see ◘ Fig. 2.2. In technical terms, the data in each *row* is called an *observation*. A *column*, represents a specific feature, is called an *attribute*. Each person, or row, is linked to various features, which in our analogy are items like socks, t-shirts, and pants. For instance, Aida might have 23 pairs of socks, 16 t-shirts, and eight pairs of pants.

2.2.6 Manipulating Data Frames

In this context, the chest of drawers can be thought of as our data frame in R. Each drawer or column represents a different item of clothing. We access these items in R in a similar way to opening a specific drawer of the piece of furniture. For example, if we want to check how many t-shirts Carl has, and Carl is the third person in our data frame, we would use the command `chest[3, 2]` in R. This command is akin to opening the second drawer (t-shirts) of the third row (Carl) of our chest of drawers.

We can also "slice" this data frame, which is just like selecting specific drawers from our chest of drawers. If we want to see only the t-shirts and pants for everyone, we use `chest[, c(2, 3)]`. The empty space before the comma indicates that we are selecting all the rows or, in our analogy, all the people. After the comma, the `c(2, 3)` specifies that we only want to look at the second and third columns, which are t-shirts and pants.

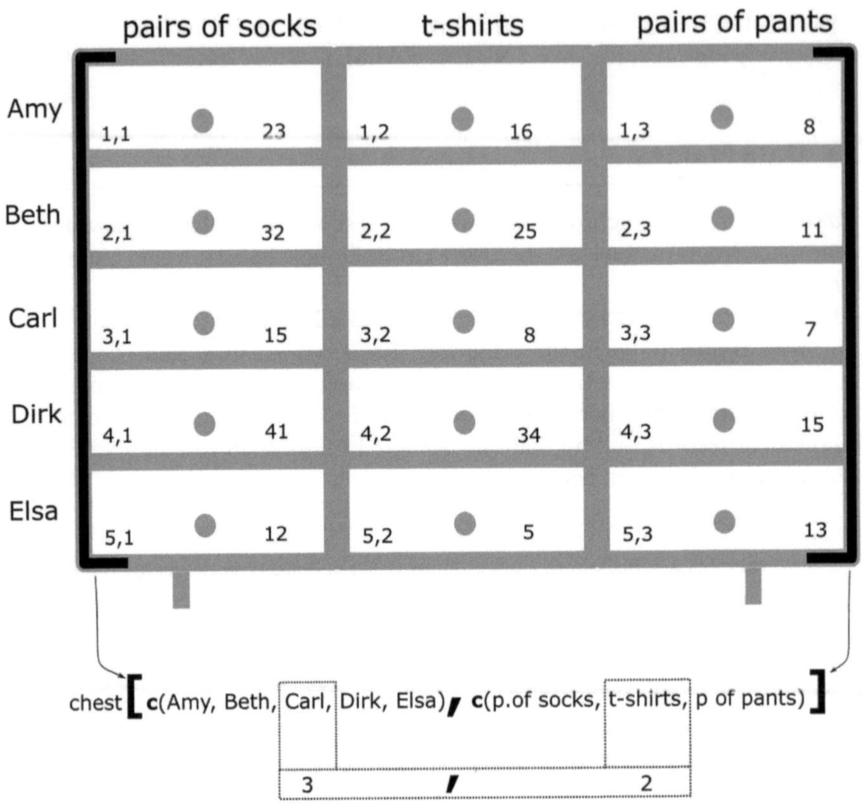

Fig. 2.2 A data frame containing various items. Authors' own figure

In this analogy, instead of actual socks, t-shirts, and pants, we are dealing with different types of data in our data frame. So, where you might imagine long socks in a drawer, in R, this could correspond to a column of strings or numbers representing that particular item or attribute.

Imagine that your chest of drawers can be part of different sets of furniture. One chest might belong to a set for a bedroom (similar to a data frame *class*), another might be part of a set of office furniture (similar to a list *class*), and so on. The set of furniture (*class*) to which the chest of drawers belongs determines how it is used. A bedroom chest of drawers might be used to store clothes, while an office version might be organized to store files and documents. In R, the *class* of an object determines how it behaves with different functions and operations. For example, functions treat a data frame (a bedroom set) differently than a basic vector (a standalone chest of drawers). The difference between *data type* and *class* is the following. The first refers to the *low-level internal structure* of how R stored data in memory. A variable can be checked for its type using the `typeof()` function, while the second is a *high-level abstraction* that focuses on how an object behaves in R. Because the word *class* is related to Object Oriented Programming, it defines how functions and methods interact with an object. As a reminder, an *object*, which stores information, is referenced by a name, which is the name of the variable.

2.3 String Containers in R

2.3.1 Empty Strings and Character Vectors

Just as we use a drawer to store garments, we can use specific structures in programming to store text strings. Let us imagine we have a chest of drawers, but we will leave these drawers empty. In the context of programming, particularly in R, text strings are categorized as belonging to a *character class*. So we use another data type now, a *character*, not an integer.

Let us consider an *empty string*, which is similar to having a chest of drawers with only one column of drawers, and those drawers are empty. We can assign an *empty string* to a variable; let us call it `empty_string`. This would be shown in R as `empty_string <- ""`, signifying a string that contains no characters. Paradoxically, even though the string is empty, it belongs to the *character class* in R.

When we are uncertain about the class type of a variable, we can easily check it using the `class()` function. For instance, typing `class(empty_string)` would confirm that empty_string is indeed a *character class* despite being empty. This is similar to confirming that an empty drawer is still a part of the chest of drawers, designed to hold items even when it currently does not.

```
# Assign an empty string to the variable "empty_string"
empty_string <- ""

# Display the value of "empty_string"
empty_string
```

```
[1] ""
```

```
# Check and display the class of "empty_string"
class(empty_string)
```

```
[1] "character"
```

Similarly, we can create an empty character vector in R using the `character()` function by setting its length argument to zero. It is important to note that `empty_character` is just a name we have assigned to our variable (object) for clarity and understanding. We could have named it anything, such as `john_doe`, ala_bama, or bugs_bunny. Choosing a descriptive name is beneficial. When we revisit the code later and need an immediate glimpse of what a specific variable might contain, the appropriate naming of variables makes them easier to read and understand.

2

```
# Create an empty character vector with a length of zero
empty_character <- character(length = 0)

# Display the content of "empty_character"
empty_character
```

```
character(0)
```

```
# Check and display the class of "empty_character"
class(empty_character)
```

```
[1] "character"
```

What if we want to create a character vector in R that is initialized (meaning it occupies spots but contains only empty placeholder values)? The procedure can be thought of as preparing a chest of drawers, where each drawer is meant to hold a character string, but initially, all the drawers are empty. In programming terms, we are talking about initializing an empty character vector, and we can set it to be a specific length, for example to have 10 elements, precisely like a chest of drawers with 10 drawers. At this stage, each "drawer" (or element in the vector) contains an *empty string* ("") —ready to hold data, but currently contains no values.

```
# Create a character vector with 10 elements, initialized as empty
↪  strings
character_vector <- character(10)

# Display the contents of "character_vector"
character_vector
```

```
[1] "" "" "" "" "" "" "" "" "" ""
```

2.3.2 Combining and Indexing Strings

We can populate our newly created character vector with words or strings by assigning them to specific positions within the vector. This is done through indexing, which allows us to access and modify elements at particular locations in the vector. For example, if we want to place the word "five" in the fifth position of our vector, we use indexing. This is done by adding square brackets `[]` after the vector's name, `character_vector`, and specifying the position we want with a number. In this case, we use the number 5 to indicate the fifth position. The corresponding R code would be `character_vector[5] <- "five"`, which assigns the string "five" to the fifth element of the vector.

```
# Assign the string "five" to the fifth element of the
↪   "character_vector"
character_vector[5] <- "five"

# Display the contents of "character_vector"
character_vector
```

```
[1] ""        ""        ""        ""        "five" ""        ""        ""
↪   ""        ""
```

As previously mentioned, a vector in R is designed for homogeneous storage, meaning it can only hold one type of data. For instance, if we add a string to a numerical vector, R will automatically convert all numerical values in the vector into strings. This is because a vector must maintain a consistent data type across all its elements, or "drawers," as we might metaphorically describe them. We can convert vector types manually if we require precise control over our types of data. To check if a vector is a character type, we use the function `is.character()`. Moving from one type to another, such as from numerical to character, is achieved using functions like `as.character()`. This operation might be performed when we want to transform numerical value types into character types. While number types are used for computations, numbers as text (character type) are interpreted as words.

Consider the following example where two variables, `x` and `y`, hold different types of data: character and numerical, respectively. We can check if they are a character type, examine their class, convert one type into another, and then verify if the conversion was successful.

```
# Assign a string to variable "x"
x <- "really, is this a character?"

# Assign the result of the sum 9+8 to variable "y"
y <- 9 + 8

# Check if "x" is of character type
is.character(x)
```

```
[1] TRUE
```

```
# Check if "y" is of character type
is.character(y)
```

```
[1] FALSE
```

```
# Get the class of "x"
class(x)
```

```
[1] "character"
```

```
# Get the class of "y"
class(y)
```

```
[1] "numeric"
```

```
# Convert "y" from numeric to character type
y <- as.character(y)

# Get the class of "y" after conversion
class(y)
```

```
[1] "character"
```

When we need to combine ("concatenate") different strings to create longer ones, the `paste()` function in R comes in handy. This has two primary arguments: `sep` and `collapse`. The `sep` argument specifies a separator to be placed between each pair of strings being brought together. This can be an empty space, a dot, a dash, or whichever symbol, word, or character you want to put between the strings. On the other hand, when set to something other than its default value of NULL, the collapse argument introduces an optional character string to separate the results. For example, if we bring together the string "My favorite book" with "has many chapters" using `paste()`, we can create a seamless single string from these two. In another scenario, we might use `paste()` to append the word "Chapter" to numbers generated from 1 to 5, separating each resulting string with a comma. Here is how it looks in R:

```
# Concatenating two strings
x <- paste("My favorite book", "has many chapters", sep = " ")
x
```

```
[1] "My favorite book has many chapters"
```

```
# Concatenating "Chapter" with numbers 1 to 5, separated by commas
x <- paste("Chapter", 1:5, sep = " ", collapse = ", ")
x
```

```
[1] "Chapter 1, Chapter 2, Chapter 3, Chapter 4, Chapter
↪  5"
```

You may have noticed that we used the same variable name, x, as in the previous example. It is important to remember that reusing a variable name in your code will overwrite its previous content with the new data. Therefore, carefully tracking the names you assign to your variables is good practice. Overwriting variables can lead to confusion or errors, particularly in more complex scripts where the same variable name might be used multiple times unintentionally. Thus, using descriptive and unique names for your variables is advisable. This approach helps to identify their purpose clearly and significantly reduces the risk of accidental overwrites, thereby enhancing the longevity and readability of your code.

2.3.3 Working with Strings

In text mining, strings are our bread and butter, and to enhance our understanding, in this section we will explore some simple examples of text manipulation. This will involve using functions that come with the base version of R, as well as additional functions that can be installed to further enhance R's text-processing capabilities. We will begin by importing the *Product Reviews* data set, as described in the Introduction, focusing on the "Title" column. To illustrate what the data look like, we will display a small subset (20 items). A larger data set would be impractical to show in a printed book. The data are selected randomly, but we ensure the reproducibility of the results by using the `set.seed()` function. This approach maintains a controlled randomness, ensuring consistent results across different runs on different computers. Throughout this chapter, we will demonstrate how the functions of the base version of R and the additional packages can be used effectively in text mining to extract meaningful insights from our data.

```
# Set global option to not automatically convert strings to
↪  factors
options(stringsAsFactors = FALSE)

# Read the CSV file "Product Reviews.csv" into a data frame
↪  "prodreviews"
# "data" is a sub-folder inside your current working directory
prodreviews <- read.csv("data/Product Reviews.csv")

# Convert the "Title" column of "prodreviews" to character type
# and store it in "prodtitle"
prodtitle <- as.character(prodreviews$Title)

# Set a seed for random number generation to ensure
↪  reproducibility
set.seed(123)

# Sample 20 titles randomly from "prodtitle" and store them in
↪  "prodtitle20"
(prodtitle20 <- sample(prodtitle, 20))
```

```
 [1] "Best tech toy of 2010-2011"
 [2] "Worked for one day!"
 [3] "Ignore the nonsense"
 [4] "Nonna162"
 [5] "Obviously only for the Tech Savvy"
 [6] "eh.."
 [7] "Excellent for what it is!"
 [8] "Does not add up at all"
 [9] "Love the product!"
[10] "Good purchase"
[11] "Great Tablet"
[12] "Not what I expected"
[13] "Less than satisfaction"
[14] "Boss tablet."
[15] "Sweet Little Tablet"
[16] "I have learned my lesson."
[17] "Lightweight 10-inch Android 2.3 tablet with so-so
↪  screen"
[18] "Kindle?"
[19] "The Kindle Fire is a great first effort"
[20] "Wifi version inferior to the 3g version"
```

As we can see, the system displays the titles in a reproducible pseudorandom sequence, thanks to the use of `set.seed()`. It is important to note that text in R is case sensitive; a computer will consider the words "great" and "Great" to be two distinct entities. This distinction is essential in text analysis and manipulation.

To get a bit of practice, let us use the `substr()` function to select a part of these strings. For instance, our goal could be to extract the first four letters of each title string. Technically, we achieve this by specifying the start and end index positions in the `substr()` function. In our case, we start from index position 1 (the first letter of a word) and end at position 4.

```
# Extracting the first four letters of each title
substr(prodtitle20, start = 1, stop = 4)
```

```
 [1] "Best" "Work" "Igno" "Nonn" "Obvi" "eh.." "Exce"
 ↪   "Does" "Love" "Good"
[11] "Grea" "Not " "Less" "Boss" "Swee" "I ha" "Ligh"
↪   "Kind" "The " "Wifi"
```

By abbreviating the titles in our data set, we might encounter a situation where some strings end up with identical sequences. These can be composed of a mix of lowercase or uppercase letters, spaces, and punctuation marks. To mitigate the potential confusion caused by such duplication, we can use the `abbreviate()` function. This creates abbreviations from each string, typically selecting the first letter of each word and ensuring a minimum of four letters are used. If a string has fewer than four words, `abbreviate()` automatically constructs abbreviations to match this length.

Beyond reducing duplication, the `abbreviate()` function serves several other purposes. It can save time, reduce computer memory usage, and enhance data anonymity. It is also handy for creating concise labels for graphs or managing large data sets where conserving space is critical.

```
# Apply the "abbreviate()" function to the "prodtitle20" vector
abbreviate(prodtitle20)
```

```
                   Best tech toy of 2010-2011
                                      "Btto2"
                         Worked for one day!
                                       "Wfod"
                         Ignore the nonsense
                                       "Igtn"
                                    Nonna162
                                       "N162"
          Obviously only for the Tech Savvy
                                     "OoftTS"
                                         eh..
                                       "eh.."
```

```
                        Excellent for what it is!
                                          "Efwii"
                           Does not add up at all
                                         "Dnauaa"
                                Love the product!
                                           "Ltp!"
                                    Good purchase
                                           "Gdpr"
                                     Great Tablet
                                           "GrtT"
                              Not what I expected
                                           "NwIe"
                           Less than satisfaction
                                           "Lsts"
                                     Boss tablet.
                                           "Btb."
                              Sweet Little Tablet
                                           "SwLT"
                        I have learned my lesson.
                                          "Ihlml"
Lightweight 10-inch Android 2.3 tablet with so-so screen
                                       "L1A2twss"
                                          Kindle?
                                           "Knd?"
                The Kindle Fire is a great first effort
                                      "TKFiagfe"
                Wifi version inferior to the 3g version
                                       "Wvitt3v"
```

In this example, each title in the "prodtitle20" vector is abbreviated, with a minimum abbreviation length of four characters.

The length of strings in a data set is a valuable statistical item, particularly in text analysis. For instance, we might be curious about the number of characters in each review title within our sample, or we might want to identify the title with the highest character count. To accomplish this, we can use the `nchar()` function to determine the length of each string and the `max()` function to find the maximum length in the "prodtitle20" data set. Applying these functions is an important step for a marketing analyst examining text data: It helps them understand how extensively people are talking about a product in the reviews. Longer titles might indicate more detailed discussions or descriptions, which can be insightful for understanding customer engagement and interest.

```
# Calculate the length of each title
nchar(prodtitle20)
```

```
[1] 26 19 19  8 33  4 25 22 17 13 12 19 22 12 19 25 56
↪  7 39 39
```

```
# Find the maximum length among these titles
max(nchar(prodtitle20))
```

```
[1] 56
```

We obtained two results from our analysis: firstly, a vector of numbers where each number represents the character count of each title in the sample data set; and, secondly, a single number indicating the maximum length of the titles. The next step is determining which title(s) correspond to this maximum length. For this, we use the `which()` function in R, which identifies the position(s) of the string(s) with the longest length. It is possible to find more than one string sharing the same maximum number of characters, i.e., that of the title of the longest string in the data set. In our case, the longest string has 56 characters.

```
# Extract the titles from "prodtitle20" that have the maximum
↪ length
prodtitle20[which(nchar(prodtitle20)==max(nchar(prodtitle20)))]
```

```
[1] "Lightweight 10-inch Android 2.3 tablet with so-so
↪  screen"
```

The code can be translated from R into plain English as follows: *Which* is the string that has the *max*imum *n*umber of *char*acters in the *prodtitle20* sample data set?

We can also determine the total number of titles in the data set and find out how many are unique. To do these, we can utilize R's `length()` and `unique()` functions. The `length()` function will tell us the total number of titles in the data set, while `unique()` will help us identify the number of unique titles. We apply these functions to the entire data set, "prodtitle."

```
# Count total titles in "prodtitle"
length(prodtitle)
```

```
[1] 40741
```

2

```
# Count unique titles in "prodtitle"
length(unique(prodtitle))
```

```
[1] 31405
```

We can see a total of 40,741 titles in our data set, out of which 31,405 are unique. This shows that the remaining 9336 titles are duplicates, i.e., they appear more than once.

Having mentioned the relevance of statistics in relation to this data set, we can gain a quick statistical overview using the `summary()` function. This function is particularly useful for analyzing the length of strings in the "prodtitle" data set. By applying `summary()` to the character lengths of the titles, we shift our focus to a broader analysis of the entire data set. This allows us to understand not just the count of titles but also the distribution of their lengths, providing insights into the data set's characteristics.

```
# Get statistical summary of title lengths in "prodtitle"
summary(nchar(prodtitle))
```

```
   Min. 1st Qu.  Median    Mean 3rd Qu.    Max.
   1.00   13.00   21.00   24.64   32.00  128.00
```

We immediately notice that the lengths of strings in our data set vary significantly: The shortest title has only one character, while the longest has 128 characters. The average (mean) number of letters per title is 24.64, with a median of 21. This range in string lengths could affect how we process and analyze our text data. For instance, very short titles might need a closer look to ensure they are meaningful, while the longer titles could be more descriptive or complex, and rich in information.

But how are these string lengths distributed across our data set? And, how many strings are there of each length? To answer these questions, let us plot a histogram, which is ideal for uncovering patterns in data sets. Histograms are very helpful for showing the frequency of groups, or "bins," of data. When creating our histogram, we will adjust the default bin width by setting the `breaks` argument. This will control the number of bins used to group our data. For our analysis, we aim to distribute the data across 20 bins. However, it is important to note that the number of breaks specified in R is treated as more of a guideline than a strict parameter. R's internal algorithms may adjust the number to produce a visually appealing histogram. While there are methods of forcing R to produce an exact number of bins, as discussed in Ogle (2018), the default behavior typically yields satisfactory results.

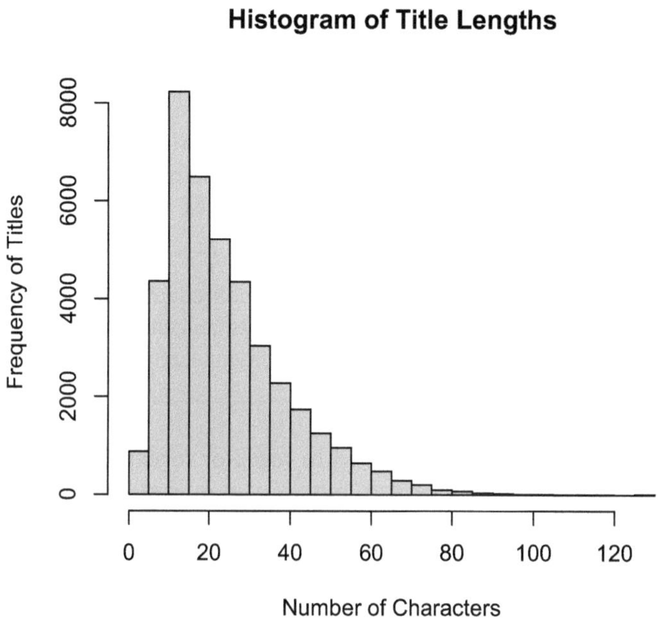

Fig. 2.3 Length of the titles in the Product Reviews data set. Authors' own figure

```
# Plot a histogram of string lengths in "prodtitle"
hist(nchar(prodtitle),
     main = 'Histogram of Title Lengths',  # Set the main title of
     ↪  the histogram
     breaks = 20,                          # Specify the number of
     ↪  bins as 20
     xlab = 'Number of Characters',        # Label for the x-axis
     ylab = 'Frequency of Titles')         # Label for the y-axis
```

We can conclude from the histogram (see Fig. 2.3) that most of the review titles in this data set, some 8237, have lengths of between 10 and 15 characters. Beyond this range, the frequency of string lengths gradually decreases. This trend indicates that shorter titles are more common; the longer the title, the less frequently it appears in the data set.

Exercise. Try to find the longest title in the entire data set using R. Determine whether there is only one or multiple titles of the maximum length. Hint: You can use the `nchar()` function to calculate the length of each title and then identify the title(s) with the maximum length. Once you find the longest title(s), explore it/them further: What do they have in common, and what might their length indicate about the content or nature of these titles?

2.4 Regular Expressions in R

2

The previous sections served as a warm-up, using R-based procedures to introduce you to the fascinating world of text analytics. Next, we will explore the basics of regular expressions, a powerful tool for searching, parsing, and manipulating text. All the examples in this section are designed to work with the base R functions, meaning you do not need to install any extra packages.

> *A regular expression (regex)* is a pattern using a collection of metacharacters and shorthand notations (including quantifiers, anchors, and character classes, etc.) for matching, extracting, and (via replacement) modifying text.

Regular expressions, often shortened to regex or regexp, are used not only in search engines and by word processors, but are also integral to many programming languages for detecting, locating, or replacing information. This section will illustrate the basic concept and some elementary functions of regular expressions in the R computing environment (Sanchez, 2013). For a more detailed exploration, see Friedl (2006) or Forta (2018).

R supports two types of regular expression paradigms: POSIX and Perl-like. The POSIX standard, an acronym for Portable Operating System Interface, comprises a set of IEEE (Institute of Electrical and Electronics Engineers) standards. These standards aim to provide a consistent and portable interface for programming and user environments across various operating systems, including but not limited to Unix-based systems. The POSIX standard has two types of regular expressions: basic regular expressions (BRE) and extended regular expressions (ERE). R uses ERE by default in its expression functions, such as `grep()`, `grepl()`, `sub()`, and `gsub()`.

Perl had a large community that has significantly contributed to the development of a rich set of regex libraries and documentation, and it was renowned for its early and robust integration of regular expressions. This makes Perl's regex particularly well suited for complex pattern-matching tasks. In R, Perl-compatible regular expressions can be used by setting the `perl = TRUE` option, which allows for the use of advanced regex features within R's regex functions. For further reading and a deeper understanding of these topics, see the following: Lewine (1991) and Gagolewski (2022).

A regular expression is a sequence of characters and metacharacters which together form a search pattern. For instance, a simple pattern like **[a-z]+** is designed to find any lowercase letter. This pattern represents a concise string that tests for a specific pattern capable of extracting or replacing substrings. Regular expressions can search for a variety of elements, including letters (e.g., "a," "b," "c,") numbers (e.g., "0," "1," "5"), or other characters (e.g., "=", "-"). To the untrained eye, these patterns might look as random as the keystrokes of a cat walking across a keyboard. If you have ever witnessed such a feline typist, you will know exactly what we mean. Rest assured, no cats were harmed in the writing of this book:

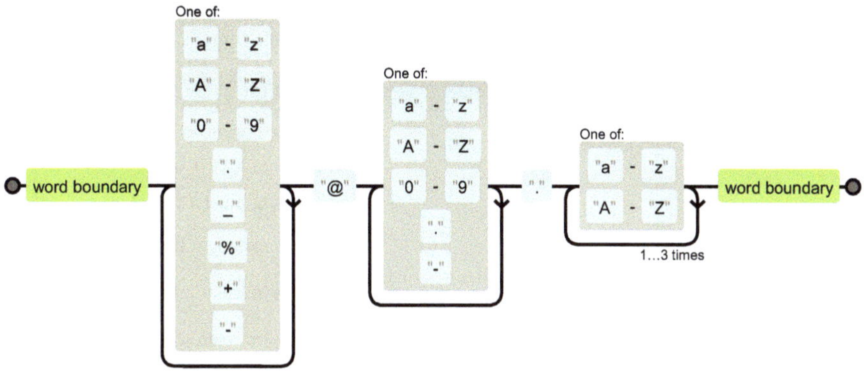

Fig. 2.4 Visualization of a regular expression for an email address. Authors' own figure

To demystify these seemingly cryptic search patterns, consider an example: that of finding all the email addresses in a corpus. An email address, such as john.doe@someserver.com, can be interpreted as a user (John Doe) located at a domain (someserver.com). Our task is to create a regular expression that captures all the email addresses in the text, regardless of the domain, whether it is Gmail, Yahoo, Outlook, or others. Constructing a regular expression for this purpose might look challenging at first. For instance, a basic pattern to match email addresses could be something like: **[a-zA-Z0-9._%+-]+@[a-zA-Z0-9.-]+\.[a-zA-Z]{2,}**. This pattern is designed to match the general structure of email addresses, but it can be pretty tricky to read for those new to regular expressions. To aid in understanding and visualizing these patterns, we can use tools provided by the `re2r` package Wenfeng (2020). This offers a way to visually break down and interpret each part of a regular expression. Figure 2.4 shows an example of what this visualization looks like.

```
# Load re2r package
library(re2r)

# Visualize email regex pattern
show_regex("\\b[a-zA-Z0-9._%+-]+@[a-zA-Z0-9.-]+\\.[a-zA-
↪  Z]{2,4}\\b")
```

Note that the `re2r` package has been removed from CRAN and may contain bugs, such as displaying quantifiers like `{2,4}` inaccurately. We have installed it from `GitHub` for educational purposes. While it has potential as a tool, you should be aware of its limitations and bugs. Another R regex enhancement tool is the `regexplain` (Gadenbuie, 2018) add-in for RStudio, which is installable from GitHub. It provides a user-friendly regex experience for crafting and understanding regular expressions within RStudio. It uses both base R functions and the `stringr` package (Wickham, 2022), on which there is more toward the end of this chapter.

■ **Table 2.1** Quantifiers. Table compiled by the authors

Quantifier	Description
*	Matches 0 or more times
+	Matches at least 1 time
?	Matches at most 1 time
`{n}`	Matches exactly n times
`{n,}`	Matches at least n times
`{n,m}`	Matches between n and m times

We notice that the regular expression contains a sequence of characters designed to capture one or more email addresses (Goyvaerts & Levithan, 2012). Let us decode this in plain English: The expression starts and ends with a word boundary \b, encapsulating the email address. The user name consists of a combination of characters from a to z (or A to Z), numbers from 0 to 9, and special characters like a dot ., an underscore _, a percentage %, a plus +, and a hyphen -, in any order. This is followed by the @ symbol found in all email addresses. After this, the server name is specified, which can include letters (both upper- and lowercase), numbers, dots, and hyphens. Finally, the domain's extension is indicated by a dot followed by 2 to 4 letters (e.g., .com, .org). It is important to note that while this pattern captures many email formats, it may not encompass all, especially more complex ones like second-level domains (e.g., john.doe@myserver.ac.at). Thus, while this is effective for most common email addresses, the regex might not detect every possible valid email format. Nevertheless, by adjusting and expanding the pattern, it is possible to tailor the regex to match a wider variety of valid email formats, accommodating different structures and domain specifications.

Let us now delve into the characters and metacharacters used in regular expressions in a structured manner. Regular expressions are composed of characters, symbols or letters, and metacharacters which have special meanings in the context of regex. One of the key aspects of regular expressions is the use of quantifiers, which allows us to specify the number of repetitions of characters in a pattern.

2.4.1 Quantifiers

Quantifiers, as detailed in Sanchez (2013), define how many times a particular character or sequence of characters need to appear in a string for a match to be found. The various quantifiers and their functions are summarized in ■ Table 2.1. These enable us to construct flexible and powerful search patterns in regular expressions.

The quantifier in a regular expression is placed after the character or a group of characters whose occurrences (repetitions) it is meant to refer to. For example, let us create a character vector in R containing eight similar strings. These strings are designed to illustrate the effect of applying various quantifiers and how they affect pattern matching.

```
# Create a vector of sample strings with varying patterns
strings <- c("x", "xy", "xz", "xzy", "xzzy", "xzzzy", "xzzzzy",
↪   "xzzzzyzy")
```

To identify patterns, such as finding all the sentences that contain a specific sequence of characters, we can use the `grep()` function. For instance, if we want to locate the sequence "xy" in our previously created vector, we would use `grep("xy", strings)`. This function returns the indices of the vector elements containing a specific sequence, allowing us to identify and extract matching patterns quickly.

```
# Identify indices of elements in vector "strings" that contain
↪   "xy"
grep("xy", strings)
```

```
[1] 2
```

The `grep()` function in R is used to identify patterns within a vector of strings. By default, it returns the indices, i.e., the positions in the vector, where the pattern you specify matches. If you set the value parameter to `TRUE`, the function's behavior changes: Instead of returning the indices, it will return the actual strings that contain the pattern. This flexibility allows you to either locate where the pattern occurs in the vector or extract the matching elements.

```
# Return elements in "strings" that contain "xy"
grep("xy", strings, value = TRUE)
```

```
[1] "xy"
```

Let us analyze all the quantifying metacharacters and understand how they perform in regular expressions.

The asterisk `*` matches no or more occurrences of the preceding character. For instance, in a pattern, it can be used to match any number of a specific character, such as z, that appears before another character, like y. So, `z*y` in a regular expression would match "y," "zy," "zzy," "zzzy," and so on, effectively capturing sequences where "z" appears any number of times (including none) before a "y."

```
# Return elements matching "xz*y" pattern in "strings"
grep("xz*y", strings, value = TRUE)
```

```
[1] "xy"          "xzy"         "xzzy"        "xzzzy"       "xzzzzy"
↪   "xzzzzyzy"
```

The function successfully captured all items in the vector where the letter "y" is preceded by no or more occurrences of "z."

Next, let us consider the plus character +. Unlike the asterisk, the plus sign matches the preceding character one or more times. It requires the preceding character to appear at least once, making it useful for patterns where the character's presence is mandatory but can repeat.

```
# Return elements matching "xz+y" pattern in "strings"
grep("xz+y", strings, value = TRUE)
```

```
[1] "xzy"         "xzzy"        "xzzzy"       "xzzzzy"
↪   "xzzzzyzy"
```

The question mark character ? in regular expressions shows that the preceding character appears at least once or not at all. This means it allows for the presence of the character to be optional, indicating that the character might appear once or never in the search pattern.

```
# Return elements matching "xz?y" pattern in "strings"
grep("xz?y", strings, value = TRUE)
```

```
[1] "xy"   "xzy"
```

The quantifier {n}, enclosed in curly brackets, is used in regular expressions to match the precise number of occurrences—"n"—of the preceding character. This allows for precise control over how many times a character appears consecutively in the string being matched.

```
# Find "xz{3}y" (three "z's" before "y") in "strings"
grep("xz{3}y", strings, value = TRUE)
```

```
[1] "xzzzy"
```

The quantifier `{n,}` in regular expressions, followed by a comma, is used to match at least "n" occurrences of the preceding character, setting "n" as the lower boundary. The absence of an upper boundary in this quantifier means it can match "n" or more occurrences, effectively extending to any (potentially infinite) number of repetitions.

```
# Find "xz{2,}y" (at least two "z's" before "y") in "strings"
grep("xz{2,}y", strings, value = TRUE)
```

```
[1] "xzzy"      "xzzzy"     "xzzzzy"    "xzzzzyzy"
```

In regular expressions, the quantifier `{n,m}` is used to match a character that appears at least "n" times but not more than "m" times. This allows us to specify a range for the number of occurrences of the preceding character, with "n" as the lower limit and "m" as the upper limit.

```
# Find "xz{0,2}y" (0 to 2 "z's" before "y") in "strings"
grep("xz{0,2}y", strings, value = TRUE)
```

```
[1] "xy"    "xzy"    "xzzy"
```

In conclusion, this section has explored the versatile and powerful role of quantifiers in regular expressions within R. We have seen how quantifiers like `*`, `+`, `?`, `{n}`, `{n,}`, and `{n,m}` help us to maintain precise control over pattern matching by specifying the number of occurrences of characters.

Exercise. Find all string titles in the "prodtitle20" variable which contain the pattern "ire." Use the `grep()` function in R for this purpose. Once you have identified these titles, continue your exploration by applying the quantifiers we have discussed above. Experiment with these quantifiers to discover a variety of patterns within the "prodtitle20" variable.

2

Table 2.2 Position of a pattern inside a string. Table compiled by the authors

Anchors and boundaries	Description
`^`	Matches the beginning of a string
`$`	Matches the end of a string
`\b`	Matches a word boundary
`\B`	Matches a nonword boundary

2.4.2 Position of Pattern Inside a String

In the following section, we will focus on anchors and boundaries in regular expressions, as detailed in sources like Bryan (2020). These elements are crucial for specifying the position of a string within a sequence of characters. Anchors denote a string's start and end, such as the circumflex (^) for the former and the dollar sign ($) for the latter. Boundaries, on the other hand, define specific positions within the string. A summary of these anchors and boundaries, along with their descriptions, is provided in Table 2.2.

We use an anchor in regular expressions to locate strings which start or end with a specific word or character. Conversely, a boundary is used to find a position between a word character (like letters and numbers) and a nonword character (like spaces or punctuation). While the beginning or end of a string could be considered a boundary, in regular expressions, anchors and boundaries are distinct concepts with specific uses. For example, if we want to capture all the sentences which start with the character sequence "Ki," we would use the ^ anchor followed by "Ki." The ^ anchor explicitly matches a string's start, so `^Ki` would find any string that begins with "Ki" (note that "Ki" and "ki" differ).

```
# Find elements in "prodtitle20" starting with "Ki"
grep("^Ki", prodtitle20, value = TRUE)
```

```
[1] "Kindle?"
```

To capture phrases which end with a specific sequence of characters, such as "et," we use the `$` anchor. This metacharacter is placed after the character sequence and ensures that the match occurs at the end of the string. For example, using `et$` would match any string that concludes with "et."

```
# Find elements in "prodtitle20" ending with "et"
grep("et$", prodtitle20, value = TRUE)
```

```
[1] "Great Tablet"          "Sweet Little Tablet"
```

A word boundary in regular expressions, denoted as `\\b`, detects a position where a word character (like a digit, a letter, or an underscore) is adjacent to a nonword character (such as the beginning of a string, a tab, or a space). In R, the backslash \ is a special escape character. Therefore, when specifying a word boundary in a regular expression within R, double backslashes must be used to escape it properly, resulting in `\\\\b`. This ensures that the regular expression engine interprets it as a word boundary.

```
# Find elements in "prodtitle20" with the word "Fire" as a whole
↪  word
grep("\\bFire\\b", prodtitle20, value = TRUE)
```

```
[1] "The Kindle Fire is a great first effort"
```

The sequence `\\bFire\\b` successfully matches the term "Fire" as a standalone word. However, if "Fire" were in lowercase, this pattern would not match terms like "firefly," "crossfire," or "unfired," where "fire" is a substring of a larger word. The pattern will match sequences like "fire!me" because "!" is not considered a word character. The word boundary `\\b` can be used flexibly: Placing `\\b` before a term (e.g., `\\bfire`) will match cases like "firefly," and placing it after a term (e.g., `fire\\b`) will match cases like "crossfire." You can use the word boundary at either or both ends of the search sequence.

`\\B` is the complement of `\\b`. It matches positions where the adjacent characters are either both word characters or both nonword characters. For example, `\\B` would identify a match within strings like "$(=%@" or in cases where word characters surround a term without forming a standalone word. This makes `\\B` useful for detecting patterns which are not distinct words or are embedded within other characters.

```
# Find elements in "prodtitle20" where "able" is part of another
↪  word
grep("\\Bable\\B", prodtitle20, value = TRUE)
```

```
[1] "Great Tablet"
[2] "Boss tablet."
```

2

Table 2.3 Common regular expression characters and their functions. Table compiled by the authors

Character	Description
.	Matches any character except newline
[...]	Matches any one of the characters inside the brackets. A dash - can specify a range, like [a-z]
[^...]	Matches any character not listed inside the brackets
|	The OR operator: matches patterns on either side of |
(...)	Groups characters. Used with quantifiers (?, *, +, {n}). Groups can be referenced with \N, where N is the group number
\	Escapes a special character's meaning, like \$, *, \+, etc. In R, use double backslashes, e.g., *

```
[3] "Sweet Little Tablet"
[4] "Lightweight 10-inch Android 2.3 tablet with so-so
↪   screen"
```

In the example above, the pattern `\\Bable\\B` is designed to detect the sequence "able" when it is part of a larger word and surrounded by other word characters. It will not identify "able" as a standalone word. However, it is important to note that this pattern will not match "able" when it is directly followed or preceded by nonword characters, such as a full stop or a space. Essentially, `\\B` requires that both sides of "able" or any other collection of word characters, to be word characters, showing where "able" is embedded within a word but not at the beginning or end of a word.

2.4.3 Common Operators

Operators in regular expressions, such as the dot (`.`) or character lists denoted by three dots embraced by square brackets (`[...]`), are essential when defining specific criteria for matches. These operators are the building blocks of regular expressions, allowing for the construction of complex search patterns. Table 2.3 presents some of the most common operators used in regular expressions. For a more comprehensive list and detailed explanation of these operators, refer to the works of Sanchez (2013) and Forta (2018).

Examine the following examples carefully to understand how the different elements in regular expressions work. The single dot (`.`) is a versatile operator in regular expressions. It matches single characters (except for newline characters).

For instance, in the pattern `f.e`, the dot (`.`) will match any character that appears between "f" and "e," such as "fle," "fee," or "fze."

```
# Match "fe" followed by any character in "prodtitle20"
grep("fe.", prodtitle20, value = TRUE)
```

```
[1] "Wifi version inferior to the 3g version"
```

The square brackets in regular expressions match any of the characters contained within them. When a hyphen is used between two letters, it creates a range, selecting all the characters that lie between them in (English) alphabetical order. For example, `[a-i]` matches any letter from "a" to "i": a, b, c, d, e, f, g, h, or i. In a pattern such as `p[ru]`, "p" can be followed by either an "r" or a "u." In a pattern like `p[a-i]`, "p" can be followed by any letter from "a" to "i."

```
# Match "p" followed by "r" or "u" in "prodtitle20"
grep("p[ru]", prodtitle20, value = TRUE)
```

```
[1] "Love the product!" "Good purchase"
```

```
# Match "p" followed by any letter from "a" to "i" in
↪  "prodtitle20"
grep("p[a-i]", prodtitle20, value = TRUE)
```

```
[1] "Not what I expected"
```

The caret symbol (^) inside square brackets (not at the beginning of the expression) inverts the character class, selecting characters that are not listed inside the brackets. For example, in a pattern like `f[^i]`, the "f" must not be followed by an "i." It matches any character following "f" except for "i." In contrast, a pattern like fi simply looks for the exact sequence "fi."

```
# Match "f" not followed by "i" in "prodtitle20"
grep("f[^i]", prodtitle20, value = TRUE)
```

```
[1] "Best tech toy of 2010-2011"
[2] "Worked for one day!"
```

```
[3] "Obviously only for the Tech Savvy"
[4] "Excellent for what it is!"
[5] "Less than satisfaction"
[6] "The Kindle Fire is a great first effort"
[7] "Wifi version inferior to the 3g version"
```

```
# Match "fi" in "prodtitle20"
grep("fi", prodtitle20, value = TRUE)
```

```
[1] "The Kindle Fire is a great first effort"
[2] "Wifi version inferior to the 3g version"
```

In regular expressions, the `OR` operator represented by the vertical bar (|) is used to match strings that contain one of multiple specified patterns. For example, using `er|re` in a regular expression will match all strings that contain either the sequence “er” or “re.”

```
# Match "er" or "re" in "prodtitle20"
grep("er|re", prodtitle20, value = TRUE)
```

```
[1] "Ignore the nonsense"
[2] "Great Tablet"
[3] "Lightweight 10-inch Android 2.3 tablet with so-so
↪   screen"
[4] "The Kindle Fire is a great first effort"
[5] "Wifi version inferior to the 3g version"
```

Capturing parentheses () are often understood less well than other operators. Quite simply, they allow us to treat multiple characters as a single unit. This can be particularly useful when applying quantifiers for extracting specific parts of a string. In the pattern `(xy)+`, the parentheses group together “xy,” so the + quantifier applies to the sequence “xy” and not just “x” or “y.” This pattern will also match strings such as “xyxy,” “xyxyxy,” and so on, where “xy” repeats one or more times.

```
# Match one or more repetitions of "ire" in "prodtitle20"
grep("(ire)+", prodtitle20, value = TRUE)
```

```
[1] "The Kindle Fire is a great first effort"
```

Capturing parentheses can work wonders in combination with `sub()` and `gsub()`, which stand for *sub*stitution and *g*lobal *sub*stitution, respectively. The sub() function replaces the first occurrence of a pattern, while gsub() replaces all occurrences. When using capturing parentheses with these functions, the text within the parentheses is the target for substitution. Capturing parentheses are used to create captured groups. Capturing parentheses are represented by the (and) symbols, and a group is formed by the characters enclosed within these parentheses, such as (xyz). We reference captured groups in the replacement string using double backslashes followed by a group number (e.g., \\1 for the first group, \\2 for the second group, etc.), where the number corresponds to the order of the group. For example, in the pattern (xy) (yz), \\1 refers to the group, (xy), and \\2 refers to the group (yz). This allows us to specify which part of the pattern should be modified or which should remain *unmodified*. By default, the gsub() function processes each element of a character vector and returns a vector of the same length, including modified and unmodified elements. To focus on certain parts, we can first select the elements which match our criteria using a function like grep(). After isolating these elements, we then apply gsub() to them. This allows us to view and work with the data that matches our substitution pattern.

```
# Identify elements containing "Kindle Fire"
matches <- grep("Kindle Fire", prodtitle20, value = TRUE)

# Apply gsub only to matched elements
modified <- gsub("(Kindle) Fire", "\\1 Big Fire", matches)

# Display modified elements
modified
```

```
[1] "The Kindle Big Fire is a great first effort"
```

In our example, we searched for the sequence "Kindle Fire." Using gsub(), we kept the "Kindle" part unchanged, while substituting "Fire" with "Big Fire." This was achieved by capturing groups and back-referencing: The "Kindle" part was captured in a group and then referenced in the replacement string to remain fixed. Another powerful application of this function is to swap two terms in a string. By placing each term in a separate group, we can use back-references in the replacement pattern to reverse their positions.

```
# Swap "Kindle" and "Fire"
gsub("(Kindle) (Fire)", "\\2 \\1", matches)
```

```
[1] "The Fire Kindle is a great first effort"
```

When we want to search for characters which are also metacharacters in regular expressions, these characters must be "escaped" because they have special

2

meanings. For example, you might need to look for a dot (.) in a string. Remember that the dot is also a metacharacter used to match any character, so you need to “escape” it to transform it into a simple character. In most regular expression engines, escaping is done with a single backslash. However, in R, because the backslash itself is an escape character, you need to use two backslashes to represent a true backslash. The first backslash escapes the second, making it a true backslash, and the second backslash then escapes the dot (\\.), treating it as a true dot.

```
# Match literal dots in "prodtitle20"
grep("\\.", prodtitle20, value = TRUE)
```

```
[1] "eh.."
[2] "Boss tablet."
[3] "I have learned my lesson."
[4] "Lightweight 10-inch Android 2.3 tablet with so-so
↪   screen"
```

Exercise 1. Using the Product Reviews data set, focus on the “Title” column. Find all titles that contain the word “love” and end with an exclamation mark “!”. Once you have identified these, use regular expressions to replace the exclamation mark at the end of these titles with a question mark “?”. Employ back-referencing in your substitution.

Exercise 2. Utilize grouping parentheses to match both “can” and “can't.” Explore how the optional character operator ? can be combined with parentheses to handle variations in word endings.

2.4.4 Character Classes

Character classes in regular expressions are powerful tools used to match specific sets of characters, such as letters, numbers, and more. In the POSIX standard for regular expressions, these classes are placed within square brackets and include additional colons and a key name, following the structure `[:keyname:]`. For example, `[:digit:]` represents all numeric digits, and `[:alpha:]` matches all alphabetical characters. ◘ Table 2.4 summarizes some of the most widely used POSIX character classes (Forta, 2018; Sanchez, 2013).

Note that POSIX character classes, shown with colons and square brackets `[:...:]`, must be used within another set of square brackets. The correct pattern for matching a specific character class, such as punctuation marks, would be `[[:punct:]]`. This pattern will match any character that is classified as a

■ **Table 2.4** POSIX character classes and their functions. Table compiled by the authors

Character	Description
`[:lower:]`	Matches lowercase letters
`[:upper:]`	Matches uppercase letters
`[:digit:]`	Matches digits, `0 1 2 3 4 5 6 7 8 9`
`[:alpha:]`	Matches alphabetic characters
`[:alnum:]`	Matches alphanumeric characters
`[:xdigit:]`	Matches hexadecimal digits, `0-9 A-F a-f`
`[:blank:]`	Matches blank characters, i.e., space and tab
`[:space:]`	Matches space characters: tab, newline, vertical tab, form feed, carriage return, space
`[:punct:]`	Matches punctuation characters
`[:graph:]`	Matches graphical (human-readable) characters
`[:print:]`	Matches printable characters
`[:cntrl:]`	Matches control characters

punctuation mark. Let us search for the titles that contain punctuation in the "prodtitle20" data set.

```
# Find titles with punctuation in "prodtitle20"
grep("[[:punct:]]", prodtitle20, value = TRUE)
```

```
[1] "Best tech toy of 2010-2011"
[2] "Worked for one day!"
[3] "eh.."
[4] "Excellent for what it is!"
[5] "Love the product!"
[6] "Boss tablet."
[7] "I have learned my lesson."
[8] "Lightweight 10-inch Android 2.3 tablet with so-so
↪ screen"
[9] "Kindle?"
```

Exercise. Try writing regular expressions to identify titles with specific character types, like numerical digits or uppercase letters. Explore several patterns, such as those with punctuation, and apply these to the entire data set. If you are up for a challenge, use the whole "prodtitle" data set.

2.4.5 Sequences

Shorthand character classes in regular expressions offer a concise notation system, similar to the more expansive character classes discussed earlier (refer to ◘ Table 2.5). These shorthand notations can often be used interchangeably with their longer character class counterparts. The syntax involves a backslash \ followed by a specific letter representing a particular set of characters. Remember, in R, you need to escape the backslash with another backslash. For a more comprehensive understanding of these shorthand character classes and their usage, consult Sanchez (2013) and Forta (2018).

Exercise. Identify titles that contain specific patterns. First, look for those which include exactly two consecutive digits. Then, search for the ones which contain non-word characters (characters that are not letters, digits, or underscores). "Exercise ends."

Important: You have seen three types of symbols in this chapter, which are borrowed from mathematics: parentheses (), brackets [], and braces {}, in other books referred to as round, square, and curly brackets. The first ones are used for grouping, the second define character classes, and the third are used to quantify specific limits.

◘ **Table 2.5** Shorthand character classes in regular expressions. Table compiled by the authors

Regex shorthand	Description
`\d`	Matches a digit character
`\D`	Matches a non-digit character
`\s`	Matches a space character
`\S`	Matches a non-space character
`\w`	Matches a word character `[A-Za-z0-9]`
`\W`	Matches a nonword character `[^A-Za-z0-9]`
`\t`	Matches a tab character
`\n`	Matches a new line character
`\r`	Matches a carriage return

2.4.6 Regular Expressions with the `stringr` Package

The `stringr` package, part of Hadley Wickham's `tidyverse` suite of tools, can be installed independently or accessed as part of the entire `tidyverse` collection (refer to the introduction for installation details; Wickham, 2022b). All main functions in `stringr` start with the prefix `str_` and are designed for efficient string manipulation and the application of regular expressions. One key advantage of using `stringr` is its standardization across the two regex standards implemented in R, which means you do not need to specify `perl=TRUE/FALSE` for regex operations (Bryan, 2020). Examples of such functions are `str_detect()` for finding patterns, `str_subset()` for extracting matching elements, and `str_split_fixed()` for splitting strings based on patterns. It is worth mentioning that the function `str_view()` checks the representation of a string and how a pattern matches.

2.4.7 Regular Expressions in Search, Search and Replace Within RStudio

RStudio helps in using regular expression patterns to search for or replace text in R, Rnw, Rmd, qmd, or other types of files. To practice your regex skills in RStudio, you can create a regex sequence and then enable the "Regex" and "Wrap" options. For instance, consider the string "Text Analytics for Digital Marketing." Using the capturing parentheses expression `(Text)(.*?)(i)` in the search box will match the sequence "Text Analyti." This pattern uses three groups. The first one captures "Text," the second captures any examples of no character or least possible number, and the third captures "i," at its first occurrence (the least possible). Similarly, `(ext)(.*?)(i)` will match "ext Analyti." The addition of the middle group `(.*?)` makes the middle group "lazy," meaning it matches the shortest possible sequence rather than the longest. The main difference between greedy (standard in R) and lazy (enabled in RStudio) matching is that the former aims to match the longest possible sequence, while the latter matches the shortest. The (`?`) is the only way to instruct the regex engine to stop at the shortest possible match for a specified quantifier. For substitution, you can replace the content of one of the groups. For example, to change "Text Analytics for Digital Marketing" to "My Text Analytics for Digital Marketing":

- In the Search box, enter `(Text)(.*)(Marketing)`.
- In the Replace box, enter `My Text\2\3`.

This means that the second and third groups remain unchanged, and only "Text" is replaced with "My text." While R's regex engines (POSIX and Perl-like) do not inherently support lazy matching, RStudio, as an integrated development environment, provides this functionality, demonstrating the flexibility different tools offer in handling regular expressions. As a short exercise using the lazy version, you can try to substitute a string inside a sentence.

Exercises. Copy and paste the following code into RStudio to begin working with a set of strings designed for practicing regular expressions:

2

```
text_strings <- c("We have to extract these numbers 12, 47, 48",
"The integers numbers are also interestings: 189 2036 314",
"',' is a separator, so please extract these numbers 125,789,1450
and also these 564,90456", "We like to to offer you 7890$ per
month in order to complete this task... we are joking", "You are
going to learn 3 things, the first one is not to extract, and
2 and 3 are simply digits.", "Have fun with our mighty test, you
are going to support science, progress, mankind wellness and you
are going to waste 30 or 60 minutes of your life.", "you can also
extract exotic stuff like a456 gb67 and 45678911ghth", "Writing 1
example is not funny, please consider that 66% is
validation+testing", "You you are a genius, I think that you like
arrays A LOT, [3,45,67,900,1974]", "Who loves arrays more than
me?", "{366,78,90,5}Yes, there are only 4 numbers inside",
"Integers are fine but sometimes you like 99 cents after the 99
dollars", "100 euro are better than 99 euro", "I like to give you
1000 numbers now: 12 3 56 21 67, and more, [45,67,7]", "Ok ok 1 2
3 4 5 and the last one is 6", "33 trentini entrarono a Trento,
tutti e 33 di tratto in tratto trotterellando")
```

Selection

Exercise 1. Select all the strings with words containing exactly two consecutive "t"s.

Exercise 2. Select all the strings with words containing exactly two "t"s (not necessarily consecutive) or exactly two "e"s (not necessarily consecutive).

Exercise 3. Select all the strings that end in exactly one digit.

Exercise 4. Select all the strings that end in two digits.

Exercise 5. Select all the strings that have more than one capital letter.

Exercise 6. Select all the strings that do not have the substring "nu."

Exercise 7. Select all the strings that contain special characters such as [, €, and so on.

Exercise 8. Select all the strings that do not contain special characters.

Exercise 9. Select all the strings that end with a punctuation mark.

Exercise 10. Select all the strings that start with a lowercase letter.

Substitution or Addition

Exercise 1. Add a punctuation mark to strings that end without one.

Exercise 2. Replace "dollars" with the $ symbol.

Exercise 3. Replace "euro" with the €symbol.

Exercise 4. Replace consecutive repeating words with a single occurrence (e.g., "Bye Bye" becomes "Bye").

Exercise 5. Replace digits separated by a space with digits separated by a comma.

Exercise 6. Replace digits separated by a comma with digits separated by a comma and a space.

Exercise 7. Capitalize words that start with a lowercase letter.

Exercise 8. Add a dollar sign at the end of strings that finish with a dot.

Exercise 9. Insert a caret sign before the dot at the end of strings.

Exercise 10. Place a caret sign at the beginning of strings that start with a lowercase letter.

Bonus Exercise: Identify and correct a phrase in the data set that contains clear grammatical errors using regular expressions.

Conclusion

This chapter was not intended to be an exhaustive exploration of regular expressions. Instead, it was designed to guide novice and intermediate users through the process of importing and manipulating text data in R, equipping you with fundamental and robust tools for finding, adding, removing, or substituting characters in your texts. We have presented regular expressions using examples and exercises aimed at simplifying complex concepts to help you understand them easily. Additionally, we have introduced some basic statistics related to text strings, illustrated with the help of a data set. With these skills and knowledge, you are now well-prepared to move on to the next chapters. We will continue the marketing analytics journey through this book by exploring essential areas such as obtaining text and text preprocessing. These chapters will build upon what you have learned so far.

2

Discussion

When cleaning UGC, where is the line between useful normalization and harmful distortion? Give an example.

Pick either a vector, list, or data frame to justify your choice of container for raw reviews.

Describe a regular expression you would trust in production and one you would not. What possible risks (false matches, locale) drove your choices?

Assemble a mini Q&A checklist of workflows for ▶ Chap. 2 (e.g., string sampling, spell/variant harmonization, regex testing).

Take Home Message

- Clean first: UGC is imperfect; spelling, variants, and context require careful task-aware normalization prior to any analysis.
- Know your containers: In R, text is contained within character vectors, lists (including list columns), and data frames; master the indexing and combinations at the start.
- Strings are data: Base R and a number of simple workflows can often satisfy most requirements; write clear code and ensure it is reproducible.
- Regular expressions are power tools: Use metacharacters, in particular quantifiers, anchors, and character classes, to help extract patterns.
- Over-normalizing can remove meaning: Always check your results against the initial question and retain the raw text.

References

AbiWord Project. (2024). *Enchant speller*. https://github.com/AbiWord/enchant.

Arasu, A., & Garcia-Molina, H. (2003). Extracting structured data from web pages. *Proceedings of the ACM SIGMOD International Conference on Management of Data*, 337–348. https://doi.org/10.1145/872757.872799

Berger, J., Humphreys, A., Ludwig, S., Moe, W. W., Netzer, O., & Schweidel, D. A. (2020). Uniting the tribes: Using text for marketing insight. *Journal of Marketing*, *84*(1), 1–25. https://doi.org/10.1177/0022242919873106

Bryan, J. (2020). *STAT 545: Data wrangling, exploration, and analysis with R*.

Coombs, C. H. (1964). *A theory of data*. John Wiley & Sons. https://doi.org/10.1037/h0047773

Forta, B. (2018). *Learning regular expressions: A hands-on guide*. Sams Publishing.

Friedl, J. E. F. (2006). *Mastering regular expressions*. O'Reilly Media.

Gadenbuie, G. (2018). *Regexplain: A tool for explaining regular expressions*. https://regexplain.rbind.io.

Gagolewski, M. (2022). Stringi: Fast and portable character string processing in r. *Journal of Statistical Software*, *103*, 1–59. https://doi.org/10.18637/jss.v103.i02

Goyvaerts, J., & Levithan, S. (2012). *Regular expressions cookbook*. O'Reilly Media.

Hitchings, H. (2008). *The secret life of words: How English became English*. Macmillan.

Hu, Y., Jing, X., Ko, Y., & Rayz, J. T. (2020). Misspelling correction with pre-trained contextual language model. *2020 IEEE 19th International Conference on Cognitive Informatics & Cognitive Computing (Icci* Cc)*, 144–149. https://doi.org/10.1109/ICCICC50026.2020.9450253

Ihaka, R., & Gentleman, R. (1996). R: A language for data analysis and graphics. *Journal of Computational and Graphical Statistics*, *5*(3), 299–314. https://doi.org/10.2307/1390807

Kabacoff, R. I. (2022). *R in action: Data analysis and graphics with R and tidyverse*. Simon; Schuster.

Lewine, D. (1991). *POSIX programmers guide*. O'Reilly Media.

Moens, M.-F., Li, J., & Chua, T.-S. (2014). *Mining user generated content*. CRC press.

Netzer, O., Lemaire, A., & Herzenstein, M. (2019). When words sweat: Identifying signals for loan default in the text of loan applications. *Journal of Marketing Research*, *56*(6), 960–980. https://doi.org/10.1177/0022243719852959

Ogle, D. H. (2018). *Introductory fisheries analyses with R*. Chapman & Hall/CRC.

Sanchez, G. (2013). Handling and processing strings in R. *Trowchez Editions, Berkeley*.

Tuomi, I. (1999). Data is more than knowledge: Implications of the reversed knowledge hierarchy for knowledge management and organizational memory. *Proceedings of the 32nd Annual Hawaii International Conference on Systems Sciences. 1999. HICSS-32. Abstracts and CD-ROM of Full Papers, Track1*, 12 pp. https://doi.org/10.1109/HICSS.1999.772795

Wenfeng, Q. (2020). *re2r: RE2 regular expression*. R package version.

Wickham, H. (2019). *Advanced R*. CRC Press.

Wickham, H. (2022). *Stringr: Simple, consistent wrappers for common string operations*.

Obtaining Textual Data for Marketing Analytics: Web Scraping, APIs, and Structured Sources

D. Dan, T. Reutterer, *Text Analytics in Marketing*, Classroom Companion: Business,
https://doi.org/10.1007/978-3-032-08086-8_3

Keywords
Electronic text · OCR · Downloads · Web scraping · DOM · CSS selector · Selenium · API · SQL and NoSQL · JSON · PDF · CSV

3

This chapter reviews modalities for gathering text in R. It opens with approaches for dealing with electronic text, and it emphasizes that collection and preparation often take a significant amount of time. It also discusses digitization and optical character recognition (OCR) workflows (and their pitfalls) for printed and handwritten sources, with consideration of the legal and ethical aspects of collecting textual data. The chapter reviews the typical pathways for acquisition, which include self-generated content, copy-and-paste content, prepackaged downloads, web scraping, and curated datasets. It also discusses the use of several packages for reading in a variety of file formats while noting issues around encoding and security. It provides a worked example of downloading and reshaping PDFs and comma-separated values (CSVs) into tidy data frames. It also compares working with API access to web scraping via the `rvest` package, along with comparing the use of browser plug-ins, programmatic scraping schema, discovering text selectors via developer tools, and cleaning up scraped text fields. The chapter also covers dynamic web pages and using `RSelenium` to automate following links and pagination. It ends with structured sources, emerging tools for AI-assisted scraping, and repositories, as well as a set of exercises.

Learning Objectives

- Understanding where to look for text to analyze.
- Downloading data sets from the Internet and importing them in R.
- Collecting unstructured data and putting them into a structured form.
- Scraping data with APIs.
- Scraping data with Web browser plug-ins.
- Programming a script that downloads data for you.
- Understanding other ways of obtaining text data.

3.1 Handling Electronic Text

Text mining and analytics provide marketing analysts with various tools for analyzing large volumes of textual data (Guyt et al., 2024). These applications and the important role they play were outlined in the introduction. In this section, we will focus on the technical aspects of text acquisition, which typically takes a considerable length of time, and it is important to acknowledge that data collection and preparation represent a significant portion of a project's duration, often up to 80%. Efficiently managing these processes can significantly reduce the frustration and inefficiency inherent in the acquisition of textual data (Frye & Schmitt, 2020).

A large proportion of data available on the Internet is unstructured (cf. Gandomi & Haider, 2015, Wedel & Kannan, 2016, Boegershausen et al., 2022). This means it is not organized in a tabular format or within a database and lacks a predefined structure. The primary types of data requiring transformation are text, images, and video. Since computers operate more effectively with structured data, converting them from unstructured to structured formats is critical in the analytical process. Therefore, before commencing data collection, it is essential to consider several fundamental questions. The foremost concern is the format of the data to be collected. This leads to the realization that data, in our case text, can be stored in various file types, such as CSV files, which are appropriate for this task. Additionally, it is good to understand the relationships within the data, the number of sources, and their acquisition methods. We speak using words, but it is through written text that we leave our imprint on the future.

Humans continuously generate text in various forms, ranging from physical mediums such as letters, articles, diaries, books, and other written formats, to virtual ones stored in file types such as *.txt*, *.doc*, *.docx*, *.pages*, *.pdf*, and *.odt* files, among others. Additionally, there are file formats with more or less familiar extensions. In text analysis or analytics, having documents in an electronic format is imperative, as it allows the text to be structured and manipulated easily.

> *Electronic text (e-text)* is the digital storage of text, which is available for reading on electronic devices, but also for searching, transforming, reasoning, and analyzing (e.g., .txt, .docx, .pdf with OCR).

Consequently, acquiring virtual text is preferable, but there are methods to convert printed text into electronic documents. Electronic text can be derived from printed material through a two-step process. The initial step involves digitization, achieved by scanning or photographing the documents. The subsequent step is to extract text from these images, using OCR systems.

> *Optical character recognition (OCR)* is software that takes images of printed text (or handwriting) and converts them into, or makes them recognizable as, machine-readable characters so they can be copied/pasted and used for analysis.

This process is often lengthy and prone to errors (Srihari, 1985), requiring specific software and human intervention for quality assurance. Proofreading is critical, demanding meticulous attention to detail to ensure the transformed text accurately reflects the original. This procedure applies to standard printed text, but the challenge intensifies with handwritten documents.

Mass digitization projects have been, and continue to be, significant endeavors. Official initiatives like Europeana, backed by the European Union, have created digital platforms housing millions of items. Another notable project is that of Google Books, launched with the ambitious goal of digitizing the world's books and making them accessible online (Thylstrup, 2019). A significant aspect of this project was the use of OCR technology, which converted the scanned images of books into machine-readable text. However, this project faced legal challenges from authors and publishers until 2016, when Google won a series of important legal battles, after which it was allowed to proceed with its scanning efforts (Rimmer, 2017). Today, a number of projects and partnerships give research groups access to this extensive database to carry out in-depth text analysis.

For those not requiring access to rare or non-digital textual sources, using existing electronic versions is a practical approach. However, although there are official repositories, shadow libraries do exist and it is important to be mindful of the copyright laws in your region, as not all digitized texts are freely available for research or other purposes.

Some ways to obtain electronic text are the following: (i) self-generated text, (ii) manual copy and paste, (iii) direct text downloads, (iv) web scraping, and (v) ready-to-use data sets. These are among the most common approaches, see ◘ Fig. 3.1. Manual copy and paste is a straightforward yet time-consuming method, ideal for small amounts of text. Directly downloading text files, such as in *pdf* format, *docx* format, or plain text files, is efficient for accessing large documents or books already in a digital format. Scraping text from documents with various file extensions often requires specialized software or scripts, especially when handling large volumes of data or complex formats. On the other hand, web scraping ranges from the simple extraction of specific pieces of text from web pages to more advanced scraping that navigates web pages and handles dynamic content. Lastly, ready-to-use data sets from online repositories are a convenient source, as these are often well-structured and ideal for analysis without extensive preprocessing. Next we describe these common ways to obtain textual data.

3.1.1 Copy and Paste

The simplest method of obtaining text that is not self-generated is through copy and paste. This involves copying text from various sources and pasting it into a simple text file stored locally on your computer. It is a three-step process: selecting the text, mainly with the help of your mouse, copying it, and then pasting it into a recipient file. You can paste different portions of text consecutively onto the same text file, making this procedure a primitive form of scraping. The procedure is similar in all operating systems, such as macOS, Windows, or Linux, with minor differences in the commands and text editing applications used. Here you have the procedure detailed for the most common commercial operating systems:

- First, open the source document or web page from which you wish to copy text.
- Click and drag your mouse over the text to highlight it.

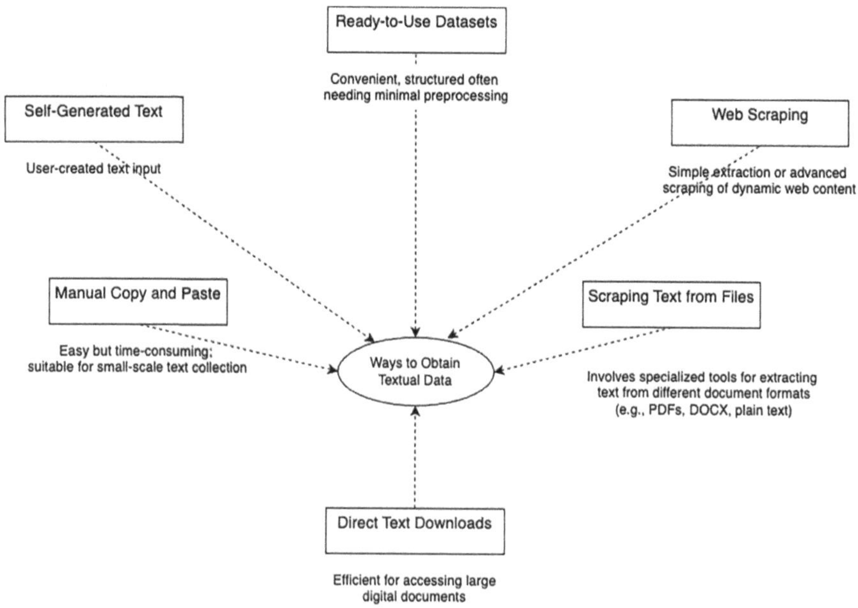

Fig. 3.1 Obtain textual data. Authors' own figure

- On OSX, press Command + C to copy the highlighted text; on Windows, use Ctrl + C.
- Next, open a text editing application. For macOS, use TextEdit; for Windows, use Notepad. Note that TextEdit defaults to rich text mode. To save your file as a .txt file, convert it to plain text by going to Format in the menu bar and selecting Make Plain Text (or use the shortcut Shift + Command + T).
- Click inside the document and press Command + V on macOS or Ctrl + V on Windows to paste the copied text.
- To save the file, click File > Save (or use Command + S on macOS or Ctrl + S on Windows). Name your file, for instance, "copied_text.txt". Navigate to the desired folder within your working directory. If you are looking for a specific folder such as "data" and it does not exist, create it. Finally, click Save.

This method is straightforward and does not require specialized software, making it an excellent starting point for anyone new to data collection.

This is how you import the file into R and visualize the text.

```
# "data" is the sub-folder inside current working directory
text_data <- readLines("data/copied_text.txt")

# Display the content of the text file
print(text_data)
```

3.1.2 Downloaded Text

3

For a marketing analyst, sourcing documents which are ready for analysis is not always straightforward. For example, literature students have the advantage of accessing many out-of-copyright texts available on the Internet. Alongside well-known resources like Google Books and Europeana, they (or anyone else) can explore sites like the Gutenberg Project, Internet Archive, Open Culture, Hathi Trust, ACLS Humanities E-Book, National Digital Library of India, Gallica, Wikisource, as well as many others. These platforms offer extensive collections of books and freely accessible texts, ideal for downloading and importing into R. The benefit of using simple text is that it allows for imports from these websites, providing an excellent opportunity to start developing text analytics skills. The goal is to have the text in a format that lends itself to structured analysis.

Fortunately, collections of documents are already prepared in structured formats such as CSV or zipped CSV files. These are often found on platforms like Kaggle, GitHub, and the repositories of various research institutes. When dealing with documents in compressed formats like *.gz* or *.zip*, it is advisable to decompress them first before importing them into R. Conversely, files in formats like *.csv* or *.xlsx* can be imported directly from the Internet via a secure HTTPS connection. Downloading files over an insecure HTTP protocol is not recommended for security reasons. Direct Internet import can be cumbersome and prone to errors for files with substantial amounts of data. Hence, it is preferable to download these files to your local machine first and then import them into R.

Let us demonstrate this by importing a data set directly. This method is suitable for smaller files: Downloading the files first is recommended for larger ones. The "sample.csv" file, an excerpt from the larger "Product Reviews.csv," contains the first 250 observations. This file is an example of a structured document. As shown in ■ Table 3.1, the first row, which is the header, lists the column names or features. Each subsequent row represents an observation, encompassing all the data related to a single purchase.

The `read.csv()` function in R is used to import the `sample.csv` file and automatically transform it into a data frame. Remember, in R, a data frame is a term used to describe a tabular data structure. The parameter `header = TRUE` within the function specifies that the first row of the CSV file should be treated as the header containing the column names rather than regular data.

■ **Table 3.1** Sample table, Excel-like. Table compiled by the authors

Review ID	Item ID	Base item ID	Review date	…
R100E6MT94PK6L	B0051VVOB2		1/8/2012	…
R100HU42LKLLD0	B0057O9O6K		4/10/2012	…
R100PBXP49AU0B	B0051VVOB2		3/26/2012	…
…	…	…	…	…

```
# URL of the file
url <- "https://danieldanlab.github.io/data/sample.csv"

# Read CSV into data frame
df <- read.csv(url, header = TRUE)

# If you want to see the data set in viewer, uncomment
# View(df)

# Keep only first 5 columns
df <- df[, 1:5]

# Display first 6 rows
head(df)
```

```
  X      Review_ID    Item_ID Base_item_ID Review_date
1 1 R100E6MT94PK6L B0051VVOB2                1/8/2012
2 2 R100HU42LKLLD0 B00570906K               4/10/2012
3 3 R100PBXP49AU0B B0051VVOB2               3/26/2012
4 4 R100U020EZR95F B0051VVOB2               6/14/2012
5 5 R101ANBUYVZCUM B004U9USEA               5/21/2011
6 6 R101MUGRC35UWS B001UHPRSW               1/29/2010
```

```
# Display last 6 rows
tail(df)
```

```
      X      Review_ID    Item_ID Base_item_ID Review_date
245 245 R10VM77VD3D76X B004Q1P0S6               12/25/2011
246 246 R10VXS69HIOF1X B0044UAQMY                6/21/2011
247 247 R10W6FDN5GFTK4 B004U78J1G   B004U78J1G  10/24/2011
248 248 R10WG1DINHPFRU B0051VVOB2               12/12/2011
249 249 R10WJVG8HFG133 B0051VVOB2               11/30/2011
250 250  R10WL5UATT2QP B004PGMFG2   B0067XX3AI   6/30/2011
```

The `df` data frame can be sliced both horizontally and vertically to suit your needs. The general syntax for this operation is `df[rows, columns]`. In this structure, the brackets encompass the entire data frame, and the comma separates the rows from the columns, in that order. To select the first row along with all its columns, you would use `df[1, ]`, where the (empty) space after the comma signifies the inclusion of all the columns. Similarly, to select specific rows and columns, for example, rows 3 to 5 and columns 2 to 9, you would use `df[3:5, 2:9]`.

3.1.2.1 Common File Type Extensions

What if the file you need to analyze does not have a `.csv` extension? In such instances, the `readtext` package (Benoit & Obeng, 2020) is handy. It is designed to read and extract text from a variety of file formats, including *.doc*, *.docx*, *.html*, *.json*, *.pdf*, *.rtf*, *.tab*, *.xls*, *.xlsx*, *.xml*, and several other related extensions. This versatile function not only extracts the text but also retrieves the document's metadata, and it can handle multiple file types simultaneously. The data extracted are stored in a data frame, our preferred tabular data format. As a side note, when importing data into R, it is not uncommon to encounter issues with character encoding. Common fixes include setting the correct file encoding on import, normalizing text to UTF-8, and checking the system locale.

The `readtext` package relies on other packages for specific file types: `pdftools` (Ooms, 2020) for PDF files and `antiword` for *.doc* documents. Installation on Windows and macOS is typically straightforward. However, Linux users might face challenges, particularly with `pdftools`, which requires a development library. On Debian/Ubuntu and similar systems, this issue can be resolved by installing the `libpoppler` development library. Other Linux distributions with different package management systems, like those using `rpm` package management, have similar solutions.

```
# Installs the libpoppler-cpp-dev library on Debian/Ubuntu systems
sudo apt install libpoppler-cpp-dev
```

Text files are often unstructured. This means that the data are not stored in a tabular form, making them difficult to work with. To illustrate this, in the next example, we have created a PDF file that simulates a real-world scenario. This file consists of two pages. The first page contains text divided into paragraphs, generated using lorem ipsum, a commonly used placeholder text which imitates Latin. The second page features a table filled with randomly generated data (Random Data Generator, 2024). While this text appears structured to our eyes, this is not the case for a computer. We will show how to extract and format this information into a structure suitable for basic text analytics. The goal is to organize the data into a simple table, with one column for each sentence and another for an incremental number to track the paragraphs, similar to the structure shown in ◘ Table 3.1. It is important to know that a PDF file is a container rather than a specific format. If the document contains text in image format rather than selectable text, use `pdf_ocr_text()` to perform OCR before parsing. Let us now download the file and extract the text from the first page of the PDF. To understand its content and structure, it is advisable to open and inspect the file, as well as any other text file, before working with it.

```
# Load necessary libraries
library(pdftools)
library(stringr)

# Define URL of the PDF file
url <- "https://danieldanlab.github.io/data/sample.pdf"

# Download PDF file
download.file(url, "sample.pdf", mode = "wb")

# Read PDF; each page becomes an element in "text"
text <- pdf_text("sample.pdf")

# Remove "Sample text" from the text
text <- str_replace(text, "Sample text", "")

# Replace newline characters with space in page 1
text[1] <- str_replace_all(text[1], "\n", " ")

# Split text at periods in page 1
text[1] <- str_split(text[1], "\\.")

# Convert to data frame
mytext <- as.data.frame(text[1])

# Name the column as "Sentence"
colnames(mytext) <- c("Sentence")

# Display first six rows
head(mytext)
```

```
                                              Sentence
1       Lorem ipsum dolor sit amet, consectetur
 ↪  adipiscing elit
2                                        Quisque sed
 ↪  venenatis mi
3  Mauris eget lectus luctus, molestie enim nec,
 ↪  tincidunt urna
4                                Nulla iaculis ut lorem a
 ↪  blandit
5              Etiam non arcu et magna tempor iaculis ac
 ↪  at erat
6            Quisque non malesuada augue, sit amet
 ↪  vulputate enim
```

Having achieved the primary goal of extracting the data, you can refine the appearance of the content in the data set further. This can be done using regular expressions and string manipulation functions to tailor the data to your specific needs.

The table on the second page of the *.pdf* file is already in a tabular format, which we will aim to keep. To accomplish this, we will use the `extract_tables()` function, which efficiently extracts the table's content and places it in a data frame. It is worth noting that in scenarios where a PDF page contains multiple tables, possibly in various locations, these can also be extracted. For more advanced options and the handling of such cases, refer to the `tabulapdf` package (Sepulveda, 2024), which offers additional tools for extracting PDF tables.

3

```
# Load tabulapdf library
library(tabulapdf)

# Extract table from second page of PDF
atable <- extract_tables(url, pages = 2, guess = TRUE, output =
↪   "tibble")

# Assign first table to mytable
mytable <- atable[[1]]

# Display top six rows of the table
head(mytable)
```

```
# A tibble: 6 x 5
  `First Name` `Last Name` Gender Education Occupation
  <chr>        <chr>       <chr>  <chr>     <chr>
1 Kate         Jones       Female Bachelor  Scientist
2 Adele        Barnes      Female Doctoral  Social Worker
3 Sofia        Campbell    Female Primary   Mathematician
4 Oscar        Parker      Male   Master    Mathematician
5 Andrew       Armstrong   Male   Bachelor  Mathematician
6 Sawyer       Taylor      Male   Doctoral  Social Worker
```

All in all, our primary goal is to extract the most crucial element for our analysis, which is text, regardless of the file format in which it is encoded. The *.pdf* file type we just discussed is only one example of a source from which we can obtain information. As you have learned, importing text data into R from common file formats is a (relatively) straightforward process. This procedure is similar to that used when extracting information from other file types, such as Excel formats (*.xls* or *.xlsx*). There are several packages in R designed for this purpose. For instance, the `readxl` package is an excellent choice for reading Excel files. When it comes to reading files from the Internet, the file's extension guides us to choose the appropriate function. For *.dat*, *.txt*, or *.csv* files, we can use the `read.table()` function. R can also import various file types from other software, such as SAS,

SPSS, or STATA. This is made possible with the `haven` package (part of the `tidyverse` suite) and its related functions, `read_sas()`, `read_sav()`, and `read_dta()`, supporting Stata *.dta* files up to version 15.0. In the next section, we will tackle more advanced procedures to structure data from the Internet effectively within R.

3.2 Web Scraping

3.2.1 Scraping for Data

It usually requires a more elaborate procedure to collect customer opinions and other user-generated content, as they are typically embedded within specific web pages. How do we collect reviews about a specific product or service? Many companies, such as Airbnb, Amazon, Booking.com, TripAdvisor, Trustpilot, and Yelp, host these data on their websites. Similarly, opinion-based text from social media platforms like X (formerly Twitter), Facebook, and Instagram can be valuable. We can access this data through a process known as web scraping (Khder, 2021; Munzert et al., 2014). As the term suggests, this involves extracting data from a surface. In a digital context, it refers to the technique of copying data embedded in an unstructured way within HTML tags to a structured format which suits the needs of data analysts, such as a CSV file.

> *Web scraping* is the automated capturing of content embedded in web pages, either as HTML or rendered via JavaScript. It takes the content (including images and metadata) and makes it available in a structured dataset for analysis.

What can we scrape from web pages? Essentially anything digital: text, numbers, images, and metadata. For instance, in the context of online product feedback, we can collect customer reviews, product ratings, customer nicknames, labels, dates, and other related data or metadata. All this can be transformed into useful information for analysis and knowledge extraction. Researchers in a number of fields, such as economics (Cavallo, 2012; Hillen, 2019), psychology (Landers et al., 2016), agriculture (Yang et al., 2010), and the hotel industry (Han & Anderson, 2021), as well as geographic data acquisition (Brenning & Henn, 2023), obtain data through scraping. Web scraping for consumer research (Boegershausen et al., 2022) plays a significant role too. There are several methods and tools which facilitate the downloading and collection of data. Some of them must be built specifically for the fields in which they are used (Bonifacio et al., 2015), while others are more generic, such as Outwit (Harvest the Web, 2024), Fminer (Web Data Extractor, 2024), or Parsehub (Free Web Scraping, 2024). Some methods need to be tailored to specific projects and frequently use computer languages such as Java, Python, or R to carry out their data crawling. These tools change data from an unstructured into a structured form, making them ready for further analysis. It is important to note that data, mainly text data, are often the core business of some companies, and they may try to block or hinder automatic parsers or robots from scraping and collecting information (Hirschey, 2014; Poggi et al., 2007). Technically, there are two main ways to scrape Internet data: using an application programming interface (API), for example, Sturm et al. (2017), or document object model (DOM) parsing (Radilova et al., 2022). APIs, provided by platforms such as X, Facebook, and TripAdvisor, offer well-established procedures for obtaining data in predefined formats such as *.csv*, *.xls*, or *.xlsx*. On the other hand, DOM parsing is carried out through programming with scripts and requires considerable effort. Additionally, some programs or plug-ins facilitate the retrieval of information without an extensive knowledge of programming.

> *An application programming interface (API)* is a published interface which allows programmatic requests (often with authorization) using a set of instructions to retrieve (or modify) data in standardized formats (e.g., CSV, JSON).

3.2.1.1 Data from Social Media, the API Concept

In the land of social media, there have been winners and losers. Some social media platforms, once ubiquitous, have now turned into little more than websites, such as Myspace, or were entirely discontinued by their creators, like Orkut and Google+. A few, however, have stood the test of time: X (formerly Twitter), one of the most scraped social media platforms, Facebook, LinkedIn, and Reddit, are just a few of these. Others are new or emerging, such as TikTok. No matter their current status, their content can be a valuable source of data. Let us briefly consider them and the collection of their data through an API.

Twitter's name was inspired by how birds communicate, with short, high-pitched calls or sounds directed to an audience which understands those messages. The titular company debuted in 2006 and is well known for its microblogging consisting of short and concise messages (Murthy, 2018). This model of communication is both efficient and information-dense. Messages, called tweets, have several key elements: *addresses* (usernames marked by @), *text* (limited to *280* characters), *hashtags* (marked by # to denote topics), and types of interaction like *replies*, *mentions*, and *retweets*.

Data from X and other social media are particularly interesting for marketing analysts because it has been, and continues to be, used extensively for viral advertising (Berger et al., 2020; Tellis et al., 2019). It has strong user engagement, a solid user base, and supports many languages. Moreover, it contains vast amounts of real-time data. The mix of user behavior and competitor strategy is crucial for understanding and analyzing marketing. It is an ideal place to monitor influencers' ideas and opinions, understand why they are followed, and use this information for marketing purposes: for example, knowing how your brand is perceived on this social media platform. Learning this can help you stay aware of potential discontent. Understanding how people "feel" about your brand and how this sentiment changes in response to your actions is vital. This type of analysis, known as "sentiment analysis," will be discussed in more detail in ► Chap. 8. Some R packages that help you scrape data from Twitter through APIs are `rtweet` (Kearney, 2019), `streamR` (Barbera, 2018), and `academictwitteR` (Barrie & Ho, 2021).

With its massive user base, Facebook has been seen as an ideal platform for promoting products, ideas, or projects. The connection between users and the "like" system made it an easy way to collect personal data for free. These can be harnessed for marketing analysis, especially for segmentation, where targeting by geographical regions can enhance communication and promote specific products. Two important R packages for dealing with data on Facebook are `Rfacebook` (Barbera et al., 2017) and `fbRads` (Daroczi et al., 2023).

LinkedIn, a popular social media platform for professionals, was set up to aid networking. Finding a job through LinkedIn has become a viable option, and the personal pages can contain a lot of interesting information, mainly about what occupies most of our time: work. This can be extracted to check for who might be important partners or influencers in marketing campaigns. Other analyses could be done to understand market dynamics, emerging trends, and information about competitors, including their workforce size or skill sets. To access data through LinkedIn's APIs via R, you can use `Rlinkedin` (Piccirilli, 2016).

Reddit, a very popular platform for sharing opinions and asking questions about products, recipes, medicines, supplements, and much more, has become a rich source of data. The impressive quantity of data and opinions makes this social media platform extremely useful for marketing analysis. The R package to interact with this platform is `RedditExtractoR` (Rivera, 2023).

All the platforms mentioned above offer, or offered, the opportunity for researchers to scrape their data through an API. An API consists of definitions and communication protocols that allow a person with a computer to connect to a server providing this technology. It is a privileged gateway to data that needs to be first identified and then transferred to your computer. APIs generally use a username and password system, plus or minus other related values, also known as keys. These alphanumeric sequences are generated for a specific user and work like credentials. APIs are interfaces; they open a door through which the user can access data directly from the service's backend. However, it is rare that you are able to do this immediately, and collecting data through APIs can be problematic. Significant issues arise due to constant changes in authorization modes, data access limitations, and managerial decisions which can restrict access. Several R packages written for this purpose become obsolete after a few years, or even months, due to internal changes in social media data accessibility policies and parameters. As such, although scraping with APIs might seem a good way forward, other methods of obtaining data may be more suitable for the task you have in front of you. Remember, while working with R packages that do API scraping, two components must be stable: the policies of the API provider and the R package.

3

3.2.2 Scraping with Your Browser

Having tools that simplify the data collection process without requiring deep technical know-how can be useful and comforting. Take the Web Scraper plug-in for Google Chrome, for example. It is a user-friendly tool for web scraping, requiring only a basic understanding of HTML and CSS. You can install it easily from the Chrome store, and, as with most plug-ins, a browser restart is needed post-installation. Web scraper stands out for its:

- Ability to navigate and scrape multiple pages with a defined structure, like "http://www.example.com/pages/[1-10]".
- Versatility in scraping various data types.
- Ability to extract dynamically generated text from client-side scripts, including AJAX and JavaScript.
- Capacity to review and export the local storage of scraped data to a CSV file.
- Ease in switching between exportable and importable sitemaps which detail the scope of a scraping project.

Setting it up involves defining the sitemap (which pages to visit) and the data to be scraped. During the scraping process, Chrome will display a series of pop-up windows showing its progress. You will receive a notification once the scraping is complete. All the data can be browsed and exported as a CSV file, ready to be imported into R for further analysis. The plug-in also allows you to export the sitemap for future use. Check out the plug-in's official web page for a comprehensive guide on using this tool.

3.2.2.1 Other Plug-ins

The world of Chrome plug-ins for data scraping is vast and varied. Take Instant Data Scraper, for example, a plug-in that simplifies the scraping process, requiring minimal technical know-how. It uses AI analysis to see what data can be extracted from an HTML page, bringing something unique to your scraper's toolbox. And for those interested in specific sites, Amazon Reviews Exporter and Amazon Data Scraper are plug-ins designed for collecting data from Amazon. Wherever the data are, it is likely there is a tool ready to help you harvest them. This is true for a range of sites that are well known to be rich in data, from Parler to Gab, and Yelp to Trustpilot. And it is not just Chrome that offers these tools; Data Miner, for instance, works with both Chrome and Microsoft Edge.

Focusing on something more practical, using Amazon Reviews Exporter's free version, you can download about ten reviews at a time (be aware that these parameters might change over time). For example, we could grab reviews for The Lord of the Rings Hardcover-Box set, March 3, 1988 from Amazon, save them as a CSV file, and then dive into the data using R.

```
# Load tibble package
library(tibble)

# Read CSV as data frame
tolkien <- read.csv("data/LordOR_amzn.csv", header = TRUE,
↪ stringsAsFactors = FALSE)

# Convert data frame to tibble for readability
tolkien_t <- as_tibble(tolkien)

# Display tibble structure
str(tolkien_t)
```

```
tibble [50 x 16] (S3: tbl_df/tbl/data.frame)
 $ id               : chr [1:50] "R177MIRDIAB6HL"
 ↪ "R1AD5LS9CM4L0R" ...
 $ username         : chr [1:50] "Karen Reynolds" "Julian F
 ↪ Waldby" ...
 $ profileURL      : chr [1:50]
 ↪ "https://www.amazon.com/gp/profile/amzn1." ...
 $ rating           : int [1:50] 5 5 5 5 5 5 5 5 5 5 ...
 $ title            : logi [1:50] NA NA NA NA NA NA ...
 $ review_url       : chr [1:50]
 ↪ "https://www.amazon.com/gp/customer-reviews" ...
 $ asin             : int [1:50] 395489326 395489326
 ↪ 395489326 395489326 ...
 $ content          : chr [1:50] "Such a nice looking
 ↪ collection. So nice" ...
 $ date             : chr [1:50] "Reviewed in the United
 ↪ States on January 2 ...
 $ format_strip     : logi [1:50] NA NA NA NA NA NA ...
 $ verified        : chr [1:50] "Verified Purchase" "Verified
 ↪ Purchase" ...
 $ helpful          : chr [1:50] "One person found this
 ↪ helpful" "" ...
 $ videoURL         : logi [1:50] NA NA NA NA NA NA ...
 $ video_cover_url: logi [1:50] NA NA NA NA NA NA ...
 $ imgs             : chr [1:50] "[]" "[]" "[]" ...
 $ normalImgs       : chr [1:50] "[]" "[]" "[]" ...
```

```
# Show first 2 entries
head(tolkien_t$content, 2)
```

```
[1] "Such a nice looking collection. So nice that it can
↪   be used as room"
[2] "decor when not being read. Hey its Lord of the Rings
↪   and a perfect set."
[3] "All the books together.  Gave me something to do
↪   whenever I got"
[4] "depressed over holidays."
```

3

As you can see, even from a small data set, as in the one above, you can extract a lot of information and save it in a structured form. And, the more data you have access to, the better and more accurate the analysis will be. All in all, there is no one-size-fits-all solution in the scraping-plug-in world. Some will work better than others, some new tools will appear on the market, and others will cease to exist. But it is important that you know, as a data analyst, that you can always find another plug-in for your data-scraper toolbox. Most of these services are not free or have a free version that allows you to collect a limited number of pages or items. Alternatively, if you need to have full control over the downloaded content, you can be creative and use your programming skills to collect information, as discussed in the next section.

3.2.3 Scraping by Programming

To the nonspecialist, a web page appears as a blend of text, images, and videos, all presented on a Web browser. However, beneath this surface lies a more complex reality of a two-layer language system made of a markup language and a style sheet that instructs the browser on what and how to display the content. The structure of the page is governed by hypertext markup language (HTML), while its visual presentation is run by cascading style sheets (CSS). HTML has an easy-to-understand syntax. It gives directives to the Web browser and embeds text in HTML pages. The text displayed on a web page is (nearly) always enclosed in HTML tags such as `<tag>`Some Text`<tag>`. The text inside the angular brackets < > can be any HTML keyword such as `<html>`, `<body>`, `<h1>`, and `<p>`, among others. The slash inside the brackets < / > signifies the end of an element. In technical jargon, the term "element" defines the opening and closing of two tags and the content between them. Once a tag is open, it must also be closed, like a bracket in mathematics. There are some exceptions, though, where the tags are self-contained and do not require closing, such as `<br>` for a line break. Some HTML tags contain attributes, such as `id` or `class`. They link HTML elements to the CSS for the aesthetic styling of the web page. An important tag in HTML is `<div>`, used in Web design and layout, and is essential for structuring the site. It is commonly used together with CSS for styling and JavaScript for functionality, so pay attention to it whenever you find it. ◘ Figure 3.2 shows the main components of an HTML element.

A simplified example of an HTML code that also includes an element like that in ◘ Fig. 3.2, can be seen in the snippet below:

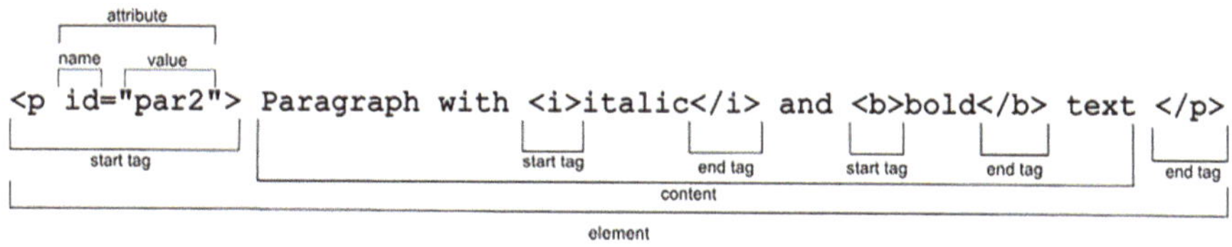

Fig. 3.2 HTML, paragraph element. Authors' own figure

```
    <!DOCTYPE html>
<html>
<head>
    <title>Book</title>
    <meta name="description" content="Marketing">
    <script type="text/javascript">
    // JavaScript code can go here
    </script>
    <link rel="stylesheet" href="style.css">
</head>
<body>
    <h1>Scraping</h1>
    <article>
        <p>
            Paragraph with <sub>subscript</sub> and
↪   <sup>superscript</sup> text.
        </p>
        <p id="par2">
            Paragraph with <i>italic</i> and <b>bold</b> text.
        </p>
    </article>
    <table>
<tr>
<td>Tablets</td>
</tr>
</table>
    <ul>
        <li>API</li>
        <li>DOM</li>
    </ul>
    <footer>
        <p>This is a footer paragraph.</p>
        <a href="https://danieldanlab.github.io">Link to a
        ↪ page</a>
    </footer>
</body>
</html>
```

Using programming languages, for example, R, Python, or Java, we can navigate through the internal elements of these web pages and retrieve valuable information. This process involves parsing the pages into a document object model (DOM) tree

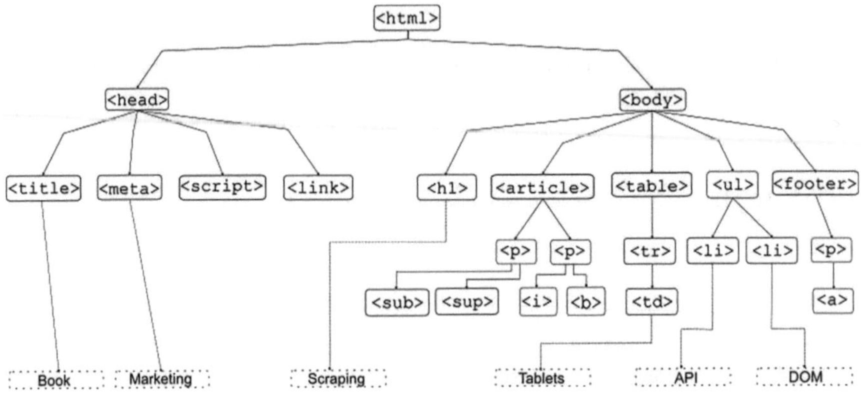

Fig. 3.3 DOM structure. Authors' own figure

structure (Keith & Sambells, 2011). Let us demystify the link between HTML and DOM. When a browser loads a web page, it parses the web page sequentially, reading the HTML tags in sequence. While parsing, it builds the DOM, and the HTML tags are transformed into DOM nodes. If, during the parsing process, there are scripts, JavaScripts, for example, or external elements such as CSS directives and images that might interrupt the process, the DOM building still goes ahead, most of the time, in parallel, with little or no interruptions. So, the DOM represents a model of a page, while HTML is a language that allows you to create the DOM. After its creation, scripts can manipulate it to change a page's content, structure, or style after it has been loaded. This procedure allows for it to be interactive, making pages dynamic and accessible alike. It is easier to locate specific data on a web page through the hierarchical tree structure of the DOM, and scraping tools can use the DOM to identify `ids`, `classes`, and `tag names` to extract the information you need. For a visual representation of how a basic HTML page, like that in the previous example, is organized by the DOM, refer to Fig. 3.3. Be aware that only the opening tags are represented; the closing section is, for the most part, a mirror of these.

The `<html>` node is the *root* of the tree; it has two branches: `<head>` and `<body>`. It tells the browser that it encapsulates all the elements of the page. The `<head>` node is like the preface of a book. Along with other elements, it provides meta-information about the content of the page. The `<meta>` tag adds information about the HTML page. It does not have a closing counterpart. `<title>`, `<script>`, and `<link>` are just some of the tags you might encounter in a header. The `<body>` node contains the main content, structured into headers, such as `<h1>`, the main content which can be made up of articles `<article>`, tables, `<table>`, unordered lists `<ul>`, and ends with the footer `<footer>`. `<h1>` is the heading tag with the largest dimensions. If you want to create smaller headings, `<h2>` to `<h6>` offer progressively smaller sizes. The `<li>...</li>` shows that we will enclose a *li*st between its tags. To make an *u*nordered *l*ist, you use the `<ul>` tag. Of course, there is a tag for an *o*rdered *l*ist too, which adds numbers or letters in front of `<ol>`. You can create a table with a unique element that has a table row `<tr>`, within which is a *t*able *c*ell defined not by `<tc>` but by `<td>`, which stands for *t*able *d*ata (or cell). For more information on HTML and CSS, see Wolf et al. (2025).

In the following example, we have imported a web page into R and removed the unnecessary part by stripping away the code and liberating the embedded text.

The `rvest` package (Wickham, 2022a) provides functions that allow us to scrape (or ha*rvest*) data by parsing the HTML content of the web page. `rvest` integrates with the `magrittr` package seamlessly, using the pipe operator `%>%` to pass output easily from one function to the next. This approach is detailed in the introductory chapter, but let us explore how things work in practice with an example.

```
# Load necessary library
library(rvest)

# Define the URL to scrape
url <- "https://webscraper.io/test-sites/e-commerce/allinone"

# Read and parse HTML at the URL
parsed_html <- read_html(url)

# Extract product titles
titles <- parsed_html %>%
  html_elements("h4 .title") %>%
  html_text()

# Extract product descriptions
descriptions <- parsed_html %>%
  html_elements(".description") %>%
  html_text()

# Extract product prices as text
prices_text <- parsed_html %>%
  html_elements(".caption .pull-right") %>%
  html_text()

# Clean and convert prices to numeric
prices <- as.numeric(gsub("\\$", "", prices_text))

# Combine extracted data into a data frame
product_data <- data.frame(titles, descriptions, prices)

# Preview the first few rows of the data frame
head(product_data)
```

The `read_html()` function is designed to parse the content of an HTML file. Once the file is parsed and stored in a variable, such as `titles`, we need to pass this variable containing the entire structure of the page and the text to the

■ **Fig. 3.4** Icon to select elements on a web page, snapshot from a Chrome browser. Google Chrome is a trademark of Google LLC. This book is not endorsed by or affiliated with Google in any way

`html_elements()` function. This will extract the text using various HTML and CSS selectors, in this case, `h4` and `.title`. If you were wondering why we use more than one selector, it is because this allows us to be specific and pinpoint the content we need to extract. It is important to be able to identify these selectors visually. An easy way to access and inspect them is through the developer's Web tools. All modern browsers can show a page's source and unveil its DOM. On some browsers, in the settings, which are usually represented by three vertical dots or lines, you need to select *More tools*, then *Developer tools*. A menu for the developer tools will appear either at the bottom of the page or on the right-hand side. The first step is to select an element on the page. Let us identify the *title* of the first item whose data we want to have downloaded. Given the repetitive nature of the code structure, identifying this for one item is usually sufficient as the other items will likely follow the same pattern. Click on the icon depicted in ■ Fig. 3.4 and then click on the title of one product; see ■ Fig. 3.5. Usually, such a procedure is applied to all the elements to be harvested from a page, regardless of the number of products. The code above is sufficient to harvest all the features you want of all the products on a page. Be aware that what you see in the developer tools of a browser is the DOM, not just the raw HTML, as it displays the current state of the DOM as it is interpreted and rendered by the browser being used.

> *A document object model (DOM)* is a computer-readable representation of a parsed, loaded web page, which can be conceptually represented as an upside-down tree; scripts and tools will search this to locate, extract, or modify elements.

The HTML snippet code will be displayed in the *Developer tools* frame underneath, allowing you to detect the path where the title is situated; see ■ Fig. 3.6.

> *A cascading style sheets (CSS) selector* is a textual pattern (e.g., `.title`, `h4 > a`) which allows you to search the DOM. CSS selectors are used by programmers to style web pages, but here they are used to scrape for the location of information and its extraction.

When examining the code, you can build an imaginary path going through both elements, `h4` and `.title`, to locate a specific title, such as "Acer Aspire 3

Fig. 3.5 Title selection of a product (screenshot from webscraper.io)

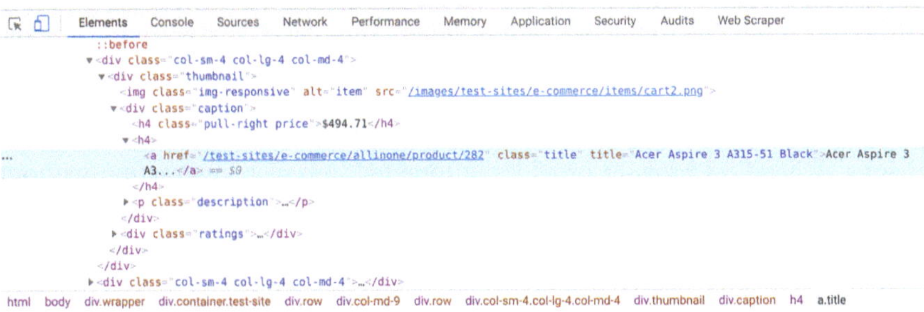

Fig. 3.6 Code snippet showing the selector path to obtain the title text (courtesy of webscraper.io)

A315-15 Black." The function is designed to extract a node containing text but does not know the path to follow. This is why we have to inspect the code and supply the function with the right elements. Essentially, it selects only the desired node, removing all the unnecessary information. This output is then passed to the `html_text()` function, which extracts the text from the node. This approach is applied in the same way to all the other variables. Note that the *prices_text* variable has a character sign before the numerical value. With the help of a regular expression you have studied, ▶ Chap. 2, we can remove that sign and convert the remaining string made by character digits into an integer. This step is always needed for subsequent mathematical computations: mathematical operations are done using numbers, not characters.

3.2.4 Scraping Dynamic Sites with Selenium

Sometimes, scraping web pages based on a static pattern is very challenging, especially when actions like clicking a link or navigating to a "next" page are required. In such cases, we need a tool which can mimic and automate human actions on a web page. Selenium (Selenium Web Browser Automation, 2024) has a set of various open-source software tools, each with a distinct method, to help do this.

> *Selenium (WebDriver)* is a browser-automation framework; via WebDriver, it uses real browsers (including headless ones) and allows you to recreate aspects of the user experience in real time (once loaded and rendered), interact with the page, and scrape dynamic elements.

Primarily used for automating tests of website functionality, Selenium can also be used as a remote control. It makes it possible for the interface elements on web pages, for example, links or pop-ups, to be accessed via scripting rather than through clicking with a mouse. It can even handle JavaScript processes as well (García et al., 2020). The procedures mentioned above are usually tricky to execute without Selenium due to the problem of integrating JavaScript with the browser.

Another component is Selenium's ability to identify the agent, essentially the browser used for scraping. Common choices include Google Chrome (the default option), Firefox, or Edge, and these can be used in their standard or headless versions. A headless browser provides automated web page interaction without a graphical user interface. It can be chosen in lieu of commonly used Web browsers to minimize interactions, and so maximizing the user's anonymity. The key packages used for this task are `RSelenium` (Harrison, 2022) and `rvest`. The former ensures that R and Selenium interact and provides a set of R bindings from the Selenium WebDriver (García et al., 2021), while the latter handles the scraping. The script starts the Selenium server sequentially and pauses the system for two seconds, allowing it to be loaded. Then, it links the driver to the browser, which opens a session and loads the external file. Eventually, the data are stored in a data frame and then saved in CSV format. However, be aware of potential compatibility issues between Chrome and the versions of its driver. In such cases, switching to Firefox or another browser might resolve the issue. Also, if a script fails due to a communication port being busy, consider closing the current session or choosing a different port. For more detailed guidance, see Aydin (2018).

Let us use this tool on a page we are already familiar with from the webscraper.io website, starting from a general page. The function `rsDriver()` may default to using the Chrome browser if not specified by the user or the user's environment. The option `verbose = FALSE` suppresses the system messages. Its default value is TRUE. We suggest experimenting with the code and its various attributes in order to understand better the true potential of these functions.

```
# Load RSelenium
library(RSelenium)

# Set URL
```

```
url <- "https://webscraper.io/test-sites/e-commerce/allinone"

# Initialize Selenium driver
# NOTE: Make sure your Chrome version matches the installed
↪ chromedriver.
# If Chrome-driver compatibility errors occur, set browser =
↪ "firefox".
driver <- rsDriver(verbose = FALSE)

# Create client
remote_driver <- driver$client

# Navigate to URL
remote_driver$navigate(url)

# Wait for page load
Sys.sleep(2)

# Click element by XPath
button_element <- remote_driver$findElement(using = "xpath",
                    value = '//*[@id="side-menu"]/li[3]/a')
button_element$clickElement()

# Get and print new URL
url1 <- remote_driver$getCurrentUrl()
print(url1)

# Scrape data (integrate here your code)

# Close driver and stop server
remote_driver$close()
driver$server$stop()
```

To sum up, the code starts by loading the necessary library and setting a target URL. It then identifies and follows a path to a specific element on the web page, simulating a click. This action leads us to a new page with an updated URL. Effectively, this code automates the process of navigating through web pages, enabling important information to be scraped without the need for manual interaction, such as clicking on links.

3.3 Structured Data Sources

3.3.1 Data from Databases: SQL, NoSQL

Structured query language (SQL) is a programming language designed for accessing and managing databases, regardless of their physical location. It is used to retrieve, write, or update inherently structured data which are stored in tables linked through a relational scheme. As has been highlighted above, structured data are the preferred format for analysts, and SQL has a distinctive syntax, which can be used to interact directly with databases. While direct SQL commands can be complex, wrapper functions are available to "conceal" the SQL jargon and simplify these commands into more user-friendly terms. To illustrate, consider a hypothetical SQL query: In the "users" table, for the `user_id` identified by number 25, select columns like `name`, `familyname`, and `address`. This example, though not connected to an actual database, demonstrates the fundamental power of SQL for manipulating data.

3

```
SELECT name, familyname, address FROM users WHERE user_id = 25
```

If we replace `name`, `familyname`, and `address` with an asterisk (*) in the SQL query, it will select all the fields from the table. Additionally, omitting the WHERE clause will result in the selection of all users, not just those matching a specific condition.

```
SELECT * FROM users
```

Structured query language (SQL) is a declarative language for the definition, query, and manipulation (including aggregation) of relational data (tables with rows and columns, joins, keys).

NoSQL is a family of non-relational data stores (e.g., document, key-value, wide-column, or graph) which often trade rigid schemas for scalability/flexibility; many document-based data store documents as .JSON.

The indisputable strength of R lies in its built-in functions, which enable the quick analysis of data and the ability to visualize results through graphs for immediate comprehension. Moreover, R, with its extensive range of packages, offers drivers for connecting to various types of databases, including MySQL, ORACLE, PostgreSQL, Impala, Amazon RedShift, and Spark, to name just a few.

You can either use the SQL syntax embedded in simple R code or use packages like `dplyr`. For the first approach, you might use a command like:

```
tbl(mydatabase, sql("SELECT name, familyname, address FROM users
↪  WHERE user_id = 25"))
```

For the second:

```
myselection <- tbl(mydatabase, "users")
myselection %>%
  filter(user_id == 25) %>%
  select(name, familyname, address)
```

In either case, whether using SQL directly or via `dplyr`, the richness and power of the `dplyr` package can work like a charm, offering a vast array of analytical possibilities.

The approach to accessing data differs slightly for NoSQL databases but retains some similarities. In NoSQL, data are often stored in JSON format with embedded attributes. For instance, in a user table within a `mydatabase` database, fields like `name`, `familyname`, and `address` are stored as attributes within a single document. This helps horizontal scalability, allowing for large amounts of data to be contained within a single table.

This brief foray into the world of databases is intended to provide a more comprehensive view of the diverse sources from which data can be acquired. However, it is important to note that throughout this book, we will primarily focus on other methods of data acquisition.

3.3.2 Use AI-Based Services to Obtain Data

Because scraping using traditional software or self-produced code can be problematic due to changing website layouts, developments in AI (especially large language models (LLMs)) offer new ways to improve web scraping, as described in Posedaru et al. (2024). The authors propose a solution involving a JavaScript application that uses natural language to extract information and save the scraped results to a JSON file. The steps include providing a URL address and a description of the data that needs to be extracted. The HTML structure is then collected, cleaned, and transferred to ChatGPT in several chunks. ChatGPT is used to detect the appropriate selectors corresponding to the data in the HTML structure, after which it generates a scraper based on these elements. Once the scraper is executed, the data are saved in a JSON file.

> *JavaScript Object Notation (JSON)* is a lightweight format (text only) for storing and exchanging structured data (i.e., key-value pairs, arrays) that is easy to parse, generate, or search in R, Python, JavaScript, etc.

There are other GPT-based tools, such as the gpt-automated-web-scraper, which generates code based on user inputs and website analysis (Breeuwer, 2024), or the ChatGPT Web Scraper API plug-in (OpenAI, 2024). These tools enable autonomous data collection using LLMs, though ChatGPT-like tools cannot scrape websites directly (as of now). Additionally, several Web services use AI to scrape data without the need for any coding, such as browser.ai, bardeen.ai, and kadoa.com.

All these tools are very promising, although some will endure and others may fade away. The important thing to understand is how to collect data while taking into account privacy and ethics.

3.4 Other Sources for Obtaining Text Data Sets

Gathering data for analysis, whether through web scraping or utilizing existing data sets, can be daunting, but readily available resources on the Web can ease this process. Notable among these are well-known data set aggregators like Kaggle and GitHub. These platforms host various data sets covering various topics, including numerical data, categorical data, and combinations thereof. In this book, we are particularly interested in data sets suitable for natural language processing (NLP) and analysis.

We have compiled a list of data sets from the Elite Data Science website (https://elitedatascience.com/datasets), which are excellent for honing your text analytics skills. We encourage you to explore these datasets and consider their potential application for marketing:

- "Game of Thrones": Explore the political landscape, characters, and battles of the popular TV series, based on George R.R. Martin's *A Song of Ice and Fire*.
- World University Rankings: Analyze three global university rankings, each with a unique methodology and different insights.
- IMDB 5000 Movie data set: Can a movie's popularity be predicted before its release?
- Enron Data Set: Email data from Enron's senior management, a resource for understanding corporate communication. This data set was originally made public and posted to the Web by the Federal Energy Regulatory Commission during its investigation.
- Amazon reviews: Examine around 35 million Amazon reviews, a rich source for sentiment analysis and customer feedback studies.
- Newsgroup classification: Practice text classification and topic modeling with 20,000 documents from 20 newsgroups.

Check our website for more links to usable data sets.

Exercise 1. Inspect the Amazon data set's first 20 and last 20 review elements. Hint: type `help(head)` and `help(tail)` in the R console to learn how to do it.

Exercise 2. Search on the Internet and extract unstructured data from PDF, doc, or docx files. Then, save them into a data frame.

Exercise 3. Choose a popular online forum or discussion board. Extract and analyze the most recent ten posts from a subreddit which relates to your interests. Hint: Investigate the structure of the forum's URLs and how posts are displayed to determine your scraping strategy.

Exercise 4. Find a website of your choice and use the Web Scraper plug-in to extract data.

Exercise 5. Find a website of your choice and use `RSelenium` and `rvest` to download a usable data set. Consider websites requiring interaction, such as clicking buttons or filling forms, to navigate to the data.

Conclusion

This chapter is a resource for those beginning their journey in text data acquisition and analysis in R. It offers practical insights into, and a tangible foundation in, various methods of and tools for data acquisition. Text is present in various file formats, and throughout this chapter, we covered methods for handling PDFs, Word documents (*doc*, *docx*), and plain text files, demonstrating how to convert these formats into structured forms suitable for analysis in R. APIs were another point of interest, particularly for collecting data from social media platforms and other online services. Web scraping techniques were tackled, using R packages such as `rvest` and `RSelenium` to extract data from both static and dynamic Web content, including handling pages that require user interaction. The discussion then shifted to working with databases and how to access structured data from both SQL and NoSQL databases. Online platforms such as Kaggle and GitHub were mentioned as valuable sources for ready-to-use data sets. The chapter also provides practical exercises that range from basic data inspection to advanced web scraping techniques. These exercises are designed to enhance the reader's hands-on experience with a variety of data sources and tools.

Discussion

Ethics and policy: When is scraping acceptable?

Compare robots.txt, terms of service, and research-based fair use; propose a decision-making checklist for, "green-light" vs. "red-light" sites.

API vs. DOM: For a social platform which rate-limits API usage, when would you still prefer the API to the DOM? Map the trade-offs for stability, completeness, compliance.

Dynamic content: Given an infinite scroll page, outline your Selenium plan for, e.g., events, waits, and pagination, to understand how to validate completeness.

Data quality: What validation steps would you add after scraping (duplicate detection, timestamp normalization, language filtering, etc.)?

Storage choice of scraped reviews: Would you choose relational tables or JSON documents? Justify your storage design for text analytics.

3

Take Home Message

- Text data can come from many sources and methods, copy/paste, direct downloads, web scraping, structured database, or AI assistance; each method is a trade-off between time, effort, and control.
- Browser plug-ins are the fastest method, although only if the task is relatively simple. Scripted DOM extraction can provide amazing flexibility. APIs are generally much "cleaner," but potentially limited by the service's policies or changes in policy.
- When scraping dynamic sites (e.g., ones using AJAX heavily), always think about when you want automation tools like Selenium to reproduce certain aspects of the user experience.
- Always consider any legal/ethical restrictions and site policies; carry out"respectful" data collection at an appropriate pace.
- After you collect data, think about how you structure and clean them so they are ready to be analyzed.

References

Aydin, O. (2018). *R web scraping quick start guide: Techniques and tools to crawl and scrape data from websites*. Packt Publishing Ltd.

Barbera, P. (2018). *streamR: Access to twitter streaming API via r*. https://CRAN.R-project.org/package=streamR

Barbera, P., Piccirilli, M., Geisler, A., & van Atteveldt, W. (2017). *Rfacebook: Access to facebook API via r*. https://CRAN.R-project.org/package=Rfacebook

Barrie, C., & Ho, J. C. (2021). academictwitteR: An R package to access the twitter academic research product track v2 API endpoint. *Journal of Open Source Software*, *6*(62), 3272. https://doi.org/10.21105/joss.03272

Benoit, K., & Obeng, A. (2020). *Readtext: Import and handling for plain and formatted text files*. https://CRAN.R-project.org/package=readtext

Berger, J., Humphreys, A., Ludwig, S., Moe, W. W., Netzer, O., & Schweidel, D. A. (2020). Uniting the tribes: Using text for marketing insight. *Journal of Marketing*, *84*(1), 1–25. https://doi.org/10.1177/0022242919873106

Boegershausen, J., Datta, H., Borah, A., & Stephen, A. T. (2022). Fields of gold: Scraping web data for marketing insights. *Journal of Marketing*, *86*(5), 1–20. https://doi.org/10.1177/00222429221100750

Bonifacio, C., Barchyn, T. E., Hugenholtz, C. H., & Kienzle, S. W. (2015). CCDST: A free canadian climate data scraping tool. *Computers & Geosciences*, *75*, 13–16.

Breeuwer, D. (2024). *GPT-based universal web scraper*. https://github.com/dirkjbreeuwer/gpt-automated-web-scraper.

Brenning, A., & Henn, S. (2023). Web scraping: A promising tool for geographic data acquisition. *arXiv Preprint arXiv:2305.19893*.

Cavallo, A. (2012). The billion prices project: Building economic indicators from online data. *Meeting of the Group of Experts on Consumer Price Indices, United Nations Economic Commission for Europe, Geneva*, *3*.

Daroczi, G., Gopal, A., & Nagy, A. (2023). *fbRads: Analyzing and managing facebook ads from r*. https://CRAN.R-project.org/package=fbRads

Free Web Scraping. (2024). https://www.parsehub.com/

Frye, M., & Schmitt, R. H. (2020). Structured data preparation pipeline for machine learning-applications in production. *17th IMEKO TC*, *10*, 241–246.

Gandomi, A., & Haider, M. (2015). Beyond the hype: Big data concepts, methods, and analytics. *International Journal of Information Management*, *35*(2), 137–144. https://doi.org/10.1016/j.ijinfomgt.2014.10.007
García, B., Gallego, M., Gortázar, F., & Munoz-Organero, M. (2020). A survey of the selenium ecosystem. *Electronics*, *9*(7), 1067.
García, B., Muńoz-Organero, M., Alario-Hoyos, C., & Kloos, C. D. (2021). Automated driver management for selenium WebDriver. *Empirical Software Engineering*, *26*, 1–51.
Guyt, J. Y., Datta, H., & Boegershausen, J. (2024). Unlocking the potential of web data for retailing research. *Journal of Retailing*, *100*(1), 130–147. https://doi.org/10.1016/j.jretai.2024.02.002
Han, S., & Anderson, C. K. (2021). Web scraping for hospitality research: Overview, opportunities, and implications. *Cornell Hospitality Quarterly*, *62*(1), 89–104.
Harrison, J. (2022). *RSelenium: R bindings for 'selenium WebDriver'*. https://CRAN.R-project.org/package=RSelenium
Harvest the Web. (2024). In *OutWit*. https://www.outwit.com/
Hillen, J. (2019). Web scraping for food price research. *British Food Journal, 121*(21), 3350–3361.
Hirschey, J. K. (2014). Symbiotic relationships: Pragmatic acceptance of data scraping. *Berkeley Tech. LJ*, *29*, 897.
Kearney, M. W. (2019). Rtweet: Collecting and analyzing twitter data. *Journal of Open Source Software*, *4*(42), 1829. https://doi.org/10.21105/joss.01829
Keith, J., & Sambells, J. (2011). *DOM scripting: Web design with javascript and the document object model*. Apress.
Khder, M. A. (2021). Web scraping or web crawling: State of art, techniques, approaches and application. *International Journal of Advances in Soft Computing & Its Applications*, *13*(3), 145–168.
Landers, R. N., Brusso, R. C., Cavanaugh, K. J., & Collmus, A. B. (2016). A primer on theory-driven web scraping: Automatic extraction of big data from the internet for use in psychological research. *Psychological Methods*, *21*(4), 475.
Munzert, S., Rubba, C., Meißner, P., & Nyhuis, D. (2014). *Automated data collection with R: A practical guide to web scraping and text mining*. John Wiley & Sons.
Murthy, D. (2018). *Twitter*. Polity Press Cambridge.
Ooms, J. (2020). *Pdftools: Text extraction, rendering and converting of PDF documents*. https://CRAN.R-project.org/package=pdftools
OpenAI. (2024). *Web scraper API ChatGPT plugin*.
Piccirilli, M. (2016). *Rlinkedin: Access to the LinkedIn API via r*. https://CRAN.R-project.org/package=Rlinkedin
Poggi, N., Moreno, T., Berral, J. L., Gavalda, R., & Torres, J. (2007). Web customer modeling for automated session prioritization on high-traffic sites. *User Modeling 2007: 11th International Conference (UM 2007), Corfu, Greece, July 25–29, 2007. Proceedings*, *4511*, 450–454. https://doi.org/10.1007/978-3-540-73078-1_63
Posedaru, B.-Ş., BăTăgan, L., Bologa, R., Plăcintă, D.-D., & Mirea, C.-M. (2024). Software architecture for improving scraping systems using artificial intelligence. *Economic Computation & Economic Cybernetics Studies & Research*, *58*(3). https://doi.org/10.24818/18423264/58.3.24.09%20
Radilova, M., Kamencay, P., Hudec, R., Benco, M., & Radil, R. (2022). Tool for parsing important data from web pages. *Applied Sciences*, *12*(23), 12031.
Random Data Generator. (2024). In *Random Data Generator*. http://randat.com/
Rimmer, M. (2017). *The foxfire of fair use: The google books litigation and the future of copyright laws*.
Rivera, I. (2023). *RedditExtractoR: Reddit data extraction toolkit*. https://CRAN.R-project.org/package=RedditExtractoR
Selenium Web Browser Automation. (2024). https://doi.org/10.70315/uloap.ulirs.2024.0101002
Sepulveda, M. V. (2024). *Tabulapdf: Extract tables from PDF documents*. https://github.com/ropensci/tabulapdf
Srihari, S. N. (1985). *Computer text recognition and error correction*. IEEE Computer Society Press.
Sturm, R., Pollard, C., & Craig, J. (2017). Chapter 11 - application programming interfaces and connected systems. In R. Sturm, C. Pollard, & J. Craig (Eds.), *Application performance management (APM) in the digital enterprise* (pp. 137–150). Morgan Kaufmann.

Tellis, G. J., MacInnis, D. J., Tirunillai, S., & Zhang, Y. (2019). What drives virality (sharing) of online digital content? The critical role of information, emotion, and brand prominence. *Journal of Marketing*, *83*(4), 1–20. https://doi.org/10.1177/0022242919841034

Thylstrup, N. B. (2019). *The politics of mass digitization*. MIT Press.

Web Data Extractor. (2024). http://www.fminer.com/

Wedel, M., & Kannan, P. (2016). Marketing analytics for data-rich environments. *Journal of Marketing*, *80*(6), 97–121. https://doi.org/10.1509/jm.15.0413

Wickham, H. (2022). *Rvest: Easily harvest (scrape) web pages*. https://CRAN.R-project.org/package=rvest

Wolf, J. et al. (2025). *HTML and CSS: The comprehensive guide*. Packt Publishing Ltd.

Yang, Y., Wilson, L., & Wang, J. (2010). Development of an automated climatic data scraping, filtering and display system. *Computers and Electronics in Agriculture*, *71*(1), 77–87.

3

Basic Text Analysis, Preprocessing, Bag-of-Words, TF-IDF, and Exploratory Statistics

D. Dan, T. Reutterer, *Text Analytics in Marketing*, Classroom Companion: Business,
https://doi.org/10.1007/978-3-032-08086-8_4

Keywords
Text preprocessing · BoW · tf-idf · Stop words · Stemming and lemmatization · N-grams · Word networks · SEO keyword strategy

4

This chapter covers the basic principles of quantitative text analysis in R and explains how to convert raw documents into numbers. Through a guided example, we collect a text from the public domain on the Web, tokenize it, and look at simple counts and rank frequency behavior. Then we provide a standardized version of this text using a reproducible preprocessing pipeline in `tm`: corpus, lowercase, stop word and punctuation removal, numbers, dictionary replaces, stems, lemmatization, and white space removal. With our cleaned data, we present the vector-space model and create term-document and document-term matrices, using one-hot, count, and term frequency-inverse document frequency (tf-idf) weights. In this section, we also include practical information about controlling the sparsity while creating the document-term matrix and notes on hapaxes or thresholding. Then we lay out exploratory tools you can apply to your text analysis, such as frequency tables, bar charts, word clouds, term associations, bigrams, and basic word networks. Throughout, there are concise scripts showing all the pertinent R code for each process and decision. At the end, you will be able to transform a heterogeneous text into text-analysis-ready matrices that summarize its content, which will then support modeling in the following chapters.

Learning Objectives

- Importing, preparing, and cleaning text data in R.
- Extracting and analyzing basic statistics for text, including word frequencies.
- Representing text numerically using models like bag-of-words and tf-idf.
- Understanding and applying the vector space model for comparing texts.
- Initiating exploratory text analysis using visual and statistical tools.

Computers work with numbers. They are incredibly efficient at this task, which is what they were initially built for: mathematical computations. Gradually, some of the real-world mechanics have been adapted and shifted to digital use. When we think about typing text, although there were once plenty of typewriters, we have now switched to computers which allow us to lay out text on a white canvas of pixels that mimics a sheet of paper. While the vast majority of people write text, just a tiny fraction analyze it, and the latter is our job here. But in text analytics, text must be made ready for interpretation by a computer, and we have the duty to ensure this process is done properly. We act at a higher level and do not see the transformation take place, but we must follow specific strategies and procedures to convert text documents into vectors of numbers. This mapping between a sequence of symbols and digits is called feature representation, feature extraction, or feature encoding (Goldberg, 2017).

Before we look at deeper meanings or more elaborate forms of analysis, there is much basic information that can be extracted from text, such as the number of words, the number of characters, the number of special characters, the number of numbers, the average word length, and so on. While all these features can be extracted, a widely used conceptual model of text known as bag-of-words (BoW) focuses on the frequency of words in a text. For applications of this concept to marketing, see, for example, Netzer et al. (2019) and Toubia et al. (2019). The name bag implies that the words are simply thrown into a container with no specific order, and this is a fitting description. Whenever we apply this simple model, our attention is directed exclusively to the occurrence of the words and their frequency, but not to the structure of the text. More details on this model will be discussed below. Curiously enough, by dismantling the text's structure, removing and modifying words or parts of them and eliminating punctuation marks, we can gain insights without having to read hundreds of pages simply by analyzing a selection of its (unordered) words. Using the techniques presented in the previous chapter, we will start by collecting a simple text from the Internet and transferring it to R, and then conducting some very basic analysis on it. After that, we will use the data set mentioned in ▶ Chap. 1, apply initial reasoned text-processing steps, and transform it into a matrix, enabling our computer to handle it efficiently. Finally, we will analyze the outcome. What we are trying to achieve is size reduction. We are aiming to filter information and extract knowledge from huge numbers of documents. To accomplish this, we have to cut and remove parts of the text, leaving only the essential (and meaningful) elements.

4.1 The Basics: A Short Use Case

Most of the time, we need to work with text downloaded from the Internet. It is nearly impossible to find text that perfectly fits our specific needs. Therefore, a text analyst first collects and cleans the text, preparing it for its analysis.

Let us explore this through a simple but comprehensive example to demonstrate the process. We will show how to extract text from the Internet, save it to our computer, and perform basic analysis with the commands discussed in the previous chapter. The example uses a text on text analytics (no pun intended) from Project Gutenberg. There are two built-in functions in R for reading information from the Internet if it is not in tabular form: `readLines()` and `scan()`. We prefer the latter for its greater flexibility.

We provide the URL of the text and store it in a variable, named `etext`. The function parameters `what` and `sep` are set to interpret the input as character strings (not numerical values) and to split the text into separate vector cells for each new line, identified by the metacharacter `\n`.

```
# Set URL of the text file
url <- "http://www.gutenberg.org/cache/epub/53/pg53.txt"

# Read text as character strings, split by newline
etext <- scan(url, what = "character", sep="\n")
```

4

```
Read 6855 lines.
```

The system indicates the number of "items" stored in the `etext` variable, signifying that the text has been segmented into smaller parts. These parts are then stored in a vector of 6855 elements. Simply typing `etext` into the console will display the entire imported text, which might be extensive and impossible to read. To inspect the first six elements of `etext` briefly, we use the `head()` function.

```
head(etext)
```

```
[1] "The Project Gutenberg eBook of Workshop on
↪   Electronic Texts:"
[2] "Proceedings, 9-10 June 1992"
[3] ""
[4] "This ebook is for the use of anyone anywhere in the
↪   United States and"
[5] "most other parts of the world at no cost and with
↪   almost no restrictions"
[6] "whatsoever. You may copy it, give it away or re-use
↪   it under the terms"
[7] "of the Project Gutenberg License included with this
↪   ebook or online"
```

The function splits the text at each occurrence of the newline metacharacter "\n", which, while invisible to our eyes, is present in the *.txt* file's structure. Examining the *pg53.txt* file, we realize that not all parts of this text are relevant for our analysis. In fact, certain sections need to be excluded to focus only on the pertinent content.

It is apparent that the meaningful content begins with the word "INTRODUCTION" and concludes with "END." However, we must note that the word "END" appears twice in the text. With the help of the `grep()` function with the `value` parameter set to TRUE, we can isolate the lines containing these key words.

```
# Identify lines containing 'INTRODUCTION' or 'END' and store the
↪  content
keyword_lines <- grep("\\bINTRODUCTION\\b|\\bEND\\b", etext, value
↪  = TRUE)
keyword_lines
```

```
[1] "INTRODUCTION"
[2] "END"
[3] "*** END OF THE PROJECT GUTENBERG EBOOK WORKSHOP
     ON ELECTRONIC TEXTS:"
[4] "PROCEEDINGS, 9-10 JUNE 1992 ***"
```

Here we want to identify the section between "INTRODUCTION" and the first occurrence of "END." We can do this by setting the `value` attribute to FALSE, which is equivalent to the default value (i.e., the attribute not appearing in the function) while we try to detect the indices in the vector where these two words appear.

```
# Find indices of lines containing 'INTRODUCTION' or 'END'
keyword_indices <- grep("\\bINTRODUCTION\\b|\\bEND\\b", etext)
keyword_indices
```

```
[1]  110 6549 6556
```

Think back to our chest of drawers analogy. Here we are interested in the drawers labeled 110, 6549, and 6556. Whatever is present in the text before index 110 and after index 6549 must be discarded. This is done by selecting the elements in the vector. In R, we use square brackets `[ ]` for indexing and the colon symbol `:` is used to denote a range, like this: `[ m : n ]`. In plain English, keep everything from index 110 to 6549. We thus overwrite the `etext` variable with the newly selected text. Let us look at the updated `etext` variable.

```
# Select the elements between keyword_indices
etext <- etext[keyword_indices[1]:keyword_indices[2]]
head(etext)
```

```
[1] "                                        INTRODUCTION"
[2] "The Workshop on Electronic Texts (1) drew together
↪  representatives of"
```

```
[3] "various projects and interest groups to compare
↪  ideas, beliefs,"
[4] "experiences, and, in particular, methods of placing
↪  and presenting"
[5] "historical textual materials in computerized form.
↪  Most attendees gained"
[6] "much in insight and outlook from the event.  But the
↪  assembly did not"
```

However, working with individual words, rather than sentence fragments, would be more efficient. This can be achieved by using `strsplit()` with pattern `\\W+`, which splits the text at nonword characters, isolating the words. This is the basic concept of tokenization, that of dividing text into constituent words.

```
# Isolate words
etext <- strsplit(etext, "\\W+")
head(etext)
```

```
[[1]]
[1] ""                "INTRODUCTION"

[[2]]
 [1] "The"                "Workshop"          "on"
 ↪   "Electronic"
 [5] "Texts"              "1"                 "drew"
 ↪   "together"
 [9] "representatives" "of"

[[3]]
[1] "various"   "projects" "and"       "interest" "groups"
↪  "to"        "compare"
[8] "ideas"     "beliefs"

[[4]]
[1] "experiences" "and"          "in"
↪  "particular"  "methods"
[6] "of"          "placing"      "and"
↪  "presenting"

[[5]]
[1] "historical"   "textual"      "materials"    "in"
↪  "computerized"
[6] "form"         "Most"         "attendees"    "gained"
```

```
[[6]]
 [1] "much"     "in"       "insight"  "and"
 ↪   "outlook"  "from"
 [7] "the"      "event"    "But"      "the"
 ↪   "assembly" "did"
[13] "not"
```

We notice that after applying the function, we end up with a different structure: a list. So each vector element includes a number of other elements. But if we altered the structure again, we would create a new vector with the function `unlist()`. In this, all the words would appear in a sequential manner from the first to the last, but without punctuation marks.

After applying `strsplit()`, the structure of our data changes from a single vector into a list. In this list, each original element, previously consisting of a line of text, is now a vector containing this line of text broken into individual words. We have multiple vectors stored inside a list. So, each "drawer" contains a vector of words, similar to a drawer containing other drawers. To further transform this structure into something more manageable, we need to flatten the list and create a single chest of drawers with one word per drawer. We use the `unlist()` function to transform our list into a single, sequential vector with a word in each "drawer" but without any punctuation marks.

```
# Vectorize
etext <- unlist(etext)
head(etext)
```

```
[1] ""           "INTRODUCTION" "The"      "Workshop"     "on"
[6] "Electronic"
```

The first six elements might (or not) be blank because of the presence of white spaces. Our focus is not on these, so we remove them. The translation of the code into plain English is as follows: From the variable `etext`, extract the indexes (remember you access the content of a specific cell using a number in squared brackets), of those "drawers" which are not empty. The exclamation mark `!` is used for negation. The line of code `etext[!etext == ""]` selects all the "drawers" which are not empty and overwrites `etext` with the filtered data. Reinspecting the variable containing the vector, we will find that the blank spaces have been removed.

```
# Remove empty spaces
etext <- etext[!etext==""]
head(etext)
```

```
[1] "INTRODUCTION" "The"            "Workshop"      "on"
[6] "Texts"
```

To extract information from this text, let us perform some basic analysis. We need to find out the vocabulary used and the total number of words. To achieve this, we use the `length()` function, which gives us the total count of words. By applying the `unique()` function, we can ensure that each word is counted only once, hence we identify the vocabulary. In simple terms, the vocabulary is the set of words used in a given text.

4

```
# Check text length
length(etext)
```

```
[1] 63301
```

```
# Check unique words number
length(unique(etext))
```

```
[1] 6725
```

The results show a total of 63,301 words spread over repeats and single values, but the vocabulary itself is actually a lot smaller, consisting of 6725 terms. Let us sort these terms alphabetically and store them in a variable. Then we can peek at a segment of this variable (which, remember, in this case is a vector) somewhere between positions 975 and 1000. Again, imagine this vector as a chest of drawers, where each term occupies its own drawer.

```
# Sort words in alphabetical order
s_etext <- sort(unique(etext))

# Take a glimpse into the vector
s_etext[975:1000]
```

```
 [1] "boldness"   "bond"    "Bonita"    "book"
 ↪   "Book"
 [6] "bookmark"   "books"   "Books"     "Boolean"
 ↪   "bordering"
[11] "Borders"    "bore"    "born"      "Borrowing"
↪  "Boston"
```

```
[16] "both"          "Both"     "bother"      "bottlenecks"
↪    "bottom"
[21] "Boulevard"    "bound"    "Bound"       "boundaries"
↪    "boundary"
[26] "bounds"
```

We can see that there are variations in words appearing in plural forms, written with capital or with lowercase letters, or with different inflections. We know that those words represent the same concept, no matter their capitalization, but for a computer, these are different, distinct words with nothing in common.

To assess the popularity of a specific word, we need to consider its frequency of use: the more often a word appears, the more popular it is. For this, we utilize the `table()` function, which counts each word's occurrence and presents all of them as if they were in an imaginary table. To check which are the most frequently used words, we then apply the `sort()` function. To view the top 25 most frequently used words, we can use the `head()` function.

```
# Sort words based on frequency
sorted_etext <- sort(table(etext), decreasing = TRUE)
head(sorted_etext, 25)
```

```
etext
       the         of        and          to           a
    ↪    in        that
      3589       2447       1758        1752        1355
   ↪   1204        1021
        is        for         on        with          be
     ↪   as           it
       740        716        471         443         441
    ↪   420         390
       one        are        not          or         The
    ↪  text          an
       362        348        346         342         338
    ↪   300         285
     which         by          s  electronic
       280        269        265         261
```

We notice that among the first words of interest are the nouns *text* and *electronic*. This is intuitive, given that the document discusses a workshop on electronic texts. Thus, even without prior knowledge of the document's content, we can identify these as key words. In any English-language text, certain words such as articles, pronouns, and prepositions occur frequently, composing about 25% of the text. These statistics (and more) can be verified with corpus analysis tools such as Sketch Engine (Kilgarriff et al., 2014). Additionally, we note that this roughly

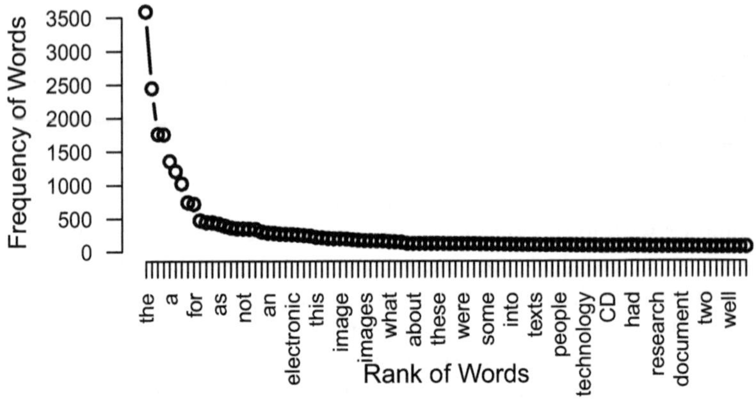

Fig. 4.1 Frequency distribution of the top 100 words (ranked by frequency). Authors' own figure

follows Zipf's empirical law (Ferrer i Cancho & Solé, 2001). This states that the frequency of a word is inversely proportional to its rank: The most frequent word appears twice as often as the second one, three times as often as the third, and so on. The larger the corpus, the closer the distribution of words aligns with Zipf's law. To confirm this visually, we have plotted the distribution of these words; see Fig. 4.1. Although not perfect, the graph exhibits a tendency which aligns with Zipf's law. For plotting, we use the `plot()` function with parameters like `xlab` for the horizontal axis (x-axis), `ylab` for the vertical axis (y-axis), and `las` for the rotation of labels on the x-axis. The suffix `lab` in these parameters is short for label.

```
plot(sorted_etext[1:100],
     type = "b",                  # Both points and lines
     xlab = "Rank of Words",
     ylab = "Frequency of Words",
     las = 2,
     cex.axis = 0.8              # Slightly reduce axis label size
     )
```

Let us analyze what we have noticed so far. Several elements in the document do not add value to our text analysis. Numbers, for example, can be removed or converted into their literal counterparts (like turning 9 into *nine*). The decision is yours. When we transformed the text from a list to a vector containing only the words, we can see the punctuation marks have been removed. They are unnecessary for an analysis using the BoW model. Similarly, empty spaces can be stripped away.

The most frequently occurring words are so frequent that they often do not add significant value to the understanding of the text, especially when it is only a computer parsing the text. These words are technically known as stop words and can be removed. Example of such words are *or*, *and*, *for*, and *the*. Depending on your expertise, you can also remove additional words that need to be left out. It is also essential to standardize word capitalization to ensure consistency, so they should appear uniformly. For example, words like *Book*, *BOOK*, and *book* represent essentially the same term and should typically be converted all to lowercase to unify their appearance. Inflected forms should be reduced to a common root. We will tackle this topic in more detail later. Carrying out properly what is often known as preprocessing the text can significantly enhance the information we extract from it.

4.2 Data Preparation and Normalization (Text Preprocessing)

To summarize, collecting text is the starting point of the whole process. Given that text must be structured and made ready for computer analysis, it is essential to normalize, or preprocess, it (Meyer et al., 2008; Miner et al., 2012). Following text correction using regular expressions (see ▶ Chap. 2), the main preliminary operations are (i) corpus preparation, (ii) lowercase transformation, (iii) stop-word removal, (iv) implicit-word removal, (v) punctuation removal, (vi) number removal or number-to-text translation and vice versa, (vii) inflectional-form reduction, and (viii) white-space contraction. We demonstrate each of them below in the sequence in which they will be applied.

4.2.1 Corpus Preparation

For our text mining procedures, we will use the `tm` package: This is an abbreviation of *t*ext *m*ining. The functions in this section refer to this, unless specified otherwise. The `tm` package works with a structure called `Corpus` (note that the plural of corpus is corpora). This is an abstract concept consisting of a collection of texts that are to be analyzed. By default, `tm` uses a volatile corpus, or `VCorpus`, which is a structure held in memory in an R object and which vanishes when destroyed.

In R, the function `options()` allows you to modify a number of default values; one of them is `stringsAsFactors`, which (in versions prior to 4.0) was set to TRUE, turning repeated strings into factors; starting from R 4.0 onward, the default is already FALSE, so you no longer need to set it manually.[1].

In this example, we are working with the data set detailed in the introductory chapter and available for download from the book's companion website. To import this data set, which is in CSV format, we use the `read.csv()` function. If you have not followed the setup instructions in the preparatory chapter, you might have a different path for where you store your data set, so please check that everything is in place to prevent errors. The data set counts several columns, but we will focus mainly on the one containing the reviews and store it in a variable called `prodreviews`. The next step is to convert the "Content" column to character

1 Factors are essentially what in statistics is called a categorical variable. If you encounter the same text value, R will automatically interpret it as a factor. For text analysis purposes, we want to treat text strings individually rather than as categories. In this case, we need to set `stringsAsFactors` to FALSE

type. This is important to ensure the consistency of the types of data because sometimes R may not infer the data types we need to work with correctly (or, perhaps better, as we desire). The text for analysis can be sourced from a directory, a vector treating each document as an individual item (in our case, the variable `prodreviews`), or a data frame. Here we will use `VectorSource`, but for more information see Feinerer and Hornik (2019). When you have a vector where each element is a different product review, as in our case, you can create a `Corpus` object from this vector using `VectorSource`.

4

To get a glimpse of the first document in our corpus we can use the function `inspect()`. The use of double squared brackets `[[ ]]` indicates that there is more than one dimension, similar to accessing elements in a list (R Core Team, 2025). `inspect(docs[[1]])` will display the contents of the first document in the corpus.

```
# Load the tm library
library(tm)

# Set string handling to non-factor
options(stringsAsFactors = FALSE)

# Load the Product Reviews data set
prodreviews <- read.csv("data/Product Reviews.csv")

# Convert "Content" column to character type
content <- as.character(prodreviews$Content)

# Create a volatile corpus
docs <- VCorpus(VectorSource(content))

# Inspect the first document in the corpus
inspect(docs[[1]])
```

```
<> Metadata: 7 Content: chars: 1384
I love my fire and highly recommend it to anyone who
wants to watch videos (netflix, hulu, amazon), read ebooks
(purchased or from the local library), surf the net and
play games. I work in the tech field and I LOVE apple
entertainment products (I own many apple products and at
work I work with several). I am very thrilled with my fire
(I LOVE IT TOO!) because it works great as an entertainment
product (and more affordable than my apple products). I
also think the fire is a great product because of Amazons
clout and support. Any tech product I buy needs to be
useable for years and updateable during those years. The
amazon market (still growing) is and will be getting better
all the time. Why? Sheer number of devices sold by Amazon
```

```
equals a large potential population of people who will
buy software equals software programmers wanting to be a
part of that market. Also in IT the biggest frustration
is having an older device and not being able to update
it or not being able to use new software or technology
because the manufacturer does not update their devices
(software) or provide backwards support. I am not saying
that Amazon will continue to provide support (that remains
to be seen), but the size, longevity, profitability and
attitude of pro consumer of a company are determining
factors and compared to other companies I would bet that
Amazon will not disappoint.
```

Inspecting the first review in our data set, the output reveals that it is a plain-text document. This output includes a metadata argument which contains seven additional elements of information, such as the author and language. If you need extra information, use the function `meta(docs[[1]])`. We also note that the text contains 1384 characters, including white spaces.

Let us start off with the real text processing. The function that does all the transformations is called `tm\_map()` and is a generic function that maps a specific function to the elements of a corpus.

4.2.2 Lowercase Transformation

For humans, the distinction between the words *hotel* and *Hotel* is minimal, and anyway, they both refer to lodgings. For computers this is different. Words have no semantic meaning to them, are just a sequence of letters, and if two words differ only through capitalization, then the two are distinct. Converting all words to lowercase ensures uniformity. This enables the accurate counting of words. Converting to uppercase is also an option, but the text becomes less readable and, in online communication, is interpreted as shouting. Remember, collecting accurate word-based statistics is essential in the BoW model. The function that can accomplish this is `tolower()` and is part of the base R program. There is an important technical detail to note, while `tm_map()` is designed to work with corpus objects; using it with some standard R functions directly can alter the structure of the content in the corpus. To ensure that the content keeps its proper format, such as `PlainTextDocument`, we use the `content_transformer()` wrapper function. By wrapping `tolower()` with `content_transformer()`, we make sure that the text is converted to lowercase while maintaining the structure of the corpus.

```
# Transform all the characters to lower case
docs <- tm_map(docs, content_transformer(tolower))
```

```
# Inspect the first document in the corpus
inspect(docs[[1]])
```

```
<> Metadata: 7 Content: chars: 1384
 I love my fire and highly recommend it to anyone who
wants to watch videos (netflix, hulu, amazon), read ebooks
(purchased or from the local library), surf the net and
play games. i work in the tech field and i love apple
entertainment products (i own many apple products and at
work i work with several). i am very thrilled with my
fire (i love it too!) because it works great as an
entertainment product (and more affordable than my apple
products). i also think the fire is a great product because
of amazons clout and support. any tech product i buy needs
to be useable for years and updateable during those years.
the amazon market (still growing) is and will be getting
better all the time. why? sheer number of devices sold by
amazon equals a large potential population of people who
will buy software equals software programmers wanting to
be a part of that market. also in it the biggest
frustration is having an older device and not being able
to update it or not being able to use new software or
technology because the manufacturer does not update their
devices (software) or provide backwards support. i am not
saying that amazon will continue to provide support (that
remains to be seen), but the size, longevity, profitability
and attitude of pro consumer of a company are determining
factors and compared to other companies i would bet that
amazon will not disappoint.
```

Observe that all the words are now lowercase. While this might not be the most reader-friendly format for us, it is effective for computer processing, and, anyway, we do not need to read the text.

4.2.3 Stop Words Removal

You should already be aware that the most frequent word in English texts is the article *the*. Comparing the word frequencies of two different texts with different topics, we would notice that the first 50 words would be likely to have similar frequencies. Such words that appear very frequently, but are also uninformative, are called stop words (Fox, 1989). Once the `tm` library is loaded, a complete list of the stop words can be found by typing `stopwords()` in R's console. As you can notice, the list includes contracted form such as *isn't*. This tells us that we need to remove the stop words *before* eliminating the punctuation. To remove the stop words (and others if needed) from our text, we use the `removeWords()` function.

Stop words are the most frequent words in a corpus (e.g., "the," "and," "of") which usually add no information to the analysis. Removing them reduces the size of the corpus (token count) and helps the model focus on the terms which provide information; in some cases, such as sentiment analysis (negations) or legal documents, selective retention can be applied.

```
# remove the stopwords and specify the language
docs <- tm_map(docs, removeWords, stopwords("english"))

# Inspect the first document in the corpus
inspect(docs[[1]])
```

```
<> Metadata: 7 Content: chars: 1071
Love fire highly recommend anyone wants watch videos
(netflix, hulu, amazon), read ebooks (purchased local
library), surf net play games. work tech field love apple
entertainment products ( many apple products work work
several). thrilled fire ( love !) works great entertainment
product ( affordable apple products). also think fire great
product amazons clout support. tech product buy needs
useable years updateable years. amazon market (still
growing) will getting better time. ? sheer number devices
sold amazon equals large potential population people will
buy software equals software programmers wanting part
market. also biggest frustration older device able update
able use new software technology manufacturer update
devices (software) provide backwards support. saying
amazon will continue provide support (remains seen), size,
longevity, profitability attitude pro consumer company
determining factors compared companies bet amazon will
disappoint.
```

We notice that the stop words have vanished from our text, and the character count has reduced. Of course, the text becomes less and less understandable for us to read.

4.2.4 Own Dictionary Words Removal

Sometimes we might need to remove other additional words. This process is often accompanied by some trial and error, along with informed decision-making. In a data set where a city name appears extensively, it becomes so prevalent in the corpus that we would like to remove it because it will not contribute any additional insights. The same `removeWords()` function can be used again. Suppose we decide to remove the word `will` from our text.

```
# Remove specific words from the corpus
docs <- tm_map(docs, removeWords, c("will"))

# Inspect the first document in the corpus
inspect(docs[[1]])
```

```
<> Metadata: 7 Content: chars: 1055
Love fire highly recommend anyone wants watch videos
(netflix, hulu, amazon), read ebooks (purchased local
library), surf net play games. work tech field love apple
entertainment products ( many apple products work work
several). thrilled fire ( love !) works great entertainment
product ( affordable apple products). also think fire great
product amazons clout support. tech product buy needs
useable years updateable years. amazon market (still
growing) getting better time. ? sheer number devices sold
amazon equals large potential population people buy
software equals software programmers wanting part market.
also biggest frustration older device able update able
use new software technology manufacturer update devices
(software) provide backwards support. saying amazon
continue provide support ( remains seen), size, longevity,
profitability attitude pro consumer company determining
factors compared companies bet amazon disappoint.
```

We notice that strictly the word *will* has been removed. It will not be removed though when it appears in any other combination, meaning as a prefix, suffix, or in the middle of a word. Also, you will observe that the number of characters has decreased and that we have some more empty spaces, exactly where the word *will* was present.

4.2.5 Punctuation Removal

Using BoW, which is centered on word frequencies, the punctuation has to be removed. Because this model overlooks semantic nuances, punctuation does not add value. `removePunctuation()` is the function designed for this task.

```
# Remove punctuation
docs <- tm_map(docs, removePunctuation)
```

```
# Inspect the first document in the corpus
inspect(docs[[1]])
```

```
<> Metadata: 7 Content: chars: 1021
  Love fire highly recommend anyone wants watch videos
netflix hulu amazon read ebooks purchased local library
surf net play games work tech field love apple
entertainment products many apple products work work
several thrilled fire love works great entertainment
product affordable apple products also think fire great
product amazons clout support tech product buy needs
useable years updateable years amazon market still growing
getting better time sheer number devices sold amazon
equals large potential population people buy software
equals software programmers wanting part market also
biggest frustration older device able update able use new
software technology manufacturer update devices software
provide backwards support saying amazon continue provide
support remains seen size longevity profitability attitude
pro consumer company determining factors compared
companies bet amazon disappoint
```

4.2.6 Removing or Transforming Numbers

Numbers may or may not be relevant to our analyses, but most of the time they are not. Nevertheless, through practical experience, you might find it beneficial to transform digits into their word equivalents (for example, `3` into `three`) or to remove them completely. A function can be easily created to map between numbers and text, if such a transformation is necessary. The function `removeNumbers()` will simply remove all numerical characters from the text.

```
# Remove numbers
docs <- tm_map(docs, removeNumbers)

# Inspect the first document in the corpus
inspect(docs[[1]])
```

```
<> Metadata: 7 Content: chars: 1021
  Love fire highly recommend anyone wants watch videos
netflix hulu amazon read ebooks purchased local library
surf net play games work tech field love apple
entertainment products many apple products work work
```

```
several thrilled fire love works great entertainment
product affordable apple products also think fire great
product amazons clout support tech product buy needs
useable years updateable years amazon market still growing
getting better time sheer number devices sold amazon
equals large potential population people buy software
equals software programmers wanting part market also
biggest frustration older device able update able use new
software technology manufacturer update devices software
provide backwards support saying amazon continue provide
support remains seen size longevity profitability attitude
pro consumer company determining factors compared
companies bet amazon disappoint
```

4.2.7 Reduction of Inflectional Forms

To reduce inflectional forms in a text, processes like stemming (Lovins, 1968) and lemmatization (Chai, 2023; Plisson et al., 2004; Toman et al., 2006) are commonly used. A stemming algorithm refers to a rule-based heuristic computational process that aims to make words uniform by reducing them to a common root (or a common stem), depending on whether we remove the prefix or the suffix. For example, a stemmer would reduce words such as *marketing*, *marketed*, or *marketization* to the word *market*. The goal is to achieve this correctly, hopefully most of the time. The `tm` package uses the `SnowballC` (Bouchet–Valat & Bouchet–Valat, 2020) package for stemming, which implements Martin Porter's version of the stemming algorithm (Porter, 1980), which focuses on suffix removal rather than prefix removal. This version has become standard for stemming in English. Be aware that the algorithm does not reduce words to a known stem word but to a neologism, for example, the words *replacement*, *replace*, or *replacing* might be reduced to *replac*. The function is `stemDocument()`. Stemming is suitable for applications such as simple search engines, or, as in our case, preliminary text analysis.

```
# Load the SnowballC library for stemming
library(SnowballC)

# Stemming
docs <- tm_map(docs, stemDocument)

# Inspect the first document in the corpus
inspect(docs[[1]])
```

```
<> Metadata: 7 Content: chars: 788
  Love fire high recommend anyon want watch video netflix
hulu amazon read ebook purchas local librari surf net play
```

```
game work tech field love appl entertain product mani appl
product work work sever thrill fire love work great
entertain product afford appl product also think fire great
product amazon clout support tech product buy need useabl
year updat year amazon market still grow get better time
sheer number devic sold amazon equal larg potenti popul
peopl buy softwar equal softwar programm want part market
also biggest frustrat older devic abl updat abl use new
softwar technolog manufactur updat devic softwar provid
backward support say amazon continu provid support remain
seen size longev profit attitud pro consum compani determin
factor compar compani bet amazon disappoint
```

Lemmatization is the dictionary- and linguistics-based process that reduces words to their dictionary form, known as the lemma, by removing inflectional endings using vocabulary and morphological analysis. For example, the words *do*, *did*, and *done* are all reduced to the lemma *do*. The package `tm` does not include a specific lemmatization function, but we could use the `textstem` package for this purpose. Since a corpus is composed of strings rather than individual words, the `lemmatize_strings()` function from `textstem` can be adapted for use with `tm`. In order to work well, lemmatizers need to understand the structure of the phrase, which is important for semantic preservation. Using a BoW approach this is disregarded, but still, lemmatization can be useful to reduce the size of the vocabulary. For training purposes, if you have your `textstem` library loaded, you can apply lemmatization to your corpus with the following code: `docs <- tm_map(docs, content_transformer(lemmatize_strings))`. Remember: this function works best when the structure of sentences is intact. Lemmatization is ideal in applications such as sentiment analysis, natural language understanding, or text-based machine learning models.

4.2.8 White-Space Deletion

The goal here is to remove the extra white space from a text document to condense instances of multiple white-space characters to a single blank space. The function which accomplishes this task is `stripWhitespace()`.

```
# White space removal
docs <- tm_map(docs, stripWhitespace)

# Inspect the first document in the corpus
inspect(docs[[1]])
```

```
<> Metadata: 7 Content: chars: 788
Love fire high recommend anyon want watch video netflix
hulu amazon read ebook purchas local librari surf net play
```

```
game work tech field love appl entertain product mani appl
product work work sever thrill fire love work great
entertain product afford appl product also think fire great
product amazon clout support tech product buy need useabl
year updat year amazon market still grow get better time
sheer number devic sold amazon equal larg potenti popul
peopl buy softwar equal softwar programm want part market
also biggest frustrat older devic abl updat abl use new
softwar technolog manufactur updat devic softwar provid
backward support say amazon continu provid support remain
seen size longev profit attitud pro consum compani determin
factor compar compani bet amazon disappoint
```


After all these steps, we have reached a point where we need to introduce text representation, a transformation that converts words and phrases into numbers or vectors, enabling computers to process textual data. This numerical representation is essential for various methods of text analysis, such as topic modeling, sentiment analysis, and machine learning algorithms applied to text data. We will analyze all of these in the following chapters.

4.3 Text Representation

Text representation is linked to a language model. But what exactly is a model? It is a simplified and interpretative representation of reality which selectively emphasizes certain features, but is not reality; for example, in geography, a model could be a map; for transportation, a train schedule; in music, the notation; in finance or marketing, graphs and/or diagrams showing hypothetical relationships between variables, such as ad spend vs. sales. Models can do more than just describe reality; they can also predict or forecast phenomena (e.g., weather forecasts) or reveal patterns (e.g., seasonality in sales data). Mathematical models might show predictions of weather patterns or the understanding of latent information, such as the seasonality of sales through a time-series graph. In the context of climate change, models can provide projections based on current data trends, such as CO_2 emissions. Statistical models are used to summarize data and reveal patterns. These models use observations to extract and infer information, helping with tasks such as classifying or predicting. In a statistical language model (or simply a language model), when you have a set of documents (a corpus), the model estimates the probability that the text in the documents was generated by that model (Aggarwal, 2018). It is important to note that models cannot perfectly mirror reality. They are abstractions which come laden with limitations and assumptions. For example, a map sacrifices details of terrain for simplicity, and a language model may miss nuanced contextual meanings.

A statistical language model also implies that there are mathematical operations, so the text needs to be transformed into mathematical values, shifting from unstructured to structured tabular formats. Like all statistical models, a language model (LM), with a specified language such as English, is designed to assign probabilities to phrases. More precisely, LMs are designed to calculate the probability or "the likelihood of a given word (or a sequence of words) to follow a sequence of words" (Beumer, 2020; Goldberg, 2017). A simple but frequently used model to represent text is the vector space model (VSM). A VSM encodes words into numerical vectors, in a similar way to how a map shows territory. However, VSMs treat words as independent dimensions, which oversimplify semantic relationships (e.g., synonyms are not inherently linked with each other). Let us see what we can work with: We have *terms*, which are basically words after they have been processed (e.g., "running" into "run"), *documents*, which can be phrases, paragraphs, articles, chapters, or books, and *corpora*, which are a collection of these documents.

4.3.1 Vector Space Model

In a VSM, the mapping is structured and gives mathematical meaning to the terms, documents, and the corpus. We know that the terms in a document appear with a certain frequency, which we can call weight and denote with a w. A single document can be denoted by a d. So, a document i in a collection of documents D that contains N unique terms (N is the vocabulary's dimension) can be represented mathematically as a vector:

$$d_i = (w_1, w_2, \ldots, w_j, \ldots, w_N)$$

where $1 \leq j \leq N$ and $i \in 1 \ldots D$ (Jurafsky & Martin, 2008)

For example, a simple document d_1 which contains the words "The more the better" can be represented by $d_1 = (1, 1, 2)$ corresponding to ("better," "more," "the"). This is a vectorial representation of the text. If you put all these vectors together, one beneath the other, the final result is a matrix. In the rows, you will have the documents in the corpus. In the columns, you will have the words in the vocabulary. Some words might appear in some documents but not in others, some might appear in all the documents, and some might appear in only one. This is the distribution of the words over the documents. The matrix is our main structure from which we extract features. Maybe the simplest technique in this model is the BoW, where the representation of the words is 1-gram, meaning that we consider one word at a time. There are also other representations based on n-grams, where n can take any number ≥ 2. In the BoW approach, it is assumed that the important unit is the word, so structure and order can be discarded. As such, the semantics of a document are given by the frequency of the words used, and the similarity with other documents is based on the similarity of word frequencies (Services, 2015). BoW performs well at representing and comparing the contents of documents.

Bag-of-words (BoW) is a representation that treats a document as a set of tokens, as if they were found in a bag. Word order and syntax are absent, but term frequency (counts) captures their topical importance and allows simple, effective comparisons to be made across documents.

To all intents and purposes, after the normalization process, we have developed a BoW model. Despite its name, hinting that it is baggy, we still need a structure for it to do computational tasks. This structure has a grid form and is called the document-term matrix (DTM) (Hofmann, 1999). The DTM is a matrix with two dimensions, (r, c) whose rows, r, represent the documents (in our case, each parcel of review content) and the columns, c, the terms in the vocabulary. Note that the vocabulary contains the total number of words that appear in the whole corpus arranged alphabetically. In the `DTM`, the frequency of a term's occurrence in a document is represented by `n` in the respective row and column. A value of 0 indicates the absence of a term in that specific document. The value n is given by the different representations of the text and there are three ways to show it: one-hot encoding, frequency vectors (or count vectors), and term frequency-inverse document frequency (tf-idf) vectors.

A document-term matrix (DTM) is made up of documents (rows) and terms (columns), with a cell (i,j) storing the weight of term j in document i (e.g., raw frequency, normalized count, or tf-idf). A DTM is the default input for many text-mining and ML workflows and is usually sparse.

▪▪ Orientation Note

Throughout this chapter, we switch between whichever matrix layout is most convenient. When we need row-wise term operations such as `row_sums()` or `findAssocs()`, we work with a term-document matrix (TDM, built with `TermDocumentMatrix()`, where rows are terms and columns are documents). When an algorithm expects one row per document—topic models, similarity measures, and the like—we use a document-term matrix (DTM, built with `DocumentTermMatrix()`, where rows are documents and columns are terms). Whenever we change orientation, we say so explicitly and show the code that constructs or transposes the object.

4.3.1.1 One-Hot Encoding

Let us take a simple example from our data set. This type of encoding uses the binary system; if a word is present in the vocabulary, it will be represented by a 1 and its absence by a 0. However, this is inefficient due to the large number of 0s. See ◘ Fig. 4.2 for a representation of this.

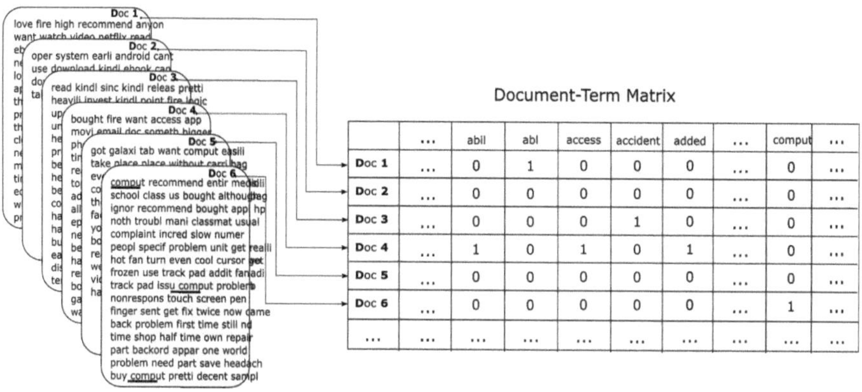

Fig. 4.2 Document-term matrix: one-hot encoding. Authors' own figure

Table 4.1 Document-term matrix. Table compiled by the authors

	...	ability	abl	access	accident	added	...	comput	...
Doc1	...	0	2	0	0	0	...	0	...
Doc2	...	0	0	0	0	0	...	0	...
Doc3	...	0	0	0	1	0	...	0	...
Doc4	...	2	0	3	0	0	...	0	...
Doc5	...	0	0	0	0	0	...	0	...
Doc6	...	0	0	0	0	0	...	3	...
...	...	...	...	...	...	...	...	...	...

4.3.1.2 Frequency Vectors

A matrix is similar to a mathematical table. The rows show the documents in the order they appear, and the columns have the words listed in alphabetical order. See Table 4.1 for a "mathematical" representation of the documents we used previously. This matrix tracks how often each word appears in each document.

For a visual representation that illustrates the relationship between documents schematically, their respective words, and the document-term matrix (DTM), see Fig. 4.3.

4.3.1.3 TF-IDF

A model that acquired a good reputation is the tf-idf measure. This is used in text analysis for document comparison or for text classification, but its origins were rooted in text information retrieval long before computers were even popular (Aizawa, 2003; Jones, 1972, 1973). Most importantly, it compares documents and shows which are more important based on specific words, in a very similar way to how a search engine prioritizes information retrieval based on search terms. The

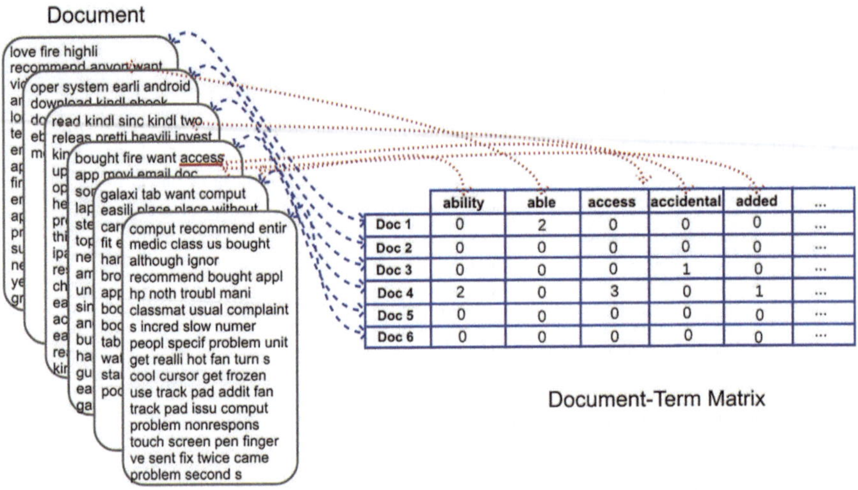

Fig. 4.3 Document-term matrix—frequency vectors. Authors' own figure

reason why tf-idf works well with a BoW approach is that both rely purely on raw-term counts, so no information about word order or syntax is needed.

> *Term frequency-inverse document frequency (tf-idf)* is a weighting scheme which increases with the term's frequency in the document (tf) and decreases with the term's frequency across the corpus (idf). Its typical form is $tf\text{-}idf(t, d) = tf(t, d) \times \log\left(\frac{N}{df(t)}\right)$, where N = the number of documents and $df(t)$ = the number of documents containing t.

The basic use of tf-idf is to assess the importance of a term in a document. This is based on statistical principles. Remember, statistics is the branch of mathematics that, among many other operations, also analyzes the frequency of a (past) event. So the more important a term is, the "heavier," or more frequent, it is expected to be.

To get an intuitive understanding of how the algorithm works, note that it is composed of two parts, the tf (*t*erm *f*requency) and the idf (*i*nverse *d*ocument *f*requency). Tf quantifies how frequently a term appears in a specific document relative to all other words in that document: the more frequent a word is, the higher the tf. Conversely, idf captures the rarity of a word in *a corpus of documents*. A word that appears in fewer documents is more significant because it is rare, and thus has a higher idf value. The product of tf and idf gives us a score (or a weight) for each word, ranking its importance with respect to the other words. Let us look at an example and examine the procedure in detail. Consider two sentences:

- Great tablet for the price.
- The best tablet.

Table 4.2 TF-IDF table (nonzero values rounded to two decimals). Table compiled by the authors

	best	for	great	price	tablet	the
n_t	1	1	1	1	2	2
tf Doc 1	0	0.20	0.20	0.20	0.20	0.20
tf Doc 2	0.34	0	0	0	0.34	0.34
idf	0.30	0.30	0.30	0.30	0	0
tf-idf × Doc 1	0	0.06	0.06	0.06	0	0
tf-idf × Doc 2	0.10	0	0	0	0	0

The sentences contain five and three terms respectively, excluding punctuation. We organize them alphabetically because it facilitates tracking and searching for specific terms. The collection of all the terms in these sentences forms the vocabulary.

In Table 4.2, we see the vector representation of the two sentences. The header row contains the terms. The first row shows the number of documents in which each term appears. The second and the third rows contain the relative *t*erm *f*requency for the first and the second documents, respectively. The word term, t, is the same as the word, w. The formula to calculate *tf* is $tf_{(t,d)} = \frac{f_{t,d}}{\sum_{t' \in d} f_{t',d}}$. This means the term frequency of t in document d is the ratio of the term's frequency f in that document to the total number of terms in the document. That total is the sum of all the number of terms $\sum_{t' \in d} f_{t',d}$ present in that specific document d. In our case, for the first sentence (which we consider a document), there are a total of five words. The word "the" appears once, so its (relative) frequency, *tf*, is $\frac{1}{5}$. The fourth row represents the *i*nverse *d*ocument *f*requency for each word in the vocabulary. Its simplified formula (simplified because sometimes after the *log*() it a 1 is added to avoid edge cases in text processing) is $idf_{(t)} = log(\frac{N}{n_t})$, where N represents the total number of documents, in our case 2, and n_t is the number of documents in which the term appears (see row one). For example, the word "the" appears in both documents, so $n_t = 2$. From algebra, we know how to compute $log(\frac{2}{2}) = log(1) = 0$. The fifth and sixth rows represent the multiplication of each document's *tf* with the corresponding *idf*.

There are several ways you can calculate *tf-idf*, but the principle remains the same: for the tf, the more frequent a term, the more important it is; see Bun and Ishizuka (2001) and Beel et al. (2017). In idf, the rarer a term is in the corpus (i.e., among all the documents), the more important it is. The word "the" will appear many times, so it will have a high tf because it is the most-used term in the English language. But this word will be penalized in the idf because it appears in all the documents: the more it appears the lower the score, so it has an inverse (document) frequency.

What tf-idf accomplishes is to find the words that are important to a document in a corpus. While tf relates to the first part of a BoW approach, the tf-idf metric will compute which words characterize the individual documents. To sum up, a word that appears frequently in one or just a few documents will have a high *tf* x *idf* score.

The `dtm` containing the tf-idf score for our main example about the tablets is shown in ◘ Table 4.2.

	…	ability	abl	access	accident	added	…	comput
Doc 1	…	0	0.0476	0	0	0	…	0
Doc 2	…	0	0	0	0	0	…	0
Doc 3	…	0	0	0	0.0358	0	…	0
Doc 4	…	0.0599	0	0.0625	0	0	…	0
Doc 5	…	0	0	0	0	0	…	0
Doc 6	…	0	0	0	0	0	…	0.1069
…	…	…	…	…	…	…	…	…

While tf-idf can exist as a standalone algorithm, it can also be applied to a BoW by replacing the word counts with their tf-idf values. The resulting matrix becomes a weighted version of BoW, where each value indicates the importance of a term in a document relative to the whole corpus. In simple terms, while BoW focuses solely on frequency, tf-idf balances frequency with importance. This is why the initial stage in the BoW model is essential, because it allows the tf-idf matrix to emphasize words that are both informative and contextually relevant.

4.3.2 Size Reduction

Now that we have explored the purpose of preparing the text and how the VSM quantifies words, a further important step before we move on to more advanced techniques to analyze text is size reduction. By now it is evident that the matrices that are created through a VSM can be huge, depending on the number of documents and the breadth of vocabulary. These matrices are often sparse, meaning that they contain a lot of zero values due to the absence of most words in most documents.

In specific cases, infrequent words do not bring much insight, and when this happens, they can be removed. However, in other cases, the words have to remain because, as you could see in the tf-idf model, they might characterize a document or enrich a text. This might give us some insights and we suggest not to dismiss the possibility of unearthing knowledge from them. The words that appear only once in a corpus are technically called *hapax legomena*, or *hapax* for short. The longer the text, the higher the probability of seeing an increase in *hapax* (Jockers & Thalken, 2020).

> *A hapax legomenon* is a term which occurs once in a corpus (plural: hapax legomena). A hapax typically adds little utility when computing global comparisons, but may be useful when doing stylistic analyses or detecting rare events; whether or not a user should prune hapax legomena is task dependent.

4.3.2.1 Sparse-Term Removal

Following data preparation and normalization (see ► Sect. 4.2), another procedure involves removing the sparse terms from the `dtm`. These are terms that appear very infrequently in a document and are recognized in a `dtm` by the fact that it contains many entries set to zero in the *j*th column and just a few entries greater than zero. To remove them, we can use the sparse option from the `removeSparseTerms()` function. The "sparsity" parameter here refers to a frequency threshold beyond which terms are discarded. Sparsity increases as it approaches 1.0 and can hold values in the interval (0, 1.0].

> *Sparsity* is the proportion of zero values in a term matrix. In general, DTMs of text are very sparse (most words occur in few documents). Controlling for sparsity in the context by pruning low-frequency words can increase the efficiency of models through the reduction of dimensionality, and often with little to no loss in signal.

Let us take an example. If we look at the sample, we can see the abundance of zeros in the matrix. If the data set were larger, words like "ability" or "access" would appear more frequently, but there would still be a lot of zeros in the columns. If a term does not have many values (again, in the columns), then the sparsity increases, bringing the index close to 1, meaning that there are a lot of zeros. If the word is present in all the documents, for example, the word "tablet," then it will fill out its column with values different from zero, making the sparsity index close to 0. We can conclude by saying that the sparsity index essentially acts as a threshold, eliminating terms whose proportion of zeros exceeds a specified level. Functions such as `removeSparseTerms(dtm, 0.95)` drop any term whose proportion of zeros exceeds the threshold. For large corpora, a threshold of between 0.95 and just below 1 is commonly used.

4.3.3 Exploratory Analysis and Visualization

4.3.3.1 Word Frequencies

After the text has been prepared, a first simple descriptive analysis can be carried out in order to search for words that most effectively represent the content (Baayen, 2001; Carroll & Roeloffs, 1969). One key point is to find the frequency for each term. We calculate this by adding up the occurrences of a term by column in a dtm. The terms are then sorted in decreasing order based on their frequency. For an overview of the data, we have shown the 20 most frequent terms along with their corresponding frequency.

This simple form of text analysis can be visualized in the form of a list, or in more visually appealing formats like plots or word clouds (Heimerl et al., 2014). Frequently, co-occurring words can be associated with each other (Church & Hanks, 1990) and can be represented graphically. This type of analysis gives us our first insights into the patterns of word co-occurrence.

Here we see the code for the term-document matrix creation, the removal of the sparse terms, and the extraction of the 20 most frequent words in that corpus. To handle the sparse terms efficiently, we use the library slam. The function row_sums() helps us identify the most frequent words.

```
library(slam)

# Create the term-document matrix, term × document
tdm <- TermDocumentMatrix(docs)

# Remove sparse terms with a threshold of 0.9
tdms <- removeSparseTerms(tdm, 0.9)

# Sort the values in decreasing order and create a data frame
v <- sort(row_sums(tdms),decreasing=TRUE)
top_terms <- data.frame(word = names(v),freq=v)

# Display the top 20 terms
head(top_terms, 20)
```

```
             word  freq
tablet     tablet 49184
use           use 46496
kindl       kindl 39523
fire         fire 36301
app           app 35770
can           can 30986
get           get 29015
ipad         ipad 28903
screen     screen 28536
one           one 27410
devic       devic 27333
like         like 27106
work         work 26595
just         just 23815
amazon     amazon 22473
great       great 22357
```

```
read          read 22115
android android 19169
want          want 18971
book          book 17854
```

4.3.3.2 Word Bar Plotting

To create a visual display of the most frequently employed words, a bar plot can be used (I.-I. Popescu et al., 2009). It is not feasible to plot all the words in the matrix due to the huge size of the corpus. Instead, a frequency threshold is set to select and display only the most prevalent terms. The threshold varies from corpus to corpus, being linked to the volume of text and the most desirable number of words. It is important to visualize the most frequent words because they will be the most important words of the topics treated in the text. The words are shown in decreasing order on the x axis and their respective occurrence depicted on the y axis; see ◘ Fig. 4.4. A bar plot allows us to identify significant words immediately. Often, the most frequent words can point to discussions about product features, and words like "tablet" and "kindle" identify key topics discussed in the corpus.

```
barplot(
  top_terms[1:20, ]$freq,
  las = 2,
  names.arg = top_terms[1:20, ]$word,
  col = "lightblue",
  ylab = "Word Frequencies",
  cex.names = 0.8,
  cex.lab = 0.9,
  cex.main = 1
)
```

We can see that the nouns *tablet*, *kindl(e)*, *fire*, *screen*, etc. with their high frequency in the text already provide significant clues to what the corpus refers

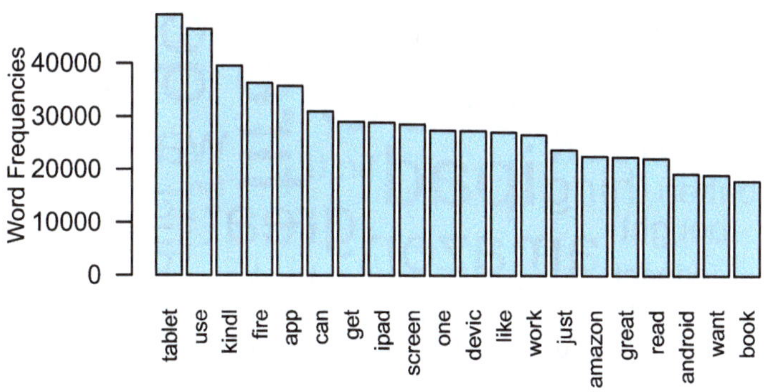

◘ **Fig. 4.4** Most frequent words. Authors' own figure

to. These words, being semantically related, point to what is predominant in these documents, the Kindle Fire tablet.

4.3.3.3 Word Cloud

A word cloud is an effective tool for providing a quick and direct visual overview of the most important words across a set of documents. It is a popular method for summarizing qualitative data (W. Cui et al., 2010; Scanfeld et al., 2010), in different fields. In marketing, word clouds can help identify key issues and themes (Abell & Jones, 2010) while in social media analysis, they offer insights into prevailing topics and language use (Xu et al., 2013). In the process of creating a word cloud, huge corpora of texts are reduced to the words that occur frequently. There is a direct relationship between the words and their appearance; bigger fonts are used for words with a higher frequency, while smaller fonts depict a lower frequency (see ◘ Fig. 4.5). In such static representations, words are considered as stand-alone entities without defined associations or relationships. The plot is created using the `wordcloud` (Fellows & Fellows, 2018) package. This visualization underscores the importance of VSMs in text analysis.

4

◘ **Fig. 4.5** Word cloud. Authors' own figure

```
library(wordcloud)

# Set seed for reproducibility
set.seed(1234)

# Create word cloud
wordcloud(
    words = top_terms$word,        # Words for the cloud
    freq = top_terms$freq,         # Their frequencies
    min.freq = 1,                  # Minimum frequency for inclusion
    max.words = 200,               # Limit on number of words
    random.order = FALSE,          # Keep words in frequency order
    rot.per = 0.35,                # Fraction of vertical words
    scale = c(3.5, 0.25)           # Scale for word size
)
```

We notice, as in the previous section, that words like *tablet*, *kindl*, *fire*, *app*, *screen*, *amazon*, and *work* are prominent. These frequently used words highlight the focus of customer reviews in the data set. Adjectives such as *great* hint at positive sentiment unless they are used in a negative context. The nouns predominantly center around topics related to the Fire tablet. From this small analysis, we can infer, even without reading every review, that the Amazon Kindle tablet is a generally well-received device. Colors in word clouds are used for aesthetic purposes or to categorize words into different themes or sentiments, not necessarily to indicate frequency. Word clouds, however, are just the starting point for more comprehensive, in-depth analyses.

4.3.3.4 Word Correlation

Words in a text are related. They are linked to other words to create meaning. To get deeper insights into our data, we can check for correlations between some of the most frequent terms and the other words in the document set (Kwartler, 2017). By correlation, in this context, we mean a measure of how words tend to appear in the same document. This can indicate a relationship or association between the terms. To analyze correlation, you can use the `findAssocs()` function from the `tm` package. The function requires you to specify the document-term matrix and the correlation threshold, which determines the minimum strength of association to be considered significant, and is set to a number between 0 and 1. If we set a correlation limit of 0.10, the function will return words that co-occur with the target word with a correlation score of *at least* 0.10. This number represents how strongly their document-level frequencies vary, rather than a probability. From an analytical point of view, using this we can unveil potential thematic or contextual connections within the documents. The correlation score computed by `findAssocs()` is based on Pearson's correlation coefficient and returns only positive correlations. This evaluates the linear relationship between the frequency vector of the target term and the frequency vectors of other terms in the document-term matrix. This method highlights terms that exhibit a significant linear relationship with the target word.

```
library(tm)
library(ggplot2)
library(ggthemes)

# Finding frequent terms
a <- findFreqTerms(tdm, lowfreq=10)
head(a)  # Display top terms
```

4

```
[1] "aaa" "aac" "aback" "abandon" "abbrevi" "abc"
```

```
# Finding word associations for "tablet", a correlation limit of
↪ 0.3
associations <- findAssocs(tdm, terms="tablet", corlimit=0.3)
# Convert associations to data frame
associations_df <- data.frame(term = names(associations$tablet),
↪ correlation = unlist(associations$tablet))
# Sort associations by correlation in ascending order
associations_df <-
↪ associations_df[order(associations_df$correlation),]

# Plotting associations
ggplot(associations_df, aes(x = correlation, y = reorder(term,
↪ correlation))) +
  geom_point(color = "blue", size = 3) +
  geom_segment(aes(x = 0, xend = correlation, y = term, yend =
  ↪ term),
               color = "lightblue", size = 0.7) +  # Add
               ↪ connecting lines for emphasis
  theme_minimal() +
  labs(
    x = "Correlation Score",
    y = "Associated Terms"
  ) +
  theme(
    axis.text = element_text(size = 10),
    axis.title = element_text(size = 12),
    plot.title = element_text(size = 14, hjust = 0.5),
    panel.grid.major.y = element_blank()  # Remove horizontal
    ↪ gridlines for a cleaner look
  )
```

The results show connections between the word *tablet* and words such as *android*, *use*, *screen*, and so on; see ◘ Fig. 4.6. These findings suggest that the terms frequently occur in the same context giving more insight into what a user thinks about a product.

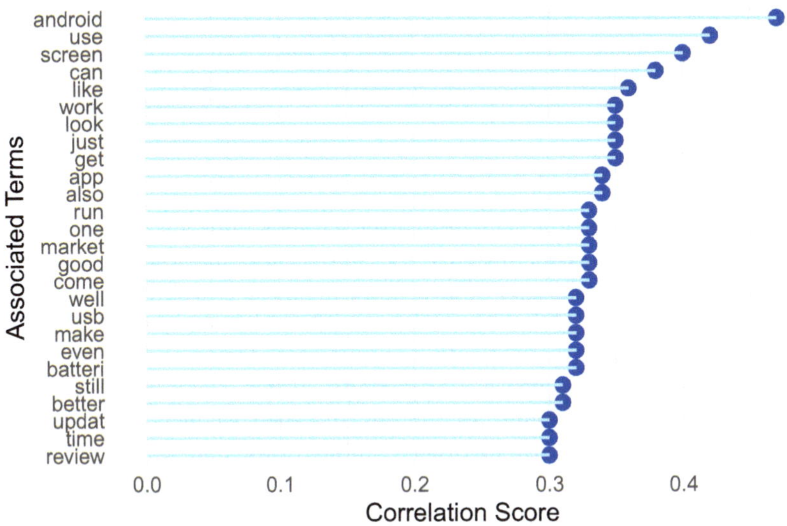

Fig. 4.6 Word association with `tablet`. Authors' own figure

4.3.4 Bigrams and Word Networks

In a VSM, text can be easily tokenized as single consecutive words, represented as a unigram. We can also use 2-grams of consecutive words, commonly known as bigrams. You can have even longer consecutive combinations, called n-grams. A bigram word cloud uses pairs of words as tokens, providing more insights into which terms are used together in reviews. A library that helps with tokenization is `RWeka` (Hornik et al., 2009) and allows for the creation of n-gram models.

```
library(RWeka)
library(wordcloud)

# Define bigram tokenizer
Bigram_Tokenizer <- function(x) NGramTokenizer(x,
↪  Weka_control(min=2, max=2))

# Create bigram term-document matrix
bitdm <- TermDocumentMatrix(docs, control = list(tokenize =
↪  Bigram_Tokenizer))

# Remove sparse terms
bitdms <- removeSparseTerms(bitdm, 0.99)

# Convert to matrix and sort by frequency
v <- sort(rowSums(as.matrix(bitdms)), decreasing=TRUE)
d <- data.frame(word = names(v), freq=v)
```

```
# Set seed for reproducibility
set.seed(1234)

# Generate bigram word cloud
wordcloud(words = d$word, freq = d$freq, random.order = FALSE)
```

As Fig. 4.7 shows, it is evident that the words Kindle and Fire pair together, but other words also provide insights: e.g., *battery life*, *touch screen*, *app store*, *sd card*, and *read books*. Bigrams offer a more nuanced understanding than single words. The easiest way to find how they are related to one another is through a word graph, which illustrates how these terms are interconnected. An important package that serves this purpose is `igraph` (Csardi & Nepusz, 2006). Using our existing data frame containing the bigrams and their frequency, we can see that some words might also exist in other combinations, and we need to separate them with the function `separate_wider_delim()` from the `tidyr` (Wickham, 2021) package. We can filter out (see package `dplyr`; Wickham et al., 2021) less frequent combinations, such as those occurring fewer than 700 times, to give better readability. Adjusting this threshold can reveal different patterns in the data. The combination of bigrams will help you understand that words in combination

Fig. 4.7 Word bigrams. Authors' own figure

provide significant insights, much more so than single words can provide. The power of word graphs is in the visualization of how different words in a corpus are connected or co-occur.

> *A bigram* is an n-gram of two consecutive tokens (e.g., "battery life"). Bigrams have a limited, local word order and often show better nuance and phrase-level meaning compared to single-word (unigram) analyses and also allow for the generation of co-occurrence graphs.

```
library(dplyr)
library(tidyr)
library(igraph)
library(ggraph)

# Separate bigrams into two words
# separate() was superseded in tidyr ≥ 2.0)
# d is the data-frame that has columns word & freq
d_2words <- d %>%
  separate_wider_delim(
    word,                  # column to split
    delim = " ",           # delimiter
    names = c("word1", "word2")
  ) %>%
  filter(freq > 700)
# Build a filtered word network
word_network <- graph_from_data_frame(d_2words)

# Inspect the word_network variable
word_network
```

```
IGRAPH a47c1b2 DN-- 110 96 --
+ attr: name (v/c), freq (e/n)
+ edges from a47c1b2 (vertex names):
 [1] kindl   ->fire      batteri->life      touch  ->screen
 ↪   read    ->book
 [5] sd      ->card       android->market    play   ->game
 ↪   easi    ->use
 [9] work    ->well       app    ->store     work   ->great
 ↪   android->tablet
[13] watch   ->movi       love   ->kindl     galaxi ->tab
 ↪  power   ->button
[17] can     ->get        custom ->servic    amazon ->prime
 ↪  can     ->use
```

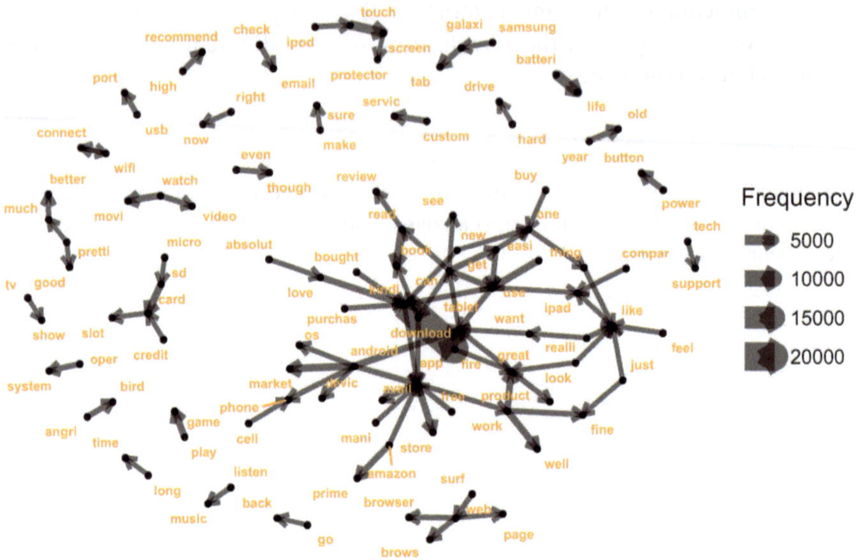

■ **Fig. 4.8** Word network. Authors' own figure

```
[21] year   ->old        angri  ->bird        much
↪  ->better   web    ->brows
[25] android->app        usb    ->port        watch  ->video
↪  high   ->recommend
[29] oper   ->system     even   ->though      surf   ->web
↪  use    ->tablet
+ ... omitted several edges
```

```
[1] "a47c1b2"
```

The a47c1b2 in the output is an internal identifier `igraph()` generates to distinguish it within the R environment, and it is not essential for the analysis. DN indicates a directed network (edges have directions). There are 110 vertices (words) and 96 edges (word pairs). Each vertex has an associated `name(v/c)` and each edge has an attribute `freq (e/n)`, indicating the frequency of the bigram occurrence. The edges list displays word pairs. `kindl -> fire` suggests a directed edge from `kindl` to `fire`, these words frequently appearing together in this order. The graph visualization (see ■ Fig. 4.8) will give a clearer picture of the co-occurring words.

The `ggraph()` function displays the information contained in the word network beautifully. The legend shows the thickness of an edge, representing the frequency of a bigram. Analyze all the words that you see in the graph for a better understanding of the underlying reviews. For example, we can notice words linked together such as *micro sd, sd card, card slot*, and *credit card*. The direction of the arrow tells you which word comes first. You can also see that Kindle Fire has the highest frequency bigram, and in the same network segment, these are linked to iPad. A lower threshold of the filter frequency would give you different insights.

4.3.4.1 Community Detection on Word Networks

You can also attempt to perform community detection on the previous graph. This is an important tool for uncovering patterns, clusters, or hidden structures represented by words that have a higher probability of appearing together in some groups than other groups; see ◘ Fig. 4.9. To understand more about this type of analysis, see Fortunato and Hric (2016). These communities often represent thematic or topical groupings in texts, providing insights into the underlying structure and content of the corpus. There are several community detection methods, such as Girvan-Newman, infomap, or label propagation (Lancichinetti & Fortunato, 2009) but a well-known one due to its fast parsing of large data sets is the so-called Louvain method (Blondel et al., 2008). In word networks, this is a popular community detection tool used to identify clusters of words that frequently co-occur in a corpus. It iteratively groups nodes (words) into communities, so that the modularity is maximized, revealing significant word clusters that might represent specific topics or themes.

An interesting application of it for marketing is in market basket analysis (Faridizadeh et al., 2018). This allows businesses to promote their products more successfully, and it is possible to discover communities with special properties, gleaning knowledge from shopping behavior. In the case of textual data, we obtain

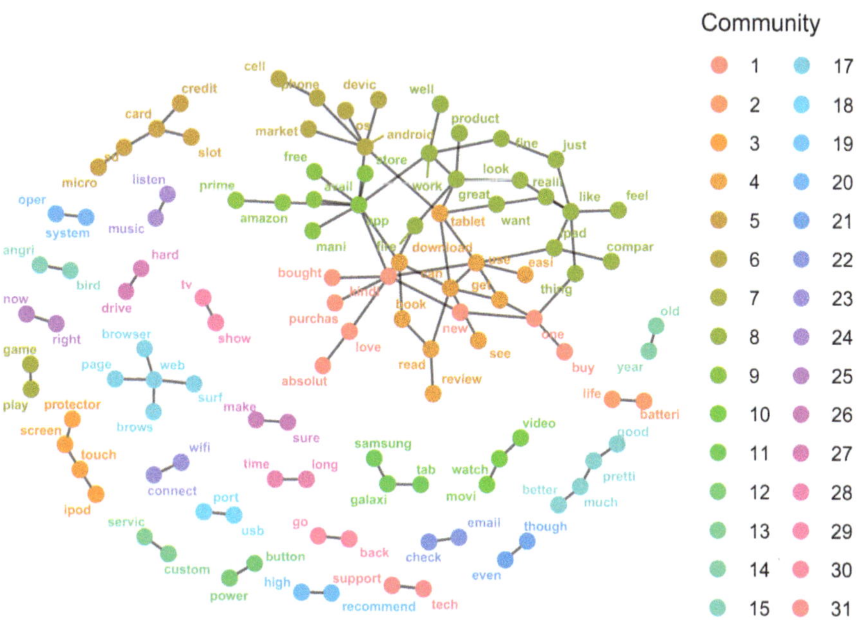

◘ **Fig. 4.9** Word network with community detection. Authors' own figure

extra knowledge from how customers put words together in their feedback and on which aspects they frequently focus.

```
# Convert to undirected graph
word_network <- as.undirected(word_network, mode = "collapse")

# Perform community detection using the Louvain method
communities <- cluster_louvain(word_network)

# Visualization of the word network with communities
ggraph(word_network, layout = 'fr') +
  geom_edge_link(edge_alpha = 0.5, show.legend = FALSE) +
  geom_node_point(aes(color = factor(communities$membership)),
  ↪   size = 3) +
  geom_node_text(aes(label = name, color =
  ↪   factor(communities$membership)),
                 repel = TRUE, fontface = "bold", size = 2,
                 ↪   show.legend = FALSE) +
  labs(color = "Community") +
  theme_void()
```

4.3.5 Some Considerations on Word Frequencies

The use of frequencies brings significant insights into the content of a corpus, and word associations give a better understanding of their co-occurrence in the text. Graphical representations are an easily grasped schematic display of the word frequencies and their associations. While these methods could be adopted for a preliminary analysis of the text, they are not sufficient for discovering patterns, latent structures, or groupings.

One of the most common activities of humans appears to be that of comparing and finding similarities. Let us use this and go deeper into our analysis, making use of the word clouds in order to compare two data sets (Kwartler, 2017). As an exercise, we have split our tablet data set into reviews which are related to Kindle Fire (the 2011 version) and the 16GB iPad2 and have selected the first 100 reviews of both of them. We know that each product on Amazon is identified by an ASIN number, and we will use those IDs to focus on two specific products. But before we do that, we have to build a function as a more compact version of what we have previously seen, something which does the preprocessing directly on the imported documents. Previously, we acted on the corpus data with the help of the `tm\_map()` function; now we will use the functions directly.

```r
library(tm)
library(magrittr)

options(stringsAsFactors = FALSE)

# Load the data
prodreviews <- read.csv("data/Product Reviews.csv")
content <- as.character(prodreviews$Content)

# Compact preprocessing (cleaning) function
preprocess <- function(feedtext) {
  feedtext %>%
    tolower() %>%
    removeWords(stopwords("english")) %>%
    removePunctuation() %>%
    stripWhitespace() %>%
    removeNumbers() %>%
    stemDocument() %>%
    return()
}

# Call the defined function
pre <- preprocess(content)

# Filter reviews by Item_ID (ASIN) and select the first 100
↪  comments for each product
kindle_reviews <- head(prodreviews$Content[prodreviews$Item_ID ==
↪  "B0051VVOB2"], 100)  # Kindle Fire 2011
ipad2_reviews <- head(prodreviews$Content[prodreviews$Item_ID ==
↪  "B0047DVWLW"], 100)  # iPad2 16GB

# Preprocess the reviews
sub_kindle <- preprocess(paste(kindle_reviews, collapse = " "))
sub_ipad2 <- preprocess(paste(ipad2_reviews, collapse = " "))

# Combine the two preprocessed review sets into a single vector
tablets <- c(sub_kindle, sub_ipad2)

# Create a corpus from the vector
corpus <- VCorpus(VectorSource(tablets))

# Create a Term-Document Matrix
tdm <- TermDocumentMatrix(corpus)
tdmmatrix <- as.matrix(tdm)

# Name the columns based on the products being compared
colnames(tdmmatrix) <- c("Kindle Fire 2011", "iPad2 16GB")
```

Now the structure is ready for displaying the commonality cloud; see ◘ Fig. 4.10. The word *commonality* indicates that the words that customers use to describe the two products are in common.

Fig. 4.10 Commonality cloud. Authors' own figure


```
commonality.cloud(tdmmatrix, max.words=200, random.order=FALSE)
```

We are trying to understand the linguistic patterns of two distinct sets of documents related to the Kindle Fire and iPad2 and see what they have in common, how many of these are discussed, and with which frequency. As bigrams are a common way to extract consecutive words, we have used the `BigramTokenizer()` function from the `RWeka` package. The custom function `extractBigrams()` is built to apply the tokenizer across the corpus. The core of the analysis lies in comparing the frequency of these common bigrams. Be aware that "lowercasing" and stemming are carried out during preprocessing. The analysis reveals the shared vocabulary between the two data sets and also the relative emphasis or prevalence of certain themes or concepts, shown by the frequency of the usage of the bigrams (see Fig. 4.11).

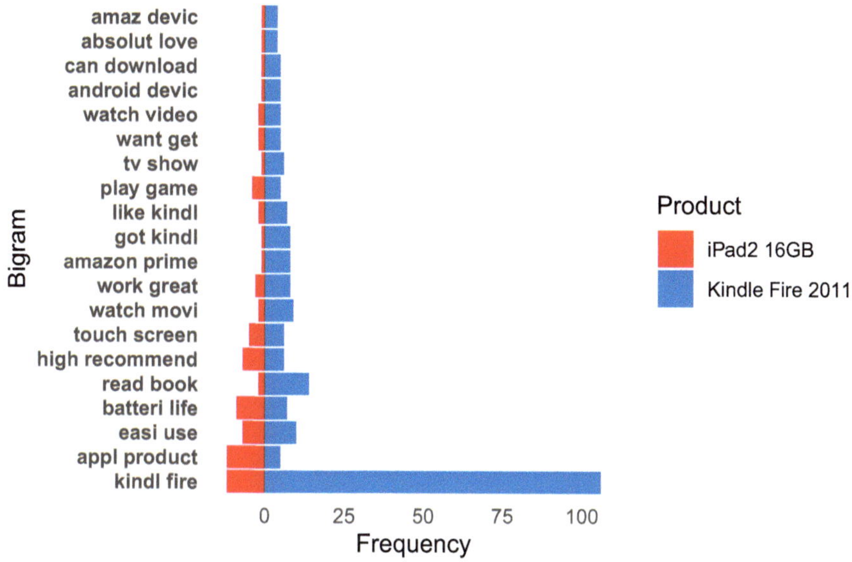

Fig. 4.11 Top 20 common bigrams for Kindle Fire2011 and iPad2 16GB. Authors' own figure

```
library(RWeka)
library(dplyr)
library(ggplot2)
library(tm)

# Bigram tokenizer function
BigramTokenizer <- function(x) NGramTokenizer(x, Weka_control(min
↪  = 2, max = 2))

# Extract bigrams for a subset of text
extractBigrams <- function(text) {
  # Extract bigrams and flatten the result to a single vector
  bigrams <- unlist(lapply(text, function(line)
↪  unlist(BigramTokenizer(line))))
  return(bigrams)
}

# Extract and process bigrams for Kindle Fire and iPad2
kindle_bigrams <- extractBigrams(sub_kindle)
ipad2_bigrams <- extractBigrams(sub_ipad2)

# Calculate frequencies
kindle_freq <- sort(table(kindle_bigrams), decreasing = TRUE)
ipad2_freq <- sort(table(ipad2_bigrams), decreasing = TRUE)

# Find common bigrams
common_bigrams <- intersect(names(kindle_freq), names(ipad2_freq))
```

```
# Select top 20 common bigrams
top_common_bigrams <- head(common_bigrams, 20)

# Prepare data frame for plotting
bigram_df <- data.frame(
  Bigram = rep(top_common_bigrams, 2),
  Frequency = c(as.numeric(kindle_freq[top_common_bigrams]),
                -as.numeric(ipad2_freq[top_common_bigrams])), #
                ↪ Make iPad2 frequencies negative
  Product = rep(c("Kindle Fire 2011", "iPad2 16GB"), each =
  ↪ length(top_common_bigrams))
)

# Create mirrored pyramid plot
ggplot(bigram_df, aes(x = reorder(Bigram, -abs(Frequency)), y =
↪ Frequency, fill = Product)) +
  geom_bar(stat = "identity") +
  coord_flip() +
  labs(x = "Bigram",
       y = "Frequency") +
  scale_fill_brewer(palette = "Set1") +
  theme_minimal() +
  theme(panel.grid.major = element_blank(), panel.grid.minor =
  ↪ element_blank(),
        axis.text.y = element_text(face = "bold"))
```

4

In contrast, a comparison cloud makes a distinction between the data sets and shows what is specific to each. It takes two or more data sets and displays the frequency of the words which are specific to each of them; see ◘ Fig. 4.12.

```
comparison.cloud(
  tdmmatrix,
  max.words = 200,
  random.order = FALSE,
  scale = c(3, 0.5),  # Adjust the size scale for words
  fixed.asp = TRUE    # Ensure the aspect ratio is fixed to make the
  ↪ cloud appear more square-like
)
```

4.3.5.1 Bigrams Comparison

Another useful method can be the comparison of mutual bigrams. With this technique, you can acquire a quick overview of how bigrams are used and with what frequency, and an immediate comparison is possible between the two; see ◘ Fig. 4.13. The steps for plotting the bigrams are as follows: First, extract them for both the Kindle Fire and iPad2 from the preprocessed text. Then, identify

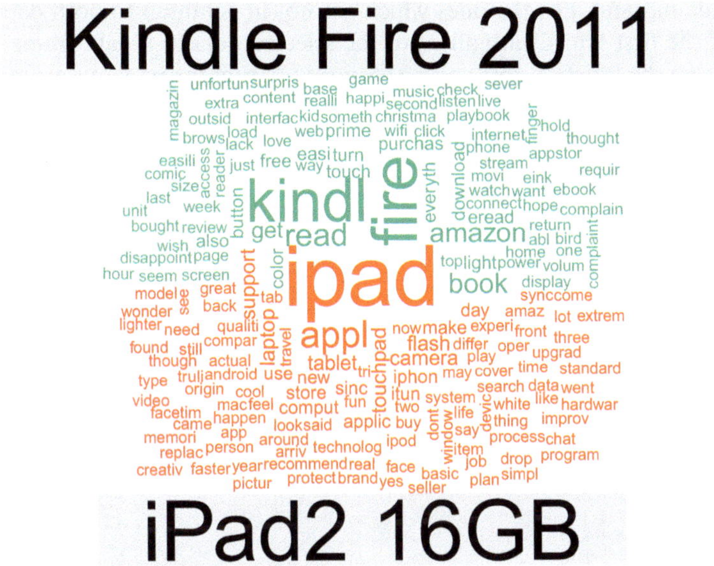

Fig. 4.12 Comparison cloud. Authors' own figure

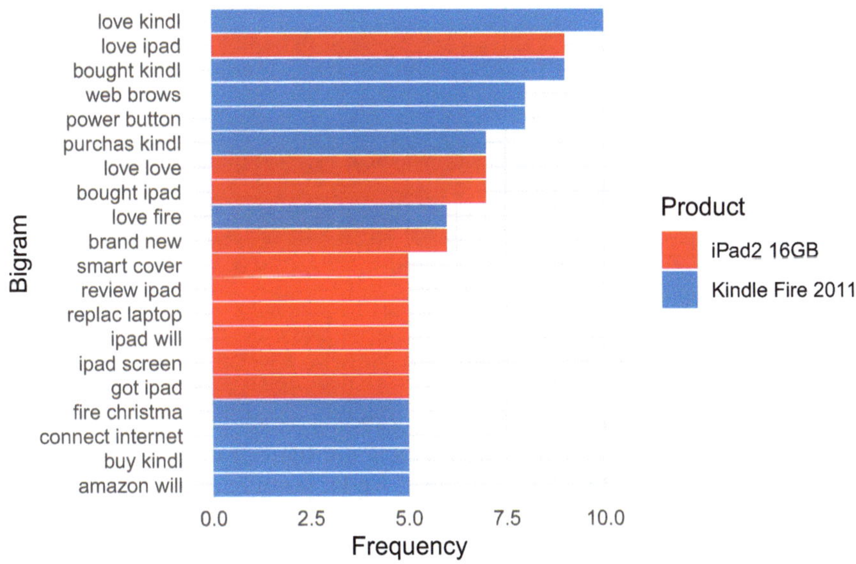

Fig. 4.13 Top ten unique bigrams for Kindle Fire 2011 and iPad2 16GB. Authors' own figure

the unique bigrams, i.e., the ones which are not in common to both data sets, by selecting the first ten. Eventually, put the selected data in a data frame and plot them. Reuse the function `extractBigrams()` from the previous example.

```
# Calculate frequencies
kindle_freq <- sort(table(kindle_bigrams), decreasing = TRUE)
ipad2_freq <- sort(table(ipad2_bigrams), decreasing = TRUE)

# Identify unique bigrams
unique_kindle <- names(kindle_freq)[!names(kindle_freq) %in%
↪ names(ipad2_freq)]
unique_ipad <- names(ipad2_freq)[!names(ipad2_freq) %in%
↪ names(kindle_freq)]

# Select top 10 unique bigrams
top_kindle <- head(sort(kindle_freq[unique_kindle], decreasing =
↪ TRUE), 10)
top_ipad2 <- head(sort(ipad2_freq[unique_ipad], decreasing =
↪ TRUE), 10)

# Convert to data frames
df_kindle <- data.frame(Bigram = names(top_kindle), Frequency =
↪ as.numeric(top_kindle), Product = "Kindle Fire 2011")
df_ipad2 <- data.frame(Bigram = names(top_ipad2), Frequency =
↪ as.numeric(top_ipad2), Product = "iPad2 16GB")

# Combine data frames
combined_df <- rbind(df_kindle, df_ipad2)

# Plot using ggplot
ggplot(combined_df, aes(x = reorder(Bigram, Frequency), y =
↪ Frequency, fill = Product)) +
  geom_bar(stat = "identity", position = position_dodge()) +
  labs(x = "Bigram", y = "Frequency") +
  scale_fill_brewer(palette = "Set1") +
  theme_minimal() +
  coord_flip()
```

All these tools are important for understanding which features both products have, or do not have, in common, how people use the words in order to describe the products, and what makes them distinct. And it is not hard to imagine that you might want to compare the reviews of what you produce or offer as a service with the reviews of your competitors.

4.3.6 Marketing Applications

How do word frequencies give insights into a set of documents and how can this be used for marketing purposes? The frequency of the words indicates that there

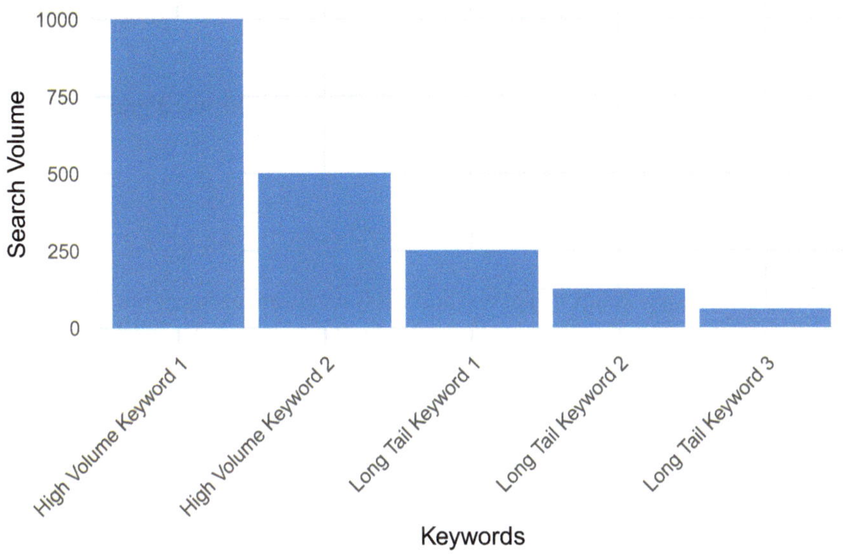

Fig. 4.14 The long tail for SEO keywords. Authors' own figure

is a tendency to describe the phenomenon, following the argument that the more you talk about something, the more important it is. But those words are perhaps the ones that are also used in a search engine, so employing them, or at least considering them as SEO keywords, is as important as checking trends with tools such as Google Trends. You can be found on the Internet if people look for you, so these words can work as hooks. But how many words should you choose for SEO? Knowing that the competition for one or two words is tight (see Fig. 4.14), the long tail (Anderson, 2013) is a very helpful place to examine. Check the search-engine results page and you will see that Google's recent advances in NLP allow you to use a more generous number of words.

Checking what you have in common with another company might help you diversify so that you can make yourself distinctive. It is also important to analyze what already differentiates you from other companies, especially the keywords that put your products in a bad light, or if your products are compared to competitors' products. You also need, in this case, to analyze not only the words themselves but also the associations of words. Another element to consider is the time of the year, when is it better to market a product? Is it perceived as a Christmas gift or a gadget for Father's Day?

Exercise 1. Make a comparison and an intersection cloud using bigrams.

Exercise 2. Create a trigram word cloud.

Exercise 3. Print an `igraph` with more than 300 occurrences of bigrams. Note the differences and how this new graph gives you more insights.

Exercise 4. Analyze and visualize the frequency distribution of trigrams across the data set.

Exercise 5. Take the iPad and Kindle subsets and make the word graphs for both of them.

Conclusion

This chapter was a walkthrough of text analysis from the importing of the basic data and preprocessing to more advanced concepts like the vector space model and word frequencies. We looked at how the transformation of text into numerical data enables us to extract information without the need to read large volumes of text. The chapter highlighted the importance of steps like normalization, stop words, punctuation, numbers, white space removal, and vocabulary reduction in general. The application of these techniques to word clouds, frequency plots, word networks, and community detection provided a visual understanding of the data, revealing underlying themes and patterns. We also plotted common words used for different products as well as distinct words used to describe specific products for easier identification. In this context, we examined the importance of using n-grams for more nuanced analyses. We explored how word frequencies can help develop SEO strategies, underscoring the significance of selecting the right keywords to improve online visibility and customer engagement.

Discussion

Keywords strategy and seasonality: Given the idea of long-tail (see ◘ Fig. 4.14) keywords, how should the head terms vs. long-tail terms be balanced for the tablets, and how should they change in December ("Christmas gift") or June ("Father's Day")?

Unigrams vs. bigrams: In the Kindle vs. iPad review comparisons, where did bigrams (for example, "battery life," "screen protector") change the insights compared to unigrams? What does the bigram direction/co-occurrence give?

Sparsity control: What pruning threshold (e.g., `removeSparseTerms` value) would you use which strikes a balance between interpretability vs. information when struggling with sparsity? When would you keep (or not) hapax legomena, and why?

Raw counts vs. tf-idf: For comparisons of the cross-product and SEO planning, when would tf-idf be the best choice, and when would raw counts communicate information better to stakeholders?

Insights from word networks: Choose an edge-frequency threshold for the bigram graph; which relationships emerge or disappear as you raise/lower it? Which community structures would you expect to find?

Take Home Message

- Preprocessing (normalization, stop-word removal, punctuation/number removal, and stemming/lemmatization) is the backbone of solid text analysis.
- BoW and DTM give simple but efficient numerical representations of text; tf-idf guarantees/ensures salience by down-weighting common terms.
- Sparsity control prunes low/no information terms (including hapax) to reduce dimensionality while retaining key signals.
- N-grams (especially bigrams) capture meaning at phrase level and often reveal different marketing insights compared to unigrams alone.
- Co-occurrence graphs illustrate the relationships between terms quickly and are a helpful tool for communicating findings.
- Word-frequency analysis can support the SEO; head terms provide reach, while long-tail terms show intent and differentiation across seasonal feeds.

References

Abell, C. H., & Jones, M. S. (2010). The power of a "word cloud" in marketing a nursing program. *Nursing Faculty Publications, 40*.

Aggarwal, C. C. (2018). *Machine learning for text*. Springer.

Aizawa, A. (2003). An information-theoretic perspective of TF–IDF measures. *Information Processing & Management*, *39*(1), 45–65. https://doi.org/10.1016/S0306-4573(02)00021-3

Anderson, C. (2013). *The long tail*. Nieuw Amsterdam.

Baayen, R. H. (2001). Word frequencies. *Word Frequency Distributions*, 1–38.

Beel, J., Langer, S., & Gipp, B. (2017). *TF-IDuF: A novel term-weighting scheme for user modeling based on users' personal document collections*. Bibliothek der Universität Konstanz.

Beumer, L. (2020). *Evaluation of text document clustering using k-means* [PhD thesis]. The University of Wisconsin–Milwaukee.

Blondel, V. D., Guillaume, J., Lambiotte, R., & Lefebvre, E. (2008). Fast unfolding of communities in large networks. *Journal of Statistical Mechanics: Theory and Experiment*, *2008*(10), P10008.

Bouchet–Valat, M., & Bouchet–Valat, M. M. (2020). Package "SnowballC." *R Package Version 0.7.0*.

Bun, K. K., & Ishizuka, M. (2001). *Emerging topic tracking system*. 2–11.

Carroll, J. M., & Roeloffs, R. (1969). Computer selection of keywords using word frequency analysis. *American Documentation*, *20*(3), 227–233.

Chai, C. P. (2023). Comparison of text preprocessing methods. *Natural Language Engineering*, *29*(3), 509–553. https://doi.org/10.1017/S1351324922000213

Church, K., & Hanks, P. (1990). Word association norms, mutual information, and lexicography. *Computational Linguistics*, *16*(1), 22–29.

Csardi, G., & Nepusz, T. (2006). The igraph software package for complex network research. In *InterJournal: Vols. Complex Systems* (p. 1695). https://igraph.org

Cui, W., Wu, Y., Liu, S., Wei, F., Zhou, M. X., & Qu, H. (2010). Context preserving dynamic word cloud visualization. *2010 IEEE Pacific Visualization Symposium (PacificVis)*, 121–128.

Faridizadeh, S., Abdolvand, N., & Rajaee Harandi, S. (2018). Market basket analysis using community detection approach: A real case. *Applications of Data Management and Analysis: Case Studies in Social Networks and Beyond*, 177–198.

Feinerer, I., & Hornik, K. (2019). Tm: Text mining package [version R package version 0.7–7]. *R Package*.

Fellows, I., & Fellows. (2018). Package "wordcloud." *R Package, Maintainer Ian and Rcpp, Linking To and Rcpp. [(Accessed on 4 February 2021)]*.

Ferrer i Cancho, R., & Solé, R. V. (2001). Two regimes in the frequency of words and the origins of complex lexicons: Zipf's law revisited. *Journal of Quantitative Linguistics*, *8*(3), 165–173.

Fortunato, S., & Hric, D. (2016). Community detection in networks: A user guide. *Physics Reports, 659*, 1–44.

Fox, C. (1989). A stop list for general text. *ACM SIGIR Forum, 24*(1–2), 19–21.

Goldberg, Y. (2017). Neural network methods for natural language processing. *Synthesis Lectures on Human Language Technologies, 10*(1), 1–309.

Heimerl, F., Lohmann, S., Lange, S., & Ertl, T. (2014). Word cloud explorer: Text analytics based on word clouds. *Proceedings of the 47th Hawaii International Conference on System Sciences*, 1833–1842.

Hofmann, T. (1999). Probabilistic latent semantic indexing. *Proceedings of the 22nd Annual International ACM SIGIR Conference on Research and Development in Information Retrieval*, 50–57.

Hornik, K., Buchta, C., & Zeileis, A. (2009). Open-source machine learning: R meets Weka. *Computational Statistics, 24*(2), 225–232. https://doi.org/10.1007/s00180-008-0119-7

Jockers, M. L., & Thalken, R. (2020). Hapax richness. In *Text analysis with R* (pp. 93–97). Springer.

Jones, K. S. (1972). A statistical interpretation of term specificity and its application in retrieval. *Journal of Documentation*.

Jones, K. S. (1973). Index term weighting. *Information Storage and Retrieval, 9*(11), 619–633.

Jurafsky, D., & Martin, J. H. (2008). *Speech and language processing, 2nd edition*. Prentice Hall.

Kilgarriff, A., Baisa, V., Bušta, J., Jakubíček, M., Kovář, V., Michelfeit, J., Rychlý, P., & Suchomel, V. (2014). The sketch engine: Ten years on. *Lexicography, 1*(1), 7–36.

Kwartler, T. (2017). *Text mining in practice with R*. John Wiley & Sons.

Lancichinetti, A., & Fortunato, S. (2009). Community detection algorithms: A comparative analysis. *Physical Review E, 80*(5), 056117.

Lovins, J. B. (1968). Development of a stemming algorithm. *Mechanical Translation and Computational Linguistics, 11*(1–2), 22–31.

Meyer, D., Hornik, K., & Feinerer, I. (2008). Text mining infrastructure in R. *Journal of Statistical Software, 25*(5), 1–54.

Miner, G., Elder IV, J., Fast, A., Hill, T., Nisbet, R., & Delen, D. (2012). *Practical text mining and statistical analysis for non-structured text data applications*. Academic Press.

Netzer, O., Lemaire, A., & Herzenstein, M. (2019). When words sweat: Identifying signals for loan default in the text of loan applications. *Journal of Marketing Research, 56*(6), 960–980. https://doi.org/10.1177/0022243719852959

Plisson, J., Lavrač, N., & Mladenic, D. (2004). *A rule based approach to word lemmatization. 3*, 83–86.

Popescu, I.-I., Mačutek, J., & Altmann, G. (2009). *Aspects of word frequencies*.

Porter, M. F. (1980). An algorithm for suffix stripping. *Program*.

R Core Team. (2025). *R: A language and environment for statistical computing*. R Foundation for Statistical Computing. https://www.R-project.org/

Scanfeld, D., Scanfeld, V., & Larson, E. L. (2010). Dissemination of health information through social networks: Twitter and antibiotics. *American Journal of Infection Control, 38*(3), 182–188.

Services, E. E. (2015). *Data science and big data analytics: Discovering, analyzing, visualizing and presenting data*. Wiley.

Toman, M., Tesař, R., & Ježek, K. (2006). Influence of word normalization on text classification. *Proceedings of InSciT, 4*, 354–358.

Toubia, O., Iyengar, G., Bunnell, R., & Lemaire, A. (2019). Extracting features of entertainment products: A guided latent dirichlet allocation approach informed by the psychology of media consumption. *Journal of Marketing Research, 56*(1), 18–36. https://doi.org/10.1177/0022243718820559

Wickham, H. (2021). *Tidyr: Tidy messy data*. https://CRAN.R-project.org/package=tidyr

Wickham, H., François, R., Henry, L., & Müller, K. (2021). *Dplyr: A grammar of data manipulation*. https://CRAN.R-project.org/package=dplyr

Xu, P., Wu, Y., Wei, E., Peng, T.-Q., Liu, S., Zhu, J. J. H., & Qu, H. (2013). Visual analysis of topic competition on social media. *IEEE Transactions on Visualization and Computer Graphics, 19*(12), 2012–2021.

Clustering Text for Marketing Segmentation, Similarity Measures, and Grouping

D. Dan, T. Reutterer, *Text Analytics in Marketing*, Classroom Companion: Business,
https://doi.org/10.1007/978-3-032-08086-8_5

Keywords
Clustering · Proximity and similarity · Euclidean distance · Cosine similarity · Linkage criteria · K-means · GMM · DBSCAN/HDBSCAN · Affinity propagation

This chapter is a step into the clustering of textual data and shows how the latent structures in words and documents can be revealed. The chapter distinguishes between distance and similarity measures for text (Euclidean vs. cosine) and how the choice of metric shapes the results. Hierarchical agglomerative clustering involves single/complete/average/Ward linkages, introducing the use of dendrograms to visualize the merging, and allowing for "cuts" to obtain a chosen number of clusters. Partitioning approaches are also illustrated using k-means (time of initialization, minimizing variance, elbow/silhouette ideas, and limitations with nonspherical shapes and outliers). Probabilistic or "soft" assignments are examined by using Gaussian mixture models and expectation-maximization. Density methods (DBSCAN/HDBSCAN) allow us to detect arbitrarily shaped clusters while also flagging noise without explicitly providing k. Affinity propagation introduces exemplars and the tuning of preferences. Throughout the chapter, R implementations show both term clustering (from TDMs) and document clustering (from DTMs). Practical guidance is provided regarding model choice, parameter tuning, and validation indices, while noting the role of the analyst's judgment. The algorithms can be linked to marketing segmentation, review analysis, and topics of discovery.

Learning Objectives

- Identifying and understanding the main clustering algorithms
- Exploring practical examples of different clustering methods
- Understanding the techniques for clustering text or documents to uncover latent patterns
- Analyzing and extracting information from clustering to aid decision-making
- Experimenting with clustering and applying it in different contexts

5.1 Grouping Text and Linguistic Elements

Humans tend to categorize (Harnad, 2017): This is a cognitive shortcut which identifies commonalities and creates groups, enabling the efficient processing of information. This is part of human cognition and allows us to act in a predetermined way when a specific, already familiar, situation arises. It also serves as a method of evaluating homogeneity in data so that we can make decisions based on a restricted number of groups with specific characteristics. It is similar to summarizing: We condense a lot of information into a few important key points that describe the whole in a concise manner.

One practical application of categorizing is clustering. This involves identifying shared characteristics within data and grouping similar items accordingly. There are several clustering techniques, as well as many fields of application. In marketing, clustering can also be referred to as segmentation, i.e., when we try to find a segment of a population that exhibits similar behaviors and patterns. Of clustering methods, one is model-based and uses statistical probability models, another is density-based clustering, which uses a model that groups objects based on objective functions, while yet another is distance-based and has a strong exploratory component. Various measures can be used for this last version, including Hamming for categorical data, Manhattan and Euclidean for continuous data, Jaccard for binary data, Mahalanobis for correlated data, or cosine similarity for text data. There are also hybrid methods which combine various clustering methods (Vries et al., 2019). A compact taxonomy of clustering families and the distance or similarity measures they typically rely on can be found in Aggarwal and Reddy (2014).

A similar concept to clustering is classification. This uses existing classes with known features: New unclassified elements are tested against these features and then assigned to the appropriate class, so classification is a supervised method (Sen et al., 2020). Clustering seeks to uncover these commonalities autonomously, often through iterative, unsupervised mathematical operations within algorithms. Often we do not know how many clusters we can have and need to conduct several trials before we can extract meaningful insights into the data. This is a brief outline of two important concepts, clustering and classification, and in this chapter, we will concentrate on the principles and application of the former.

In clustering, the goal is to extract latent groups, or clusters, that contain a certain number of elements. These clusters may range from those which contain a single element to those in which all elements within a data set are present. In any clustering algorithm, the concept of similarity is twofold: high similarity (homogeneity) within clusters and marked dissimilarity (heterogeneity) between different clusters, as illustrated in ◘ Fig. 5.1. When applying a clustering algorithm, several factors are of interest, including the number of clusters generated, their relative distances, sizes, shapes, and densities.

Text clustering gives us a quick overview of the content of a corpus by extracting its most representative features. Grouping together the words that are most closely related to each other (Struhl, 2015) helps us to identify underlying topics and themes. These methods can be very useful, for example, when clustering search results or finding similar word groups in emails from customers. Such insights are essential in refining segmentation strategies and discovering recurring issues in customer communications, and so helping to develop one-to-one marketing.

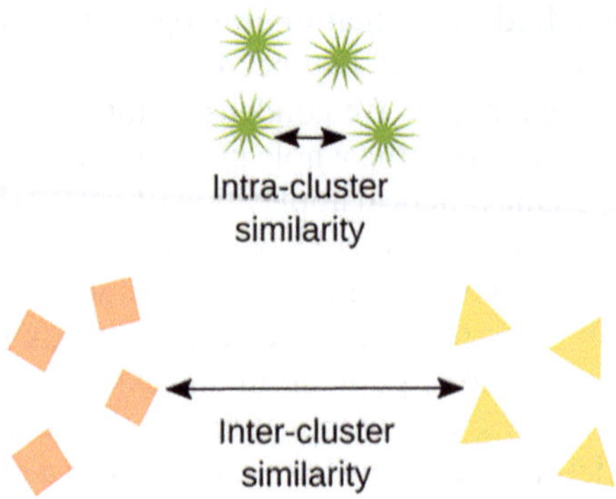

Fig. 5.1 Cluster similarity. Authors' own figure

5

5.2 Proximity and Similarity

5.2.1 Euclidean Distance

In text mining, clustering can be applied at various levels, for entire books, chapters, paragraphs, sentences, or even individual words. Clustering words mean grouping terms that appear at similar frequencies across different documents (see the definition of document in the introductory chapter), while clustering documents allows us to understand the similarities between them. Authorship attribution is one practical application, where texts are grouped to assign them to specific authors. Each author's unique writing style, manifested through their use of stop words, distinctive expressions, word frequencies, and punctuation, becomes an identifier for such analyses (Stamatatos et al., 2016). Research has also shown gender-based differences in writing styles, indicating potential gender segmentation in texts (Cheng et al., 2011).

Frequency (i.e., how many times a term appears in a text) allows us to use algorithms that involve the concept of Euclidean distance (Huang et al., 2008). Documents with a high degree of similarity of word frequencies are considered closer in terms of Euclidean distance, meaning that the distance between them is minimal. A simple example will help to grasp the basic concept.

Consider an unlikely scenario of three documents, each containing just two words. Each word's occurrence in a document is quantified by its frequency, expressed as the number of times it appears. To demonstrate this concept, we will use R to replicate the data presented in Table 5.1 where the numerical representation of our example is shown.

To begin our analysis, we define the variables `doc1`, `doc2`, and `doc3` containing the frequency counts of two specific words within the respective documents. The function `rbind()` is used to merge the individual `doc` vectors into a single data frame consolidating them in terms of row. It is worth noting the existence of `cbind()`, a complementary function that consolidates columns.

After binding these vectors, we use the function `rename()` to assign meaningful column names to the newly formed table stored in the variable `docs`: `bank` and `engine`. To represent the co-occurrence frequencies of these two words visually

Table 5.1 Example: word frequencies in three documents. Table compiled by the authors

	Bank	Engine
doc1	20	11
doc2	22	12
doc3	12	27

across the documents, we construct a scatterplot. The function `ggplot()` and its associated attributes are used to display our data. The function `geom_point()` is applied to generate a scatterplot, and `labs()` and `geom_label()` enhance the plot by adding labels and creating an aesthetically pleasing layout, see Fig. 5.2.

```
# tidyverse library
library(tidyverse)

# Example, the word bank (appears 20 times in the first document),
# engine (appears 11 times in the same document)
doc1 <- c(20, 11)
doc2 <- c(22, 12)
doc3 <- c(12, 27)

docs <- rbind(doc1, doc2, doc3) %>%
  as.data.frame %>%
  rename(bank=1, engine=2)

ggplot(docs, aes(x=bank, y=engine)) +
  geom_point() +
  labs(x="bank", y="engine") +
  geom_label(label=rownames(docs), nudge_x = 0.35, nudge_y = 0.35)
```

After we bind the documents and the words together in a tabular structure, the data frame, we can calculate the distance between the documents. Note that the concept of distance is associated with the concept of similarity: The smaller the distance, the higher the similarity. Figure 5.2 gives a visual interpretation of this concept, illustrating that `doc1` and `doc2` are closer to one another when compared with `doc3`. Mathematically, this can be calculated using Euclidean distance (Jockers & Thalken, 2020). On a two-dimensional plane, this is analogous to the hypotenuse in the theorem of Pythagoras. Be aware that Euclidean distance is not the only method that can be used to calculate the distance between two or more elements. The work of Deza and Deza (2009) offers an extensive overview of distance metrics covering a wide range of calculation methods.

The equation to calculate the distance between `doc1` and `doc2` uses w to represent word frequencies in the documents. It is essential to understand that $1^{st}w_{doc_1}$, $1^{st}w_{doc_2}$, etc., represent the frequencies of the first words in `doc1` and

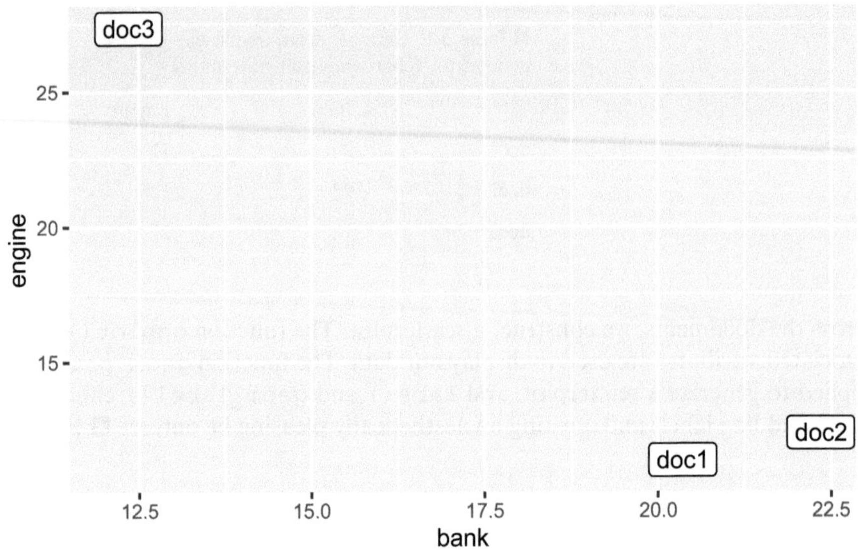

Fig. 5.2 Documents similarity. Authors' own figure

doc2, respectively. The pattern continues for all words, up to the nth word. This is a simplification which assumes that both documents contain exactly the same set of words. For words that are present in one document and absent in the other, their frequency in the document where they are absent is considered to be zero. The equation calculates the Euclidean distance by summing the squares of differences in word frequencies for each word across the two documents and then taking the square root of this sum.

$$dist(doc_1, doc_2) = \sqrt{(1^{st}w_{doc_1} - 1^{st}w_{doc_2})^2 + (2^{nd}w_{doc_1} - 2^{nd}w_{doc_2})^2 + \ldots + (n^{th}w_{doc_1} - n^{th}w_{doc_2})^2}.$$

In our case, we do not have n words, but only two: *bank* and *engine*. Let us calculate the distance between the documents and round the result to the first two decimals.

$$dist(doc_1, doc_2) = \sqrt{(20 - 22)^2 + (11 - 12)^2} = 2.24$$

$$dist(doc_1, doc_3) = \sqrt{(20 - 12)^2 + (11 - 27)^2} = 17.89$$

$$dist(doc_2, doc_3) = \sqrt{(22 - 12)^2 + (12 - 27)^2} = 18.03.$$

As was expected from the scatterplot, the Euclidean distance between documents d_1 and d_2 is considerably smaller than the distance between d_1 and d_3 or between d_2 and d_3. To facilitate the calculation of these distances, especially in cases involving many documents with multiple features, we can use the R function `dist()`. This efficiently calculates the distances of pairs between the documents.

```
# Compute pairwise distances between documents
dist(docs)
```

```
          doc1      doc2
doc2  2.236068
doc3 17.888544 18.027756
```

Euclidean distance is a simple method for calculating proximity, but in marketing it is not used frequently due to its sensitivity to the magnitude of the term frequencies. Another metric, called cosine similarity, is preferred because it measures the angle between vectors. We will discuss this in more detail in ► Chap. 10. In marketing applications, cosine similarity helps in the analysis of text similarity, such as clustering customer reviews or segmenting product descriptions (Berger et al., 2020).

Euclidean distance is the straight-line distance between two vectors (e.g., documents) and is the square root of the sum of the squared differences between the corresponding elements of the vectors. It is important to normalize data to avoid bias in the results.

5.2.2 Cosine Similarity

We can calculate the cosine similarity of two vectors by using the data from the previous session. We can consider a document as a vector, with the elements of the vector being the frequencies of the words in a document (Han et al., 2022). The cosine similarity between two vectors $\vec{A}$ and $\vec{B}$ is defined as

$$\mathrm{sim}(\vec{A}, \vec{B}) = \frac{\sum_{i=1}^{n} A_i \cdot B_i}{\sqrt{\sum_{i=1}^{n} A_i^2} \cdot \sqrt{\sum_{i=1}^{n} B_i^2}}. \tag{5.1}$$

Note on Terminology. We call the quantity in Eq. 5.2.2 *cosine similarity* (ranges 0–1). When a clustering routine needs a distance, we would use

$$d_{\cos}(A, B) = 1 - \mathrm{sim}_{\cos}(A, B),$$

which we refer to as *cosine distance*.

> *Cosine similarity* is the cosine of the angle between two vectors. The cosine distance is 1− (cosine similarity) and is often used in clustering.

5

In Eq. 5.2.2, A_i and B_i are the i-th components, in our case word frequencies, of the two vectors. The numerator represents their dot product, while the denominator is the product of their Euclidean magnitudes. We have the three documents represented as vectors, $\vec{doc_1} = (20, 11)$, $\vec{doc_2} = (22, 12)$, $\vec{doc_3} = (12, 27)$. The cosine similarity between $\vec{doc_1}$ and $\vec{doc_2}$ is calculated as

$$\text{sim}(\vec{doc_1}, \vec{doc_2}) = \frac{(20 \cdot 22) + (11 \cdot 12)}{\sqrt{20^2 + 11^2} \cdot \sqrt{22^2 + 12^2}} = \frac{572}{22.83 \cdot 25.07} \approx 0.999.$$

Similarly, we can calculate the cosine similarity between $\vec{doc_1}$ and $\vec{doc_3}$, and between $\vec{doc_2}$ and $\vec{doc_3}$. The closer the similarity measure between the two vectors is to 1, the more similar they are. In R we can use the package `lsa` to speed up the computation.

```
# lsa library
library(lsa)

# Example data: term frequencies
doc1 <- c(20, 11)
doc2 <- c(22, 12)
doc3 <- c(12, 27)

# Combine into a matrix
docs <- rbind(doc1, doc2, doc3)

# Calculate cosine similarity matrix
# lsa::cosine() expects term vectors
# in columns, hence the transpose
cosine_sim_matrix <- cosine(t(docs))

# View the cosine similarity matrix
cosine_sim_matrix
```

```
          doc1      doc2      doc3
doc1 1.0000000 0.9999939 0.7962479
doc2 0.9999939 1.0000000 0.7941278
doc3 0.7962479 0.7941278 1.0000000
```

It is easy to observe that `doc1` and `doc2` are the most similar, while `doc3` is less.

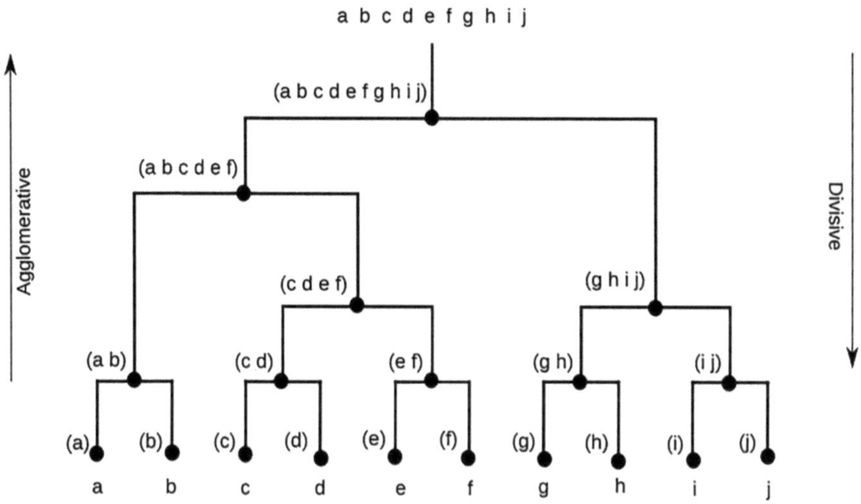

Fig. 5.3 Hierarchical agglomerative/divisive clustering dendrogram. Authors' own figure

5.3 Hierarchical Agglomerative Clustering

If we do not want to cluster or find document similarities, but we need to focus on the words, a directly related application, exemplifying the principles discussed in ▶ Sect. 5.2.1, is hierarchical clustering (HC), one of the simplest forms of clustering. HC has two primary methodologies: agglomerative and divisive. In agglomerative (or bottom-up) clustering, each element initially represents a distinct cluster. Then, they are merged, or agglomerated, into increasingly larger clusters, culminating in a single, comprehensive cluster. In the divisive (or top-down) clustering, the algorithm begins with one large cluster which is systematically divided into smaller and smaller ones, ultimately reaching the level of individual elements with a tree-like taxonomy. The analogy with a tree (dendrogram) is straightforward: The end branches are individual objects, the nodes where they divide signify the clusters, and the root contains the entire data set, as illustrated in ◘ Fig. 5.3.

> *A dendrogram* is a tree-like diagram showing hierarchical clustering results. The leaves represent individual items, while the internal nodes are merges (clusters). Branch heights reflect intercluster dissimilarities.

We have learned how to calculate the distance between objects using Euclidean distance, but a cluster contains one or more than one element. So, if the distance between individual elements is well understood, how can we calculate the distance between clusters? There are several ways to do this. The distance between two clusters can be given by the distance between either the closest or furthest elements contained in the two clusters. Or it is possible to calculate the mean distance

Table 5.2 Linking criteria. Table compiled by the authors

Single Linkage	This is the distance between the closest members of the two clusters	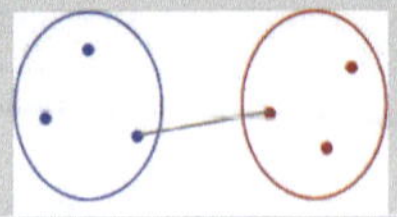
Complete Linkage	This is the distance between the members that are farthest apart	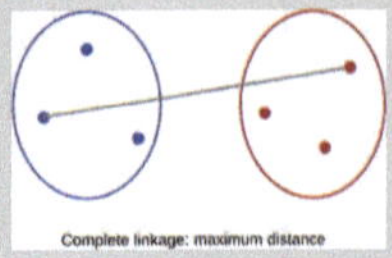
Average Linkage	This method involves looking at the distances between all the pairs and averages all of the distances, also called UPGMA	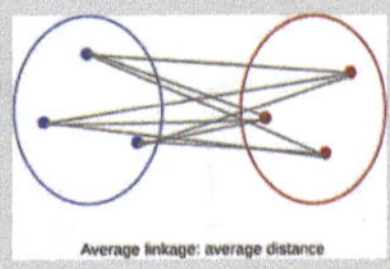
Ward Linkage	This method minimizes the within-cluster variance	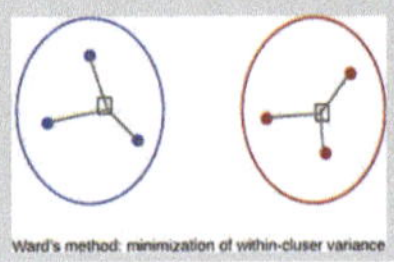

5

between all the pairs of elements, one from each cluster. Both of these methods, known collectively as linkage criteria, influence the shape and size of the clusters formed. To better visualize these concepts, Table 5.2 provides diagrams and succinct descriptions.

Apart from the linkage methods presented in Table 5.2, there are other procedures, such as the combined weighted algorithm discussed by Maqbool and Babri (2004). While these other methods offer nuanced approaches to clustering, their practical use is somewhat limited.

To illustrate the workings of HAC, consider a scenario with six elements (referred to as "words") across two dimensions (labeled as "documents"). This example is a slightly more complex than the one above, but is still accessible to beginners. We have applied HAC using a single-linkage method. Notice that in the previous example, the focus was on the clustering of documents, while now the clustering revolves around words. We hypothesized that these words appear with varying frequencies within the documents, meaning that in each document, the six words appear a certain number of times. The words have a similar characteristic if they appear with a similar frequency in the documents that hold them (Table 5.3).

The first step in starting to perform HAC is to calculate the distances between the elements, in this case, the words. Words that exhibit similar frequencies across documents will be positioned closer to each other in the conceptual space. A visual representation of this arrangement, if plotted on a canvas, would resemble the configuration shown in Fig. 5.4.

■ **Table 5.3** Table containing six words and their frequencies in the corpus. Table compiled by the authors

Word	Document1	Document2
Word1	40	53
Word2	22	38
Word3	35	32
Word4	26	19
Word5	8	41
Word6	45	30

```
# Relevant libraries
library(ggplot2)
library(ggrepel)

# Create a data frame for six words and their frequencies in two
↪ documents
words_data <- data.frame(
  Word = c("Word1", "Word2", "Word3", "Word4", "Word5", "Word6"),
  Document1 = c(40, 22, 35, 26, 8, 45),
  Document2 = c(53, 38, 32, 19, 41, 30)
)

# Calculate Euclidean distances
dist_matrix <- dist(words_data[, 2:3], method = "euclidean")
print(dist_matrix)

# Plotting using ggplot2
ggplot(words_data, aes(Document1, Document2, label = Word)) +
  geom_point() +
  geom_text_repel() +
  labs(x = "Frequency in Document 1",
       y = "Frequency in Document 2") +
  theme_minimal()
```

```
         1        2        3        4        5
2 23.43075
3 21.58703 14.31782
4 36.76955 19.41649 15.81139
5 34.17601 14.31782 28.46050 28.42534
6 23.53720 24.35159 10.19804 21.95450 38.60052
```

The distance between `Word1` and `Word2` can be calculated using the Euclidean metric, and `Document1` is represented on the X -axis, `Document2` on the Y-axis:

5

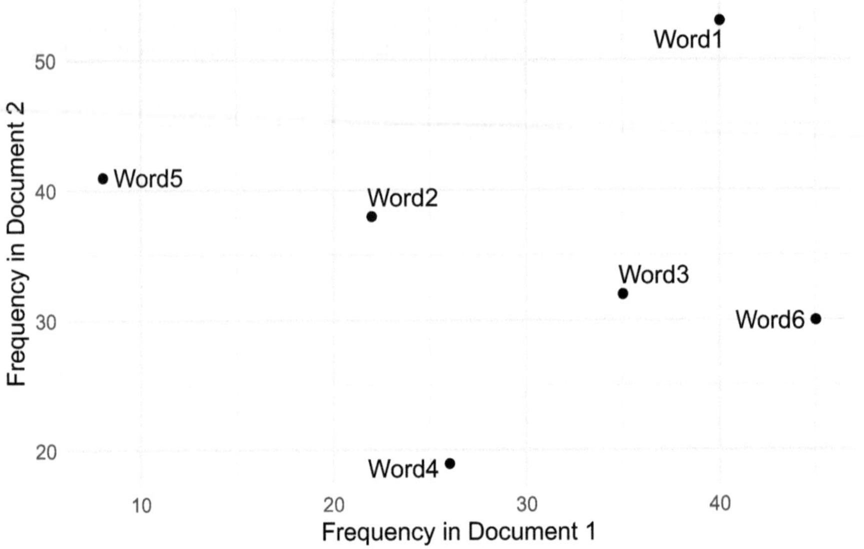

Fig. 5.4 Six words, two documents. Authors' own figure

$$dist(Word1, Word2) = \sqrt{(40-22)^2 + (53-38)^2} = 23.43.$$

We can calculate the distance between all the pairs of words in the same way, (Word1, Word3), (Word1, Word4), (Word1, Word5), etc., and put them into a distance matrix, see Table 5.4.

Table 5.4 Initial pairwise Euclidean distances among words. Table compiled by the authors

	Word1	Word2	Word3	Word4	Word5	Word6
Word1	0.00					
Word2	23.43	0.00				
Word3	21.59	14.32	0.00			
Word4	36.77	19.42	15.81	0.00		
Word5	34.18	14.32	28.46	28.43	0.00	
Word6	23.54	24.35	**10.20**	21.95	38.60	0.00

You can see that the diagonal of the distance matrix is always zero, because the distance between a word and itself is null. In symmetric-distance matrices the values above and below the diagonal mirror each other, hence only one part, usually the lower, is displayed for simplicity. For example, the distance between `Word1` and `Word3` is the same distance as the one between `Word3` and `Word1`. Using the

Fig. 5.5 Clustering `Word3` and `Word6`. Authors' own figure

Euclidean distance formula, we can calculate these distances and then apply single-linkage clustering, which is also known as the minimum method. In other words, we search for the minimum value between two elements. Initially, all the elements form clusters on their own, resulting in six separate clusters. The minimum value between two values is between `Word3` and `Word6`, as highlighted in Table 5.4, leading to their combination into the first cluster. There are two vertical lines which represent the individual clusters, merging into a single line that represents the new cluster. The number 1 in Fig. 5.5 states that this is the first cluster, and the vertical line indicates at what height on the dendrogram the cluster was produced, in this case at *10.20*. The height represents the distance or difference between the clusters. If two clusters join at a low height, it suggests they are quite similar or close to each other. Conversely, if two clusters join at a higher height, it indicates a greater degree of dissimilarity or distance, suggesting that the clusters are less alike.

After the initial clustering, we can update the distance matrix to show the newly formed cluster, see Table 5.5. In this revised matrix, the distances have been recalculated to account for the clusters of elements that have just been created. We must be consistent and apply the single-linkage criterion each time. In this updated scenario, the minimum distance can now be seen between `Word2` and `Word5`, highlighted in bold in the table. This indicates that these two words are the next closest pair.

Note: In single linkage, the algorithm picks the smaller of the two intercluster distances (bolded above).

We can also focus on finding the minimum distance between the newly formed cluster and the remaining individual words or existing clusters. To do this, we have to look for the smallest value among these recalculated distances. In this case, the

Table 5.5 Distances after merging Word3 and Word6 (single linkage). Table compiled by the authors

	Word1	Word2	(Word3, Word6)	Word4	Word5
Word1	0.00				
Word2	23.43	0.00			
(Word3, Word6)	(**21.59**, 23.54)	(**14.32**, 24.35)	0.00		
Word4	36.77	19.42	(15.82, 21.96)	0.00	
Word5	34.17	**14.32**	(28.46, 38.60)	28.42	0.00

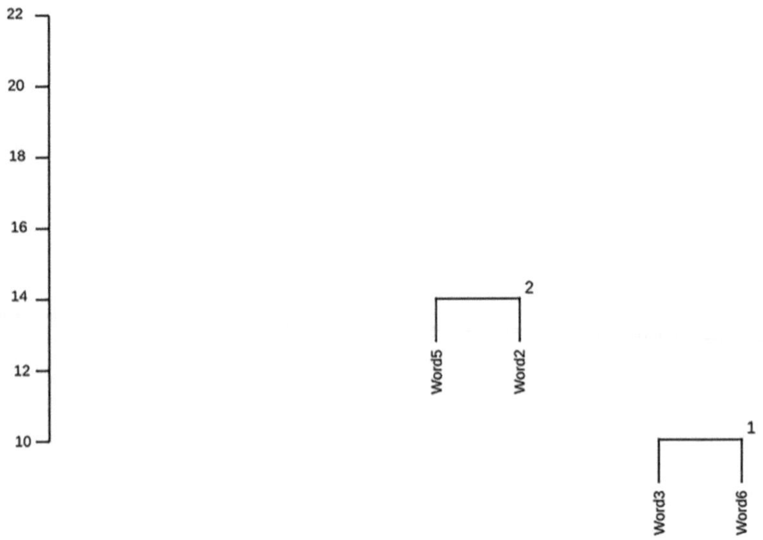

Fig. 5.6 Clustering `Word2` and `Word5`. Authors' own figure

next smallest distance is observed between `Word2` and `Word5`, indicating that these two entities will form the next cluster. In Fig. 5.6 this is marked as number 2.

We hope that by now the hierarchical clustering procedure is clear. As shown in Fig. 5.7 at the end of the process, we will have one single comprehensive final cluster, here labeled as Cluster 5. Note that the number of clusters can be determined by cutting the dendrogram at a specific height. To sum up, the dendrogram's horizontal axis displays the clusters, while the vertical axis represents the sequence and scale of cluster amalgamation, with the numerical values indicating the proximity or similarity between the merged clusters.

Determining the optimal number of clusters in a data set is often challenging, as there is no definitive answer. Several heuristic methods, commonly referred to as stopping rules, may offer a degree of guidance by generating a score or index, helping you come to a decision about the ideal number of clusters. The choice of

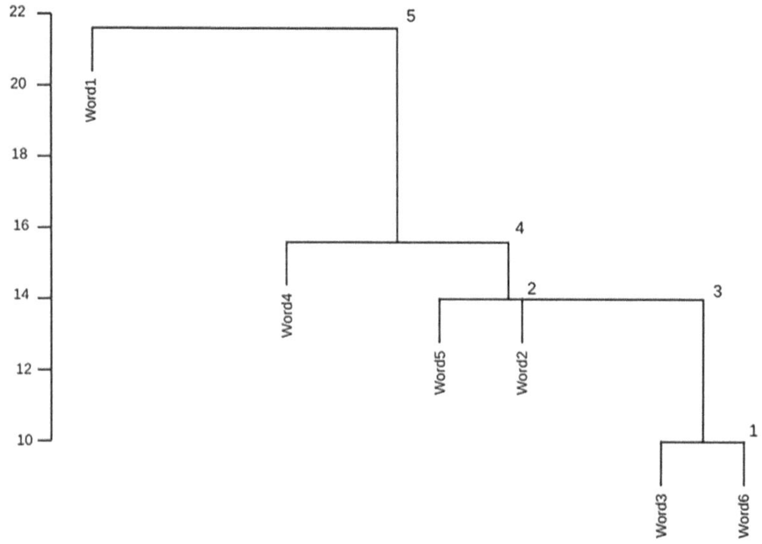

Fig. 5.7 Clustering `Word1` with all the other clusters. Authors' own figure

an appropriate number of clusters and how well data are clustered is subjective and influenced by various factors, including which distance metric is used.

Some of the prominent stopping rules or indices dealing with clustering validation include the Bayesian information criterion (BIC), Akaike information criterion (AIC), silhouette score, Davies-Bouldin index, homogeneity score, completeness score, V-measure, the Calinski-Harabasz index, Duda-Hartigan's rule, among others. It is crucial to note that while these mathematical methods can deliver an optimal result, the clusters formed may not always align with intuitive or meaningful groupings in practical scenarios.

In applying HAC to our data set, we have introduced variation. Instead of using the conventional Euclidean distance, we opted for the Canberra distance (Kocher & Savoy, 2017), and instead of single linkage, we employ Ward's method (Strauss & Maltitz, 2017). As we have already mentioned, we can also employ the cosine distance (Maimon & Rokach, 2010). For assessing the optimal number of clusters, we used the Hartigan index (Purwitasari et al., 2011), which calculates the maximum difference between the levels of the index's hierarchy.

```
# Loading libraries
library(factoextra)
library(NbClust)
library(proxy)

# Reproducibility function
set.seed(123)
```

```
# Convert "docs" to matrix
m <- as.matrix(docs)

# Canberra distance matrix
d <- dist(m, method = "canberra")

# Ward's method clustering
hc <- hclust(d, method = "ward.D")

# Optimal cluster count
nb <- NbClust(m, distance = "canberra", min.nc = 2, max.nc = 5,
              method = "ward.D", index = "all")
```


*** : The Hubert index is a graphical method of determining the number of clusters. In the plot of Hubert index, we seek a significant knee that corresponds to a significant increase of the value of the measure, i.e., the significant peak in Hubert index second differences plot.

*** : The D index is a graphical method of determining the number of clusters. In the plot of D index, we seek a significant knee (the significant peak in Dindex second differences plot) that corresponds to a significant increase of the value of the measure:

- Among all indices:
- 6 proposed 2 as the best number of clusters.
- 9 proposed 3 as the best number of clusters.
- 1 proposed 4 as the best number of clusters.
- 6 proposed 5 as the best number of clusters.

***** Conclusion *****

- According to the majority rule, the best number of clusters is 3.

```
optimal_clusters <- nb$Best.nc[1]

# Clustering result
hc_result <- hcut(d, k = optimal_clusters, hc_method = "ward.D")
```

To visualize the hierarchical clustering results as a dendrogram, see ◘ Fig. 5.8. To do this we used the function `fviz_dend()` from the `factoextra` package (Kassambara & Mundt, 2020). It uses `ggplot2` to create aesthetically informative dendrograms. For the calculation of the distances between the clustered items, we used the `dist()` function, with the cosine distance measure from the `proxy` package (Meyer & Buchta, 2021).

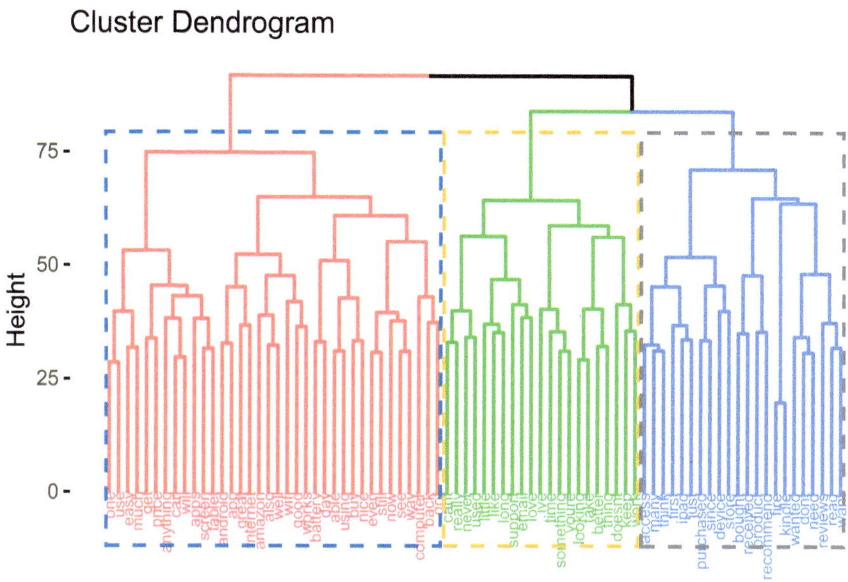

Fig. 5.8 Cluster dendrogram. Authors' own figure

```
# Dendrogram visualization
fviz_dend(hc_result, rect = TRUE, rect_border = "jco", rect_lty =
↪  2, cex = 0.5)
```

We can also visualize the cluster plot, see Fig. 5.9.

```
# Cluster visualization
fviz_cluster(hc_result, data=m, ellipse.type = "norm")
```

In this analysis, we used a weighted version of the term-document matrix, see ► Chap. 4. Unlike the regular TDM, which employs plain word frequencies, the weighted version contains a numerical statistic and considers the significance of words across the entire corpus.

The removal of most of the words was done to manage the complexity and ensure clarity of the visualization. Try doing this without the removal of the words (inadvisable) to see the chaos that ensues.

The clustering process grouped words that had a similar importance across the documents. Yes, *kindle fire* is one such case, and as you can see the words *kindle* and *fire* frequently occur together in the context of this data set. It is the experience and

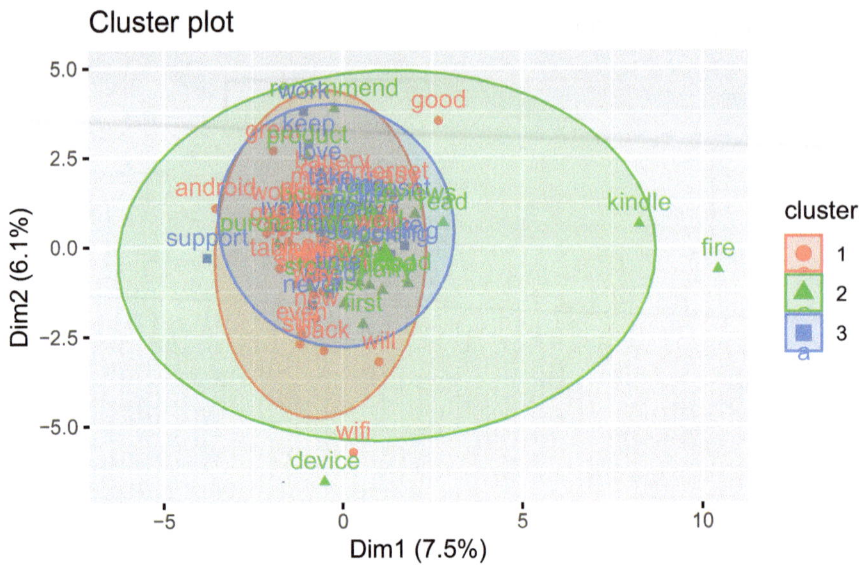

Fig. 5.9 Cluster plot. Authors' own figure

the knowledge of the analyst that make sense of the clusters and the underlying semantic relationships and patterns.

The `NbClust()` function yielded 3 as the best number of clusters using the Hubert index. Ideally, we would apply all the indexes to the function and choose the mode (the most frequent number). Unfortunately, not all of them are suitable for hierarchical clustering. Nevertheless, for all those that can be treated in this way, the mode is 3.

The choice of the best linking criterion or distance metric in hierarchical clustering is subject to debate, as highlighted in sources such as Gower and Legendre (1986). There is a consensus that the choice largely depends on the specific circumstances of the data and the analyst's experience. As we have already mentioned, Euclidean distance might not always be appropriate as it tends to group documents based on length rather than semantic content. In such cases, cosine similarity, which focuses on the orientation rather than the magnitude of vectors, can offer a more nuanced understanding of the textual data. Here is an example which demonstrates how these changes can shape the final result (see Fig. 5.10).

```
library(proxy)  # for cosine similarity calculation
library(cluster)  # for hierarchical clustering

# Compute the similarity matrix
similarity_matrix <- simil(m, method = "cosine")

# Converting similarity to distance
```

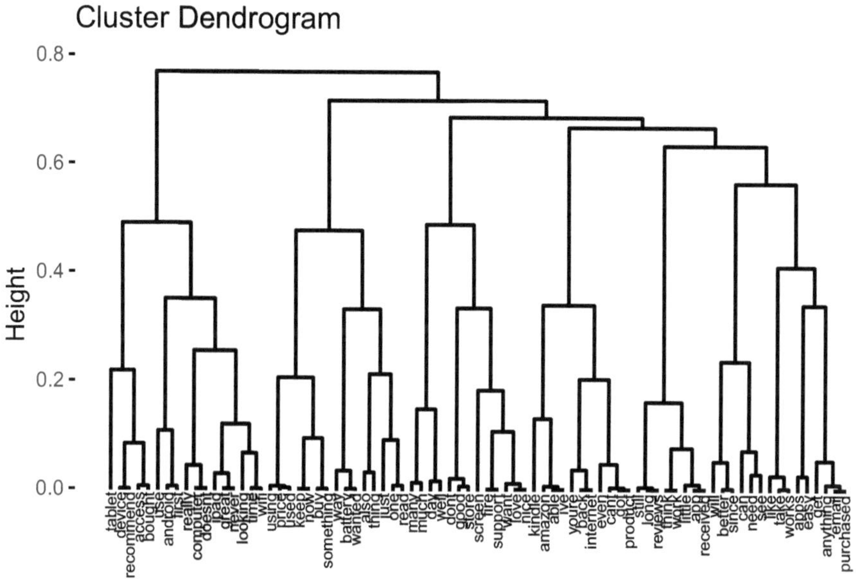

Fig. 5.10 Hierarchical clustering with cosine similarity calculation. Authors' own figure

```
distance_matrix <- 1 - similarity_matrix

# Performing hierarchical clustering
hc <- hclust(as.dist(distance_matrix), method = "ward.D")  # or
↪  any other method

# Plotting the dendrogram
fviz_dend(hc, cex = 0.5, rect = TRUE, k_colors = "jco",
↪  rect_border = "jco", rect_lty = 2)
```

5.4 K-Means Clustering

K-means clustering is a partitioning method that segments a data set into a predetermined number of clusters, denoted by "k." The data set is divided into partitions, where each data point belongs to only one group. The objective is to partition the data set into k clusters to maximize the similarity of the data within each cluster and minimize that between clusters. To do this, it plays with the concepts of between and within. The process begins by specifying "k," although finding the optimal "k" can be challenging, and methods like the elbow or silhouette technique are often employed (see Saputra et al., 2020). The algorithm randomly selects the initial "k" centroids (cluster centers), either from the data points or random locations. Each point is then assigned to its nearest centroid based on

Euclidean distance (or other distance metrics). The centroids are recalculated as the mean of all the points within their clusters, and points are reassigned to the closest new centroids. This process repeats until points no longer switch clusters or a maximum number of iterations have been reached (typically 10 in R). The goal is to minimize within-cluster variance, making k-means suitable for spherical clusters; it may face challenges when confronted by clusters of varying densities or nonspherical shapes.

5

> *Within-cluster sum of squares (WCSS)* is the sum of the squared distances of each element of the cluster to its centroid. Through k-means you can optimize the assignment of elements to centroids (and the centroid locations) to minimize WCSS, in favor of compact, spherical clusters.

Let us apply the k-means algorithm to our data set consisting of six words and two documents. Because k-means clustering involves a degree of randomness in its initial assignments, this can lead to different outcomes from separate runs. The randomness is managed in R using the `kmeans()` function's `nstart` parameter, which carries out multiple initial configurations (25 in our case) to find the best starting point, see ◘ Fig. 5.11. This approach helps mitigate the algorithm's tendency to converge to local optima. To make the algorithm's process easier to understand, we will use the `animation` library in R to create a visual clustering sequence (see ◘ Fig. 5.12 for the result after the first iteration, ◘ Fig. 5.13 for the result after the second iteration, and ◘ Fig. 5.14 for convergence).

For our example, we will place the data into a table (using the `dt` variable) and choose to segment it into two clusters, showing how k-means clustering partitions the data without the hierarchical structure seen in other methods such as HAC. The version printed here is not that spectacular, you see only the final result, but once you have run the code on your machine, you will appreciate and understand the power of animation as an educational tool.

```
library(animation)

# Example, six words with their frequencies
Rowname <- c("Word1", "Word2", "Word3", "Word4", "Word5", "Word6")
Document1 <- c(40, 22, 35, 26, 8, 45)
Document2 <- c(53, 38, 32, 19, 41, 30)

# Create the data set
dt <- cbind(Document1, Document2) %>%
  as.data.frame %>%
  `rownames<-`(Rowname)

# Set a random seed for reproducibility
set.seed(123)
```

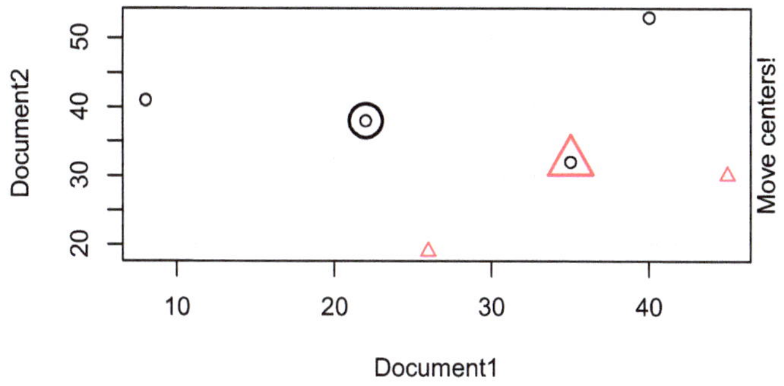

Fig. 5.11 K-means initialization. Authors' generated figure

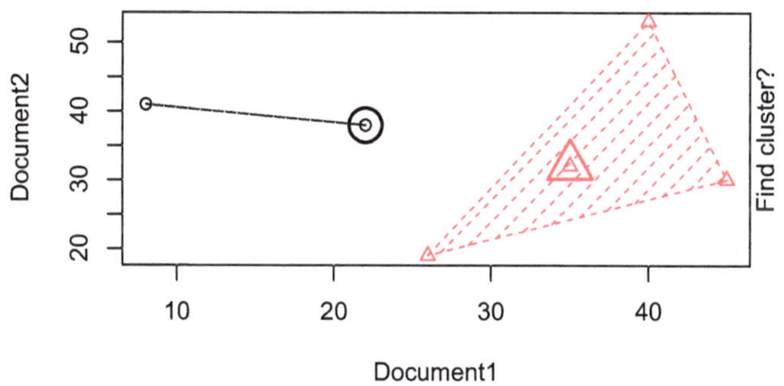

Fig. 5.12 K-means after first iteration. Authors' generated figure

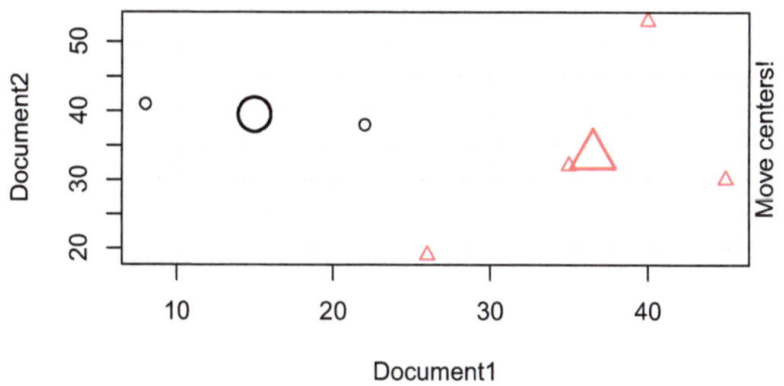

Fig. 5.13 K-means after second iteration. Authors' generated figure

```
# Perform animated k-means with 2 clusters
kmeans.ani(dt, 2)
```

Several limitations need to be taken into account for k-means clustering. One is that the algorithm may perform poorly when cluster sizes and densities vary

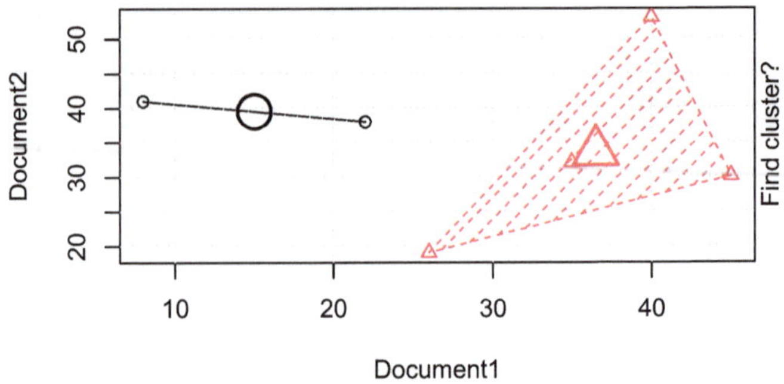

5

■ **Fig. 5.14** K-means converged. Authors' generated figure

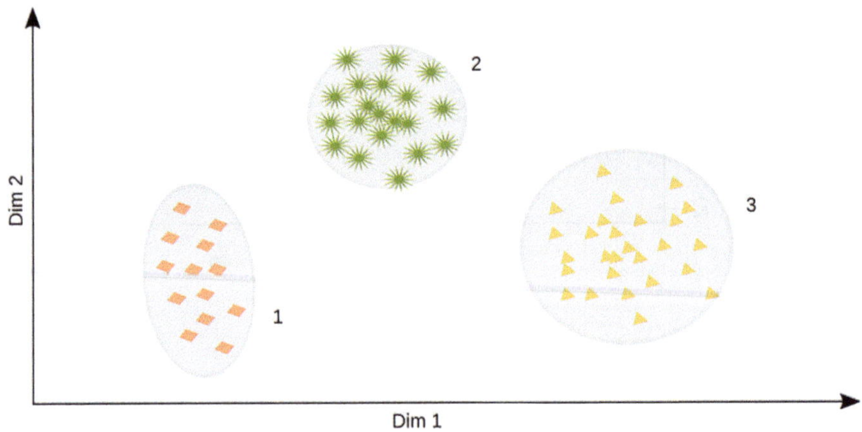

■ **Fig. 5.15** K-means clustering situations. Authors' own image

significantly. Another one is that the presence of outliers can skew the clustering results, as k-means clustering is sensitive to extreme values. Additionally, this technique assumes clusters are roughly spherical in shape, meaning it struggles with nonspherical (e.g., elongated or oblong) clusters. In a two-dimensional space, k-means is most effective when data points within a cluster are equidistant from the cluster center, forming a circular pattern. However, this occurs rarely in real-world data, as illustrated by the oblong shape of cluster 1 in ■ Fig. 5.15, which is not ideal for this form of clustering.

In our example, we analyzed the reviews data set using the k-means clustering algorithm, employing the `kmeans()` function in R. However, we let `NbClust()` find the optimal number of clusters. The `nstart` parameter sets the number of initial random centroid configurations to try, with the algorithm selecting the configuration that yields the most stable arrangement of clusters. Empirical observations suggest that a higher value often benefits smaller data sets by enhancing the stability of the clusters. We use the `fviz_cluster()` function to visualize the clustering results, which offers several helpful formatting options.

The `repel` argument helps to prevent label overlap, enhancing readability, while `show.clust.cent` plots the centroid of each cluster, providing a clear visual representation of the clustering. After plotting (see ◘ Fig. 5.16), it is possible to examine the cluster assignment of individual words through the cluster attribute in the `km` object (accessible via `km$cluster`). This analysis allows us to understand how words from the reviews can be grouped into distinct clusters.

```
library(RColorBrewer)

# Reproducibility function
set.seed(123)

# Transform into a matrix
tdm_matrix <- as.matrix(docs)

# Calculate the optimal number of clusters using NbClust
nckm <- NbClust(tdm_matrix, distance = "canberra", min.nc = 2,
↪  max.nc = 10, method = "kmeans", index = "ch")
nbc <- as.vector(nckm$Best.nc[1])  # Extracting the optimal
↪  cluster number

# Perform k-means clustering with the optimal number of clusters
km <- kmeans(tdm_matrix, centers = nbc, nstart = 30)

# Generate a color palette based on the number of clusters
palette <- brewer.pal(nbc, "Set1")
```

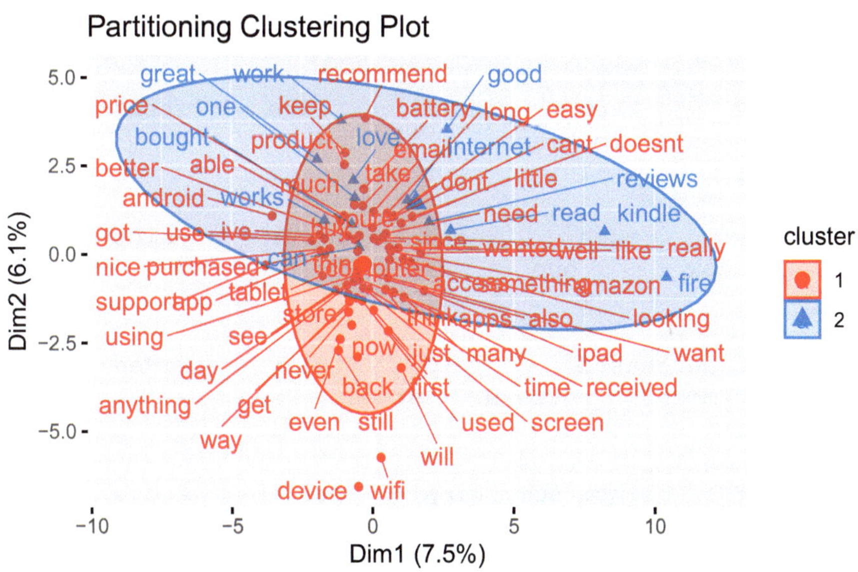

◘ **Fig. 5.16** K-means clustering. Authors' own figure

```
# Visualize the clusters using the same data matrix used in kmeans
fviz_cluster(list(data = tdm_matrix, cluster = km$cluster),
             palette = palette,
             main = "Partitioning Clustering Plot",
             ellipse.type = "norm",
             repel = TRUE,
             show.clust.cent = TRUE
)

# Print cluster assignments
km$cluster
```

5

```
     able    access      also    amazon   android
  ↪  anything      app      apps
        1         1         1         1         1
     ↪ 1         1         1
     back   battery    better    bought       buy
  ↪  can       cant  computer
        1         1         1         2         1
     ↪ 2         1         1
      day    device    doesnt      dont      easy
   ↪  email      even      fire
        1         1         1         1         1
     ↪ 1         1         2
    first       get      good       got     great
 ↪  internet      ipad       ive
        1         1         2         1         2
     ↪ 2         1         1
     just      keep    kindle      like    little
  ↪  long   looking      love
        1         1         2         1         1
     ↪ 1         1         2
     many      much      need     never      nice
  ↪  now        one     price
        1         1         1         1         1
     ↪ 1         2         1
  product purchased      read    really  received
↪  recommend   reviews    screen
        1         1         2         1         1
     ↪ 1         2         1
      see     since something     still     store
   ↪  support    tablet      take
        1         1         1         1         1
     ↪ 1         1         1
```

```
thing        think        time        use        used
  ↪  using        want      wanted
    1            1           1           1           1
      ↪  1           1           1
  way        well        wifi        will        work
    ↪  works        youre
    1            1           1           1           2
      ↪  2           1
```

We determined our data set's optimal number of clusters using the k-means method and by applying the `ch` index. This resulted in an optimal cluster count of 2. This process enables us to visually inspect and understand the distribution of words across the clusters.

The k-means algorithm has several variations tailored to different characteristics of the data. One such variation is k-medians, where the cluster's center is determined by the median rather than the mean, offering a robust defense against outliers (Arora et al., 1998). Another variation, k-medoids, designates a real data point as the center of the cluster, usually the most centrally located point in the cluster, enhancing the clarity of the interpretation of the clusters (Rousseeuw & Kaufman, 1987). Spherical k-means clustering is particularly useful for high-dimensional data. In this approach, data points are considered to be vectors on a unit sphere, and the cosine similarity is used as the distance metric, making it suitable for text and other high-dimensional data (Dhillon & Modha, 2001).

K-means clustering is a widely used algorithm due to its simplicity and computational efficiency, making it suitable for large data sets with multiple variables. The algorithm's core requirement is that the number of clusters (k) is specified, and it adapts to new partitions by simply changing this value. It performs efficiently when clusters are spherical or circular in a 2D plane, often resulting in tightly grouped clusters, allowing for clear interpretation when compared to hierarchical clustering.

However, selecting the optimal number of clusters can be challenging, and results may vary between runs due to the algorithm's sensitivity to the initial conditions. This inconsistency is a notable limitation. Moreover, it typically assumes the clusters are of approximately equal sizes, which may not align with the underlying distribution of the data. Another limitation is its exclusive focus on numerical data, which relies on calculating the Euclidean (or other types of) distance between points.

5.5 Gaussian Mixture Model Clustering

Gaussian mixture model (GMM) clustering, often used in conjunction with the expectation-maximization (EM) algorithm, is a sophisticated method for identifying underlying patterns in data (Bouman et al., 1997). This approach assumes that data points are generated using a combination of several Gaussian (or normal) distributions, each representing a distinct cluster. The term "mixture" in GMM reflects this concept of multiple, potentially overlapping, Gaussian distributions within the data set. Unlike the "hard" approach of k-means clustering, where each data point is assigned to one cluster, GMM adopts a "soft"-clustering technique. Each data point is associated with probabilities denoting its likelihood of belonging to different clusters, allowing for more nuanced and probabilistic classifications. In GMM, each Gaussian distribution within the model is defined by its own mean and covariance, shaping the cluster's appearance in the data space. The EM algorithm plays an essential role in GMM by iteratively estimating and refining these parameters, aiming to maximize the fit of the model to the data.

> *Expectation-maximization (EM)* is an iterative procedure used by probabilistic models with latent variables. The E-step calculates the posterior membership probabilities, taking into account the current data; the M-step updates the parameters to maximize the expected likelihood under these posteriors.

This model is handy in scenarios where data do not conform to the spherical cluster assumed by k-means clustering, as shown by cluster 1 of ◘ Fig. 5.15. For instance, GMM can handle elongated or irregularly shaped clusters effectively. In R, the Gaussian mixture model can be implemented using the `GMM()` function from the `ClusterR` package (Mouselimis, 2023). The process typically involves converting data into a suitable format (such as a data frame) and specifying the number of clusters. The `predict_GMM` function assigns each data point to clusters based on the probabilities calculated by `GMM()`. It is advisable to explore the functions' parameters and settings to understand their application. We will now explore this type of clustering using three clusters.

```
library(ClusterR)
library(factoextra)

# Reproducibility function
set.seed(123)

# Transform into a matrix
gmm <- as.matrix(docs)

# Fit Gaussian mixture model
nbc <- 3
gmm_model <- GMM(gmm,
                 gaussian_comps = nbc,
                 dist_mode      = "maha_dist",      # Initial
                 ↪  k-means metric
                 seed_mode      = "random_subset",
                 km_iter        = 10,
                 em_iter        = 10,
                 verbose        = FALSE,
                 var_floor      = 1e-10)
```

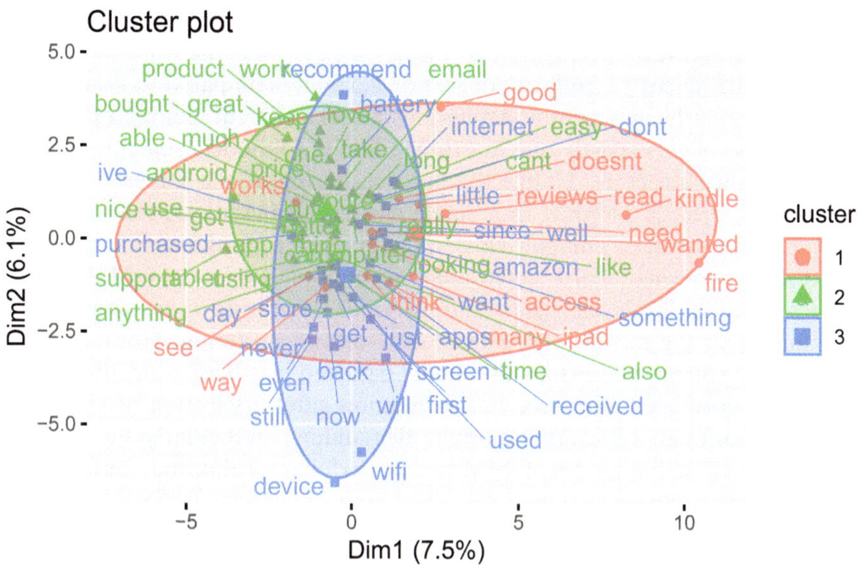

Fig. 5.17 Gaussian mixture model clustering. Authors' own figure

```
# Posterior assignment
gmm_labels <- predict_GMM(gmm,
                          CENTROIDS   = gmm_model$centroids,
                                                       COVARIANCE
                          ↪  = gmm_model$covariance_matrices,
                          WEIGHTS     =
                          ↪  gmm_model$weights)$cluster_labels

# Visualize clusters  (high-dimensional -> PCA for 2-D plot)
fviz_cluster(list(data = gmm, cluster = gmm_labels),
             ellipse.type = "norm",
             repel        = TRUE)

# Inspect a few assignments
head(data.frame(word = rownames(gmm), cluster = gmm_labels))
```

```
      word cluster
1     able       2
2   access       1
3     also       2
4   amazon       3
5  android       2
6 anything       2
```

In ◘ Fig. 5.17, we can see better clustering compared to that produced by k-means clustering. It is also possible to check which clusters the words belong to.

GMM introduces a significant degree of flexibility compared to k-means clustering, particularly in accommodating clusters of different shapes, orientations, and variances. This is partly due to GMM's ability to model each cluster with its own covariance structure. Unlike the hard clustering of the k-means approach, where each object is assigned to a single cluster, GMM allows for probabilistic assignments to clusters. This soft-clustering approach is particularly advantageous in text analytics where words often relate to multiple topics. In GMM, centroid updates consider both the mean and variance, capturing more complex data structures than the mean-only updates of k-means clustering. However, GMM assumes that you have Gaussian distributed data and may have difficulties working with highly correlated data sets. It also requires careful selection of the number of clusters and can be computationally demanding, particularly for large data sets. Despite these limitations, GMM is a powerful algorithm that performs well, especially where data exhibit complex, overlapping clustering patterns.

5.6 Density-Based Clustering

DBSCAN (Density-Based Spatial Clustering of Applications with Noise) is ideal for data sets where clusters are not necessarily spherical, offering, like GMM, a flexible alternative to methods such as k-means clustering. Its original formulation relies on two parameters, an ϵ-neighborhood radius and a minimum number of points (`minPts`), but the more recent extension HDBSCAN removes the need to fix ϵ in advance. DBSCAN forms clusters from dense regions of data points, while HDBSCAN varies the radius automatically to capture clusters at multiple density levels and identifies outliers in low-density areas. Unlike some algorithms, it does not require you to specify the number of clusters, as these emerge naturally from the data based on its density. When ϵ is fixed (standard DBSCAN), a point that falls inside the ϵ-neighborhood of several clusters is usually assigned to the first cluster examined; HDBSCAN resolves such ties by preferring the most stable cluster across scales. Choosing the right ϵ can be challenging, as it significantly affects the resulting clusters, which is precisely why HDBSCAN's ability to dispense with this parameter is attractive, leaving primarily `minPts` to tune (Ozkok & Celik, 2017).

> ϵ *(epsilon)* is the neighborhood radius used by DBSCAN, together with the minimum number of points (`minPts`) to form a dense region. HDBSCAN focuses on `minPts` and a minimum cluster size, obviating the setting of ϵ.

HDBSCAN (hierarchical density-based spatial clustering of applications with noise) extends DBSCAN's capabilities by transforming its flat clustering into a hierarchical structure. This method extracts clusters based on their stability over varying levels of density, with no need for the user to specify ϵ. It is particularly good at handling data sets with clusters of different densities, automatically determining the optimal scale for ϵ and revealing consistent clusters over a range of densities.

We will use the HDBSCAN algorithm, available in the dbscan package, to explore density-based clustering. This approach requires setting one key hyper-parameter (minPts, the minimum cluster size), which often depends on the data set and objectives of the clustering. HDBSCAN's ability to identify stable clusters without predefined parameters like ϵ makes it a robust and user-friendly choice when confronted with complex data sets.

```
library(dbscan)
library(factoextra)

# Ensure reproducibility
set.seed(123)

# Transform into a matrix
m <- as.matrix(docs)

# Adjust minPts as needed
# Here we use 2 for demonstration, commonly 5-10
# is a starting range
hd <- hdbscan(m, minPts = 2)
# Cluster summary
print(hd)
```

```
HDBSCAN clustering for 79 objects.
Parameters: minPts = 2
The clustering contains 2 cluster(s) and 13 noise points.

 0  1  2
13  3 63

Available fields: cluster, minPts, coredist,
 ↪  cluster_scores,
                     membership_prob, outlier_scores, hc
```

```
# hd$cluster == 0 are "noise" points converted to NA
cl <- factor(ifelse(hd$cluster == 0, NA, hd$cluster))

# Visualize clusters
fviz_cluster(
  list(data = m, cluster = cl),
  palette     = "jco",
```

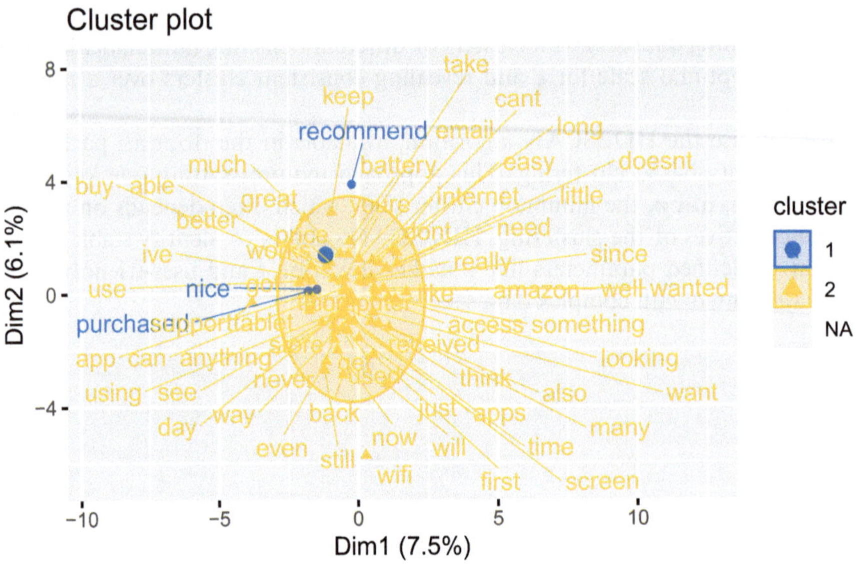

■ **Fig. 5.18** HDBSCAN clusters of product review terms. Authors' own figure

```
    ellipse.type = "norm",
    repel        = TRUE,
    na.rm        = TRUE
  )
```

We can see in ■ Fig. 5.18 how it has created two clusters. With a bigger data set the clustering would yield better results.

DBSCAN and its variant HDBSCAN separate clusters into those of high and low density, but face difficulties when the densities are similar. Unlike in other clustering algorithms, the clusters can take any shape, outliers are dealt with well, and there is no need to set the number of clusters manually. However, you must tune the ϵ and the minimum points parameters. The order of the data has an influence on the final result, and you need sufficient data to separate dense areas; otherwise, you obtain poor results.

As a practical example, it is possible to apply DBSCAN to the data set and find clusters based on the reviews. Using the clusters, we can see similarities between reviews, for example, if one customer writes about the screen, memory, and connection of a tablet, and another one about the screen and memory, then it is useful to enquire about the connection between the two. In a commercial setup, if one customer talks about products 1, 2, and 3, and another one only about the first two, a system of recommendation might propose the third product to the second customer.

5.7 Affinity Propagation Clustering

Affinity propagation clustering (APC), as defined by Frey and Dueck (2007), Dueck and Frey (2007), and Dueck (2009), introduces the concept of "exemplars." These are the foundational elements, or the core nodes, of a data set around which clustering is performed. The idea is that all the elements are potential exemplars, and a message system between data points identifies a subset of exemplars and their clusters iteratively.

An exemplar is the characteristic data point identified by affinity propagation, around which other points cluster; the algorithm exchanges messages of "responsibility" and "availability" between points to select exemplars and form clusters.

This is carried out by the `apcluster` package (Bodenhofer et al., 2011). Unlike in the other clustering algorithms, the data can be of any shape and of variable density. Importantly, the basic version of APC will calculate the optimal number of clusters by propagating "preferences" (self-similarities) through the data. However, the default preference value is very low and can yield many tiny clusters. You can tune this behavior either (i) by supplying your own vector of preferences, or (ii) more simply, by setting the `q` argument (e.g., `q` = 0.5 chooses the median similarity as the preference). Nevertheless, the `apclusterK()` function in the `apcluster` package provides a mechanism to specify the cluster count. In this, the first parameter, `s`, calculates the similarity function using the negative squared distances by default, although alternative similarity measures, such as the Spearman correlation, can be employed to capture the relationships within certain data sets.

The second parameter, `x`, represents the distance matrix we derived from on our previous analysis using k-means clustering. Despite the possibility of setting a predetermined number of clusters via K, adjusting the preference (or `q`) in `apcluster()` often gives a more interpretable solution without fixing K in advance, because the algorithm can still adaptively discover a natural cluster structure while avoiding an overabundance of micro-clusters.

```
# Affinity propagation library
library(apcluster)


# negDistMat computes the similarity matrix
similarity_matrix <- negDistMat(as.matrix(docs), r=2)

# Apply clustering
apck <- apclusterK(s=similarity_matrix, K=3)
```

```
Trying p = -0.006489952
   Number of clusters: 77
Trying p = -0.01611412
   Number of clusters: 52
Trying p = -0.1123558
   Number of clusters: 4
Trying p = -0.5400968 (bisection step no. 1 )
   Number of clusters: 1
Trying p = -0.2727587 (bisection step no. 2 )
   Number of clusters: 1
Trying p = -0.1390897 (bisection step no. 3 )
   Number of clusters: 3

Number of clusters: 3 for p = -0.1390897
```

```
# Convert data from a cluster type into a data frame
apckmelt <- data.table::melt(apck@clusters)

# Visualize the data
fviz_cluster(list(data = as.matrix(docs)[apckmelt$value,], cluster
↪  = apckmelt$L1),
             ellipse.type = "norm",
             repel = TRUE)

# Check which words belong to each cluster
apck
```

```
APResult object

Number of samples       =  79
Number of iterations    =  138
Input preference        =  -0.1390897
Sum of similarities     =  -2.322368
Sum of preferences      =  -0.417269
Net similarity          =  -2.739637
Number of clusters      =  3

Exemplars:
   can cant think
Clusters:
   Cluster 1, exemplar can:
      amazon bought can great love one reviews works
   Cluster 2, exemplar cant:
      cant doesnt good ipad like much price since work
```

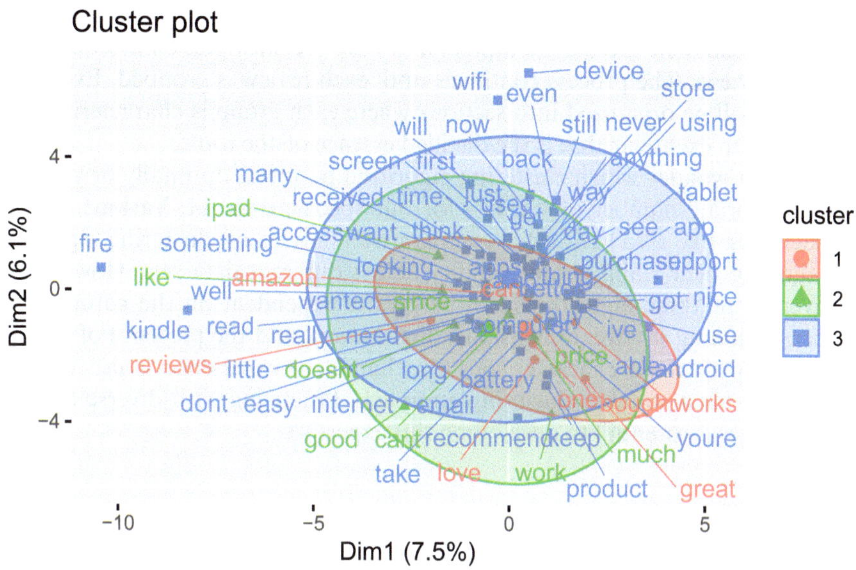

■ **Fig. 5.19** Affinity propagation clustering. Authors' own figure

```
Cluster 3, exemplar think:
   able access also android anything app apps back
   ↪  battery better buy
   computer day device dont easy email even fire first
   ↪  get got internet ive
   just keep kindle little long looking many need
   ↪  never nice now product
   purchased read really received recommend screen see
   ↪  something still store
   support tablet take thing think time use used using
   ↪  want wanted way well
   wifi will youre
```

We notice that each cluster has an "exemplar" cluster, a prominent word that best represents the cluster. It is a word that should define the other words which are contained in the same cluster. It might be considered the "topic" of the cluster and can be the thematic focus of a cluster. In our case, the exemplars are: can, cant, and think. Check the words in each cluster and see if you can relate them to their exemplar, see ■ Fig. 5.19.

The exemplars are chosen based on a message passing between data points regarding their suitability as the most representative points of a cluster. To demonstrate this, think of the reviews data set in our book. We want to group reviews which are similar. Each review can "send a message" to the other reviews, revealing its topic. If another review has the same topic, they will group. Some reviews will receive many messages back, showing that they are popular within that topic. These reviews become their groups' exemplars and have the strongest connections to all the other reviews. The process continues until each review is grouped. Eventually, the corpus will be organized into sections where each group is characterized by a topic led by an exemplar that is the distilled essence of the topic.

We might wonder which clustering algorithm performs optimally or yields the most appropriate number of clusters for our specific data set. Various methods and packages, like `cValid`, offer comparative analyses of clustering algorithms by evaluating their stability and validity across different data sets. However, the effectiveness of these algorithms can be greatly dependent on the nature of the data set, including its size, dimensions, distribution, and the presence of outliers. Familiarity with these characteristics and hands-on experience is crucial when selecting the most suitable clustering approach. Practicing with diverse data sets and challenges is essential to developing this expertise.

5.8 Document Clustering

In marketing, clustering similar elements enables more effective segmentation. As an illustration, let us apply a method such as HDBSCAN to cluster documents. Unlike in previous approaches, we will use a document-term matrix (DTM) instead of a term-document matrix (TDM), focusing on clustering documents with similar features.

Although we have processed the documents by removing elements like stop words and numbers, this analysis aims to reveal insights based on the documents' reduced set of features. For this purpose, we are using the same underlying code but applying it to a DTM. This is achieved by transposing the matrix so that rows and columns are switched, effectively turning the document features into the primary axis for clustering. This allows us to examine the thematic similarities between documents more directly. Clustering in this space groups reviews that exhibit comparable vocabularies or topics, which is precisely what analysts need for persona building and content-strategy design in marketing segmentation (Cozzolino & Ferraro, 2022; Wedel & Kamakura, 2000).

```
library(dbscan)

# Matrix transposition
dtm <- t(as.matrix(docs))

# Calculate the hdbscan cluster
clustering.dbscan <- hdbscan(dtm, minPts = 2)

# Visualize the clusters created with hdbscan
fviz_cluster(list(data = as.matrix(dtm), cluster =
↪  clustering.dbscan$cluster),
```

```
               ellipse.type = "norm",
               repel = TRUE)

# Clustering details
clustering.dbscan
```

```
HDBSCAN clustering for 50 objects.
Parameters: minPts = 2
The clustering contains 2 cluster(s) and 45 noise points.

 0  1  2
45  3  2

Available fields: cluster, minPts, coredist,
↪  cluster_scores,
                  membership_prob, outlier_scores, hc
```

In cluster 2, there are only two elements, documents 16 and 35. In R, type `content[16]` and `content[35]` to compare the documents, see ◘ Fig. 5.20.

The two reviews seem to be similar in terms of length and content. To hone your skills, you can try various combinations of clustering methods, distances, and parameters.

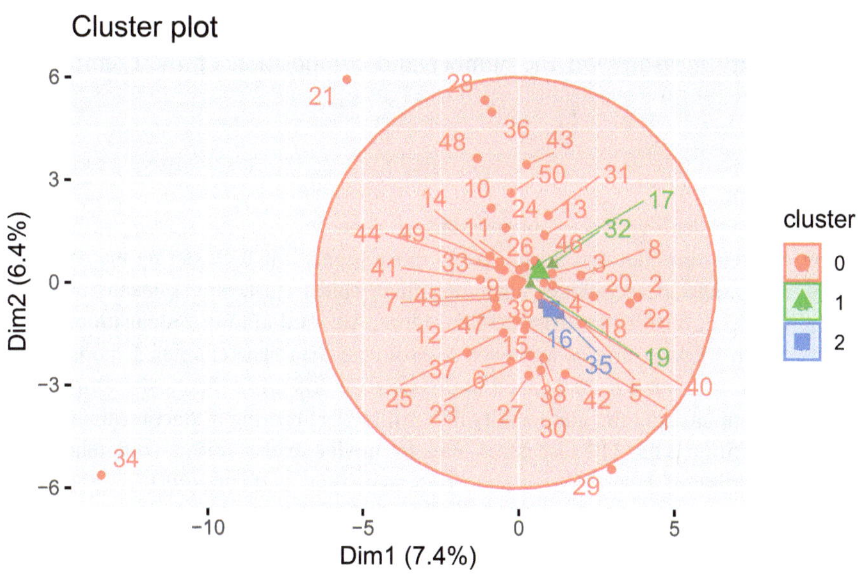

◘ **Fig. 5.20** Document clustering with DBSCAN. Authors' own figure

More generally, you can apply these techniques to any corpus in order to extract their meaning in terms of topics, but also similarities and differences between and within clusters.

Exercise 1. Hierarchical clustering. Apply hierarchical clustering using various distance metrics (e.g., Euclidean, Manhattan) and linkage methods (e.g., single linkage, average linkage, complete linkage). Analyze how different combinations affect the structure of the dendrogram.

Exercise 2. K-means clustering. Experiment with the k-means algorithm by varying the number of clusters (K). Evaluate how the choice of K influences the cohesion and separation of the clusters.

Exercise 3. Gaussian mixture models (GMM) clustering. Apply GMM clustering to varying numbers of components (clusters). Experiment with different types of covariance (e.g., full, tied, diagonal, spherical) and initialization methods to observe their effects on the shapes and sizes of clusters.

Exercise 4. HDBSCAN clustering. Run hdbscan() several times, varying only `minPts` (e.g., 2, 5, 10, 20), and observe how the minimum-cluster-size setting changes (i) the number of clusters reported and (ii) the share of points labeled as noise.

Exercise 5. Affinity propagation clustering. Investigate the use of different affinity propagation methods provided by the `apcluster` package, such as `apcluster()` and `apclusterL()`. Explore the impact of preference values and similarity measures on the number and composition of the exemplars and clusters.

Conclusion

This chapter deals with the fundamentals of clustering analysis, starting with basic step-by-step examples and advancing to more sophisticated clustering methods. It covers a range of techniques, including hierarchical clustering, k-means clustering, Gaussian mixture models (GMM), DBSCAN, and affinity propagation, each selected to show its unique approach to grouping data. The chapter demonstrates how these methods can be applied to diverse data sets using practical examples of coding, emphasizing the adaptability and utility of clustering in uncovering hidden patterns within data. The discussion aims to provide readers with a comprehensive understanding of how different clustering algorithms perform and their potential application to text analytics in marketing.

Discussion

Cosine vs. Euclidean: Which of these performs best when confronted with sparse, high-dimensional text vectors? Is normalization a viable option?

Linkage in HAC: Compare the linkage criteria applied to a term-frequency table; in which ways does the choice of clusters influence the interpretation in a marketing context?

GMM vs. k-means: Do soft assignments add value to marketing? How is density influenced by tuning `minPts` (and ϵ values for DBSCAN)? When do they yield over- or under-clustering?

Affinity preferences: Which preferences (or `q`) can be used in APC to avoid micro-clustering while retaining nuance?

Document clustering Q&A: How can you assess cluster coherence (e.g., top terms, exemplar reviews) and detect "noise" using a DTM-based HDBSCAN?

Take Home Message

- In high-dimensional sparse text, use cosine similarity; whenever you have normalized, comparable scales, use Euclidean.
- The type of linkage influences the structure of the cluster in HAC.
- Although k-means is fast and intuitive, it needs compact and spherical types of cluster. Its sensitivity to initialization is a weak point.
- GMM is a valid alternative to k-means because it handles elements in clusters which overlap and have nonspherical structures through EM and probabilistic memberships. It is useful for detecting nuance.
- DBSCAN/HDBSCAN does not need k to discover shaped clusters and outliers; by tuning `minPts` (and ϵ for DBSCAN), you can check the stability.
- When dealing with document clustering, you should operate on a DTM (not TDM). Verify the validity via top terms and exemplar documents.

References

Aggarwal, C. C., & Reddy, C. K. (2014). *Data clustering: Algorithms and applications* (1st ed.). Chapman & Hall/CRC. https://doi.org/10.5555/2535015

Arora, S., Raghavan, P., & Rao, S. (1998). Approximation schemes for Euclidean k-medians and related problems. *Proceedings of the Thirtieth Annual ACM Symposium on Theory of Computing*, 106–113. https://doi.org/10.1145/276698.276718

Berger, J., Humphreys, A., Ludwig, S., Moe, W. W., Netzer, O., & Schweidel, D. A. (2020). Uniting the tribes: Using text for marketing insight. *Journal of Marketing*, *84*(1), 1–25. https://doi.org/10.1177/0022242919873106

Bodenhofer, U., Kothmeier, A., & Hochreiter, S. (2011). APCluster: An R package for affinity propagation clustering. *Bioinformatics*, *27*(17), 2463–2464. https://doi.org/10.1093/bioinformatics/btr406

Bouman, C. A., Shapiro, M., Cook, G. W., Atkins, C. B., & Cheng, H. (1997). *Cluster: An unsupervised algorithm for modeling gaussian mixtures*.

Cheng, N., Chandramouli, R., & Subbalakshmi, K. P. (2011). Author gender identification from text. *Digital Investigation*, *8*(1), 78–88. https://doi.org/10.1016/j.diin.2011.04.002

Cozzolino, I., & Ferraro, M. B. (2022). Document clustering. *Wiley Interdisciplinary Reviews: Computational Statistics*, *14*(6), e1588. https://doi.org/10.1002/wics.1588

Deza, M. M., & Deza, E. (2009). Encyclopedia of distances. In *Encyclopedia of distances* (pp. 1–583). Springer. https://doi.org/10.1007/978-3-662-52844-0

Dhillon, I. S., & Modha, D. S. (2001). Concept decompositions for large sparse text data using clustering. *Machine Learning*, *42*, 143–175. https://doi.org/10.1023/A:1007612920971

Dueck, D. (2009). *Affinity propagation: Clustering data by passing messages*. University of Toronto Toronto, ON, Canada.

Dueck, D., & Frey, B. J. (2007). Non-metric affinity propagation for unsupervised image categorization. *2007 IEEE 11th International Conference on Computer Vision*, 1–8. https://doi.org/10.1109/ICCV.2007.4408853

Frey, B. J., & Dueck, D. (2007). Clustering by passing messages between data points. *Science*, *315*, 972–977. https://doi.org/10.1126/science.1136800

Gower, J. C., & Legendre, P. (1986). Metric and euclidean properties of dissimilarity coefficients. *Journal of Classification*, *3*(1), 5–48. https://doi.org/10.1007/BF01896809

Han, J., Pei, J., & Tong, H. (2022). *Data mining: Concepts and techniques*. Morgan Kaufmann.

Harnad, S. (2017). To cognize is to categorize: Cognition is categorization. In *Handbook of categorization in cognitive science* (pp. 21–54). Elsevier. https://doi.org/10.1016/B978-008044612-7/50056-1

Huang, A. et al. (2008). Similarity measures for text document clustering. *Proceedings of the Sixth New Zealand Computer Science Research Student Conference (NZCSRSC2008), Christchurch, New Zealand*, *4*, 9–56.

Jockers, M. L., & Thalken, R. (2020). Hapax richness. In *Text analysis with R* (pp. 184–192). Springer. https://doi.org/10.1007/978-3-030-39643-5_8

Kassambara, A., & Mundt, F. (2020). *Factoextra: Extract and visualize the results of multivariate data analyses*. https://cran.r-project.org/package=factoextra

Kocher, M., & Savoy, J. (2017). Distance measures in author profiling. *Information Processing & Management*, *53*(5), 1103–1119. https://doi.org/10.1016/j.ipm.2017.04.004

Maimon, O., & Rokach, L. (2010). *Data mining and knowledge discovery handbook*. https://doi.org/10.1007/978-0-387-09823-4

Maqbool, O., & Babri, H. A. (2004). The weighted combined algorithm: A linkage algorithm for software clustering. *Eighth European Conference on Software Maintenance and Reengineering, 2004. CSMR 2004. Proceedings.*, 15–24. https://doi.org/10.1109/CSMR.2004.1281402

Meyer, D., & Buchta, C. (2021). *Proxy: Distance and similarity measures*. https://cran.r-project.org/package=proxy

Mouselimis, L. (2023). *ClusterR: Gaussian mixture models, k-means, mini-batch-kmeans, k-medoids and affinity propagation clustering*. https://cran.r-project.org/package=ClusterR

Ozkok, F. O., & Celik, M. (2017). A new approach to determine eps parameter of DBSCAN algorithm. *International Journal of Intelligent Systems and Applications in Engineering*, *5*(4), 247–251. https://doi.org/10.18201/ijisae.2017533899

Purwitasari, D., Priantara, I. W. S., Kusmawan, P. Y., Yuhana, U. L., & Siahaan, D. O. (2011). The use of Hartigan index for initializing k-means++ in detecting similar texts of clustered documents as a plagiarism indicator. *Asian Journal of Information Technology*, *10*(8), 341–347.

Rousseeuw, P.J., & Kaufman, P. (1987). Clustering by means of medoids. *Proceedings of the Statistical Data Analysis Based on the L1 Norm Conference, Neuchatel, Switzerland*, *31*.

Saputra, D. M., Saputra, D., & Oswari, L. D. (2020). Effect of distance metrics in determining k-value in k-means clustering using elbow and silhouette method. *Sriwijaya International Conference on Information Technology and Its Applications (SICONIAN 2019)*, 341–346. https://doi.org/10.2991/aisr.k.200424.051

Sen, P. C., Hajra, M., & Ghosh, M. (2020). Supervised classification algorithms in machine learning: A survey and review. In *Emerging technology in modelling and graphics* (pp. 99–111). Springer. https://doi.org/10.1007/978-981-13-7403-6_11

Stamatatos, E., Tschuggnall, M., Verhoeven, B., Daelemans, W., Specht, G., Stein, B., & Potthast, M. (2016). Clustering by authorship within and across documents. *Working Notes Papers of the CLEF 2016 Evaluation Labs. CEUR Workshop Proceedings/Balog, Krisztian [Edit.]; Et Al.*, 691–715.

Strauss, T., & Maltitz, M. J. von. (2017). Generalising ward's method for use with Manhattan distances. *PloS One*, *12*(1), e0168288. https://doi.org/10.1371/journal.pone.0168288

Struhl, S. (2015). *Practical text analytics: Interpreting text and unstructured data for business intelligence*. Kogan Page Publishers.
Vries, N. J. de, Olech, Ł. P., & Moscato, P. (2019). Introducing clustering with a focus in marketing and consumer analysis. *Business and Consumer Analytics: New Ideas*, 165–212. https://doi.org/10.1007/978-3-030-06222-4_3
Wedel, M., & Kamakura, W. A. (2000). *Market segmentation: Conceptual and methodological foundations* (2nd ed.). Springer. https://doi.org/10.1007/978-1-4615-4651-1

Text Classification, LDA, KNN, SVM, Neural Networks, and FastText

D. Dan, T. Reutterer, *Text Analytics in Marketing*, Classroom Companion: Business,
https://doi.org/10.1007/978-3-032-08086-8_6

Keywords
Supervised text classification · Linear discriminant analysis · KNN · SVM · Cross-validation · Confusion matrix · Evaluation metrics · Class imbalance · Stacking

This chapter tackles text classification presenting a complete process for categorizing documents into known categories. The tablet-review data set is used to discuss how to vectorize the text (bag-of-words, tf-idf), how to lemmatize it, how to tweak sparsity, how to split the data into train/validation/test sets, and how to select models using cross-validation and hyper-parameter tuning. We evaluate models using confusion matrices, precision, recall, and F1 and address class imbalance by comparing these with the no-information rate (NIR). Core classifiers include linear discriminant analysis (LDA), k-nearest neighbors (KNNs) (with distance metrics and the curse of dimensionality), and support vector machines (SVMs) (linear, radial, polynomial), making use of margin, cost (C), and kernel parameters. The chapter adds a shallow neural network baseline (nnet) and builds FastText for rapid, accurate sentence classification using subword n-grams. The chapter further describes stacking ensembles, shows how to combine different algorithms to provide better generalization and discusses the risks of overfitting. Practical advice is provided on how to update training labels, interpret probabilities, and translate results into marketing activities, such as email triage and brand monitoring. Exercises are included to reinforce the implementation of, and comparisons across, models and preprocessing decisions.

6

Learning Objectives

- Understanding supervised text classification and its end-to-end workflow.
- Applying key algorithms such as LDA, KNN, SVM, neural nets, and FastText to real review data.
- Evaluating models with confusion-matrix metrics and addressing class imbalance.
- Tuning hyper-parameters with cross-validation to reduce over-fitting and improve generalization.
- Boosting performance with ensemble methods and translating results into marketing insights.

6.1 What Is in a Class?

The term "class" originates from the Latin word "classis," which initially denoted a "fleet" or the "levy" itself before it acquired the meaning of a group of citizens in a census (see Livy, 1919, *s.v.* `classis`; Glare, 1982). In the latter sense, it was used in ancient Rome to categorize citizens within the Centuriate Assembly based on wealth and property. This system, attributed to the reforms of Servius Tullius, the sixth king of Rome, divided society into several classes. The wealthiest were assigned to the upper classes and received an allowance to purchase a war-horse, being granted significant political power as members of the cavalry. In contrast, the lower classes consisted of those with less wealth, who armed themselves with lighter equipment and therefore enjoyed only limited political influence. This classification primarily determined military duties and voting rights, reflecting the organization of society by economic status. It later remained the basis for regular taxation, because there was a constant need for revenue, even though wars occurred less frequently (Cornell, 2012). The assignment of a citizen to one of the five classes took into account several factors, such as the kind of armor they possessed, wealth, and age, among others.

Some two thousand five hundred years later, we have developed several methods of classification, one of them being manual. Due to the incredible amount of data we deal with, however, this is very impractical for the processing of information. In practice, humans therefore label only a small sample, and machine learning models scale those labels up to the remaining data. In ▸ Chap. 5, we explored a method known as clustering. Both classification and clustering aim to achieve the same goal, that of putting data into categories using algorithms. Clustering uses unsupervised learning, where the algorithm, with the help of mathematical formulas, attempts to group elements with common characteristics without predefined categories. This means we interpret the categories after the algorithm has done its work.

On the other hand, classification involves supervised learning. Here, we start with a training set, a collection of documents already categorized into classes or categories. The algorithm learns from these existing categories to create a model, or a modus operandi, through which to categorize the new data. This process is essential when data need to be sorted automatically to save time and obtain accurate results.

For instance, a customer relationship manager dealing with hundreds of incoming emails daily could use an automated system to sort these emails into the correct departments, such as Finance, Logistics, or Complaints. Another classic application in a direct marketing context is Recency–Frequency–Monetary value (RFM) classification, which involves segmenting customers based on the recency, the frequency, and the monetary value of their previous interactions with a firm (see, e.g., Bult & Wansbeek, 1995, Gönöl et al., 2000, Berry & Linoff, 2009). The applications of automatic classification are many and varied.

This chapter focuses on classification using the same tablet data set as in the previous chapters. Note that there is a "Brand" column which we will use for classification. Each review in the data set is associated with a brand. The goal is for each new, unlabeled review, to be processed by the model and assigned to the correct category of brand.

This chapter will cover the following types of classification algorithms: linear discriminant analysis (LDA), k-nearest neighbors (KNNs), support vector machines (SVMs), and neural networks (NNs). To complete the chapter, we will use a library, FastText, for the efficient learning of word representation and sentence classification. It is optimal for its speed of execution and accuracy, especially with large data sets.

6.2 Supervised Machine Learning Models

In this section, we will focus on employing supervised machine learning algorithms. Our primary elements are the text content of the review and its association with a specific brand. Using these well-understood elements, the algorithm will generate a model. This enables the classification of new, unlabeled content, ensuring that the correct brand label is assigned accurately.

The entire process is depicted in ◘ Fig. 6.1, showing a typical machine learning workflow when applied to a corpus of documents. This procedure is consistent across different types of data sets. Initially (step I in ◘ Fig. 6.1), we provide the algorithm with a set of documents which have already been classified, each review tagged with a brand label. This data set is known as the training set, offering the algorithm a comprehensive framework for how reviews correlate with brands. Through the analysis of these associations and specific rules governing classification, the machine constructs a model based on the data, particularly the words within each review.

In the subsequent step, II, we introduce a collection of unlabeled documents to the model already established. The expectation is for these documents to be accurately classified according to the model's guidelines. Computers excel when identifying regularities within data, using these patterns to make efficient and precise predictions. Essentially, this is a task of predicting the following: Given a set of reviews, the machine will, using a certain degree of probability, predict the appropriate assignment of the review to the brand.

The algorithm's accuracy is evaluated using a testing set, typically comprising 20% of the total data set. As shown in ◘ Fig. 6.1, this evaluation is an integral part of the workflow. After the training phase (step I), the classification model is applied to the testing set (step II), which is processed by the model as if it were unlabeled. The outcomes of this classification are then compared against the actual labels (known as ground-truth values). While the train-test split is commonly 80:20, other configurations are also possible, such as a training, validation, and test split (e.g., 80:10:10). In these setups, the validation set is used to fine-tune the model, while the test set is reserved exclusively for evaluating its performance. The higher the congruence between how the algorithm assigns the material and the original labels, the greater the algorithm's accuracy. Accuracy alone, however, can be misleading

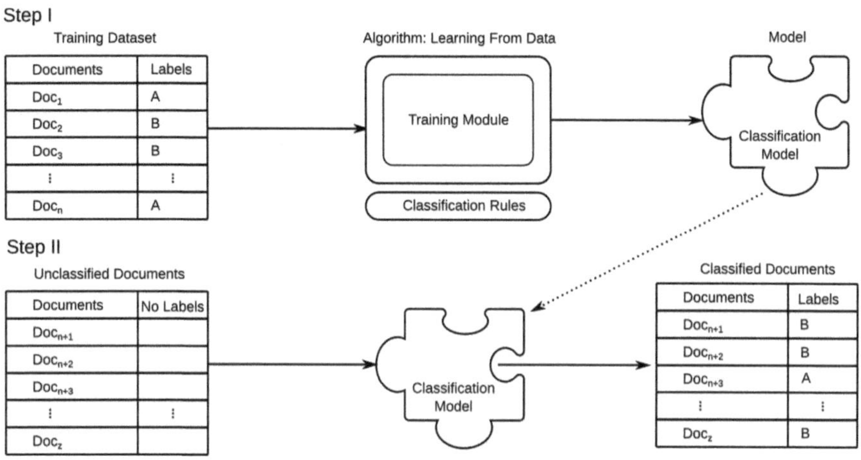

Fig. 6.1 Supervised learning. Authors' own figure

whenever the class distribution is highly skewed. In such cases, a classifier that always predicts the majority class can achieve a seemingly impressive accuracy equal to the No-information rate (NIR), yet it provides no practical value. Metrics that look at each class separately such as precision, recall, and the F_1 score remain informative even when, say, 90% of the reviews belong to one brand. Although the Apple-Samsung example is nearly balanced, the same evaluation toolkit will be crucial when you face real-world data sets where one class is rare.

With the current state of technology, it is not possible to guarantee that algorithms will perform flawlessly. However, they are efficient enough to reduce manual effort significantly. When data are misclassified, human intervention becomes necessary. A robust approach includes regularly updating the training data set after correcting any errors. This process not only introduces new vocabulary and scenarios to the model but also enhances the accuracy of its predictions.

Classification algorithms vary in effectiveness, with some outperforming others based on the specific requirements of the data and the context of how it is applied. Broadly, we can categorize these algorithms into two types: linear and nonlinear. Linear classification uses a straight line (or a hyperplane in higher dimensions) to divide data into distinct classes, which, obviously, works well for linearly separable data. On the other hand, nonlinear classification employs more complex boundaries to separate classes, enabling it to handle data with intricate patterns or overlaps.

6.2.1 Data Set Preparation

As discussed in previous chapters, text data must be converted into a vectorized format and organized into a matrix or, more simply, a table. This format allows the computer to process the numerical data efficiently. The process begins by importing the data set into the R programming environment from a local source or the Internet. (If you need to re-familiarize yourself with this step, reread the introductory sections of this book for detailed guidance.) Next, we focus on a subset of the data by selecting two brands for analysis, such as Apple and Samsung, though you could choose any brands featured in the data set which are of interest. This selection effectively narrows down the data set horizontally. We then refine the data set further by retaining only the columns essential for classification, namely, "Content" and "Brand." This involves slicing the data set vertically, ensuring we have a focused and manageable data set for our analysis. But first we need to load the necessary libraries and the data set.


```
# Set global option to avoid automatic conversion of strings to
↪  factors
options(stringsAsFactors = FALSE)

# Load necessary libraries
library(tm)
library(caret)
library(tidyverse)
library(SnowballC)
library(textstem)
library(kableExtra)
library(caretEnsemble)

# Read the classified data set, directly filter, and select required
↪  data
dt <- read.csv("data/Product Reviews.csv") %>%
  filter(Brand %in% c("Apple", "Samsung")) %>%
  select(Content, Brand)
```

With a data set comprising two columns, one of which identifies two brands, we have established a division: One segment will serve as the training set, and the other as the test set. The test set allows us to simulate a scenario where the test portion is unlabeled to evaluate the algorithm's performance. By applying the model to the test set, we can compare its predictions against the known classifications. By now, preparing the data set should be familiar to you and certain commands are provided for you to explore during the training sessions. Using the `%>%` operator, preprocessing and other related tasks are integrated seamlessly within a document-term matrix, one for the training set and another for the test set. We encourage you to read the comments embedded in the code to understand each step better. You can also comment and remove the comments from the functions and check the results.

```
# Set the seed for reproducibility
seed <- 123
```

```
set.seed(seed)

# Assign "train" or "test" to each observation in the data set
dt$Type <- sample(c("train", "test"), nrow(dt), replace = TRUE,
↪  prob = c(0.8, 0.2))

# Check the distribution of the brands over the Type variable
table(dt$Brand, dt$Type)
```

```
          test train
  Apple    372  1520
  Samsung  365  1419
```

We can see that the distribution of reviews by brand is reasonably balanced.

```
# Create a corpus from the Content column for preprocessing
library(tm)
library(SnowballC)
corpus <- VCorpus(VectorSource(dt$Content))

# Preprocess the corpus and create a Document Term Matrix
dtm <- corpus %>%
  tm_map(content_transformer(tolower)) %>% # Convert to lowercase
  tm_map(content_transformer(removeWords), stopwords("english"))
  ↪  %>% # Remove stopwords
  tm_map(removePunctuation) %>% # Remove punctuation
  tm_map(removeNumbers) %>% # Remove numbers
  # tm_map(stemDocument) %>% # Stemming (commented out)
  tm_map(content_transformer(lemmatize_words)) %>% # Lemmatization
  tm_map(stripWhitespace) %>% # Remove whitespace
  DocumentTermMatrix() %>%
  # weightTfIdf() %>% # Tf-Idf weighting (commented out)
  removeSparseTerms(0.98) # Adjust for sparsity

# Check the dimensions of the DTM
dim(dtm)

# Convert the DTM to a data frame
dtm_df <- as.data.frame(as.matrix(dtm))

# Ensure dtm_df and dt contain the same number of documents, then
↪  add Brand and Type
dtm_df <- bind_cols(dtm_df, dt[ , c("Brand", "Type")])

# Split the data frame into training and testing sets and remove
↪  the Type column
dtm_train <- filter(dtm_df, Type == "train") %>% select(-Type)
dtm_test <- filter(dtm_df, Type == "test") %>% select(-Type)
```

```
# Clean up the workspace
rm(dtm, corpus, dtm_df)
```

6.2.2 Linear Discriminant Analysis

LDA is a robust algorithm for classifying, especially when distinguishing between more than two classes. While logistic regression, which is another algorithm, is widely used for binary classification (Komarek, 2004), it faces challenges in dealing with multiclass scenarios, where multinomial logistic regression or LDA is more suitable (Torkkola, 2001). In marketing, both techniques are standard when the task is to describe market segments which have been derived previously (and which are built by using a clustering method); for an overview, refer to Wedel and Kamakura (2000) or Reutterer and Dan (2021). The word "discriminate" means to separate, and LDA uses a linear discrimination function to separate classes, addressing some of the limitations of logistic regression, such as instability in cases of well-separated classes or small data sets. It is important to distinguish LDA from another, non-related, soft-clustering algorithm called latent Dirichlet allocation despite sharing the same abbreviation. We will discuss the latter in the next chapter. Classification LDA assumes that, within each class, the predictor variables are jointly multivariate normal and that all classes share the same covariance matrix (i.e., $\Sigma_1 = \Sigma_2 = \cdots = \Sigma_K$), a form of homoskedasticity that can be sensitive to outliers (Balakrishnama & Ganapathiraju, 1998).

Linear discriminant analysis (LDA) classification is a generative technique which assumes that across classes there are class-conditional multivariate normal features with equal covariance matrices. It detects linear decision boundaries, maximizes separation, and provides baselines for analyses with high-dimensional text features (document-term matrix—DTMs).

Several algorithms can extend LDA's principles, including quadratic discriminant analysis (Tharwat, 2016), flexible discriminant analysis (Hastie et al., 1994), and regularized discriminant analysis (Friedman, 1989). In machine learning, model parameters are estimated from training data to make predictions. The caret package in R, standing for *C*lassification *A*nd *RE*gression *T*raining, facilitates this process with functions for data splitting, preprocessing, feature selection, model tuning through cross-validation, resampling, and variable importance estimation (Kuhn et al. 2013). For model tuning, caret's `trainControl()` function is versatile, allowing the use of various validation techniques, including k-fold cross-validation, a method we explore within the context of LDA. Cross-validation divides the training set into K segments, or folds, typically between 5 and 10, to

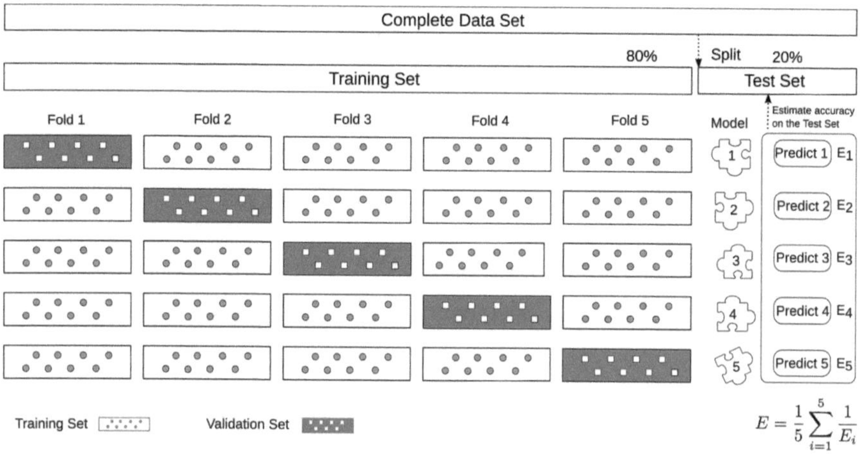

Fig. 6.2 Supervised learning: cross-validation. Authors' own figure

train and validate the model iteratively, enhancing its reliability and performance (Forman & Scholz, 2010).

Figure 6.2 shows the cross-validation process using a fivefold example. This means there are five iterations, each incorporating a unique combination of folds. In every iteration, a model is trained on the training set and then applied to the validation set to make predictions (Bishop & Nasrabadi, 2006). The discrepancy between the model's predictions and the ground-truth labels of the validation fold is measured as misclassification. The overall error rate E is calculated as the average of the errors from each iteration i. A common misunderstanding is the belief that the best-performing model from these iterations is selected for future classification tasks. However, this approach does not fully align with best practice. Cross-validation serves as a method to estimate how well the algorithm is likely to perform on unseen data. It provides a measure of the model's generalizability rather than of selecting a specific model for use. It is also important to note that the test set remains untouched during cross-validation and is reserved exclusively for final evaluation.

> *Cross-validation (k-fold)* estimates generalization by dividing the training data into *k* folds and repeatedly holding out each fold in turn, using an average value for validation across folds. It is used for the comparison and tuning of models using hyper-parameters, but without using the test set.

The final model, intended for operational use, is trained on the entire training data set without folding, using the hyper-parameters chosen (or validated) during cross-validation (Cawley & Talbot, 2010). Once this model has been developed, it can then be evaluated using the test set, with performance metrics providing

Table 6.1 Fivefold cross-validation with ten documents. Table compiled by the authors

Fold	Validation set	Training set
Fold 1	Doc1, Doc2	Doc3, Doc4, Doc5, Doc6, Doc7, Doc8, Doc9, Doc10
Fold 2	Doc3, Doc4	Doc1, Doc2, Doc5, Doc6, Doc7, Doc8, Doc9, Doc10
Fold 3	Doc5, Doc6	Doc1, Doc2, Doc3, Doc4, Doc7, Doc8, Doc9, Doc10
Fold 4	Doc7, Doc8	Doc1, Doc2, Doc3, Doc4, Doc5, Doc6, Doc9, Doc10
Fold 5	Doc9, Doc10	Doc1, Doc2, Doc3, Doc4, Doc5, Doc6, Doc7, Doc8

insights into its effectiveness with the help of a confusion matrix. A confusion matrix is shown in tabular form and used to evaluate the performance of classification models. It categorizes predictions into four categories: true positives (correct positive predictions), false positives (incorrectly predicted as positive), false negatives (incorrectly predicted as negative), and true negatives (correct negative predictions). When the class distribution is imbalanced, it is common to improve the overall accuracy with metrics such as precision, recall, and an F1-score (Saito & Rehmsmeier, 2015).

To understand better how cross-validation works, let us link image Fig. 6.2 with table Table 6.1 to pass from the abstract concept in the image to a simple application in the form of a table. We will use an example of a data set containing ten documents. Before folding, the documents are usually shuffled at random (Breiman & Spector, 1992) to avoid any order-related bias.

Table 6.1 corresponds to the left portion of Fig. 6.2, showing the 80% of the data set designated as the training set. In machine learning, "training" refers to the process of teaching an algorithm to recognize patterns, relationships, and features that lead to specific outcomes. For example, when applying classification LDA to textual data, such as a document-term matrix (DTM), the predictors are the text features extracted from the reviews, such as the frequencies of words or other linguistic properties. These features help the algorithm identify which discriminate most between the two brands, revealing patterns that distinguish the brands in terms of language, word usage, or specific terms.

This training process enables the development of models in k with different configurations through k-fold cross-validation, where the data set is divided into folds for sequential validation. Each fold serves as a validation set while the remaining folds are used for training. In our data set, cross-validation involves identifying the conditions or features that distinguish between products A and B, as well as testing the model's ability to generalize.

But how effective is this model at predicting the classification of an unseen review? For illustration, consider a simplified data set comprising only five reviews. With k=5, a fivefold validation is effectively equivalent to leave-one-out cross-validation (LOOCV) in this case: It uses each review sequentially as a validation point, initially, the first review, then the second, and so on until the fifth. A unique model is trained during each iteration, excluding the validation review from the training process. The errors from each model are averaged to determine the overall performance, with the algorithm optimizing itself to minimize this error.

Subsequently, the model's ability to generalize is assessed by evaluating its accuracy, or using other relevant metrics, for the test data set. This was initially set aside, ensuring that it can provide a final, unbiased evaluation of the model's performance.

```
# Set 10-fold CV, save predictions, enable class probabilities
control <- trainControl(method = "cv", number = 10,
↪  savePredictions = "final", classProbs = TRUE)

# Set seed for reproducibility
set.seed(seed)

# Train LDA model, optimize for accuracy, 5 tuning iterations
lda <- train(Brand ~ ., data = dtm_train, method = "lda",
↪  trControl = control, metric= "Accuracy", tuneLength = 5)

# Display model summary
lda
```

```
Linear Discriminant Analysis

2939 samples
 804 predictor
   2 classes: 'Apple', 'Samsung'

No preprocessing
Resampling: Cross-Validated (10 fold)
Summary of sample sizes: 2645, 2646, 2645, 2645, 2645,
↪  2645, ...
Resampling results:

  Accuracy   Kappa
  0.7727195  0.5429092
```

The results from training the model can be summarized by entering the variable name of where the model is stored. This summary includes the number of classes, number of samples, predictor variables (the terms from the document-term matrix after preprocessing), the type of cross-validation used, and the evaluation metrics: accuracy and kappa. Accuracy is particularly relevant for binary classification tasks, especially if the data set is balanced (Koyejo et al., 2014), while kappa, or Cohen's kappa, is more informative in scenarios where there is a class imbalance, as it accounts for the possibility of the agreement occurring by chance (Wang et al., 2019).

Cohen's κ is a metric which adjusts the observed accuracy for chance-level agreement: $\kappa = (p_o - p_e)/(1 - p_e)$, where p_o is the observed agreement and p_e is the expected chance agreement. It is useful when class distributions are imbalanced; $\kappa \approx 0$ means chance level, 1 means a perfect agreement.

To apply the trained model to the test data set, we use the `predict()` function. This not only classifies the new data but also provides probabilities for the assigning of each class, offering deeper insights into the model's confidence in its predictions.

```
# Predict with LDA model on test data
lda.predict <- predict(lda, newdata = dtm_test)
```

Now let us generate a confusion matrix by comparing the predictions made by the classification model against the real, true labels of the data. This matrix helps us to evaluate the model's performance by showing the true positives, false positives, false negatives, and true negatives. There are multiple metrics to assess how well a model fit can be evaluated, through measures such as accuracy and error rate, as well as some class-specific measures which evaluate its performance for the individual classes rather than the overall data set, such as precision, recall, and F-measures (Anandarajan et al., 2019).

The `caret` package in R provides comprehensive support for these metrics for evaluating a model's performance thoroughly.

```
# Evaluate model performance on the test set using a confusion
↪  matrix
cfm <- confusionMatrix(lda.predict, as.factor(dtm_test$Brand))
print(cfm)
```

```
Confusion Matrix and Statistics

          Reference
Prediction Apple Samsung
   Apple     325     108
   Samsung    47     257

               Accuracy : 0.7897
                 95% CI : (0.7585, 0.8186)
    No Information Rate : 0.5047
    P-Value [Acc > NIR] : < 2.2e-16
```

```
                  Kappa : 0.5787

 Mcnemar's Test P-Value : 1.441e-06

            Sensitivity : 0.8737
            Specificity : 0.7041
         Pos Pred Value : 0.7506
         Neg Pred Value : 0.8454
             Prevalence : 0.5047
         Detection Rate : 0.4410
   Detection Prevalence : 0.5875
      Balanced Accuracy : 0.7889

       'Positive' Class : Apple
```

```
# Obtain classification probabilities for each brand in the test
↪ set
lda.predict.p <- predict(lda, newdata = dtm_test, type = "prob")

# Display probabilities for the first six documents as percentages,
↪ rounded to two decimals
head(round(lda.predict.p * 100, 2))
```

```
   Apple Samsung
4  90.13    9.87
5  92.70    7.30
8  99.99    0.01
11 67.03   32.97
16 93.08    6.92
20 98.90    1.10
```

Examining the probabilities which a model uses to assign texts to specific brands can provide deeper insights into the algorithm's confidence in classifying objects. This analysis helps us understand that inaccurate classification may arise from ambiguities and similarities in the language used to describe different brands. In the following section, we will explore a different classification algorithm and compare its performance with linear discriminant analysis (LDA).

The accuracy of the test set, rounded to four decimals, is 0.7897 and quantifies the proportion of correct predictions of the total predictions made by a model. Conversely, the error rate measures the proportion of incorrect predictions, essentially serving as the inverse of accuracy, calculated as Error rate = 1−Accuracy. Here we are investigating metrics which assess how accurately individual classes are predicted when evaluating class-specific performance. *Precision* measures the proportion of correct predictions for a specific class out of all the predictions made for that class, highlighting the model's accuracy in identifying that class among all

Table 6.2 Confusion matrix

	Actual Apple	Actual Samsung	Total predicted
Predicted Apple	325	108	372
Predicted Samsung	47	257	365
Total actual	433	304	737

classes it attempts to identify. *Recall*, on the other hand, focuses on the proportion of correct predictions for a specific class out of all the actual instances of that class, indicating the model's ability to capture all the instances. The *F-measure*, or F1 score, harmonizes precision and recall into a single metric, calculated as $F_i = 2 \times \frac{precision \times recall}{precision+recall}$, where i represents the class. This balance makes the F-measure a valuable tool for assessing a model's overall effectiveness in class-specific predictions, especially when using data sets which are imbalanced.

Using the confusion matrix, which assesses which products were actually Apple or Samsung and were classified correctly (or not), we can calculate all the measures mentioned above. See Table 6.2 for better guidance.

With the numbers we obtained, let us calculate the accuracy: $\frac{325+257}{737} = 0.7897$. The error rate is $1-0.7897 = 0.2103$. Precision for the Apple tablets is $\frac{325}{\mathbf{433}} = \mathbf{0.7506}$ and precision for the Samsung tablets is $\frac{257}{\mathbf{304}} = \mathbf{0.8454}$. Recall for the Apple products is $\frac{325}{\mathbf{372}} = \mathbf{0.8737}$, while for the Samsung products, it is $\frac{\mathbf{257}}{\mathbf{365}} = \mathbf{0.7041}$.

Calculating the F-measure is straightforward using the formula given in the paragraph above.

> *A confusion matrix* shows predicted values vs. actual values with four counts: TP (true positives: predicted positive and actually positive), FP (false positives: predicted positive but actually negative), FN (false negatives: predicted negative but actually positive), and TN (true negatives: predicted negative and actually negative). From these you can obtain the overall accuracy and other metrics such as precision (TP/(TP+FP)), recall (TP/(TP+FN)), and F1 (harmonic mean of precision and recall), which are fundamental under class imbalance.

6.2.2.1 A Word About Accuracy

Assessing what constitutes "good" accuracy in machine learning is nuanced, influenced by factors such as the specifics of the application, complexity of the problem, and class distribution within the data set. A fundamental measure, baseline accuracy, represents the success rate of the most naive model that always predicts the most frequent class. For a model to be considered effective, its accuracy must substantially exceed this baseline, indicating genuine learning rather than mere replication of existing class distributions. Simple, well-defined problems might warrant accuracies approaching perfection, whereas the messiness of real-world data, characterized by noise and class overlap, means that for more complex issues accuracy will not meet the same level. The presence of imbalanced classes further complicates matters, making high overall accuracy potentially deceptive. Here, metrics such as precision, recall, and the F1 score, particularly in relation to the performance of minority classes, offer a better assessment of a model's efficacy. Moreover, the benchmark for "good" accuracy is not universal but varies across domains. For example, the thresholds for acceptability in spam detection vs. medical diagnostics diverge significantly due to the difference in consequences resulting from errors.

In the following section, we will explore a different classification algorithm and compare its performance with linear discriminant analysis (LDA).

6.2.3 K-Nearest Neighbor Classification

The KNN algorithm is simple and effective for tasks involving classification and regression. Classification using KNN aims to assign entities to predefined categories, whereas regression predicts a numerical value. Our focus here will be on its use in classification.

A unique element of KNN classification is that nothing is ordained before the model is used. This means that, unlike algorithms which learn parameters to make predictions for classification, KNN relies on the data set itself, identifying the *k*'s most similar instances (or "neighbors") to a given point to make a prediction. New data are evaluated during the running time against preexisting data. The concept of "similarity" is quantified through distance metrics, making KNN a distance-based algorithm, and Euclidean distance is an excellent candidate for this.

> *K-nearest neighbors (KNN)* is a non-parametric, instance-based method. To classify a new text vector, we use a distance metric, such as Eucledian, and find its instances of k-closest training and decide using majority labeling. The control of bias variance and robustness is determined by the choice of k, scaling and distance metric.

When the algorithm needs to make a prediction, it searches through the training data set (i.e., the preexisting data) to find the instances (neighbors) nearest to *k*. The prediction is then made by assigning the new instance to one of the predefined categories, based on the majority class among its nearest neighbors.

Determining the optimal number of neighbors, *k*, is essential for the algorithm's performance, with the best value typically identified through experimentation and validation techniques. KNN's principle is straightforward: to classify an entity based on the majority vote of the classes or average outcome of the target values of its *k*-nearest neighbors (Brownlee, 2016). This vote, or outcome, is based on the calculation of similarity between the new instance and its neighbors; see ◘ Fig. 6.3. Note that in order to derive a unanimous decision of assignment, the value for *k* must always be odd. Choosing an odd value for *k* prevents ties in *binary*

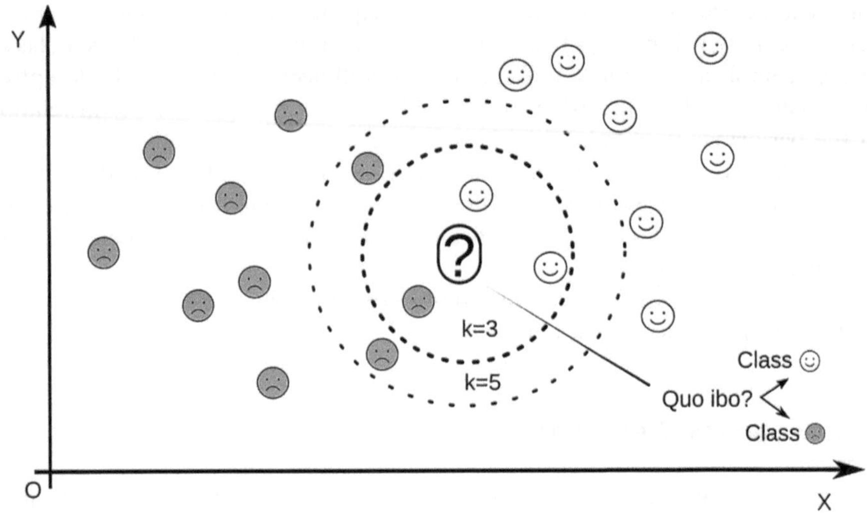

Fig. 6.3 KNN classification. Authors' own figure

classification because one class must receive a majority of the votes. With three or more classes, however, ties can still occur even when k is odd; common tiebreakers include distance-weighted voting, reducing k, or breaking the tie at random. While KNN is known for its ease of use and understanding, especially in scenarios with a small number of predictors, its efficiency diminishes as the dimensions of the data set increases, a phenomenon known as the "curse of dimensionality." Further reading is recommended for a more detailed exploration of KNN and its use (e.g., Tan, 2006).

In our example, we use exactly the same data set we prepared for the LDA classification analysis. The training and testing data sets are reused here, so the application of KNN classification is immediate. In this analysis, we use the DTM to detect which textual features are predictive of the two brands under study, focusing on how KNN classification identifies patterns in the data.

```
# Configure 10-fold CV with class probabilities
ctrl <- trainControl(method = "cv", number = 10, classProbs =
↪  TRUE)

# Train kNN, optimizing accuracy, with 5 k values
set.seed(seed)  # Ensure reproducible results
knn <- train(Brand ~ ., data = data.frame(dtm_train), method =
↪  "knn", trControl = ctrl, metric = "Accuracy", tuneLength = 5)

# Display model summary
knn
```

```
k-Nearest Neighbors

2939 samples
 804 predictor
   2 classes: 'Apple', 'Samsung'

No preprocessing
Resampling: Cross-Validated (10 fold)
Summary of sample sizes: 2645, 2646, 2645, 2645, 2645,
↪   2645, ...
Resampling results across tuning parameters:

  k   Accuracy   Kappa
   5  0.7985686  0.5916877
   7  0.7876831  0.5692389
   9  0.7778192  0.5488217
  11  0.7733881  0.5396807
  13  0.7638655  0.5198805

Accuracy was used to select the optimal model using the
↪   largest value.
The final value used for the model was k = 5.
```

The system identified the optimal performance as $k = 5$, where the model's predictive accuracy reached 79.8569%. It is important to note that variations in the size and diversity of the data set could lead to improved accuracy. Moreover, the preprocessing significantly influences the results. In this analysis, employing a bag-of-words (BoW) model (see ▶ Sect. 4.3.1) alongside lemmatization (see ▶ Sect. 4.2.7) yielded the highest accuracy. For a comprehensive comparison of the results under various conditions, see ◘ Table 6.3. This discussion presents the best-case scenario based on the current data set and preprocessing methods. You are encouraged to experiment with different preprocessing options to try and enhance the model's performance. The fact that lemmatization outperforms stemming here is unsurprising. Stemming chops words down to the most basic root (e.g., "running," "runs" → "run"), but it can also conflate unrelated terms ("universe" and "university" are both reduced to "univers"). Lemmatization, by returning valid dictionary forms, keeps more semantic information while still reducing sparsity, which typically helps classifiers that rely on token overlap; see Sch et al. (2008).

We can also visualize the predictive performance with a varying k; see ◘ Fig. 6.4.

```
# plot and identify best k
ggplot(knn)
```

The process for making predictions (or classifications) mirrors that of the earlier example. To evaluate the algorithm's performance for the test data set, we have used a confusion matrix.

Table 6.3 KNN, various preprocessing methods. Table compiled by the authors

k	Model	Word root	Accuracy
7	BoW	Stem	0.7842
5	**BoW**	**Lem**	**0.7914**
9	Tf-Idf	Stem	0.6189
5	Tf-Idf	Lem	0.6250

Bold indicates the highest accuracy; here, $k = 5$ with BoW + lemmatization yields the best accuracy (0.7914).

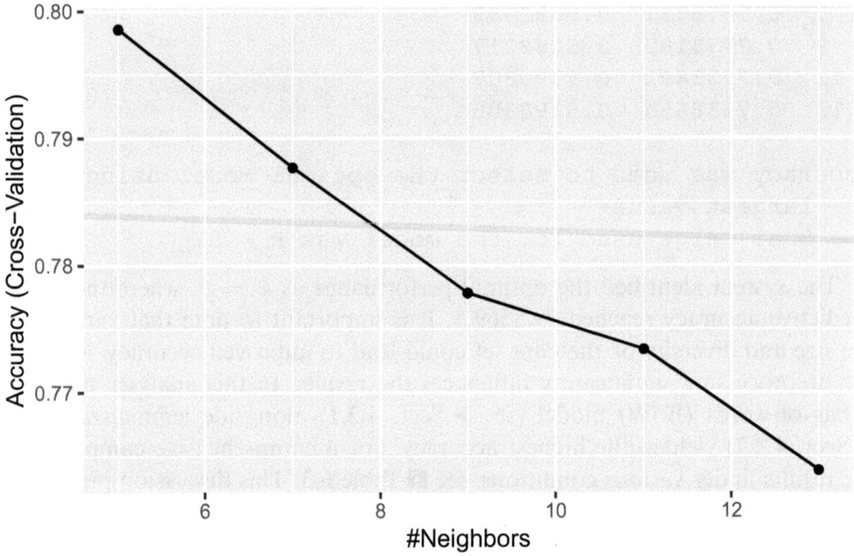

Fig. 6.4 Plot and identify best k. Authors' own figure

```
# Predict labels for the test data set using the trained kNN model
knn.predict <- predict(knn, newdata = data.frame(dtm_test))

# Evaluate the model's performance on the test set using a
↪  confusion matrix
cfm <- confusionMatrix(knn.predict, as.factor(dtm_test$Brand))
```

In this case, the accuracy for the testing set is 0.7734, which is slightly worse than the LDA classification, but otherwise more or less equivalent.

6.2.4 Support Vector Machine Classification

Support vector machine (SVM) classification is a well-known and widely used procedure that performs well in binary classification and multi-class classification (Cui & Curry, 2005). It is known to need little tuning when creating a model. We need to introduce the concept of the maximal-margin classifier here to explain the internal workings of SVM classification. Usually, we have *n* input variables, such as the words in a vocabulary. Classification means separation and is done through a hyperplane. For example, in a three-dimensional space, a hyperplane will have two dimensions, while in a three-dimensional space the hyperplane has one dimension, basically a line. For simplicity, let us take a two-dimensional space. In ◘ Fig. 6.5, we can see the optimal solution SVM finds for the position of the separation line for distinguishing two classes out of an infinity of possible solutions through which the line can pass.

The model classifies new elements based on their position relative to the decision boundary: Elements on one side of the line (where the line-model equation yields a value greater than zero) are assigned to one class, while those on the other side (with values less than zero) are classified as part of the opposite class. Classification becomes challenging for values that lie close to the decision boundary. At the heart of this model is the distance between the decision boundary and the nearest points on either side of it which belong to both classes. The optimal decision boundary, known as the maximal-margin hyperplane, is the one that maximizes this distance, ensuring the most precise separation between (in our case: two) classes. The points nearest to this hyperplane are called support vectors, as they "support" the positioning of the hyperplane, playing an essential role in defining a robust

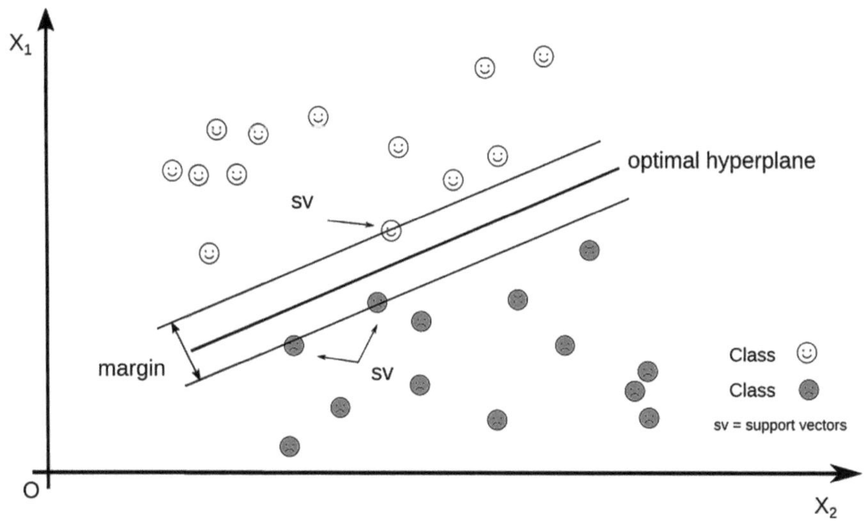

◘ **Fig. 6.5** Support vector machine classes separation. Authors' own figure

separator. During training, the model aims to identify this optimal hyperplane, maximizing the margin for a given data set (Brownlee, 2016).

In scenarios where perfect separation is not feasible, the soft-margin classifier offers a more flexible solution. It introduces a parameter, denoted as C (for "cost"), which adjusts the model's tolerance for misclassifications. Tuning the C parameter allows for some points to cross the boundary, effectively balancing the trade-off between a strict separation and allowing for misclassifications. A higher C value tends to reduce misclassifications by enforcing stricter margins. Like KNN, SVMs are also exposed to the *curse of dimensionality*. In a space with tens of thousands of word features, many vectors lie almost equidistant from one another, which can make any flexible kernel overfit the noise. Regularization through the C parameter (and, in the nonlinear case, appropriate choices of γ or degree d) acts as a safeguard by penalizing overly complex hyperplanes.

6

The construction of the hyperplane for SVM is achieved through linear algebra operations known as the dot product, also referred to as the inner product. For instance, consider two vectors represented by [1, 2] and [3, 4]; their inner product is calculated as the sum of the products of their corresponding elements: $1 \times 3 + 2 \times 4$. Prediction with an SVM is based on a decision function that combines those inner products between the input feature vector (x) and the *support vectors* (x_i):

$$f(x) = b + \sum_i \boldsymbol{\alpha_i}\, \mathbf{y_i}\, \mathbf{K}(\mathbf{x_i}, \mathbf{x})$$

where $(K(x_i, x))$ is the kernel (for a linear SVM, $(K(x_i, x) = (x_i, x)))$ and $(y_i \in \{-1, +1\})$ are the class labels of the support vectors, and (α_i) and (b) are coefficients estimated during training; see Sch and Smola (2002). (If you restrict the kernel to the linear dot product and absorb the labels into the weights, the equation reduces to the familiar form $(f(x) = b + \sum_i w_i\,(x_i, x))$.)

The prediction for a new data point involves using the dot product between the input features and the support vectors. This operation, known as the kernel function, essentially measures similarity, or from another perspective, the distance between data points.

When dealing with a linear combination of input features, we employ a linear kernel. However, to facilitate classification in scenarios where the data are not separable by a line, inputs can be transformed into higher dimensions using polynomial or radial kernel techniques. These allow for complex separations with curved lines. We will explore the performance of these various kernels to determine which offers the best separation.

> *A support vector machine (SVM)* finds the maximal-margin hyperplane, where the parameter C controls the regularization (the trade-off between margin width and classification errors). Linear SVMs applied to text corpora are strong and efficient, while nonlinear kernels typically require additional tuning procedures to avoid overfitting.

6.2.4.1 Linear SVM

The linear SVM kernel is the simplest of various types of kernels used in SVM models. It excels in scenarios with many features, making it particularly well suited for text classification. Joachims (1998), Sebastiani (2002), and Gao and Sun (2010) suggest that linear kernels are efficient and perform well for high-dimensional data such as texts due to their straightforward computation. Compared to more complex kernels, linear kernels are faster, as they are less computationally intensive. The formula for the linear kernel is:

$$K(x, x_i) = \sum(x * x_i)$$

This equation represents the dot product of the input vector x and a support vector x_i, effectively measuring the distance between new data points and the support vectors. The training process for a model using a linear kernel typically involves cross-validation, something you have seen before, to ensure the model generalizes well for unseen data.

```
library(kernlab)
# Set 10-fold CV with class probabilities and save predictions
ctrl <- trainControl(method="cv", number=10,
↪  savePredictions="final", classProbs=TRUE)

# Tuning grid for "C" parameter
# A cost of zero forces a degenerate solution, we start at 0.1
tG <- expand.grid(C = seq(0.1, 2, length = 5))

# Train SVM with linear kernel, tuning "C"
set.seed(seed)
svm.linear <- train(Brand~., data=dtm_train, method="svmLinear",
↪  trControl=ctrl, preProcess = c("center","scale"), tuneGrid=tG)

# Predict and evaluate with linear kernel SVM
svm.linear.predict <- predict(svm.linear, newdata=dtm_test)
confusionMatrix(svm.linear.predict, as.factor(dtm_test$Brand))
```

```
Confusion Matrix and Statistics

          Reference
Prediction Apple Samsung
   Apple     334      70
   Samsung    38     295

               Accuracy : 0.8535
                 95% CI : (0.8258, 0.8782)
    No Information Rate : 0.5047
```

```
    P-Value [Acc > NIR] : < 2.2e-16

                  Kappa : 0.7067

 Mcnemar's Test P-Value : 0.002855

            Sensitivity : 0.8978
            Specificity  : 0.8082
         Pos Pred Value : 0.8267
         Neg Pred Value : 0.8859
             Prevalence : 0.5047
         Detection Rate : 0.4532
   Detection Prevalence : 0.5482
      Balanced Accuracy : 0.8530

       'Positive' Class : Apple
```

Results can be significantly improved by adjusting the parameters. However, this has a trade-off, meaning that more extensive tuning may lead to increased training times but can yield superior outcomes. To assess the effectiveness of the tuned parameters, results can be compared with those obtained using other models, such as LDA and KNN, discussed earlier in this chapter. Metrics like accuracy, precision, and the F1-score provide a basis for evaluating whether tuning the parameters leads to meaningful improvements compared to other models.

6.2.4.2 SVM Radial

In the context of SVM, particularly when employing the radial basis function (RBF) kernel, two critical parameters are introduced: the cost parameter (C) and the gamma parameter γ (sometimes referred to as σ). The cost parameter C addresses the trade-off between minimizing training errors and ensuring simplicity of the model for better generalization, essentially controlling how much misclassification is tolerated. On the other hand, the gamma parameter γ influences the decision boundary's shape; lower values of γ may result in more linear decision boundaries, while higher values allow for more complex, curved boundaries that can closely fit the training data. The influence of γ is captured by the RBF kernel formula:

$$K(x, x_i) = e^{-\gamma * \sum((x-x_i)^2)}$$

This formula shows how the similarity between any two data points x and x_i is calculated, with γ modulating the impact of the distance between these points on their calculated similarity. The values for γ typically range from $0 < \gamma < 1$, allowing for a wide spectrum of decision-boundary complexity. The radial kernel, with its ability to create complex polygons of separation, is a powerful method, especially for data sets that are not separable linearly, enabling the model to capture intricate patterns within the data. In caret's `svmRadial`, the default value for γ is actually $1/p$, where p is the number of features.

```
# Set seed for reproducible results
set.seed(seed)

# Train SVM with radial basis function kernel on training data
svm.radial <- train(Brand ~ ., data = dtm_train, method =
↪  "svmRadial", trControl = ctrl, tuneLength = 10)

# Predict labels on test data
svm.radial.predict <- predict(svm.radial, newdata = dtm_test)

# Evaluate predictions using a confusion matrix
confusionMatrix(svm.radial.predict, as.factor(dtm_test$Brand))
```

```
Confusion Matrix and Statistics

          Reference
Prediction Apple Samsung
   Apple     339      73
   Samsung    33     292

               Accuracy : 0.8562
                 95% CI : (0.8287, 0.8807)
    No Information Rate : 0.5047
    P-Value [Acc > NIR] : < 2.2e-16

                  Kappa : 0.712

 Mcnemar's Test P-Value : 0.0001519

            Sensitivity : 0.9113
            Specificity : 0.8000
         Pos Pred Value : 0.8228
         Neg Pred Value : 0.8985
             Prevalence : 0.5047
         Detection Rate : 0.4600
   Detection Prevalence : 0.5590
      Balanced Accuracy : 0.8556

       'Positive' Class : Apple
```

The accuracy shows minimal difference when compared to the linear case. Fine-tuning the parameters could potentially enhance the results marginally. However, this increased flexibility comes at a cost: It may lead to overfitting, where the model performs well using the training data but struggles to generalize unseen data.

6.2.4.3 Polynomial Kernel SVM

The polynomial kernel extends the concept of the linear kernel, allowing for more complex, nonlinear decision boundaries. While it sometimes may be less accurate or efficient than its linear counterpart, it offers flexibility in capturing more complex patterns within the data. The polynomial kernel is defined as:

$$K(\mathbf{x}, \mathbf{y}) = \left(\mathbf{x}^{\top}\mathbf{y} + c\right)^{d}.$$

Here, c is a nonnegative constant (offset or bias), and d represents the degree of the polynomial, which must be greater than 1 for the kernel to exhibit nonlinear properties. When $d = 1$, the polynomial kernel simplifies to the linear kernel. The term “polynomial” suggests the ability to model curved lines, enabling the separation of classes through curved boundaries rather than straight lines. Obviously, choosing different values for d can lead to more complex decision boundaries and might better fit the training data, but this will increase the risk of overfitting. Also, a higher d will result in increased computational complexity affecting training time and requiring more computer resources.

```
# Set seed for reproducible results
set.seed(seed)

# Train SVM with polynomial kernel on training data
svm.poly <- train(Brand ~ ., data = dtm_train, method = "svmPoly",
↪  trControl = ctrl, tuneLength = 5)

# Predict labels for test data using the trained model
svm.poly.predict <- predict(svm.poly, newdata = dtm_test)

# Evaluate model performance with a confusion matrix
confusionMatrix(svm.poly.predict, as.factor(dtm_test$Brand))
```

```
Confusion Matrix and Statistics

          Reference
Prediction Apple Samsung
   Apple     335      71
   Samsung    37     294

               Accuracy : 0.8535
                 95% CI : (0.8258, 0.8782)
    No Information Rate : 0.5047
    P-Value [Acc > NIR] : < 2.2e-16
```

```
                  Kappa : 0.7066

 Mcnemar's Test P-Value : 0.001496

            Sensitivity : 0.9005
            Specificity : 0.8055
         Pos Pred Value : 0.8251
         Neg Pred Value : 0.8882
             Prevalence : 0.5047
         Detection Rate : 0.4545
   Detection Prevalence : 0.5509
      Balanced Accuracy : 0.8530

       'Positive' Class : Apple
```

Presenting the three SVM options together helps us to make decisions about their use and allows us to compare their relative performance quickly. Graphical representation is usually a necessary aid in such cases (see Fig. 6.6). Presenting the three SVM options together also helps us to decide which to choose and allows for a quick comparison of their relative performance. For instance, the polynomial kernel often performs well in scenarios with nonlinear relationships, but its effectiveness depends heavily on the choice of degree and regularization parameters. Compared to the linear kernel, it may offer more flexibility at the cost of increased computation time and a higher risk of overfitting. The radial kernel can model more complex patterns, but requires the careful tuning of parameters like gamma to avoid underfitting or overfitting.

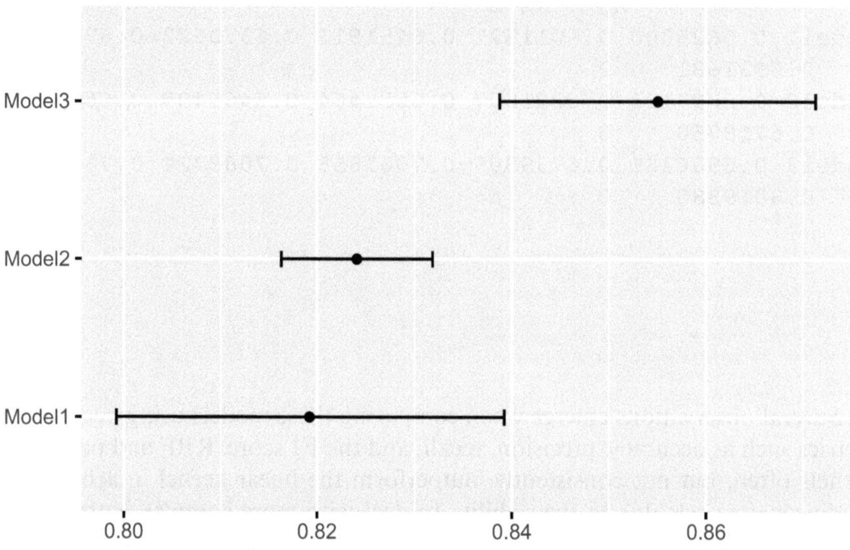

Fig. 6.6 Model performance comparison. Authors' own figure

```
# Aggregate resampling results for SVM models with different
↪  kernels
svm <- resamples(list(svm.linear, svm.radial, svm.poly))

# Summarize the performance metrics of the models
summary(svm)
```

```
Call:
summary.resamples(object = svm)

Models: Model1, Model2, Model3
Number of resamples: 10

Accuracy
            Min.   1st Qu.    Median      Mean   3rd Qu.
      ↪    Max. NA's
Model1 0.7823129 0.8010204 0.8231293 0.8192374 0.8366041
↪   0.8469388    2
Model2 0.8061224 0.8154762 0.8282313 0.8240928 0.8320564
↪   0.8367347    0
Model3 0.8265306 0.8375850 0.8534977 0.8550533 0.8656463
↪   0.9013605    0

Kappa
            Min.   1st Qu.    Median      Mean   3rd Qu.
      ↪    Max. NA's
Model1 0.5625000 0.6011521 0.6451912 0.6370622 0.6716049
↪   0.6921681    2
Model2 0.6097163 0.6291597 0.6551464 0.6465499 0.6627008
↪   0.6718750    0
Model3 0.6506361 0.6739805 0.7061855 0.7088224 0.7305667
↪   0.8019880    0
```

```
# Visualize the performance comparison using ggplot
ggplot(svm)
```

Several observations emerge when comparing these models using performance metrics such as accuracy, precision, recall, and the F1 score. RBF and polynomial kernels often, but not consistently, outperform the linear kernel in accuracy for nonlinear data sets due to their ability to deal with more complex patterns. This increased flexibility can sometimes lead to a trade-off between precision and recall, with the RBF kernel generally providing a good balance between the two for diverse data sets. The F1 score, which combines precision and recall, tends to be better for models using RBF and polynomial kernels in nonlinear settings, reflecting its greater adaptability.

These observations are evident in the plot and output derived from the coding above. For example, the RBF kernel shows improved F1 scores and a better balance of precision and recall compared to the linear kernel. The polynomial kernel has a higher degree of accuracy in scenarios where nonlinear relationships dominate. The computational trade-offs and increased risk of overfitting with more complex kernels, such as RBF and polynomial, are also reflected in the results, requiring us to tune the performing parameter and cross-validation for better performance.

The decision on which kernel to use should take into account the data set's characteristics, the computational resources available, and the balance required between interpreting the model and its complexity. Experimentation and cross-validation remain essential for determining the optimal kernel and parameter settings for any classification task, ensuring the model is accurate and generalizable.

6.2.5 Ensemble Learning

What if you could put more than one model together to obtain better prediction accuracy and higher overall performance? A technique that can assist in such a situation is called ensemble learning. The Oxford Dictionary gives a definition of the word "ensemble as "a small group of musicians, dancers or actors who perform together." We can think of our system as an orchestra. Each machine learning model is a musician, and each does its best so that they all contribute to a collective performance which is more than the sum of its parts.

Ensemble algorithms can be categorized into three types: bagging, boosting, and stacking. Bagging involves training multiple models on different subsamples of a training data set, allowing for parallel processing and reducing variance. Boosting, on the other hand, trains models sequentially (in a chain), with each focusing on correcting its predecessor's errors, effectively reducing bias. Unlike the first two, stacking combines predictions from diverse models, using an additional model (often called a meta-model) to determine the best way to combine these predictions, in a similar way to how an orchestra's conductor ensures the musicians play together.

Each method has its pros and cons, and choosing between them is determined by the challenge at hand. For further insights into these methods, see Tattar (2018). Our focus here will be on stacking. See the example in ◘ Fig. 6.7.

Utilizing the `caret` package, we can assemble various models under a meta-model that optimizes the combination of their predictions for the best outcome. Following the setup of control attributes for training, we then compile a list of machine learning algorithms, such as LDA, KNN, and linear SVM. Using the `caretList()` function, these models are trained, and the accuracy of their predictions is assessed collectively, showing the power of ensemble learning in achieving optimal results. This is accomplished by specifying resampling methods,

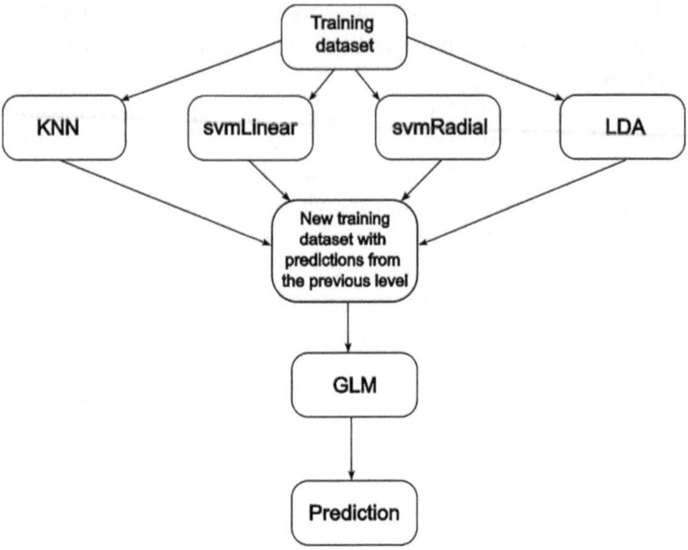

Fig. 6.7 Stack ensemble algorithm (example). Authors' own figure

such as cross-validation, using the `resamples()` function from the `caret` package. This allows for comparison of the performance of the models and enhances the reliability of the stacking.

```
# Set a 10-fold cross-validation scheme, enabling class
↪  probability predictions and saving all predictions
ctrl <- trainControl(method="cv", number = 10, classProbs=TRUE,
↪  index=createFolds(dtm_train$Brand, k = 10), savePredictions =
↪  "all")

# Define a list of machine-learning algorithms for ensemble
↪  learning
algorithmList <- c('lda', 'knn', 'svmLinear')

library(caretEnsemble)
set.seed(seed)  # Ensure reproducible results

# Train models specified in the algorithm list with the defined
↪  control settings
models <- caretList(Brand ~ ., data = dtm_train, trControl = ctrl,
↪  methodList = algorithmList, tuneLength = 10)

# Compare the models' performance using resampling
results <- resamples(models)

# Summarize the comparative performance of the models
summary(results)
```

```
Call:
summary.resamples(object = results)

Models: lda, knn, svmLinear
Number of resamples: 10

Accuracy
                 Min.   1st Qu.    Median      Mean    3rd
                  ↪ Qu.      Max. NA's
lda       0.5576560 0.5642479 0.6068053 0.6006904
 ↪  0.6181474 0.6797732    1
knn       0.6378072 0.7121928 0.7251418 0.7181979
 ↪  0.7377127 0.7682420    0
svmLinear 0.6748582 0.6875178 0.7009452 0.7135846
 ↪  0.7219282 0.8370510    0

Kappa
                 Min.   1st Qu.    Median      Mean    3rd
                  ↪ Qu.      Max. NA's
lda       0.1197228 0.1340173 0.2130066 0.2004211
 ↪  0.2363048 0.3551089    1
knn       0.2567923 0.4135803 0.4418663 0.4262784
 ↪  0.4670586 0.5308638    0
svmLinear 0.3434394 0.3676854 0.3986043 0.4233009
 ↪  0.4407455 0.6735033    0
```

The comparison of models can be represented by a graph; see ◘ Fig. 6.8. You can clearly see the best model of the three. Be aware that the lines represent an interval, given by the accuracy of the ten folds. The mean is represented by the dot and it is the value to be used. Note that in our application, the KNN algorithm performs slightly better than the SVM with a linear-kernel function, and the accuracy is 0.7181979.

```
# Plot the results
ggplot(results)
```

Now, using the models trained previously as the base layer, we can employ a generalized linear model (GLM) as the meta-learner. The GLM serves as a highly efficient prediction model, synthesizing the base models' outputs to enhance the overall performance.

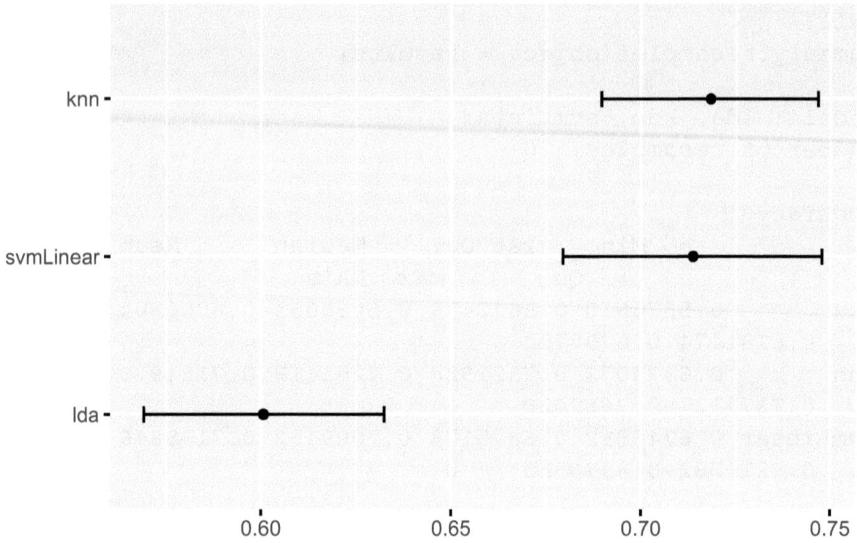

Fig. 6.8 Algorithm performance comparison. Authors' own figure

```
# Configure 10-fold CV, saving predictions and probabilities
stackControl <- trainControl(method="cv", number=10,
↪  savePredictions=TRUE, classProbs=TRUE)

# Stack models using GLM as meta-learner, optimizing for accuracy
stack.glm <- caretStack(models, method="glm", metric="Accuracy",
↪  trControl=stackControl, tuneLength = 10)

# Display stacked model summary
stack.glm
```

```
A glm ensemble of 3 base models: lda, knn, svmLinear

Ensemble results:
Generalized Linear Model

26451 samples
    3 predictor
    2 classes: 'Apple', 'Samsung'

No preprocessing
Resampling: Cross-Validated (10 fold)
Summary of sample sizes: 23806, 23806, 23806, 23806,
 ↪  23805, 23806, ...
```

```
Resampling results:

  Accuracy   Kappa
  0.7640567  0.5256692
```

The analysis demonstrates that the ensemble system, using stacking, has enhanced the predictive accuracy, elevating it from 0.7181979 to 0.7640567. This improvement underscores the efficacy of bringing together diverse models to achieve a superior performance.

Stacking can lead to better accuracy, provided these models exhibit low correlation in their predictions. The underlying rationale is that each model brings unique insights or captures different patterns within the data, thereby complementing each other. When models generate largely uncorrelated predictions, it indicates that they excel in different elements of the task. This diversity enables the meta-learner, or the classifier that integrates these predictions, to discern the most effective way of amalgamating the strengths of each model, thereby optimizing the overall predictive performance. However, if the predictions from the sub-models are highly correlated (with correlation coefficients exceeding 0.75), this implies that the models are likely to be capturing similar patterns and making analogous predictions. In such scenarios, the advantage of ensemble learning diminishes, as the aggregation of predictions offers little incremental value over the individual predictions. But this is not the case here, since the correlations are modest. The incremental increase in accuracy is 0.7640567. The accuracy, although modest, signifies the advantage of employing a stacked ensemble over relying solely on a single SVM model. See also the scatterplot matrix of model predictions in ◘ Fig. 6.9.

```
# Correlation matrix between model predictions
modelCor(results)
```

```
          lda       knn svmLinear
lda         1        NA        NA
knn        NA 1.0000000 0.2160285
svmLinear  NA 0.2160285 1.0000000
```

```
# Scatterplot matrix (splom) to visually examine the correlations
↪  between model predictions
splom(results)
```

The NA correlations between LDA and the other two models (KNN and svmLinear) suggest that the value either was not calculated or was not applicable. Although moderate, the positive correlation between KNN and svmLinear indicates some level of agreement in their predictions, suggesting they might be recognizing similar patterns in the data.

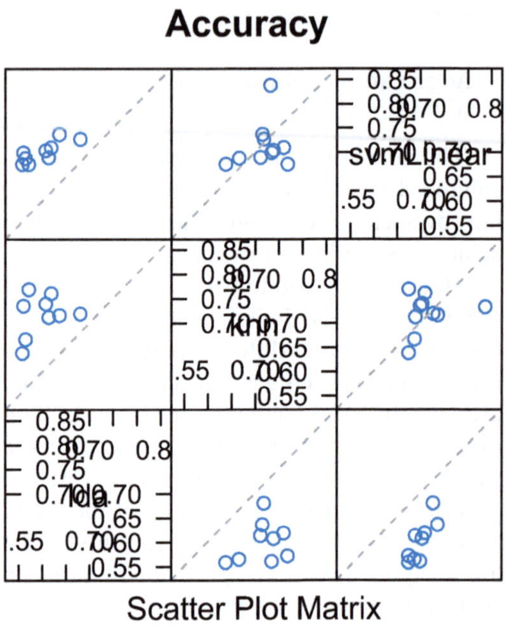

Fig. 6.9 Scatterplot matrix of model predictions. Authors' own figure

6

6.3 Neural Networks

The fascination with understanding how our brain thinks and what can be done in computer terms in order to mimic and outperform our reasoning has received a lot of attention in the academic literature. The move from understanding the biological neural cells of the natural neural network to the algorithmic constructs of an artificial neural network (ANN) is remarkable. ANNs, a subset of machine learning algorithms, employ interconnected nodes across a number of layers to process data, emulating the human brain's intricate network of neurons and synapses (Fig. 6.10). While these algorithms have proven incredibly potent, they are not always the optimal solution for every problem. Their performance can vary based on several factors, including the task's complexity, the size of the data set, and the computational resources available. Despite these limitations, ANNs have achieved remarkable success across a wide range of applications, from image recognition (Quraishi et al., 2012) to fraud detection (Asha & KR, 2021; Krambia-Kapardis et al., 2010), to medical diagnoses (Yen & Tsao, 2024), to the classification of natural language patterns (Goldberg, 2017), which is our area of interest.

In the following example, we will turn to the R package `nnet`. `caret` can interface with it to train neural network models, allowing users to use `caret`'s convenient functions such as model training and parameter tuning, while using the neural network algorithms provided by `nnet`. Despite the seemingly mystical aura surrounding neural networks, the core steps in using them for classification remain straightforward and familiar: data preparation, setting up the model, network training, and performance evaluation.

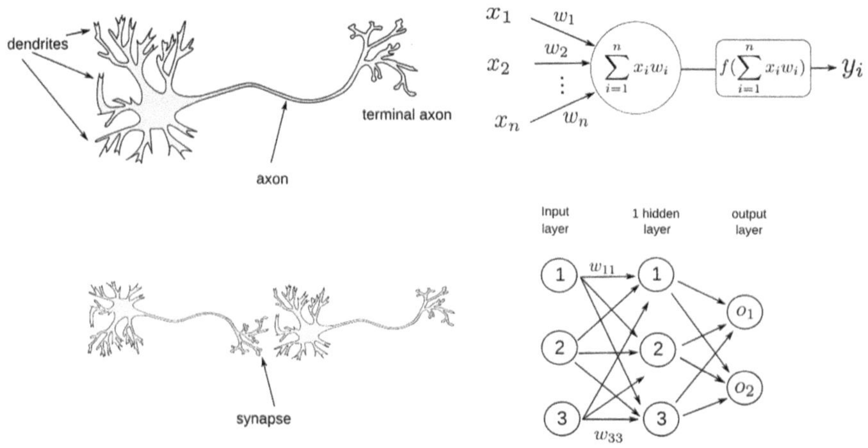

Fig. 6.10 Neural networks. Authors' own figure, partly inspired from https://commons.wikimedia.org/wiki/File%3ADerived_Neuron_schema_with_no_labels.svg

```
# Define a grid for tuning the decay parameter and the number of
↪  units in the hidden layer
nnetGrid <- expand.grid(decay = c(0, 0.01, .1), size = c(1:10))

# Determine the maximum number of units in the hidden layer from
↪  the grid
maxSize <- max(nnetGrid$size)

# Calculate the maximum number of weights for the neural network
# Formula: M(p+1)+M+1, where M is the number of hidden units, and
↪  p is the number of inputs
numWts <- maxSize * (length(dtm_train) + 1) + maxSize + 1

# Set a 10-fold cross-validation scheme (see the ensemble method)
ctrl <- trainControl(method="cv", number = 10, classProbs=TRUE,
↪  index=createFolds(dtm_train$Brand, k = 10), savePredictions =
↪  "all")

# Load the nnet package for neural network training
library(nnet)

# Set a random seed for reproducible results
set.seed(seed)

# Train the neural network model using the specified control
↪  parameters and tuning grid
NNModel <- train(Brand ~ ., data = dtm_train, method = "nnet",
↪  trace = FALSE,
                 trControl = ctrl, tuneGrid = nnetGrid, # Include
                 ↪  the tuning grid in the training process
                 na.action = na.omit, MaxNWts = numWts)
```

```
# Predict the test set using the trained neural network model
NNPredictions <- predict(NNModel, dtm_test)

# Evaluate the model's performance with a confusion matrix
confusionMatrix(NNPredictions, as.factor(dtm_test$Brand))
```

```
Confusion Matrix and Statistics

          Reference
Prediction Apple Samsung
   Apple     335      46
   Samsung    37     319

               Accuracy : 0.8874
                 95% CI : (0.8623, 0.9093)
    No Information Rate : 0.5047
    P-Value [Acc > NIR] : <2e-16

                  Kappa : 0.7747

 Mcnemar's Test P-Value : 0.3799

            Sensitivity : 0.9005
            Specificity : 0.8740
         Pos Pred Value : 0.8793
         Neg Pred Value : 0.8961
             Prevalence : 0.5047
         Detection Rate : 0.4545
   Detection Prevalence : 0.5170
      Balanced Accuracy : 0.8873

       'Positive' Class : Apple
```

The accuracy achieved with this model surpasses previous results, underscoring neural networks' potential for enhancing our ability to predict classifications. However, this improvement comes at a cost: training takes noticeably longer. The `nnet` package fits a shallow neural network (one hidden layer), so the computational burden is still moderate. Deeper architectures with many layers would require substantially more time and resources.

6.4 FastText

FastText (Bhattacharjee, 2018) is a powerful library developed by Facebook's AI research team and designed for efficient text classification and embedding words (more on this topic can be found in ▶ Chap. 10). During its training process, it stands out by using sub-word information, such as character n-grams, alongside whole words. This approach enables FastText to handle texts with rare words or misspelling effectively, capturing their meanings based on sub-word patterns. In R, the `fastTextR` package serves as an interface with this library, offering training for text classification models, generating word embedding, and conducting nearest-neighbor searches within the embedding space. FastText's efficiency is particularly notable when working with large data sets, allowing for the rapid training of models without compromising their accuracy. Another key strength of FastText is its support for multiple languages, making it an excellent tool for multilingual text analysis. FastText can be used for various natural language processing (NLP) tasks, including sentiment analysis, where it helps identify emotional tones in product reviews; language modeling, enhancing the performance of predictive-text systems; and named entity recognition, where it helps classify the names of people, organizations, and locations in unstructured text, which is an exciting feature for any marketing analyst looking for brands or brand names in text. In the following chapters, we will tackle all these topics. Meanwhile, here is an example of how FastText can be used for classification tasks using our tablet data set.

```
library(fastTextR)

set.seed(seed)

# Split data into training and testing sets
idx <- sample(seq_len(nrow(dt)), size = 0.8 * nrow(dt))
data_train <- dt[idx, ]
data_test  <- dt[-idx, ]

# Prepare training and testing data
prepare_data <- function(data, file_name) {
  labels_texts <- paste0("__label__", tolower(data$Brand), " ",
↪  tolower(data$Content))
  normalized <- ft_normalize(labels_texts)
  writeLines(normalized, con = file_name)
}

prepare_data(data_train, "tablets.train")
prepare_data(data_test,  "tablets.test")

# Set training parameters
cntrl <- ft_control(word_vec_size = 10L, learning_rate = 0.3,
↪  max_len_ngram = 2L,
                    min_count = 1L, nbuckets = 10000000L, epoch =
                    ↪  10L, nthreads = 4L)
```

```
# Train model and save
model <- ft_train(file = "tablets.train", method = "supervised",
↪ control = cntrl)
ft_save(model, "tablets.bin")

# Load model and predict
model <- ft_load("tablets.bin")
test_text  <- ft_normalize(tolower(data_test$Content))  # raw
↪ text, no labels
test_pred  <- ft_predict(model, newdata = test_text, k = 1L)

# Evaluate model
confusion_matrix <- table(Truth       = paste0("__label__",
↪ tolower(data_test$Brand)),
                          Prediction = test_pred$label)
print(confusion_matrix)
```

```
                  Prediction
Truth              __label__apple __label__samsung
  __label__apple              341               31
  __label__samsung             35              329
```

```
# Calculate and print accuracy
accuracy <- sum(diag(confusion_matrix)) / sum(confusion_matrix)
print(sprintf("Accuracy: %0.4f", accuracy))
```

```
[1] "Accuracy: 0.9103"
```

Compared to our previous results, the accuracy seems to be exceptionally high, and this shows the model's power in classifying documents quickly and efficiently.

There are other tools to classify text, such as Keras (Ramasubramanian et al., 2019). It is a comprehensive neural network library for both R and Python. It is used extensively in building and training advanced deep learning models for text classification, supporting complex architectures such as convolutional neural networks (CNNs) and recursive neural networks (RNNs), although it can also be applied to textual data.

6.5 Classification and Its Role in Marketing Analytics

Machine learning classification techniques are useful in modern marketing analytics, offering new tools to help understand and predict consumer behavior (Ali Hakami & Hosni Mahmoud, 2022). There is an abundance of textual data generated by users from reviews, social media, and surveys. Classifiers can understand patterns and trends that unveil customer preferences and perceptions of brands. Through the algorithms presented in this chapter, an analyst can categorize customer feedback, supporting customer service and product development, see Noori (2021), and also classify sentiment in reviews. This topic will be tackled in depth in ▶ Chap. 8.

For example, methods like the ones we have described in this chapter can categorize customer feedback, identifying common themes or pain points associated with a product, paving the way for binary separations into good/bad, or more nuanced understanding, such as classification using a Likert scale. Another potential application could be in classifying the feedback for new brands to understand which existing brands customers perceive as being similar.

Exercise 1. Naive Bayes brand classification. Use the tablet data set to classify brands with a naive Bayes model. Evaluate the accuracy and generate a confusion matrix.

Exercise 2. Tablet categorization with Keras. Use a Keras model to categorize tablets from their descriptions. Focus on the model architecture and the evaluation of performance.

Exercise 3. FastText vs. naive Bayes. Select a data set, classify it with FastText, and then compare its performance and training time against a naive Bayes model.

Exercise 4. SVM customer feedback categorization. Use SVM to categorize customer feedback. Preprocess the data, train the SVM, and assess the accuracy.

Exercise 5. Ensemble learning for feedback classification. Use ensemble learning to classify feedback. Experiment with different algorithms, noting the training time and accuracy.

Conclusion

This chapter has explored various facets of text classification using different machine learning models and tools such as LDA, KNN, SVM, ensemble learning techniques, and FastText, as well as a few other tools. We used these models in R, emphasizing the importance of preprocessing text, choosing the right model architecture, and evaluating the performance of the model through metrics such as accuracy, precision, recall, and the F1 score. The discussion highlighted the nuanced considerations involved in determining “good” accuracy, factoring in baseline accuracy, problem complexity, class distribution, domain-specific benchmarks, and the cost of misclassifying. Specific exercises have applied these concepts, ranging from brand classification and tablet categorization to comparing model efficiencies and execution times.

Discussion

In imbalanced data sets, which metric would you choose? The Apple vs. Samsung example reports accuracy and κ/F1. When could accuracy give misleading results? When would you prioritize per-class recall or macro-F1? Explain the business impact (e.g., false-positive vs. false-negative costs).

Some results obtained and reported in tables suggest that lemmatization can outperform stemming. Imagine an experiment which discriminates between BoW and tf-idf, or between stemming and lemmatization; define the criteria for success.

Compare linear discriminant analysis, KNN, and SVM (linear/RBF/poly) for high-dimensional DTMs for speed, interpretability, tuning, and generalization. Which baseline advance-modeling ladder would be appropriate for a different data set?

Think of a stratified k-fold CV protocol for a corpus, showing where the selection of features and scaling occur to avoid train-test problems. Why should the test set remain untouched until the end?

Choose two or three diverse base learners, such as LDA, KNN, svmLinear, and a meta-model. How would you generate out-of-fold predictions for the meta-features? How would you validate the full stack without optimistic bias?

Take Home Message

- Design a clean process: Split into train/validation/test; use k-fold CV to tune; leave the test set untouched until the final evaluation.
- Linear models (LDA, linearSVM) are strong baselines in sparse, high-dimensional text; nonlinear kernels may be helpful but require extensive tuning (C, γ, degree).
- Under class imbalance, evaluate metrics such as accuracy, precision, recall, F1, and Cohen's κ. Use a confusion matrix to make the values visible.
- Preprocessing is essential because the choice of tokenization/DTM and lemmatization vs. stemming can yield different results.
- Ensembles/stacking can result in better performance if validated properly with out-of-fold predictions and robust CV.
- In business terms, the choice of document features, metrics, and thresholds provides different actionable insights.

References

Ali Hakami, N., & Hosni Mahmoud, H. A. (2022). The prediction of consumer behavior from social media activities. *Behavioral Sciences*, *12*(8), 284. https://doi.org/10.3390/bs12080284

Anandarajan, M., Hill, C., Nolan, T., Anandarajan, M., Hill, C., & Nolan, T. (2019). Classification analysis: Machine learning applied to text. *Practical Text Analytics: Maximizing the Value of Text Data*, 131–149. https://doi.org/10.1007/978-3-319-95663-3_9

Asha, R., & KR, S. K. (2021). Credit card fraud detection using artificial neural network. *Global Transitions Proceedings*, *2*(1), 35–41. https://doi.org/10.1016/j.gltp.2021.01.006

Balakrishnama, S., & Ganapathiraju, A. (1998). Linear discriminant analysis-a brief tutorial. *Institute for Signal and Information Processing*, *18*(1998), 1–8.

Berry, M. J., & Linoff, G. S. (2009). *Data mining techniques*. John Wiley & Sons.

Bhattacharjee, J. (2018). *fastText quick start guide: Get started with facebook's library for text representation and classification*. Packt Publishing Ltd.
Bishop, C. M., & Nasrabadi, N. M. (2006). *Pattern recognition and machine learning* (Vol. 4). Springer.
Breiman, L., & Spector, P. (1992). Submodel selection and evaluation in regression. The x-random case. *International Statistical Review*, *60*(3), 291–319. https://doi.org/10.2307/1403680
Brownlee, J. (2016). *Master machine learning algorithms: Discover how they work and implement them from scratch*. Jason Brownlee.
Bult, J. R., & Wansbeek, T. (1995). Optimal selection for direct mail. *Marketing Science*, *14*(4), 378–394. https://doi.org/10.1287/mksc.14.4.378
Cawley, G. C., & Talbot, N. L. C. (2010). On over-fitting in model selection and subsequent selection bias in performance evaluation. *Journal of Machine Learning Research*, *11*, 2079–2107.
Cornell, T. (2012). *The beginnings of rome: Italy and rome from the bronze age to the punic wars (c. 1000–264 BC)*. Routledge.
Cui, D., & Curry, D. (2005). Prediction in marketing using the support vector machine. *Marketing Science*, *24*(4), 595–615. https://doi.org/10.1287/mksc.1050.0123
Forman, G., & Scholz, M. (2010). Apples-to-apples in cross-validation studies: Pitfalls in classifier performance measurement. *ACM Sigkdd Explorations Newsletter*, *12*(1), 49–57. https://doi.org/10.1145/1882471.1882479
Friedman, J. H. (1989). Regularized discriminant analysis. *Journal of the American Statistical Association*, *84*(405), 165–175. https://doi.org/10.1080/01621459.1989.10478752
Gao, Y., & Sun, S. (2010). An empirical evaluation of linear and nonlinear kernels for text classification using support vector machines. *2010 Seventh International Conference on Fuzzy Systems and Knowledge Discovery*, *4*, 1502–1505. https://doi.org/10.1109/FSKD.2010.5569327
Glare, P. G. W. (Ed.). (1982). *Oxford latin dictionary*. Oxford University Press.
Goldberg, Y. (2017). *Neural network methods in natural language processing*. Morgan & Claypool Publishers. https://doi.org/10.1007/978-3-031-02165-7
Gönöl, F. F., Kim, B.-D., & Shi, M. (2000). Mailing smarter to catalog customers. *Journal of Interactive Marketing*, *14*(2), 2–16. https://doi.org/10.1002/(SICI)1520-6653(200021)14:2%3C2::AID-DIR1%3E3.0.CO;2-N
Hastie, T., Tibshirani, R., & Buja, A. (1994). Flexible discriminant analysis by optimal scoring. *Journal of the American Statistical Association*, *89*(428), 1255–1270. https://doi.org/10.1080/01621459.1994.10476866
He, H., & Garcia, E. A. (2009). Learning from imbalanced data. *IEEE Transactions on Knowledge and Data Engineering*, *21*(9), 1263–1284. https://doi.org/10.1109/TKDE.2008.239
Joachims, T. (1998). Text categorization with support vector machines: Learning with many relevant features. *European Conference on Machine Learning*, 137–142. https://doi.org/10.1007/BFb0026683
Komarek, P. (2004). *Logistic regression for data mining and high-dimensional classification*. Carnegie Mellon University.
Koyejo, O. O., Natarajan, N., Ravikumar, P. K., & Dhillon, I. S. (2014). Consistent binary classification with generalized performance metrics. *Advances in Neural Information Processing Systems*, *27*.
Krambia-Kapardis, M., Christodoulou, C., & Agathocleous, M. (2010). Neural networks: The panacea in fraud detection? *Managerial Auditing Journal*, *25*(7), 659–678. https://doi.org/10.1108/02686901011061342
Livy. (1919). *Ab urbe condita, book 1* (B. O. Foster, Ed.). Harvard University Press.
Noori, B. (2021). Classification of customer reviews using machine learning algorithms. *Applied Artificial Intelligence*, *35*(8), 567–588. https://doi.org/10.1080/08839514.2021.1922843
Quraishi, M. I., Choudhury, J. P., & De, M. (2012). Image recognition and processing using artificial neural network. *2012 1st International Conference on Recent Advances in Information Technology (RAIT)*, 95–100. https://doi.org/10.1109/RAIT.2012.6194487
Ramasubramanian, K., Singh, A., Ramasubramanian, K., & Singh, A. (2019). Deep learning using keras and tensorflow. *Machine Learning Using R: With Time Series and Industry-Based Use Cases in R*, 667–688. https://doi.org/10.1007/978-1-4842-4215-5_11
Reutterer, T., & Dan, D. (2021). Cluster analysis in marketing research. In *Handbook of market research* (pp. 221–249). Springer. https://doi.org/10.1007/978-3-319-57413-4_11

Saito, T., & Rehmsmeier, M. (2015). The precision-recall plot is more informative than the ROC plot when evaluating binary classifiers on imbalanced datasets. *PLOS ONE, 10*(3), e0118432. https://doi.org/10.1371/journal.pone.0118432

Schölkopf, B., & Smola, A. J. (2002). *Learning with kernels: Support vector machines, regularization, optimization, and beyond.* MIT press.

Schütze, H., Manning, C. D., & Raghavan, P. (2008). *Introduction to information retrieval* (Vol. 39). Cambridge University Press Cambridge.

Sebastiani, F. (2002). Machine learning in automated text categorization. *ACM Computing Surveys (CSUR)*, *34*(1), 1–47. https://doi.org/10.1145/505282.505283

Tan, S. (2006). An effective refinement strategy for KNN text classifier. *Expert Systems with Applications*, *30*(2), 290–298. https://doi.org/10.1016/j.eswa.2005.07.019

Tattar, P. N. (2018). *Hands-on ensemble learning with R: A beginner's guide to combining the power of machine learning algorithms using ensemble techniques*. Packt Publishing Ltd.

Tharwat, A. (2016). Linear vs. Quadratic discriminant analysis classifier: A tutorial. *International Journal of Applied Pattern Recognition*, *3*(2), 145–180. https://doi.org/10.1504/IJAPR.2016.079050

Torkkola, K. (2001). Linear discriminant analysis in document classification. *IEEE ICDM Workshop on Text Mining*, 800–806.

Wang, J., Yang, Y., & Xia, B. (2019). A simplified cohen's kappa for use in binary classification data annotation tasks. *IEEE Access*, *7*, 164386–164397. https://doi.org/10.1109/ACCESS.2019.2953104

Wedel, M., & Kamakura, W. A. (2000). *Market segmentation: Conceptual and methodological foundations*. Springer Science & Business Media. https://doi.org/10.1007/978-1-4615-4651-1

Yen, C.-T., & Tsao, C.-Y. (2024). Lightweight convolutional neural network for chest x-ray images classification. *Scientific Reports*, *14*(1), 29759. https://doi.org/10.1038/s41598-024-80826-z

6

Topic Modeling for Marketing Insights, Latent Dirichlet Allocation, and Structural Topic Models

D. Dan, T. Reutterer, *Text Analytics in Marketing*, Classroom Companion: Business,
https://doi.org/10.1007/978-3-032-08086-8_7

Keywords
Topic modeling · Latent Dirichlet allocation · LDAvis · Seeded LDA · Sentence-based LDA · STM · LDA tuning

This chapter introduces topic modeling as a way to gain insights into marketing. It shows the intuition behind latent Dirichlet allocation (LDA) and its generative process, followed by an explanation of how to make inferences from LDA using collapsed Gibbs sampling. To clarify the procedure, we provide a step-by-step example, as well as a practical implementation of LDA in R, including dictionary-driven seeded LDA and "residual" topics. The principle is extended to sentence-level and sequential LDA to capture continuity within reviews. Tools for visualization and interpretation are provided, including tables of top terms and an interactive walk-through of the topic structure using `LDAvis`. We also introduce structural topic models, allowing us to link topics to document metadata. Topical prevalence and topical content are estimated, and then brands are compared over time, allowing for variation in topic proportions. Recommendations are provided to help determine the optimal number of topics, considering coherence/exclusivity, held-out likelihood, residuals, and upper/lower bounds. In the examples, themes related to product features, customer service, gifting "holiday" seasonality, and brand positioning reveal how data can help marketing decisions.

Learning Objectives

- Understanding what a topic model is.
- Understanding the workings of latent Dirichlet allocation topic modeling.
- Learning how to apply LDA topic modeling.
- Understanding what a structural topic model is.
- Extracting information from structural topic models.

7.1 Identifying Latent Themes in Text Data

According to the Oxford Dictionary, a topic is "a subject that you talk, write, or learn about". Or in other terms, it can be understood as a theme. For instance, a newspaper may cover several topics, such as politics, crime, lifestyle, the economy, and sport. Each of these topics is characterized by (combinations of) specific words, something that readers recognize intuitively. For our tablet data set and marketing, topics could be the characteristics of certain products, comparisons of brands, and evaluations of and sentiments about products and services (such as value for money, product quality, or customer service), to name but a few.

But what exactly constitutes a model? Depending on the field, it could refer to many elements of an area of research; however, the idea of a model for marketing is linked with disciplines such as data science and statistics. The latter deals with data-driven models such as linear regression, which summarizes or describes data sets, ultimately aiming to predict new data points. Statistical models try to explain an idealized and simplified reality through mathematics (Micceri, 1989). In statistics, mathematical formulas can be represented by beautiful graphs and curves that are extremely precise, but real data do not correspond to those shapes. Complex realities are thus transformed into idealized, simplified mathematical representations. Perfect straight lines or circles will never describe real data exactly; these shapes do not exist in the real world. However, the closer the representations are to a mathematical model, the better we can compare different data sets. We do this because we need to establish benchmarks for comparison. Comparison is not just a theoretical exercise but a practical tool enabling decision-making, helping marketers to evaluate strategies, forecast trends, and understand customer behaviors more effectively.

The generic and somewhat pompous definition of topic modeling is that it is an unsupervised statistical model used in text analytics which clusters words into topics without predefined classes, revealing latent themes within large text corpora.

> *Topic modeling* comprises a group of models which are unsupervised and identify regularly appearing themes (topics) from the patterns of word use within a corpus. Each document is a combination of topics, and each topic is represented by a distribution of words, allowing for the broader investigation of themes without labels.

This technique is essential for analyzing customer reviews or social media discourse, helping us to detect trends, sentiments, and emerging issues without reviewing each document manually. Typical applications in marketing include the analysis of social media posts or online product reviews (e.g., Tirunillai & Tellis, 2014, Büschken & Allenby, 2016), but also purchasing histories (e.g., Jacobs et al., 2016) or online browsing (e.g., Schröder et al., 2019; Trusov et al., 2016). For an extensive overview of the application of topic modeling in marketing, see Reisenbichler and Reutterer (2019). From a practical perspective, topic modeling can inform marketing strategies by identifying the focus of customers, such as the features of products or service quality. For instance, in a data set of online hotel reviews, topics such as "cleanliness" or "service" can be found and further analyzed for sentiment, frequency, and trends over time, providing insights to help address the concerns of customers. Determining the optimal number of topics k is a critical step in topic modeling. It is often approached using educated guesses informed by existing knowledge or systematic methods like coherence scores. Choosing the right k, alongside the interpretation of the words that characterize topics, should, if the practitioners are skilled enough, lead to a blend of art and science.

Some commonly used topic-modeling techniques in marketing are the latent Dirichlet allocation (LDA; D. M. Blei et al., 2003), structural topic model (STM; Roberts et al., 2014, 2016), correlated topic modeling (CTM; D. Blei & Lafferty, 2006), nonnegative matrix factorization (NMF; D. Lee & Seung, 2000), latent semantic analysis (LSA; Landauer et al., 1998), or dynamic topic models (DTM; D. M. Blei & Lafferty, 2006). For a more complete list, see Jelodar et al. (2019), but in this chapter, we will focus on topic modeling using LDA and STM.

7.2 Latent Dirichlet Allocation

One of the most studied topic modeling algorithms is the LDA. The algorithm aggregates words into topics based on their distribution across documents, uncovering the "hidden" topics that characterize the corpus. In practice, we have a set of documents which contain topics characterized by specific words. The topic exists at a conceptual level, like a # (hashtag) (e.g., #screenquality) which describes the theme of a tweet or an Instagram image. The intuition behind LDA as a generative model is that writing a document or a review of a product is driven by themes someone wants to share and adds them to the document. In our data set concerning tablets, one obvious topic might be that of the characteristics of a device, for example, the screen. Is it bright? Is it responsive? Or we might consider the connectivity. Is it fast? 5G, Bluetooth or Wi-Fi? Screen and connectivity are themes or topics. These are identified by words that are specific to the topic, but also by words which are shared by multiple topics. In a review, as in any written document, some themes will be more prevalent than others. If the customer service fell short of a person's expectations, the theme will emerge. And the words which characterize it would be more prevalent for this than for other topics. Let us consider a review which talks about *connectivity* (in 15% of the words contained in the document), about the *screen* (25%), *customer service* (50%), and *value for money* (10%); see ◘ Fig. 7.1. If we represent this as a probability distribution over the review, it looks like a vector [0.15, 0.25, 0.50, 0.1]. Note that the sum of the topics must be 1.

> *Latent Dirichlet allocation (LDA)* is a generative topic model in which a document is represented as a probability distribution of topics, and each topic is represented as a probability distribution of words. The Dirichlet priors shape these distributions and encourage interpretable topics. This algorithm is especially popular in marketing for corpora of reviews or other similar texts.

Each review has a unique distribution of topics, but this is not all. Each topic is characterized by words; for example, customer service contains words with the following proportions: bad (0.03), back (0.02), never (0.015), and so on. Each of these words in the vocabulary, i.e., the whole words used in the tablet-review corpus, is distributed with a relative frequency over that topic [..., 0.02, ..., 0.03, ..., 0.015,

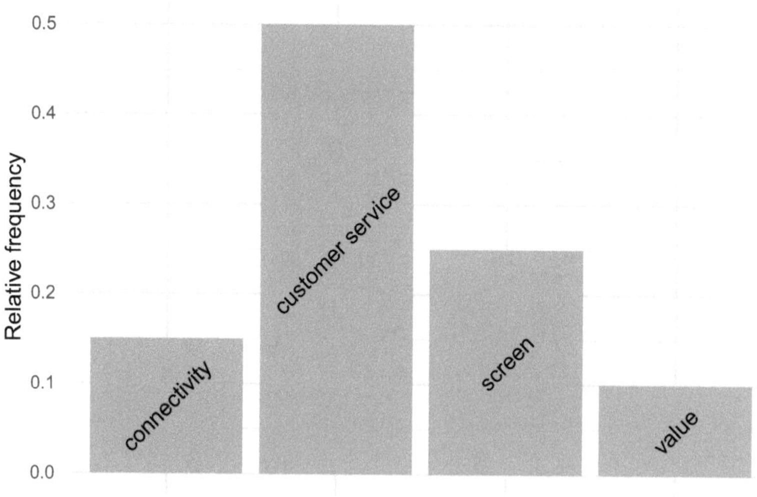

Fig. 7.1 Topic distribution for a single review. Authors' own figure

…]. This proportion is the same within the scope of that topic, no matter which review you take from the corpus. So, there are two distributions: a mixture of topics from documents and a mixture of words from topics. Because these are all probabilities, we have a probabilistic model here. The single vectors described in previous chapters are characteristic of a multinomial distribution, but a conjugate prior distribution over a multinomial distribution is characteristic of the Dirichlet distribution, hence the name of the algorithm.

To summarize, the LDA model is based on two assumptions: K hidden topics are distributed across the entire collection of reviews, and each review can be represented as a probabilistic distribution of these topics. Each topic is, in turn, a probabilistic distribution of words from the data set's vocabulary.

Let us demystify this algorithm further and understand how it functions. To see how LDA is implemented, look at Fig. 7.2 (figure produced by the authors, inspired by D. M. Blei et al., 2003).

Let us define the terms that appear in the image, and then detail how the algorithm works.

M is the fixed total number of documents. In a specific corpus D, documents are indexed by $i \in \{1, ..., M\}$

N is the number of words in a given document i. N_i represents how many words document i holds, i.e., it is the length of the document.

α is the (hyper)parameter of the Dirichlet prior to the distribution of topics by document. This describes how topics are distributed in each document.

β is the (hyper)parameter of the Dirichlet prior to the word distribution by topic. This describes how words are distributed inside each topic.

θ_i is the topic distribution for document i, modeled as a random variable characterized by a Dirichlet distribution $\theta_i \sim \mathcal{D}(\alpha)$.

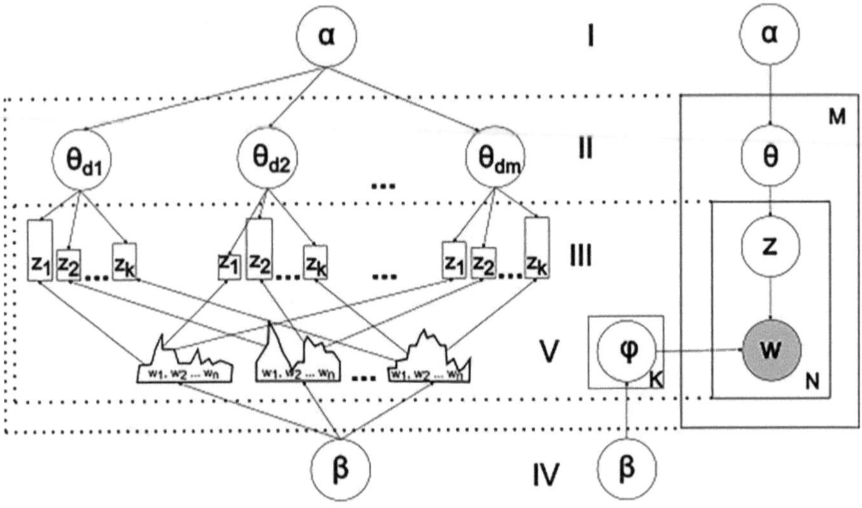

7

Fig. 7.2 Latent Dirichlet allocation. Based on "Smoothed LDA.png" (Wikimedia Commons, CC BY-SA 3.0); see Credits for details

ϕ_k is the word distribution for topic k, where $k \in \{1, ..., K\}$, modeled as a random variable characterized by a Dirichlet distribution $\phi_k \sim \mathcal{D}(\beta)$

z_{ij} is the topic for the jth word in the ith document. The topic is $z_{i,j} \sim Multinomial(\theta_i)$.

w_{ij} is a specific word, j, in document i. The words are $w_{i,j} \sim Multinomial(\phi_{z_{i,j}})$

A multinomial distribution with one trial is known as a categorical distribution.

The algorithm has a two-step process. The first part is called the generative model (GM), which describes how documents are created from a set of latent topics. The second step is called the inference or estimation procedure (EP) and involves estimating the parameters of the GM, for example, the topic distributions for each document and the word distributions for each topic from the documents. It is through this that we "learn" the hidden structure of the topic.

The first step describes how LDA assumes the data are generated and consist of five layers. In layer I in Fig. 7.2, a Dirichlet distribution characterized by parameter α is used to create the distribution of topics over each document. If $\alpha < 1$, each document will tend to contain a few dominant topics (i.e., the distribution is sparse). If $\alpha > 1$, the document will tend to contain topics which are distributed more evenly (Hagg et al., 2022). In layer II, parameter θ of a multinomial distribution determines the shape of the distribution of topics over each document. In other words, α shapes the multinomial θ, so each θ_d will be different from document to document, as shown in layer III. In IV, we have another Dirichlet distribution with parameter β, this time for all the words of the vocabulary. If $\beta < 1$, a topic will tend to be dominated by a smaller set of characteristic words. Starting with the first word of the first document to the last word in the last document, the algorithm will randomly conceptually "assign" each word to a topic, based on θ_d. In layer V, the topic's word distribution ϕ_k is shared across documents, but be aware that each document's topic mixture θ_d is different. Because each topic k has a separate ϕ_k, it defines its own "theme," characterized by specific words.

The second step (EP) uses methods such as collapsed Gibbs sampling (our focus here) or variational inference (VI) to estimate θ_d for each topic from the corpus. We do not know the true value of these parameters, and we can only observe the words in each document, but we aim to infer the latent topic assignments and distributions. In Gibbs sampling, each word's topic assignment is resampled, based on the current assignment of all the other words, until a stable words-over-topics posterior distribution is reached. Over many repetitions, the estimates for ϕ_k and θ_d converge to reach a stable state. In this context, "converge" means that the model parameters (ϕ_k and θ_d) reach a point where their distribution stops changing significantly. When Gibbs converges, we have an estimate for each document's mix of topics θ_d and how the words are distributed within each topic ϕ_k.

It is important to use a practical example to understand the underlying mechanism of Gibbs sampling: Once we have looked at that, we will provide the mathematical formulas. Let us use a simplified corpus made up of four documents that resemble the data set in this book:

Doc_1: This tablet has a bright screen.

Doc_2: The RAM memory of the tablet is sufficient.

Doc_3: The tablet connects to Wi-Fi.

Doc_4: The tablet connects to Wi-Fi and has a superb screen.

To further simplify this, we assume we have only two topics, T_1 and T_2, which represent two themes, "hardware" for T_1 and "connectivity" for T_2. LDA (D. M. Blei et al., 2003) does not assign labels to topics and gives them only generic names such as $Topic_1$, $Topic_2$, and so on. We have to figure out the topic name based on the words assigned to it. Whenever we apply LDA, we must preprocess the data set, as we did in the previous chapters for the bag-of-words (BoW) approach, such as removing punctuation and stop words or making all words lowercase. This way, our vocabulary, in alphabetical order, becomes {bright, connects, memory, screen, sufficient, superb, tablet, wi-fi}. Initially, LDA assigns the words *randomly* to one of the two topics.

Doc_1: tablet(T_1), bright (T_1), screen(T_2)

Doc_2: tablet(T_2), memory(T_1), sufficient(T_2)

Doc_3: tablet(T_1), connects(T_2), wi-fi(T_1)

Doc_4: tablet(T_2), connects(T_1), wi-fi(T_2), superb(T_1), screen(T_2)

Based on these, we can create a table to count the number of occurrences of each word in each topic (Heinrich, 2005); see ◘ Table 7.1.

Now we need a document-topic contingency table (◘ Table 7.2), showing the number of words in each topic assigned to each document.

We need to count the words in each topic.

T_1: tablet (2) + bright (1) + memory (1) + connects (1) + wi-fi (1) + superb (1) = seven words

Table 7.1 Term-topic matrix. Table compiled by the authors

Term	T1	T2
tablet	2	2
bright	1	0
screen	0	2
memory	1	0
sufficient	0	1
connects	1	1
wi-fi	1	1
superb	1	0

7

Table 7.2 Document-topic matrix. Table compiled by the authors

Doc	T1	T2
1	2	1
2	1	2
3	2	1
4	2	3

T_2: tablet (2) + screen (2) + sufficient (1) + connects (1) + wi-fi (1) = seven words

The vocabulary size V is made up of eight terms: tablet, bright, screen, memory, sufficient, connects, wi-fi, superb.

Now we have arrived at the second step of the algorithm. Following the initial random assignment, Gibbs sampling is now used to reassign the words to the existing topics until we obtain convergence, i.e., until the algorithm does not reassign these words to topics anymore. Let us update the topic assignment for the term "screen," which was initially assigned to Document 1. We must (temporarily) remove one instance of "screen" from its current assignment T_2, adjust the counts, and calculate the conditional probability for each topic. The adjusted count for T_1 is unchanged; it holds seven terms, while the adjusted count for T_2 holds six terms. You will see a (– 1) in the formula. The result is that we have temporarily removed a term which needs to be freshly assigned to a topic.

In collapsed Gibbs sampling, the conditional probability of assigning the current word token w to topic k is (Griffiths & Steyvers, 2004; Heinrich, 2005; Steyvers & Griffiths, 2007):

$$P(T_k|w_d) \propto \left(\frac{n_{k,w} + \beta}{\sum_{w'} n_{k,w'} + V\beta}\right) \times \left(\frac{n_{d,k} + \alpha}{\sum_{k'} n_{d,k'} + K\alpha}\right)$$

where

- $n_{k,w}$ is the count of word w assigned to topic k, excluding the current instance.
- $n_{d,k}$ is the count of all words in document d assigned to topic k, excluding the current instance.
- $\sum_{w'} n_{k,w'} + V\beta$: total words in topic k plus $\beta\times$ vocabulary size.
- $\sum_{k'} n_{d,k'} + K\alpha$: total words in document d plus $\alpha\times$ number of topics.
- V is the vocabulary size.
- K is the number of topics.

Be aware that this formula may appear in other books or articles in a different but similar form (Wallach et al., 2009), each of them after a similar outcome.

Assuming hyperparameters $\alpha = 0.1$ (for document-topic distributions) and (Asuncion et al., 2012) $\beta = 0.01$ (for topic-term distributions), we can calculate the probability of the term "screen" to see if it belongs to T_1 or to T_2.

$P(T_1|\text{screen})$ is proportional to:

Term-topic:

$$\frac{(n_{T_1,\text{screen}} + \beta)}{\text{Total words in} T_1 + V \times \beta} = \frac{0 + 0.01}{7 + 8 \times 0.01}$$

Document-topic:

$$\frac{(n_{Doc_1,T_1} + \alpha)}{\text{Total words in } Doc_1 + 2 \times \alpha} = \frac{2 + 0.1}{3 + 2 \times 0.1}$$

Combined probability for T_1 proportional to: $\frac{0.01}{7.08} \times \frac{2.1}{3.2} = 0.001608$

$P(T_2|\text{screen})$ is proportional to:

Term-Topic:

$$\frac{(n_{T_2,\text{screen}} - 1 + \beta)}{\text{Total words in } T_2 - 1 + V \times \beta} = \frac{1 + 0.01}{6 + 8 \times 0.01}$$

Document-Topic:

$$\frac{(n_{Doc_1,T_2} - 1) + \alpha}{(\text{Total words in } Doc_1 - 1) + 2 \times \alpha} = \frac{0 + 0.1}{2 + 2 \times 0.1}$$

Combined probability for T_2 proportional to: $\frac{1.01}{6.08} \times \frac{0.1}{2.2} = 0.00754$

After the calculations, we need to compare the results and check where "screen" is most likely to belong. We notice that "screen" has a higher chance of being assigned to T_2, because $0.00754 > 0.001608$, but the final outcome depends on the many iterations assigning and reassigning the word to a topic. This is done for each word in each document. In the end, what changes from the initial random assignment of words to topics is the distribution of words depicted in layer IV. The shapes you see in ◘ Fig. 7.2 will change. This example has simplified many of the steps, but it shows the core process of LDA using Gibbs sampling.

7.2.1 Applying Simple LDA

To put into practice what has been illustrated, we will use our tablet data set and apply simple LDA with the default values, so no fine-tuning will be required, at least at the beginning. For this example, although there are many R packages which carry out LDA, we will be using `seededlda` (Watanabe et al., 2022). We will show later on why the package has this name and why we have chosen it. Although the computer we used for running the code is capable of multi-threading, for reproducibility reasons, we have to use a single thread. This is because the `set.seed()`, at least while working with this package, can only ensure reproducibility for random functions when operating with one thread. If you use multi-threading, the results may vary slightly across runs despite `set.seed()`. The data set is the one we have already used in previous chapters of this book. The data preprocessing was performed according to the package's specifications.

7

At this point, we are trying to find five topics ($k = 5$) and display the most frequent terms associated with each topic. Previously, we have seen how each topic is described by a word distribution, ϕ_k, and each document is characterized by a topic distribution, θ_d. To help us interpret the results, here we show only the top ten words in each ϕ_k, but bear in mind that each topic has probabilities for every term in the vocabulary.

```
# Fit an LDA model to the DFM with 5 topics
set.seed(42)
tlda <- textmodel_lda(dfmt, k = 5, verbose = FALSE)
# Display terms associated with each topic
seededlda::terms(tlda, n=10)
```

```
      topic1        topic2     topic3      topic4
    ↪   topic5
 [1,] "apple"       "browser" "usb"       "christmas"
 ↪   "support"
 [2,] "tab"         "button"  "keyboard" "watch"
 ↪   "service"
 [3,] "xoom"        "access"  "card"      "book"
 ↪   "customer"
 [4,] "galaxy"      "book"    "sd"        "old"
 ↪   "days"
 [5,] "samsung"     "page"    "asus"      "perfect"
 ↪   "unit"
 [6,] "flash"      "reader"  "archos"    "laptop"
 ↪   "return"
 [7,] "people"      "content" "windows"   "happy"
 ↪   "tried"
```

```
 [8,] "os"          "cloud"    "memory"   "prime"
  ↪   "received"
 [9,] "experience" "store"    "google"   "gift"
  ↪   "update"
[10,] "iphone"      "volume"   "flash"    "year"
 ↪    "problems"
```

The words might give us some indication of the interpretation of the topics. For example, `topic 4` is related to Christmas gifts and `topic 5` to customer service, and so it can be labeled by us as `gifts` and `customer_service`. We can check and see with which document, represented by a title and a date, a topic is associated. By examining θ_d, we know how topics are distributed over each document. However, the top words give us a hint of how to label and interpret each topic based on the ϕ_k values.

> *Topic-word distribution* (ϕ) is a probability vector over the vocabulary for each topic k. The terms which are assigned a high probability are the most important words that define and help you interpret the topics (e.g., screen, display, resolution for a topic dealing with computer hardware).

```
# Extract document-level variables from the LDA model's data
dat <- docvars(tlda$data)
# Assign the most probable topic to each document based on the LDA
 ↪  model
dat$topic <- seededlda::topics(tlda)
# Display the first 10 rows of some selected columns
head(dat[,c("Review_date", "topic", "Title")], 10)
```

```
   Review_date  topic         Title
1     1/8/2012 topic1         Love My Kindle Fire!
2    4/10/2012 topic5         Not the best Tablet or a
 ↪  good buy
3    3/26/2012 topic2         Had it 3 months, would not
 ↪  purchase again
4    6/14/2012 topic4 College Grad - I use it waaaay more
 ↪  than my lap top!
5    5/21/2011 topic4         Better than I expected.
6    1/29/2010 topic5         Pick a different computer
7   11/26/2011 topic3         Great for travel and general
 ↪  use
8     5/6/2012 topic1         Highly Underestimated Tablet
9    6/29/2011 topic1         Lenovo ThinkPad X220 Tablet
10   6/21/2011 topic4         A little disappointment
```

In the output above, a row corresponds to a document (i.e., a review), the `Topic` column shows the most probable topic assigned to that document. The other two columns, `Review_date` and `Title`, help us identify documents, and we can check how the model has clustered them by topic. We know that each document has the topic distribution θ_d, but for clarity, we display only the topic with the highest probability.

> *Document-topic distribution* (θ) is a probability vector over topics for a document; by tuning the model, the analyst has a valid tool for comparing documents to segment customers (e.g., reader vs. buyer), or track topical prevalence over time (e.g., lookback).

7

It is possible to increase and decrease the number of topics to understand better which themes can be found in the text. To speed up the execution time, one can parallelize `seededlda` by adding a `batch_size` option and enable convergence `auto_iter=TRUE`, for example, `textmodel_lda(dfmt, k = 5, batch_size = 0.01, auto_iter = TRUE)`.

7.2.2 Seeded LDA

Let us assume that you, as an analyst, already know the topics (e.g., from a previous study on a different, but related corpus of text), but you want LDA to group the words in the topics with increased precision. Seeded LDA allows for semi-supervised topic modeling, acknowledging that you might have prior knowledge of your data set and you can provide a dictionary that links words to topics which have already been labeled. These "seeded" words provide a starting point for the algorithm, meaning that the random assignment, as in the first step of the LDA above, becomes "informed" by the dictionary. In order to perform this, we need a dictionary function and an `yml` file to store the information. Each line defines a topic's label, such as "hardware" or "functionality," and associates it with a list of "seed words" which are strongly related to that topic. The structure of the file, `dictionary.yml`, looks like this.

hardware: [ram, gb, storage, slot, external, camera, power, wi-fi, battery, button]
functionality: [video*, games, *books, email, social, media, reader, browser]
customer_service: [service, support, customer, return]
names: [amazon, apple, ipad, xoom, samsung, galaxy, google]
experience: [screen*, display, resolution, glass*, touch, thin, light]

where the * represents a placeholder that captures plurals or other inflectional forms. For example, video* could match video or videos, and *books can capture terms like books, songbooks, or notebooks.

> *Seeded LDA* is a semi-supervised variant (of LDA) which uses a dictionary of seed words (one list for each topic) to initialize topics. This facilitates the early assignment of words to user-specified topics and anchors the model within domain knowledge. It also allows for the discovery of additional words and (potentially) the identification of residual topics which were not identified through the seeding process.

When we employ seeded LDA, the algorithm uses the seeded words to initialize (guide) the assignments so that the model places them (and similar words) in the right topic. Compared to the LDA described above, the random-assignment step is replaced with an "informed" assignment based on domain knowledge.

```
library(seededlda)
# Create the dict variable containing the seeded words
dict <- dictionary(file = "data/dictionary.yml")

# Fit a seeded LDA model to the DFM with 5 topics
set.seed(42)
# Add auto_iter = TRUE for faster convergence
lda_seed <- textmodel_seededlda(dfmt, dict, auto_iter = TRUE)

# Display terms associated with each topic
terms(lda_seed, n = 10)
```

```
     hardware   functionality customer_service names
      ↪   experience
[1,] "camera"   "email"       "support"          "apple"
↪   "display"
[2,] "power"    "browser"     "service"          "google"
↪   "light"
[3,] "button"   "videos"      "customer"         "samsung"
↪   "christmas"
[4,] "usb"      "reader"      "return"           "galaxy"
↪   "resolution"
[5,] "storage"  "media"       "days"             "xoom"
↪   "old"
[6,] "keyboard" "access"      "unit"             "tab"
↪   "laptop"
[7,] "card"     "content"     "tried"            "os"
↪   "happy"
[8,] "sd"       "book"        "update"           "asus"
↪   "perfect"
```

```
 [9,] "slot"      "store"          "problems"          "flash"
  ↪  "book"
[10,] "windows"   "cloud"          "received"
 ↪  "transformer" "watch"
```

Notice that all the topic labels are described nicely by the seeded words, grouping other pertinent words to those topics. We might notice that some words in the dictionary file do not appear as the top words in the results. This might be because those words, although they belong to that topic, might not be so prevalent in the corpus. You can list more than ten terms using the function `terms(lda_seed, 20)`, for example. Let us assume that you are aware that the five topics above are represented in your data set (e.g., based on previous studies or observations of other review data), but you have a hunch that there may be more topics that might be useful. In this case, you can use seeded LDA with residual topics, which is a combination of both the seeded and unseeded options. We demonstrate this below.

```
# Fit a seeded LDA model to the DFM with 7 topics
set.seed(42)
# Add auto_iter = TRUE for faster convergence
lda_res <- textmodel_seededlda(dfmt, dict, residual = 2, auto_iter
 ↪  = TRUE)
# Display terms associated with each topic
terms(lda_res)
```

```
      hardware   functionality customer_service names
       ↪  experience
 [1,] "camera"    "email"          "support"           "apple"
  ↪  "display"
 [2,] "power"     "browser"        "service"           "google"
  ↪  "light"
 [3,] "button"    "videos"         "customer"          "samsung"
  ↪  "resolution"
 [4,] "usb"       "reader"         "return"            "galaxy"
  ↪  "keyboard"
 [5,] "storage"   "media"          "unit"              "xoom"
  ↪  "bit"
 [6,] "card"      "access"         "days"              "tab"
  ↪  "hold"
 [7,] "sd"        "content"        "update"            "os"
  ↪  "volume"
 [8,] "slot"      "store"          "tried"             "asus"
  ↪  "though"
```

```
 [9,] "keyboard" "book"          "received"
  ↪  "transformer" "pretty"
[10,] "windows"  "cloud"         "problems"         "flash"
 ↪   "screens"
      other1     other2
 [1,] "people"   "christmas"
 [2,] "anything" "book"
 [3,] "slow"     "perfect"
 [4,] "card"     "laptop"
 [5,] "reviews"  "happy"
 [6,] "bad"      "old"
 [7,] "store"    "gift"
 [8,] "worth"    "wife"
 [9,] "cheap"    "prime"
[10,] "give"     "year"
```

Note that the two extra detected topics, called `other1` and `other2`, represent new information. The first one seems to refer to tablets as gifts for Christmas, and the second seems to be a comparison between tablets and laptops or computers. From a marketing point of view, the appearance of `other1` might be interesting for understanding when (and where) such a product can be advertised, and the other topic reveals competition with other categories of product.

7.2.3 Applying Sequential Sentence-Based LDA with Seeded Words

Sentence-based LDA (see, e.g., Büschken & Allenby, 2016) is an interesting way to tokenize a corpus into documents as sentences. In this, each sentence in a review represents a document. Several studies have pointed out that when people leave a review, topics are expressed in sentences, rarely with two or more topics in a single sentence. Achieving this is solved using the `corpus_reshape()` function. In this case, we will consider the corpus as a merged list of sentences. Let us apply sequential LDA and check the results. The result of the document-feature matrix (DFM), which is the equivalent of the document-term matrix, will show as many documents as the number of sentences (i.e., documents), and the sparsity of such a matrix is very high. Use `print(dfmt)` to print it out. The sequential LDA algorithm incorporates the topics discovered for the previous sentence when modeling the next one, effectively acknowledging that neighboring sentences in a review often share related subjects. The previous sentence does not force a topic into the following one, but influences the model's estimation of whether it belongs there. In this case, each sentence's topic distribution is "guided" but not determined by the preceding one, showing a bias toward continuity.

```
library(seededlda)
library(quanteda)

# Prepare the corpus
corp <- corpus(prodreviews, text_field ="Content") |>
    corpus_reshape(to = "sentences")

# Tokenize and create the dfmt
toks <- quanteda::tokens(corp, remove_punct = TRUE, remove_symbols
↪ = TRUE,  remove_numbers = TRUE, remove_url = TRUE)

dfmts <- dfm(toks) |>
    dfm_remove(stopwords("en")) |>
    dfm_remove("*@*") |>
    dfm_trim(max_docfreq = 0.1, docfreq_type = "prop")

# Enable the sequential algorithm, set gamma to 0.5
# A lower value of gamma would impact the classification of the
↪ current sentence
lda_seq <- textmodel_lda(dfmts, k = 5, gamma = 0.5,
                         batch_size = 0.01, auto_iter = TRUE,
                         verbose = FALSE)
print(lda_seq)
```

```
Call:
textmodel_lda(x = dfmts, k = 5, auto_iter = TRUE, gamma =
↪  0.5,
    batch_size = 0.01, verbose = FALSE)

5 topics; 442,621 documents; 60,203 features.
```

After running the `textmodel_lda()` function, we obtain the topics which are displayed in ◘ Table 7.3. Each column represents the words that the model thinks are most characteristic of that topic. By examining these terms, we can analyze, sentence by sentence, which concept each topic encapsulates.

7.2.4 Visualizing LDA Topics

Topics, and how they are related to each other, can be visualized with the use of the `LDAvis` package (Sievert & Shirley, 2014). This R package is an interactive Web-based tool designed for visualizing the output of LDA topic models. The plots show the relationships between topics and emphasize the importance of each topic and the top terms associated with each topic. The tool is mostly self-explanatory and helps us interpret the results.

Table 7.3 Top terms for each topic (sentence-based LDA). Table compiled by the authors

topic1	topic2	topic3	topic4	topic5
screen	kindle	tablet	tablet	apps
just	fire	one	screen	android
device	books	ipad	can	app
get	love	product	use	tablet
button	amazon	get	ipad	can
touch	can	just	like	use
one	read	amazon	good	device
can	use	first	battery	like
like	great	now	great	market
user	reading	android	usb	great

```
library(LDAvis)
library(topicmodels)

# Coerce to base matrices
phi   <- as.matrix(lda_seq$phi)    # K x V  topic-term probs
theta <- as.matrix(lda_seq$theta)  # D x K  doc-topic probs

# Find required quantities
json <- createJSON(phi = phi,
                   theta = theta,
                   doc.length = rowSums(dfmt),
                   vocab = colnames(dfmt),
                   term.frequency = colSums(dfmt)
)

serVis(json)
```

Figure 7.3 is a static visualization of the topics generated using LDA. On the left-hand side, we can see a map displaying the distances between topics. These can be interpreted as their degree of similarity. When topics are close to each other or overlapping, they share more terms. The map is generated using multidimensional scaling, a technique which projects high-dimensional data into a two-dimensional plane while preserving distances between pairs as much as possible. Each of the five topics is represented by a circle (the marginal topic distribution) whose size is proportional to the prevalence of the topic in the data set. We can see that the sizes are similar. The navigation between topics to get more detail can be done through the controls such as "Selected Topic," while "Top-30 Most Salient Terms" ranks the

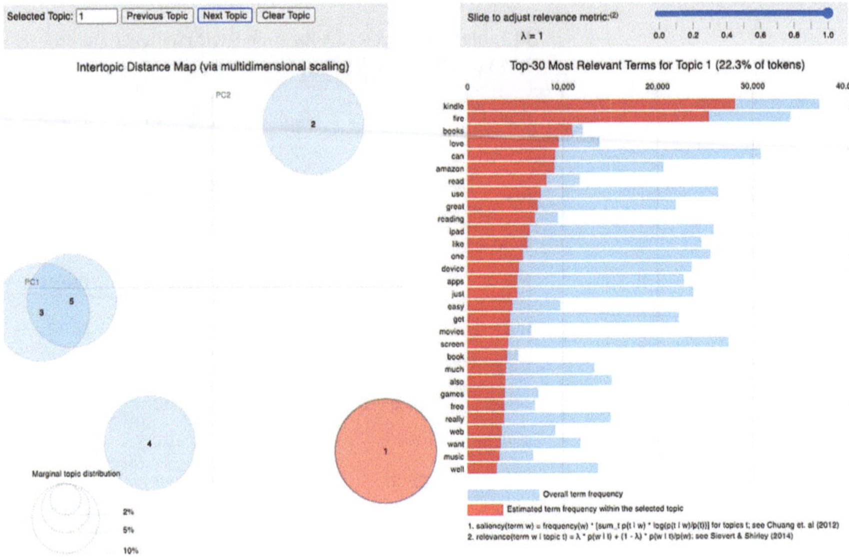

Fig. 7.3 `LDAvis`. Authors' own figure

words based on a combination of their frequency and relevance to the topic. The latter can be adjusted through the parameter λ, which controls the balance between the relevance and exclusivity of terms. When $\lambda = 0$, the focus is on the terms which are unique to the topic, showing their exclusivity, while when $\lambda = 1$, the ranking unveils the most frequent terms within the topic, even if they are common across the whole corpus. λ allows to us to see the space between the specificity and generality of the terms. It gives the ratio between the probability of a term occurring within a topic and its marginal probability across the corpus. The visual representation allows us to see which terms are combined with which topics quickly.

7.3 Structural Topic Models

A structural topic model (STM; Roberts et al., 2013, 2014) was created with existing topic models in mind (i.e., LDA; D. M. Blei et al., 2003) and correlated topic modeling (CTM; D. M. Blei & Lafferty, 2007). While LDA assumes that topics are independent, CTM relaxes this assumption by allowing topics to be correlated. This approach can be suitable for the cases where certain topics have the tendency to occur at the same time. STM complements this by allowing users to add extra information about each document, known as metadata addition, about each document to be analyzed within the topic modeling framework. This procedure helps marketers discover topics and link them to covariates represented by the related document metadata, because topical prevalence and topical content can be a function of these (Roberts et al., 2019). Technically, metadata which influence the popularity of topics are referred to as topical prevalence covariates, and variables (words) which define the themes of topics are called topical content covariates.

> *A structural topic model (STM)* is an extension of regular topic models. It incorporates document-level covariates into the topic model. Topical prevalence (how much a topic appears) can be affected by covariates. Topical content (which words constitute a topic) helps us investigate effects such as brand or time in reviews.

In this section, we will use the R `stm` package (Roberts et al., 2019) and its functions for textual data and their associated metadata. In our case, this can be the review, as the text, the associated brand, the review's date, and its rating are metadata. We can use the `quanteda` package to import the text and metadata, and then preprocess and transform the document into a document-term matrix. From the `prodreviews` variable, which contains the data set, we can select the Content, Brand, Review_date, and Rating columns. The function `prepDocuments()` uses the package `tm` to preprocess the data.

The workflow and some of the most important features of the `stm` package are illustrated in ◘ Fig. 7.4.

Notice that during the data-ingestion stage, the data set is loaded into R's memory. Then, the relevant columns are selected, and the text, together with the metadata, is preprocessed. An important part is the selection of the brands we want to focus on. We will use Amazon and Apple and aim to extract background information regarding them.

```
library(stm)
library(tm)
library(dplyr)
library(lubridate)

# Preprocessing
options(stringsAsFactors = FALSE)

# Read product reviews from a CSV file into a data frame
prodreviews <- read.csv("data/Product Reviews.csv")

# Select the desired columns
data <- prodreviews[, c("Content", "Rating", "Brand",
↪ "Review_date")]

# Transform the character content of Review_date into date type
data$Review_date <- mdy(data$Review_date)

# Select the year 2012
data <- data %>% filter(year(Review_date) == 2012)
```

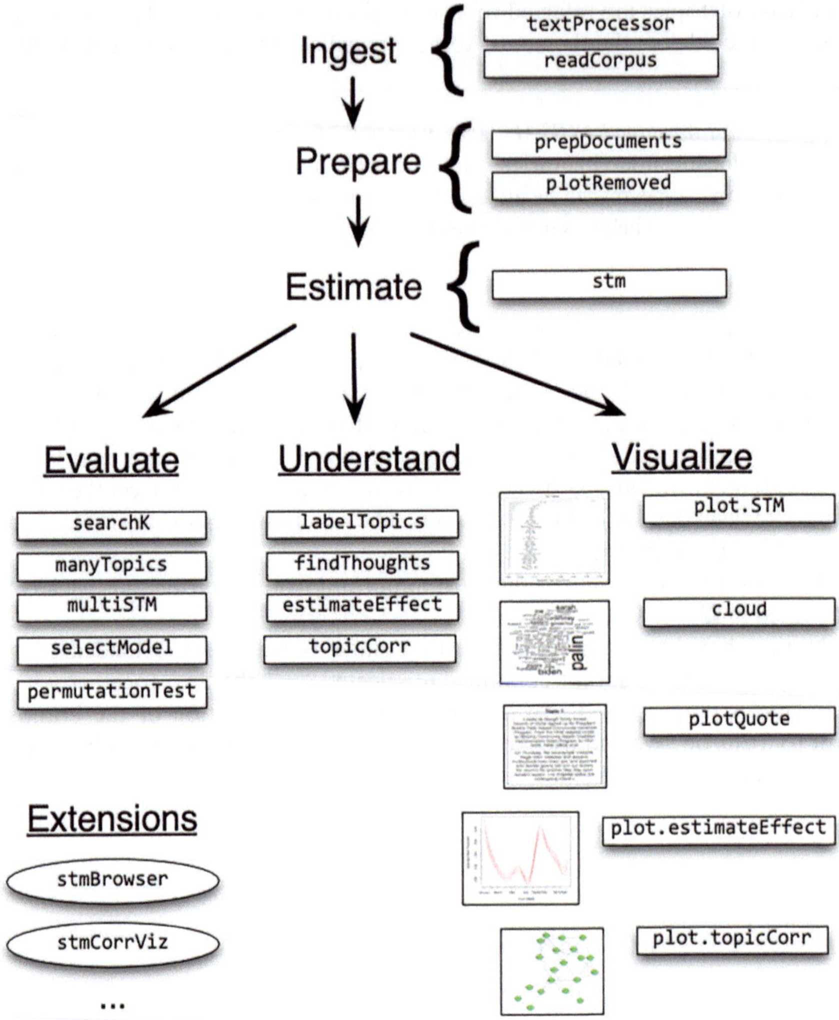

Fig. 7.4 Analysis workflow and stm package features. (Reproduced from Roberts et al. (2019), JSS, Fig. 2, CC BY 3.0; see Credits for details)

```
# Use the strftime to transform the date into a number (day of the
↪  year)
data$Review_date <- as.integer(strftime(data$Review_date, format
↪  ="%j"))

# Select the relevant rows (Amazon and Apple)
data <- subset(data, Brand == "Amazon" | Brand == "Apple")

# Set seed for reproducibility
set.seed(42)
```

```
# Process the text data
processed <- textProcessor(documents = data$Content, metadata =
↪  data)
```

After this, we need to prepare the corpus by linking the text with metadata using the `prepDocuments()` utility function. In building the model, we can set a threshold (e.g., through the option `lower.thresh`) for the minimum number of documents in which a word must appear. Note that this has an influence on the rare words. The threshold helps reduce noise by excluding terms that occur infrequently and might not be helpful for the topic modeling. After we have chosen a threshold, we can also extract some important variables, such as the documents as a large list in `docs`, the vocabulary as a character vector in `vocab`, and the metadata as a table in `meta`.

```
# Associate text with metadata
out <- prepDocuments(documents = processed$documents,
                     vocab = processed$vocab,
                     meta = processed$meta, lower.thresh = 15)
```

```
Removing 15119 of 17310 terms (32987 of 483031 tokens)
↪  due to frequency
Removing 3 Documents with No Words
Your corpus now has 10235 documents, 2191 terms and
↪  450044 tokens.
```

```
# Extract variables
docs <- out$documents
vocab <- out$vocab
meta <- out$meta
```

Next we can estimate a topic STM model by passing the output to the `stm()` function. `K` represents the number of topics we want to model. The `prevalence` option refers to how the proportions of topics vary across the documents. The covariates can be encoded through a formula which accommodates multiple covariates and variables that can be factorial or continuous. In this example, prevalence is a function of the `Brand` variable, which generally includes many brands, but in our case only two. In the model, you can set the maximum number of iterations through the `max.em.its` option. Spectral initialization is a great optimization tool for getting the same results each time we apply the `stm()` function (Roberts et al., 2016). Be aware that this might terminate the model before convergence is reached. Check the package's manual for more options (Roberts et al., 2019).

```
# Fitting the example model
productsFit <- stm(documents = out$documents, vocab = out$vocab,
                   K = 5, prevalence =~ Brand,
                   max.em.its = 75, data = out$meta,
                   init.type = "Spectral", verbose = FALSE)
```

Now we can try to understand and interpret the model estimates and use the functions. labelTopics() will display the most likely words associated with the topics. By default, it uses multiple methods to identify representative words for each topic (highest prob, FREX, lift, and ccore). In the example below, the output from labelTopics() shows the results for all the four methods you can see under "Topic's Top Words," and allows you to compare the different ways topics are represented. The words for each topic vary depending on the method used. To clarify the effects of using these methods, *highest prob* lists the most frequent words within each topic and also some common words, reducing specificity. *FREX*(*FR*equency and *EX*clusivity) identifies words which are both frequent and exclusive to a topic, making them more distinctive. The words that rank highly in FREX occur frequently in the topic and are unique to it, in a similar way to tf-idf *Lift* identifies words which are common within and specific to one topic, compared to those which can be found across the entire corpus. It can be helpful in highlighting unique terms for smaller topics. *Score* uses a combination of the log frequency inside one topic and the penalizing of the word's log frequency across all topics; the goal is to find words which are common in a specific topic but uncommon elsewhere.

```
# Find which words belong to which topic
(lT <- labelTopics(productsFit))
```

```
Topic 1 Top Words:
     Highest Prob: amazon, kindl, problem, work, one,
      ↪  get, fire
     FREX: return, custom, credit, servic, call,
      ↪  password, told
     Lift: non, paperweight, spoke, worthless, refund,
      ↪  rep, south
     Score: non, custom, return, problem, credit, call,
      ↪  amazon
Topic 2 Top Words:
```

```
     Highest Prob: app, devic, amazon, fire, use, screen,
      ↪ tablet
     FREX: browser, volum, cloud, button, content, googl,
      ↪ speaker
     Lift: clever, launcher, onboard, robust, wallpap,
      ↪ root, upsid
     Score: clever, android, app, devic, browser, button,
      ↪ volum
Topic 3 Top Words:
     Highest Prob: love, great, use, can, one, game, get
     FREX: game, kid, play, daughter, wife, love, gift
     Lift: toss, hubbi, girl, bus, appoint, grandson,
      ↪ granddaught
     Score: love, toss, game, great, christma, play, gift
Topic 4 Top Words:
     Highest Prob: ipad, tablet, appl, use, new, app,
      ↪ like
     FREX: appl, ipad, iphon, con, camera, itun, compar
     Lift: retina, con, lte, sim, facetim, dictat, imac
     Score: con, ipad, appl, retina, iphon, camera,
      ↪ tablet
Topic 5 Top Words:
     Highest Prob: kindl, fire, book, read, love, use,
      ↪ purchas
     FREX: color, kindl, book, fire, librari, read, enjoy
     Lift: proud, sun, sunglass, anti-glar, paperback,
      ↪ lamp, beach
     Score: kindl, fire, book, proud, read, love, color
```

Let us better understand the model's results by using visualizations. We can explore the words associated with each topic by plotting them. The top three words associated with the list from the highest prob method appear in ◘ Fig. 7.5.

```
plot(productsFit, type = "summary", xlim = c(0, 0.8))
```

According to the plot displayed in ◘ Fig. 7.5, topic 3 (characterized by words like "love," "great," and "use") represents a major topic, followed by 5, 1, and 2. Topic 4 is a relatively minor topic.

In case we want to see which documents are associated with which topics, we can use the `findThoughts()` function. This retrieves the most representative documents for a topic, based on their proportion in the STM model. By examining these documents, we have the chance to better understand the content of a topic. We have shortened the documents to 200 characters as a dimensionality reduction and checked the documents associated with topics 4 and 5. The documents selected for

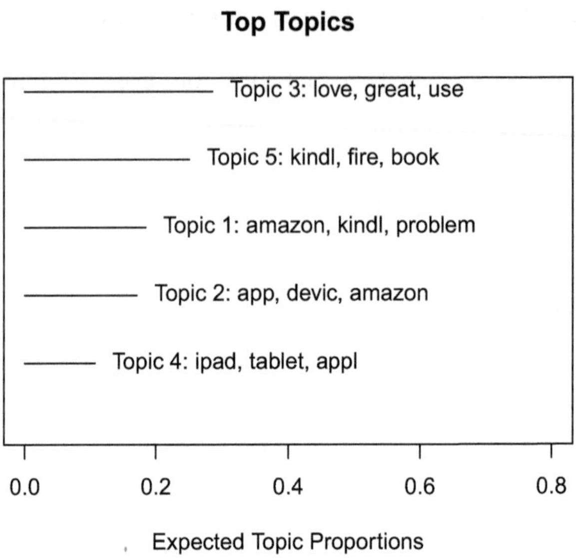

Fig. 7.5 Topic proportions. Authors' own figure

each topic are the ones which are most strongly aligned with it. The example code below uses the `labelTopics()` function, which helps us explore the documents strongly associated with the words identified by the various labeling methods.

```
# Select the first 200 text characters, to simplify
shortdoc <- substr(meta$Content, 1, 200)

# Find 2 documents associated with topic 4
thoughts1 <- findThoughts(productsFit, texts = shortdoc, n = 2,
topics = 4)$docs[[1]]

# Find 2 documents associated with topic 5
thoughts2 <- findThoughts(productsFit, texts = shortdoc, n = 2,
topics = 5)$docs[[1]]

# Plot the results
par(mfrow = c(1, 2), mar = c(0.5, 0.5, 1, 0.5))
plotQuote(thoughts1, width = 30, main = "Topic 4")
plotQuote(thoughts2, width = 30, main = "Topic 5")
```

The results in Fig. 7.6 show excerpts of the first 200 characters of the most representative two documents for topics 4 and 5. These give us an insight into what the topics are about, providing a qualitative view which complements the model's quantitative approach.

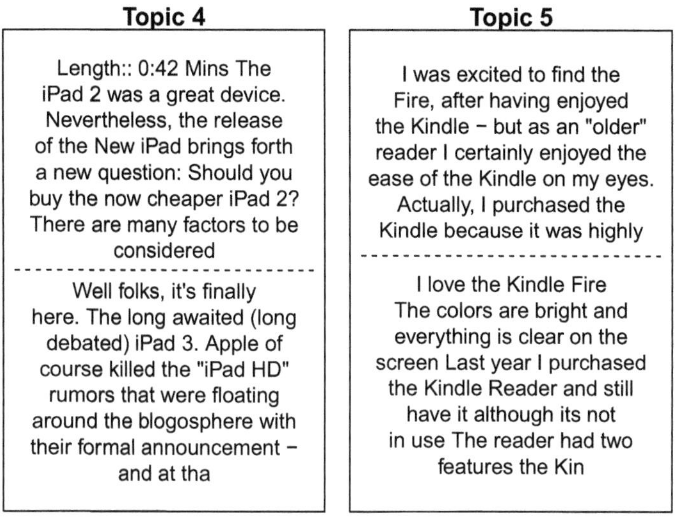

Fig. 7.6 Topic representative document excerpts. Authors' own figure

7.3.1 Estimating Metadata-Topic Relationships

The main function in the `stm` package for evaluating the link between topics and metadata is `estimateEffect()`. For *K* topics, it identifies their relationships and the associated uncertainty by employing, generally, the topical-prevalence model used in estimating STM. The topical-prevalence model is similar to a regression model; the topic proportions represent the dependent variable, while metadata (e.g., `Brand`, `Review_date`, and `Rating`) are the independent variables which explain how the prevalence of topics varies across documents. As an input, the function can take selected topics and a link formula for the metadata. There are several options for estimating this link function. To speed up processing time, you can choose `uncertainty = "None"`, but this will not give the estimation uncertainty, or you can use `"Global"`, which does consider the estimation uncertainty of the topic proportions (Roberts et al., 2019). The estimated relationships can be useful in interpreting and validating the topics (Grimmer, 2010; Grimmer & Stewart, 2013). First, we need to transform the `Brand` column into a categorical variable, called a factor in R. Then we need to estimate the effect of the covariates; in this case, we have the `Brand`, the `Review_date`, and the product's `Rating` provided in a document ranging from 1 to 5 in the `productsFit` topic model. The function `s()` applies a spline to the `Review_date` variable. This allows us capture nonlinear trends over time. The role of a spline is to create a smooth curve that models variations in topic prevalence as a continuous, nonlinear function applied to a variable, in our case `Review_date`. The `summary()` function gives a summary of the estimated effect of the topic.

```
# Convert "Brand" to a categorical variable
out$meta$Brand <- as.factor(out$meta$Brand)

# Estimate the effect of the covariates on topics
prep <- estimateEffect(1:5 ~ Brand +s(Review_date)+Rating,
↪  productsFit, meta = out$meta, uncertainty = "Global")

# Summarize the estimated effect on topic 1
summary(prep, topics = 1)
```



```
Call:
estimateEffect(formula = 1:5 ~ Brand + s(Review_date) +
↪  Rating,
    stmobj = productsFit, metadata = out$meta,
     ↪  uncertainty = "Global")


Topic 1:

Coefficients:
                    Estimate Std. Error t value Pr(>|t|)
(Intercept)        0.5073540  0.0152189  33.337   <2e-16
↪  ***
BrandApple         0.0021788  0.0091619   0.238    0.812
s(Review_date)1    0.0001916  0.0250403   0.008    0.994
s(Review_date)2   -0.0045212  0.0181252  -0.249    0.803
s(Review_date)3    0.0006369  0.0200575   0.032    0.975
s(Review_date)4   -0.0029373  0.0181413  -0.162    0.871
s(Review_date)5    0.0066960  0.0189622   0.353    0.724
s(Review_date)6   -0.0164561  0.0183642  -0.896    0.370
s(Review_date)7    0.0043552  0.0210460   0.207    0.836
s(Review_date)8    0.0085997  0.0235965   0.364    0.716
s(Review_date)9   -0.0092256  0.0249329  -0.370    0.711
s(Review_date)10   0.0309149  0.0225915   1.368    0.171
Rating            -0.0765808  0.0017751 -43.142   <2e-16
↪  ***
---
Signif. codes:  0 '***' 0.001 '**' 0.01 '*' 0.05 '.' 0.1
↪  ' ' 1
```

Analyzing the output, we can come to the following conclusions: The intercept has a significantly high t-value; this means that the base level of the topic proportion is markedly different from zero. The coefficient for brand Apple is very small

(0.0004276) and has a high p-value (p = 0.961, so is statistically insignificant), meaning that Apple is not strongly associated with topic 1 when compared with Amazon. The coefficients for the spline function applied to `Review_date` are all statistically insignificant, so the date of the review does not influence topic 1. The coefficient for `Rating` is negative (−0.0770018) and highly significant (p<2e−16), meaning that higher ratings are associated with a lower prevalence of topic 1. In other words, topic 1 is more prevalent in reviews with lower ratings; inspection of the topic's key words and representative documents confirms that it centers on complaints and service issues, so it plausibly captures user unhappiness. This information can be used by the companies to focus on specific themes and to address the concerns of users.

In marketing, comparing brand associations is essential for brand management. The change in topic proportions as a function of associated brands can be evaluated using `method="difference"`. In our case, this means taking the words from the score method value in `productsFit` and plotting the change in topic proportion between the two brands, Apple and Amazon. The `Score` method captures the frequent words in a topic while penalizing their prevalence across all the topics. This is ideal for identifying specific terms within each topic.

```
# Using apply to concatenate labels for each row
custom_labels <- apply(lT$score, 1, function(x) paste(x, collapse
↪ = ", "))

# Plot the results
plot(prep, covariate = "Brand", topics = c(1, 2, 3, 4, 5),
     model = productsFit, method = "difference", cov.value1 =
     ↪ "Apple",
     cov.value2 = "Amazon", xlab = "More Amazon ... More Apple",
     xlim = c(-0.5, 0.5), labeltype = "custom", custom.labels =
     ↪ custom_labels)
```

From the plot in ◘ Fig. 7.7,we can see that topics 1, 2, 3, and 5 are more strongly associated with Amazon, while topic 4 is more associated with Apple. It is evident that topic 1, the most negative, is defined by words related to customer service, at least for some users. Marketers can make use of the information which is now easy to see: The Kindle Fire might be an important Christmas gift. These insights can help us understand how specific brands dominate certain themes.

There are variables which can be treated as continuous; `Review_date` is such an example. Plotting the relationship between the time (Year 2012) and its effect on topic 4 would yield interesting results; see ◘ Fig. 7.8. Remember, the variable `prep` contains the estimated effects.

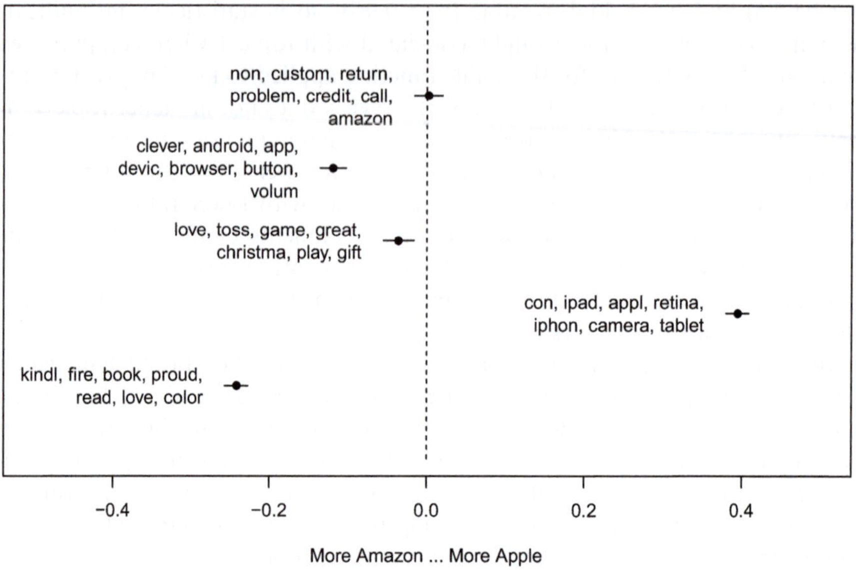

Fig. 7.7 Effect of Amazon vs. Apple. Authors' own figure

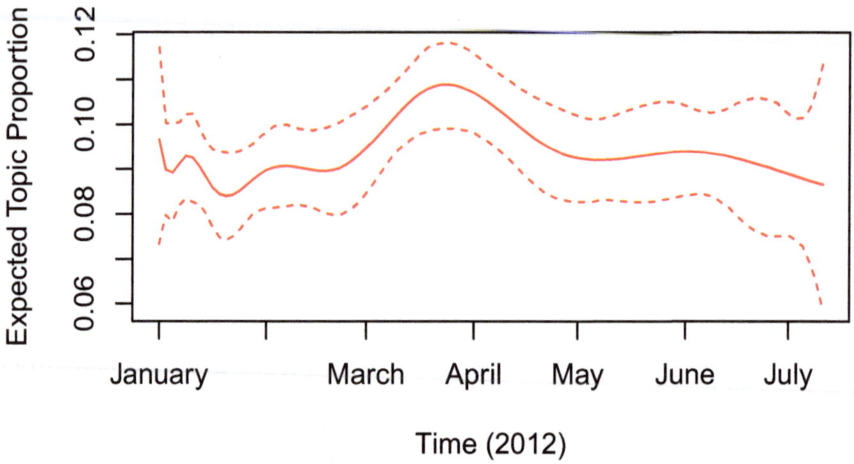

Fig. 7.8 The effect of "Review_date" on topic 4. Authors' own figure

```
# Plot the effect of 'Review_date' on topic 4
plot(prep, "Review_date", method = "continuous", topics = 4, model
↪  = productsFit, printlegend = FALSE, xaxt = "n",
xlab="Time (2012)")
# Create a sequence of dates incremented by month.
monthseq <- seq(from = as.Date("2012-01-01"), to =
↪  as.Date("2012-07-11"), by = "month")
```

```
# Extract the month name
monthnames <- months(monthseq)

# Add custom x-axis labels to the plot
axis(1, at = as.integer(strftime(monthseq, "%j")), labels =
↪  monthnames)
```

Because there is a bump starting from March and April and going down in May, we might imagine Apple held a special event in 2012. And indeed, on March 7, 2012, Apple hosted an event, announcing it with the tagline "We have something you really have to see. And touch.", where they presented the third generation iPad, a model with a Retina display and a dual-core Apple A5X processor with quad-core graphics. So, the timeline of this topic shows that something exceptional for Apple happened during that time interval.

7.3.2 Topical Content

To check the influence of a topical content covariate, we need to understand how the vocabulary used to describe a particular topic varies as a function of this. It is achieved by fitting the STM with a content variable such as `Brand`. When we include a content covariate, we examine how the words associated with each topic differ depending on the value of the covariate (e.g., Apple vs. Amazon for `Brand`). We do this by fitting a completely new model, and thus the new topics may differ from the previous example where no content covariate was used.

```
# Fit the model with the Brand content
dataContent <- stm(out$documents, out$vocab, K = 5,
 prevalence =~ Brand + s(Review_date), content =~ Brand,
 max.em.its = 75, data = out$meta, init.type = "Spectral",
 verbose = FALSE)
```

7.3.3 Visualizing STM Topics

The following examples showcase three complementary ways to plot STM output.

7.3.3.1 Influence of Topical Content

To visualize the influence of a topical content covariate (in our case `Brand`), we can use the plot method for the newly created STM object with the `option = "perspectives"`. This visualization compares the vocabulary used within

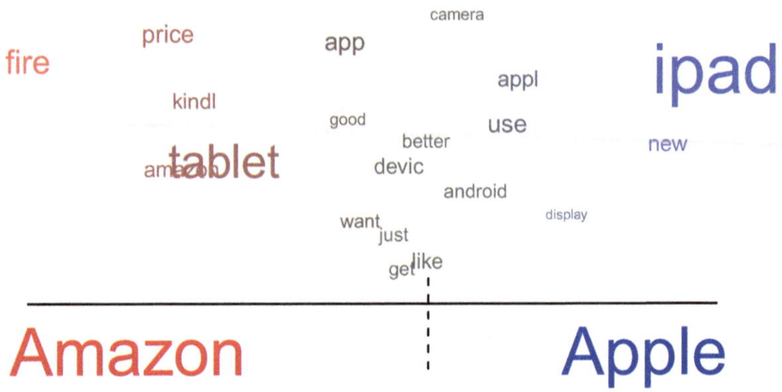

Fig. 7.9 Brand-specific vocabulary in topic 4. Authors' own figure

7

a specific topic (e.g., topic 4) with different values of the covariate (e.g., Apple vs. Amazon for `Brand`). This function displays which words within a topic are more associated with one covariate value than another. In the vocabulary differences by brand for topic 4, that of Apple, the terms identified by the `covariate` output show how the vocabulary varies between Apple and Amazon.

```
# Plot vocabulary differences by Brand for Topic 4
plot(dataContent, type = "perspectives", topics = 4)
```

The larger words on each side of the plot, see Fig. 7.9, are those most strongly associated with the covariate level (Apple or Amazon) for topic 4.

```
# Label the top words for Topic 4
(lT2 <- labelTopics(dataContent, 4))
```

```
Topic Words:
 Topic 4: thinner, processor, macbook, nexus, gen,
  ↪  higher, acer

 Covariate Words:
 Group Amazon: small, owner, capabl, download, seri, say,
  ↪  amazon
 Group Apple: ibook, imac, appl, wherea, industri,
  ↪  profession, frame
```

```
Topic-Covariate Interactions:
Topic 4, Group Amazon: green, pad, creativ, clever,
 ↪  mirror, damn, window
Topic 4, Group Apple: seller, packag, condit, scratch,
 ↪  citi, human, durabl
```

From inspecting the visualization, we see that for Apple the emphasis is on words such as ibook, imac, appl, wherea, industri, profession, frame, while for Amazon it is on small, owner, capabl, download, seri, say, amazon. There are obviously distinct vocabulary patterns for topic 4 based on the `Brand` covariate. For Amazon, words like "small," "owner," and "capable" are prominent, perhaps reflecting the tablet's usability and the experience of owners. For Apple, terms like ibook, imac, or profession underline the products' branding and professional associations. Words such as "creativity" and adaptability (through to words like "green" and "clever") show the interactive nature of the Amazon product, while the Apple reviews highlight the durability of the products and also the condition of the products, related to the sellers and packaging. Insights which might be of use here for Amazon could be the usability of the product, ownership experience, and a high degree of versatility, appealing to a broad audience, while for Apple, branding and professional associations appeal to consumers who are industry focused.

7.3.3.2 Comparing Words Across Two Topics

We can also use the `plot()` function to check the contrast in words across two topics; see ◘ Fig. 7.10.

```
# Plot the contrast in words across topics 4 and 5
plot(dataContent, type = "perspectives", topics = c(5, 4))
```

To further explore the content, we can create a word cloud for a specific topic; see ◘ Fig. 7.11.

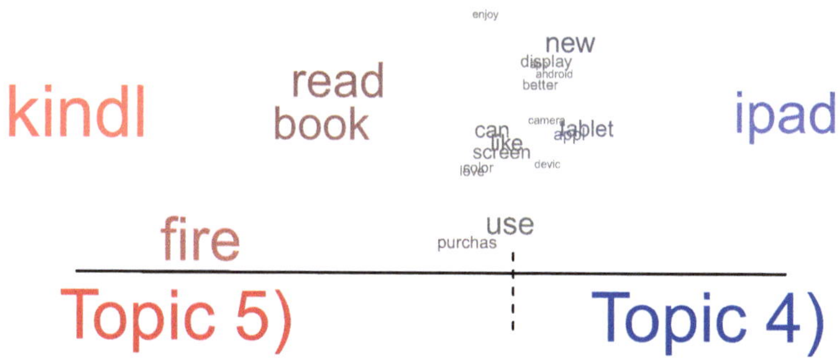

◘ **Fig. 7.10** Contrast in words across topics 4 and 5. Authors' own figure

Fig. 7.11 Wordcloud, topic 4. Authors' own figure


```
# Create a word cloud for Topic 4
cloud(dataContent, topic = 4)
```

Topic correlations can be investigated too. These can identify groups of topics which tend to appear together in documents, possibly revealing latent structures. The correlations can be visualized after calculating the topic correlation matrix using the function `topicCorr()`.

```
# Calculate and plot topic correlations
mod.out.corr <- topicCorr(dataContent)
plot(mod.out.corr)
```

To interpret the topic correlation plot, we need to define its components. Each node in the plot represents a topic, and each edge signifies the correlation between two topics. Positive correlations are typically depicted with solid lines, while negative correlations are often shown with dashed lines; when an edge is solid and carries no explicit "+" or "–" label, it should be read as positive by default. Thicker lines indicate stronger correlations. Groups of tightly connected nodes may form clusters, showing topics which frequently occur together in documents. In our

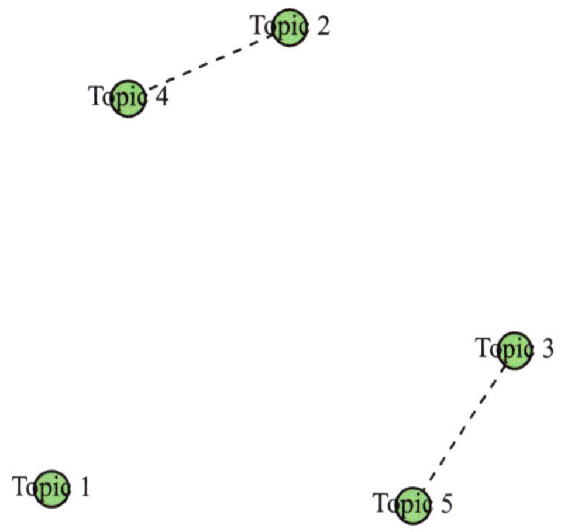

Fig. 7.12 Topic correlations. Authors' own figure

example, we can see that topics 4 and 2, as well as topics 5 and 3, are negatively correlated, whereas topic 1 appears to be more detached from the other topics (Fig. 7.12).

7.3.3.3 Topic Interactions and Correlations

It is also possible to explore complex relationships between covariates and topics in STM. To understand how the interactions between covariates can reveal how one variable can moderate the effect of another, we can estimate a model including a term which interacts with `Brand` and `Review_date`.

```
tabletInteraction <- stm(out$documents, out$vocab, K = 5,
prevalence =~ Brand * Review_date, max.em.its = 75, data =
↪  out$meta, init.type = "Spectral", verbose = FALSE)
```

We have reestimated the model to consider the interaction between the brand and the day and transformed this linearly. Using the function `estimateEffect()`, we have included the same interaction and prepared these objects for plotting, showing the interaction over time.

```
prep <- estimateEffect(c(4) ~ Brand * Review_date,
↪  tabletInteraction, meta = out$meta, uncertainty = "None")

# Plot interaction effect for Apple
plot(prep, covariate = "Review_date", model = tabletInteraction,
  method = "continuous", xlab = "Days", moderator = "Brand",
  moderator.value = "Apple", linecol = "blue", ylim = c(0, 0.60),
  printlegend = FALSE)
```

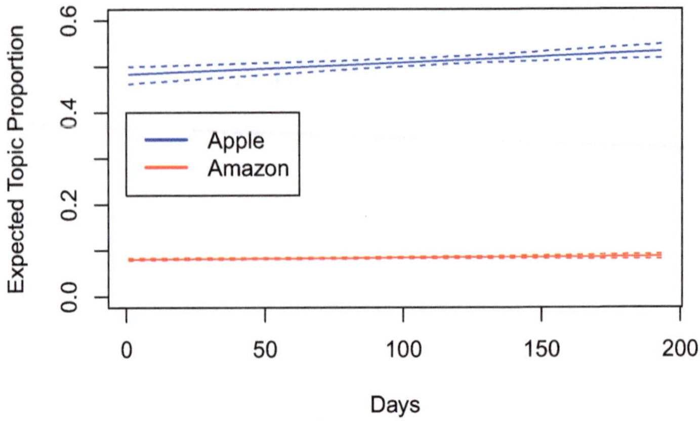

■ **Fig. 7.13** Brand interaction over time for topic 4. Authors' own figure

7

```
# Add interaction effect for Amazon
plot(prep, covariate = "Review_date", model = tabletInteraction,
  method = "continuous", xlab = "Days", moderator = "Brand",
  moderator.value = "Amazon", linecol = "red", add = TRUE,
  printlegend = FALSE)

legend(0, 0.4, c("Apple", "Amazon"), lwd = 2,
  col = c("blue", "red"))
```

The plot in ■ Fig. 7.13 shows the prevalence of topic 4 as a linear function of time, with the brand set to either Apple or Amazon. Other variables in the model are held at their sample medians. From the graph, it is clear that Apple is discussed widely in topic 4, slightly increasing over time, while Amazon is underrepresented and discussed without much variation over time.

Again, we can explore the topic correlations using the `tabletInteraction` model. Positive correlations indicate that both topics are likely to be discussed within the same document.

```
# Calculate the topic correlations
mod.out.corr <- topicCorr(tabletInteraction)

# View the correlation matrix
mod.out.corr$cor
```

```
           [,1]        [,2]        [,3]        [,4]
     ↪    [,5]
[1,]  1.0000000 -0.14830514 -0.45067563 -0.16832829
↪   -0.32473195
```

```
[2,] -0.1483051  1.00000000 -0.46675733 -0.03698267
↪  -0.30964228
[3,] -0.4506756 -0.46675733  1.00000000 -0.22282036
↪  0.01811152
[4,] -0.1683283 -0.03698267 -0.22282036  1.00000000
↪  -0.35590402
[5,] -0.3247319 -0.30964228  0.01811152 -0.35590402
↪  1.00000000
```

```
# Plot the topic correlation network
plot(mod.out.corr)
```

Unlike in ◘ Fig. 7.12, which shows the influence of the brand covariate, in ◘ Fig. 7.14 we can see the general co-occurrence of the topics and their opposition across the data set. The negative correlation between topics 3 and 5 highlights a divergence in their thematic content, while the independence of topics 1, 2, and 4 indicates that these topics cover distinct, nonoverlapping themes.

Given the significant number of visualizations and information that can be extracted from the data, this paves the way for further exploration, for example, in the exercises at the end of this chapter.

7.3.4 Determining the Number of Topics Using STM

As specified in the `stm` manual (Roberts et al., 2019), there is no clear way to decide which is the best number of topics for a given corpus (Grimmer & Stewart, 2013). While the `stm()` function accepts a fixed number for modeling the topics, `searchK()` uses a data-driven approach to select the number of topics. The

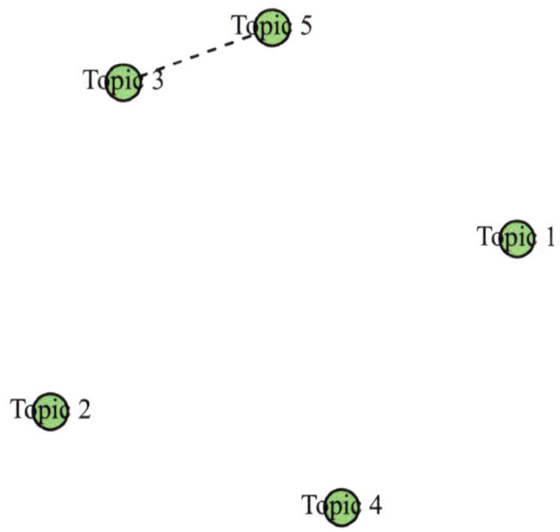

◘ **Fig. 7.14** Topic correlation in the `tabletInteraction` model. Authors' own figure

function performs several automated tests to help the analyst choose the number of topics. For example, it is possible to estimate an STM model of three to seven topics and compare the results for each of the criteria. The default initialization is spectral initialization because of its stability. This function will also calculate a range of quantities of interest, such as average exclusivity, semantic coherence, held-out likelihood, residuals, bound, lower bound, and EM iterations. Exclusivity generally increases with the number of topics k, indicating the presence of more distinct topics. Semantic coherence decreases with k, with a higher degree of coherence suggesting more meaningful topics and some difficulty in interpreting them. The held-out likelihood becomes less negative as k increases, with higher values being better. Residuals decrease with increasing k, with lower residuals being preferable. The bound (or lower bound) increases with k, where higher values are advantageous and lead to a better fit between the model and the data. Expectation-maximization (EM) iterations vary, and, typically, fewer iterations indicate better convergence, but this depends on other factors as well.


```
storage <- searchK(out$documents, out$vocab, K = 3:7,
                   prevalence =~ Brand + s(Review_date),
                   data = out$meta, verbose = FALSE)
```

When selecting the best k from a range of topic models, we should consider the factors given above (i.e., exclusivity, semantic coherence, held-out likelihood, residuals, bound, and the number of EM iterations). Let us analyze these metrics for the new results:

```
  K   exclus     semcoh   heldout residual    bound
  ↪   lbound em.its
1 3 7.844596 -45.95754  -6.23322 2.949842 -3652465
  ↪  -3652463      15
2 4 8.263599 -53.05257 -6.191949 2.820366 -3639002
  ↪  -3638999      12
3 5 8.497192 -54.77616 -6.180974 2.764601 -3633537
  ↪  -3633533      13
4 6 8.735331 -55.94213 -6.174675 2.719773 -3629253
  ↪  -3629247      14
5 7 8.899694 -62.23335 -6.176115 2.691574 -3625151
  ↪  -3625143      16
```

The optimal number of topics, based on the metrics, appears to be 7. For example, it has a high exclusivity compared to $K = 6$; this means that topics at $K = 7$ are more distinct than those at $K = 6$. Despite having the lowest semantic coherence (the topics may be less susceptible to interpretation), it performs well for the held-out likelihood, showing the least-negative value (meaning that it generalizes unseen data better), residuals (with the best fit to the data), and bound (being the best for both high and low). The low number of EM iterations indicates that the model is stable and not overfitted. So $K = 7$ appears to offer a good balance between the metrics if data fit and generalization are important for predictive modeling or explanatory purposes; otherwise, it might be better to choose $K = 5$ for more meaningful and easily understood topics if you prefer an easier interpretation and semantic coherence.

There are other ways to select the number of topics, for example, using LDA tuning. This might be a useful tool to help optimize topic modeling performance by selecting an optimal number of topics. By tuning the LDA parameters, we can create models that represent the topics in the corpus better, allowing the analyst to interpret the results and gain insights which can lead to action. The `ldatuning` package (Nikita & Nikita, 2016) allows for the analysis of some metrics which either show minimization (Arun et al., 2010; Cao et al., 2009) or maximization (Griffiths & Steyvers, 2004). We have loaded the data set to R, preprocessed it, and then applied several metrics, such as "Griffiths2004," "CaoJuan2009," "Arun2010," and a method, such as "Gibbs."

```
library(ldatuning)
library(quanteda)
library(topicmodels)
options(seededlda_threads = 4)

# Read product reviews from a CSV file into a data frame
prodreviews <- read.csv("data/Product Reviews.csv")


# Select the desired columns
data <- prodreviews[, c("Content", "Rating", "Brand",
↪   "Review_date")]

# Transform the character content of Review_date into date type
data$Review_date <- mdy(data$Review_date)

# Select the year 2012
data <- data %>% filter(year(Review_date) == 2012)

# Use the strftime to transform the date into a number (day of the
↪  year)
data$Review_date <- as.integer(strftime(data$Review_date, format
↪   ="%j"))

# Select the relevant rows (Amazon and Apple)
data <- subset(data, Brand == "Amazon" | Brand == "Apple")

# Create a text corpus from the "Content" column of the product
↪  reviews data frame
corp <- corpus(data, text_field = "Content")
dtm <- quanteda::convert(
         quanteda::dfm(
           quanteda::tokens(
```

```
                corp,
                remove_punct    = TRUE,
                remove_symbols  = TRUE,
                remove_numbers  = TRUE,
                remove_url      = TRUE
              )
            ),
            to = "topicmodels"
          )

result <- FindTopicsNumber(
  dtm      = dtm,
  topics   = 3:7,
  metrics  = c("Griffiths2004", "CaoJuan2009", "Arun2010"),
  method   = "Gibbs",
  control  = list(seed = 42),
  mc.cores = 4L,
  verbose  = FALSE
)
FindTopicsNumber_plot(result)
```

7

```
Warning: The `<scale>` argument of `guides()` cannot be
↪  `FALSE`. Use "none" instead as
of ggplot2 3.3.4.
i The deprecated feature was likely used in the ldatuning
↪  package.
  Please report the issue at
  ↪  <https://github.com/nikita-moor/ldatuning/issues>.
```

From the plots (see ◘ Fig. 7.15), it is easy to see that K =7 is the best number of topics, found by either minimizing or maximizing the values, with both converging and producing similar results.

To acquire topics of high quality, we need to consider several factors. One of them is the quality and quantity of the corpus and its preprocessing. Another is the variety of topics in the corpus. The number of grams (n-grams) may also influence the context and coherence of topics: Here we have worked with 1-grams, but two or more grams would add value to the final results. Last but not least, the fine-tuning of parameters will optimize the model's performance to achieve better accuracy and greater insights.

Exercise 1. Other packages used for LDA topic modeling. Use another package, such as `tm` from CRAN to perform LDA.

Exercise 2. A bigram approach for better insights. Use a bigram approach using the `seededlda` package and check the results.

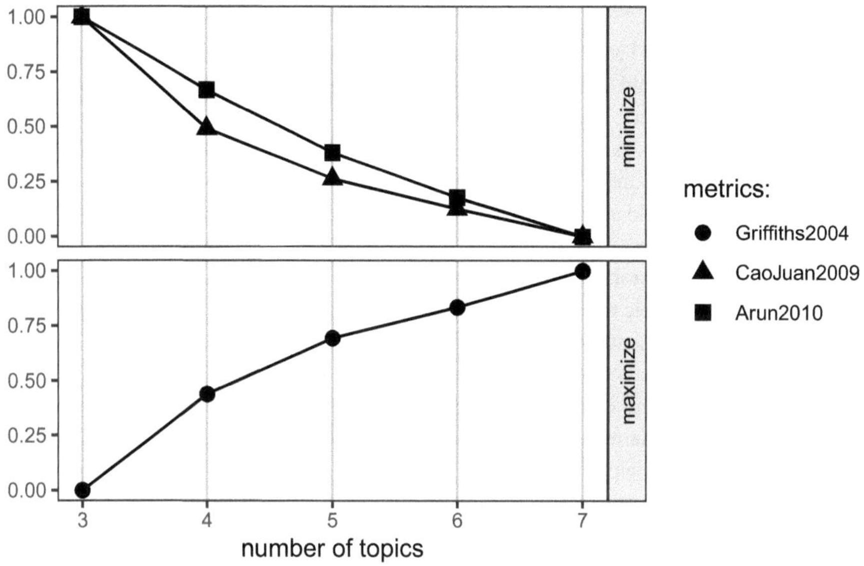

Fig. 7.15 Find the optimal number of topics. Authors' own figure

Exercise 3. Topic modeling with residuals. Use the topic modeling with residuals and seeded words at sentence level using the `seededlda` package. You can get more information on this package by reading the package's manual.

Exercise 4. Bigrams in the `stm` package. Use the `stm` package with bigrams for simple topic extraction.

Exercise 5. Covariates and bigrams. Use the stm package with different covariates and bigrams to compare two brands.

Conclusion

The chapter began with an introduction to topic modeling, showing the simple mathematical formulas which power the latent Dirichlet allocation (LDA) algorithm. It provided a simple example of how topics are derived and how words in a corpus are assigned to specific topics. Next, we looked at a practical application of LDA using the same data set and using the `seededlda` package. To give a more complete overview of the LDA, we looked at important examples, such as seeded LDA, which initializes topics around keywords, or sentence-based LDA, which treats each sentence as a distinct document. The chapter then explored another topic modeling technique, the structural topic model (STM), to expand the scope of topic modeling from a marketing perspective.

7

Discussion

Choosing k: Your STM/LDA algorithms use several metrics and suggest k =7. In which situation would you choose a smaller or a larger k? Which value would you use for interpretability, and which for niche insights?

Seed dictionary design: Which would be your sources or techniques for building a seeded LDA dictionary? Stakeholder elicitation? Term harvesting from existing similar corpora? Wildcard rules like screen*? Pilot runs? Prune/expand? How would you detect and correct bias introduced by poorly chosen seeded words?

Sentence vs. document granularity: A sentence-based LDA indicates there is a very low level of topic mixing per sentence, most of the time assigning one topic per sentence. When are sentence tokens versus full reviews preferable? Discuss the effects on sparsity, computation, and interpretability.

Interpreting θ and ϕ: Prepare a checklist for labeling topics using ϕ (top words) and auditing documents with high θ to confirm labels; add a plan for checking and validation with the help of humans.

Using STM with covariates: For the "Brand" and time ("Review_date") columns in the data set, outline some hypotheses (e.g., Apple vs. Amazon vocabulary shifts) and how would you test them using the `estimateEffect()` function and perspective plots. How would you avoid post-selection bias?

`LDAvis` λ control: Describe how different values of λ from 0 to 1 replace exclusivity with frequency. Develop a routine for analyzing topic labeling.

Take Home Message

- Model the basics first: Start with classic LDA to explore θ (document-topic) and ϕ (topic-word) patterns. Use `LDAvis` to check the labels visually.
- Make an informed choice of K: Balance held-out fit, exclusivity, and coherence. Do not look for a single metric; choose a k appropriate for your business question.
- Take advantage of existing domain knowledge: Seeded LDA can connect topics to marketing concepts while still finding residual themes.
- If needed, go for more precision: Sentence-based LDA uses one or two topics per sentence and can hone insights for review analytics.
- Include metadata in your analysis: STM links topics to metadata and separates prevalence from content to explain variation in themes.
- Validate before making decisions: Establish topic labels before making important decisions and tailoring marketing campaigns to the data.

References

Arun, R., Suresh, V., Veni Madhavan, C., & Narasimha Murthy, M. (2010). On finding the natural number of topics with latent dirichlet allocation: Some observations. *Advances in Knowledge Discovery and Data Mining: 14th Pacific-Asia Conference, PAKDD 2010, Hyderabad, India, June 21-24, 2010. Proceedings. Part i 14*, 391–402. https://doi.org/10.1007/978-3-642-13657-3_43

Asuncion, A., Welling, M., Smyth, P., & Teh, Y. W. (2012). On smoothing and inference for topic models. *arXiv Preprint arXiv:1205.2662*.

Blei, D. M., & Lafferty, J. D. (2006). Dynamic topic models. *Proceedings of the 23rd International Conference on Machine Learning*, 113–120. https://doi.org/10.1145/1143844.1143859

Blei, D. M., & Lafferty, J. D. (2007). A correlated topic model of science. *Annals of Applied Statistics, 1*(1), 17–35.

Blei, D. M., Ng, A. Y., & Jordan, M. I. (2003). Latent dirichlet allocation. *Journal of Machine Learning Research, 3*(Jan), 993–1022.

Blei, D., & Lafferty, J. (2006). Correlated topic models. *Advances in Neural Information Processing Systems, 18*, 147.

Büschken, J., & Allenby, G. M. (2016). Sentence-based text analysis for customer reviews. *Marketing Science, 35*(6), 953–975. https://doi.org/10.1287/mksc.2016.0993

Cao, J., Xia, T., Li, J., Zhang, Y., & Tang, S. (2009). A density-based method for adaptive LDA model selection. *Neurocomputing, 72*(7-9), 1775–1781. https://doi.org/10.1016/j.neucom.2008.06.011

Griffiths, T. L., & Steyvers, M. (2004). Finding scientific topics. *Proceedings of the National Academy of Sciences, 101*(suppl_1), 5228–5235. https://doi.org/10.1073/pnas.0307752101

Grimmer, J. (2010). A bayesian hierarchical topic model for political texts: Measuring expressed agendas in senate press releases. *Political Analysis, 18*(1), 1–35. https://doi.org/10.1093/pan/mpp034

Grimmer, J., & Stewart, B. M. (2013). Text as data: The promise and pitfalls of automatic content analysis methods for political texts. *Political Analysis, 21*(3), 267–297. https://doi.org/10.1093/pan/mps028

Hagg, L. J., Merkouris, S. S., O'Dea, G. A., Francis, L. M., Greenwood, C. J., Fuller-Tyszkiewicz, M., Westrupp, E. M., Macdonald, J. A., & Youssef, G. J. (2022). Examining analytic practices in latent dirichlet allocation within psychological science: Scoping review. *Journal of Medical Internet Research, 24*(11), e33166. https://doi.org/10.2196/33166

Heinrich, G. (2005). *Parameter estimation for text analysis*. Citeseer.

Jacobs, B. J., Donkers, B., & Fok, D. (2016). Model-based purchase predictions for large assortments. *Marketing Science, 35*(3), 389–404. https://doi.org/10.1287/mksc.2016.0985

Jelodar, H., Wang, Y., Yuan, C., Feng, X., Jiang, X., Li, Y., & Zhao, L. (2019). Latent dirichlet allocation (LDA) and topic modeling: Models, applications, a survey. *Multimedia Tools and Applications, 78*, 15169–15211. https://doi.org/10.1007/s11042-018-6894-4

Landauer, T. K., Foltz, P. W., & Laham, D. (1998). An introduction to latent semantic analysis. *Discourse Processes, 25*(2-3), 259–284. https://doi.org/10.1080/01638539809545028

Lee, D., & Seung, H. S. (2000). Algorithms for non-negative matrix factorization. *Advances in Neural Information Processing Systems, 13*, 535–541.

Micceri, T. (1989). The unicorn, the normal curve, and other improbable creatures. *Psychological Bulletin, 105*(1), 156. https://doi.org/10.1037/0033-2909.105.1.156

Nikita, M., & Nikita, M. M. (2016). *Package "ldatuning"*.

Reisenbichler, M., & Reutterer, T. (2019). Topic modeling in marketing: Recent advances and research opportunities. *Journal of Business Economics, 89*(3), 327–356. https://doi.org//10.1007/s11573-018-0915-7

Roberts, M. E., Stewart, B. M., & Airoldi, E. M. (2016). A model of text for experimentation in the social sciences. *Journal of the American Statistical Association, 111*(515), 988–1003. https://doi.org/10.1080/01621459.2016.1141684

Roberts, M. E., Stewart, B. M., & Tingley, D. (2019). Stm: An R package for structural topic models. *Journal of Statistical Software, 91*(2), 1–40. https://doi.org/10.18637/jss.v091.i02

Roberts, M. E., Stewart, B. M., Tingley, D., Airoldi, E. M., et al. (2013). The structural topic model and applied social science. *Advances in Neural Information Processing Systems Workshop on Topic Models: Computation, Application, and Evaluation, 4*, 1–20. https://doi.org/10.32614/CRAN.package.stm

Roberts, M. E., Stewart, B. M., Tingley, D., Lucas, C., Leder-Luis, J., Gadarian, S. K., Albertson, B., & Rand, D. G. (2014). Structural topic models for open-ended survey responses. *American Journal of Political Science, 58*(4), 1064–1082. https://doi.org/10.1111/ajps.12103

Schröder, N., Falke, A., Hruschka, H., & Reutterer, T. (2019). Analyzing the browsing basket: A latent interests-based segmentation tool. *Journal of Interactive Marketing, 47*(1), 181–197. https://doi.org/10.1016/j.intmar.2019.05.003

Sievert, C., & Shirley, K. (2014). LDAvis: A method for visualizing and interpreting topics. *Proceedings of the Workshop on Interactive Language Learning, Visualization, and Interfaces*, 63–70. https://doi.org/10.3115/v1/W14-3110

Steyvers, M., & Griffiths, T. (2007). Probabilistic topic models. In *Handbook of latent semantic analysis* (pp. 439–460). Psychology Press.

Tirunillai, S., & Tellis, G. J. (2014). Mining marketing meaning from online chatter: Strategic brand analysis of big data using latent dirichlet allocation. *Journal of Marketing Research*, *51*(4), 463–479. https://doi.org/10.1509/jmr.12.0106

Trusov, M., Ma, L., & Jamal, Z. (2016). Crumbs of the cookie: User profiling in customer-base analysis and behavioral targeting. *Marketing Science*, *35*(3), 405–426. https://doi.org/10.1287/mksc.2015.0956

Wallach, H., Mimno, D., & McCallum, A. (2009). Rethinking LDA: Why priors matter. *Advances in Neural Information Processing Systems*, *22*.

Watanabe, K., Xuan-Hieu, P., & Watanabe, M. K. (2022). *Package "seededlda"*. Repository CRAN.

Sentiment and Emotion Analysis in Marketing, Lexicons, Machine Learning, and Aspect-Based Methods

D. Dan, T. Reutterer, *Text Analytics in Marketing*, Classroom Companion: Business,
https://doi.org/10.1007/978-3-032-08086-8_8

Keywords
Sentiment analysis · Polarity · Emotion classification · Lexicon-based methods · Sentiment.ai · ABSA · Emojis and emoticons · Topic-sentiment over time · Profanity in reviews

This chapter helps to differentiate sentiment from emotion, discusses why both are important for marketing insights, and works at different levels of analysis—document, sentence, phrase, and aspect—using straightforward examples of reviews. It differs between facts and opinions and identifies potential deception/spam. The methods include lexicon-based scores with domain accuracy, machine learning, corpus-based hybrids, and advanced transfer learning/transformers and ABSA. Readers will also compare packages in R—sentimentr, syuzhet (Bing/NRC/Afinn), SentimentAnalysis (QDAP/Harvard IV), vader, and sentiment.ai with transformers—and readers are given suggestions for how to work with emojis/emoticons. The pipeline will show how to score reviews to monitor brand sentiment over time, mine bigrams and word networks representing polarized sentiments, and reveal the drivers of praise and complaint. Star ratings and sentiment scores can be contrasted, and alignments can help identify meaningful deviations. Sentence-level assessment is used to localize negative passages; the basic classes of emotion (joy, sadness, anger, fear, disgust) are classified and visualized. An example is given of how to model topic-sentiment dynamics over time using seeded LDA in order to compare brands. Lastly, it includes the detection of profanity.

8

Learning Objectives

- Understanding what sentiment analysis is
- Learning how to do sentiment analysis
- Learning how to deal with sentiment over a timeline
- Understanding what to do with emojis Learning how to use bigrams to better understand polarities
- Learning how to use word networks to extract polarized information
- Correlating sentiment scores and user ratings
- Extracting usable information from topics, sentiment, and timelines
- Learning how to classify emotions
- Tackling profanity in reviews

8.1 Meaning, Levels, and the Tasks of Sentiment Analysis

Sentiment analysis is a widely used technique in text analytics. The word "sentiment" is often interchangeable with "emotion," and it has specific meanings in disciplines, such as literature, the visual arts, or psychology, and scholars often disagree about its meaning. The word originates from the Old French term "sentement" (modern spelling "sentiment"), and, according to the *Oxford English Dictionary*, is: "What one feels with regard to something; mental attitude (of approval or disapproval, etc.); an opinion or view as to what is right or agreeable." In our context, sentiment is an opinion expressed in a text, be it a review or feedback which can be positive, negative, or neutral. Emotions in text may reveal the expression of specific feelings, such as happiness, joy, anger, disgust, or surprise, and can be detected through analysis. And so another term for sentiment analysis is emotion detection in text corpora (Alslaity & Orji, 2024). In this chapter, we will analyze both sentiment and emotion. Sentiment analysis is applied to several fields, such as: finance (Tirunillai & Tellis, 2012) to predict stock-market movements and assess economic indicators; healthcare (Denecke & Deng, 2015) to improve patient care; customer service (Kumar et al., 2016) to improve customer care; entertainment (Baid et al., 2017) to understand reactions to movies or concerts; product development (Fang & Zhan, 2015) to improve product features; psychology (Wang et al., 2013) to analyze emotional states; politics (Bakliwal et al., 2013) to understand opinions or voter sentiments; the social sciences in general (Pozzi et al., 2016) to understand societal trends; and marketing (Berger et al., 2020) to analyze the valence of texts in social media posts, consumer reviews, and other customer- and firm-generated content.

> *Sentiment (as understood here)* is an opinion expressed in a text which can be either positive, negative, or neutral, different from but related to emotions, signaling specific feelings such as joy or anger. In marketing analytics, it is used as a label or score attached to a document, sentence, phrase, or topic.

In marketing, sentiment analysis can provide valuable insights into disaggregated and aggregated opinions about products and services over a specific period of time on a particular topic, or in comparison with competing brands (see, e.g., Lee and Bradlow, 2011). Depending on the language used, customers can also be classified by gender and age, allowing for better market segmentation (see, e.g., Hartmann et al., 2019).

To carry out sentiment analysis, the corpus we want to analyze has to be broken down into a number of conceptual levels. We will use an example to help us understand this better. Let us take a document, in our case a short review: "I purchased this tablet for Christmas and have mixed feelings about it. The tablet quality was fantastic, but the Wi-Fi connection was disappointing." The highest level is that of the document, where sentiment analysis can be performed on each document of a collection. In our review, we have only one document. If the

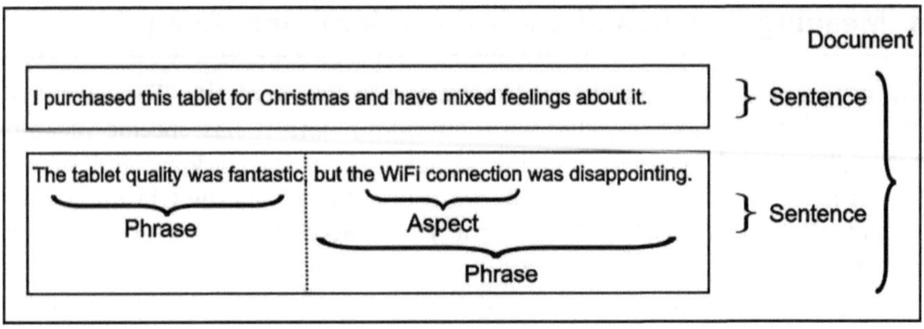

Fig. 8.1 Sentiment analysis levels. Authors' own figure

8

document is a chapter, page, or paragraph, its polarity can be assessed as positive or negative. The next level is that of the sentence. In some instances, it is much better to examine a document at sentence level because the polarities of the sentences can be aggregated, see Büschken and Allenby (2016). We then move on to the phrase level. In the sentence, "[t]he tablet quality was fantastic, but the Wi-Fi connection was disappointing," the first phrase, "[t]he tablet quality was fantastic," has a positive sentiment, while the second one, "but the Wi-Fi connection was disappointing," has a negative sentiment. Instead of giving an averaged sentiment for the whole sentence, phrase-based sentiment analysis focuses instead on its component parts. The last one is the aspect level. Sentiment analysis focuses on specific aspects (topics) of a phrase. For example, "tablet quality" (the aspect) is associated with "fantastic," which has a positive sentiment, while "Wi-Fi connection" is associated with "disappointing," which has a negative sentiment, see Fig. 8.1.

Granularity is the level of analysis at which we compute sentiment, whether document, sentence, phrase, or topic. At topic level, it connects an attribute (e.g., a Wi-Fi connection) with a modifier (e.g., disappointing)

In terms of sentiment analysis, information can be thought of as being divided into facts and opinions. According to (Liu et al., 2010), facts are statements intended to be objective, while opinions are often representative of people's biases, emotions, states of mind, or interests and are subjective. A document is deemed to be subjective if it contains a significant number of adjectives (Hatzivassiloglou & Wiebe, 2000; Rittman et al., 2004). The measuring of opinion is of great importance because it can influence companies' or people's behavior in unpredictable ways (Atwal et al., 2022). Sentiment classification is one of the main tasks for categorizing text as being positive or negative, and the most common form is polarity detection (Cambria et al., 2015). Cross-lingual classification uses one language as training data to classify documents in another language (Olsson et al., 2005). Cross-domain classification is similar; it uses a sentiment classifier trained on one source domain and used on another (Bollegala et al., 2015). Both classifications are useful to cut the costs of annotating data. Deception detection and opinion spam detection are processes focused on identifying and classifying intentionally designed fake reviews aimed at misleading and influencing readers (Rosso & Cagnina, 2017).

Sentiments can be expressed explicitly (e.g., "slow and unresponsive touchscreen experience") or implicitly (e.g., "I could use it for only 5 minutes"). Both sentences are an expression of a negative sentiment, and there are several techniques such as subjectivity detection, polarity detection, and sentiment strength detection (Saad, 2014), which carry out this task. Aspects, or topics, can be identified using LDA (see ▶ Chap. 7); there are sentiment analysis aspect models, which consider the sentiment toward a specific topic to be included in the topic model (Lu et al., 2011). For this, we can use, for example, syntax-based, supervised, unsupervised, or hybrid machine learning (Schouten & Frasincar, 2015).

8.2 Sentiment Analysis Methodology

Several methods are available for performing sentiment analysis: lexicon-based, machine-learning-based, or hybrid approaches (Dhaoui et al., 2017; Rohini et al., 2016). We also include an additional category that covers transfer learning and aspect-based sentiment analysis (ABSA) (Wankhade et al., 2022). The lexicon-based approach is the most common. It uses a dictionary and assigns scores to words. This can be problematic, though, because, depending on the context, words can have a positive or negative polarity, so domain detection is important (Han et al., 2018). Such an algorithm takes a text, compares it against a dictionary that has scores annotated with a specific polarity, and then aggregates them to form a final score (Taboada et al., 2011). Given that we have studied classification (see ▶ Chap. 6), we now have several ways of carrying out text classification. We need to assign a score to a text, something that is frequently seen on collections of opinions on the Internet: for example, a review with a score ranging from 1 and 5 stars. A hybrid method is corpus-based, a text classification problem that uses an annotated data set based on a lexicon (Abdulla et al., 2013). ◘ Figure 8.2 summarizes four families of sentiment analysis methods: (i) lexicon-based (dictionary and corpus lexicons, domain detection, and aggregation of polarity scores), (ii) machine-learning-based (linear classifiers, k-nearest neighbor, decision trees, probabilistic classifiers such as Naive Bayes/MaxEnt/Bayesian network, and neural networks such as convolutional neural networks (CNNs) and recurrent neural networks (RNNs), including long short-term memory (LSTM)), (iii) hybrid (corpus-based) approaches that combine lexicons with labeled data (e.g., lexicon-augmented classifiers, weakly supervised lexicon expansion, and model ensembling), and (iv) additional/advanced methods—transfer learning, transformers, and aspect-based sentiment analysis (ABSA). Note that we do not refer to all the approaches that were discussed in ▶ Chap. 6. Typical outputs are polarity (positive/negative/neutral) or a rating (e.g., 1–5 stars). Advanced techniques, such as transformer-based

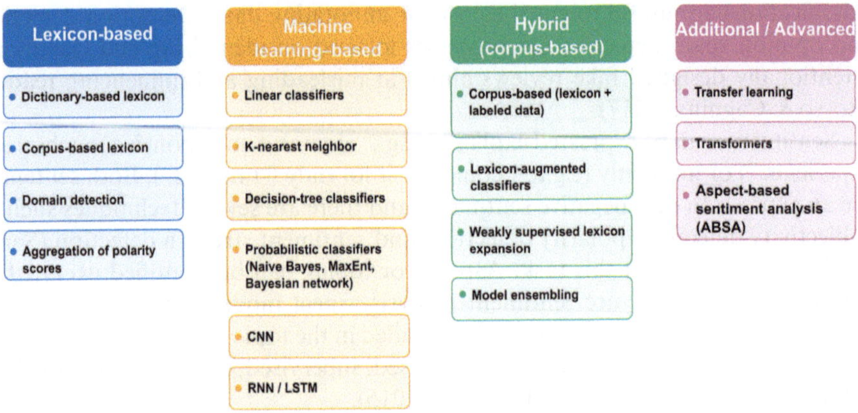

Fig. 8.2 Sentiment analysis: approaches and methods. Authors' own figure

models, are discussed in ► Chap. 10, where the contextual relationships in text data are explored more fully.

Lexicon-based refers to dictionaries of words mapped onto polarities/intensities and aggregates into a text score.
Machine learning learns classifiers/regressors from texts which have been labeled, such as linear models, trees, or CNN/RNN/LSTM algorithms.
Hybrid methods augment ML with lexicons (e.g., weak supervision, lexicon-seeded features).
Other methods use advanced learning (e.g., transformers) and ABSA to detect which aspect is being praised/criticized.

8.3 Performing Sentiment Analysis in R

In R, several packages can be used to carry out sentiment analysis. `sentiment` (Rinker, 2021), `syuzhet` (Jockers, 2015), and `SentimentAnalysis` (Proellochs & Feuerriegel, 2023) all use a lexicon-based approach, employing dictionaries of words associated with a sentiment score. `sentimentr` uses the Jockers Rinker sentiment lexicon, based on a combination of several lexicons.

syuzhet is a lexicon package which supports Bing, NRC, AFINN lexicons.
vader is a rule-based "valence aware" scoring method which handles negation, intensifiers, punctuation, and capitalization.
sentimentr is a sentence/phrase-aware scoring method (Jockers-Rinker lexicon) with valence shifters.
SentimentAnalysis is a wrapper over multiple dictionaries (e.g., Harvard IV, Loughran-McDonald).

It takes into account several interesting elements, such as negators, amplifiers, and de-amplifiers, with which to fine-tune the sentiment scores. The result is an intensity polarity scale with a range of very negative to very positive [−1,1], passing through a neutral. `syuzhet` uses scores from different dictionaries, including: Bing (Hu & Liu, 2004) to classify words as a positive or negative binary without an intensity; the NRC emotion lexicon (Khoo & Johnkhan, 2018; Mohammad & Turney, 2010), developed at the National Research Council of Canada (NRC), which associates words with eight basic emotions, such as anger, fear, anticipation, trust, surprise, joy, and disgust, and also flags positive and negative sentiment; and Afinn (Aung & Myo, 2017), which assigns integer scores to words, ranging discretely from [− 5, 5]. `SentimentAnalysis` supports several lexicons, including the QDAP dictionary (Rinker et al., 2018), the Harvard IV dictionary (Frankel et al., 2022), and many more. `vader` (Roehrick, 2020) takes the Valence-Aware Dictionary for Sentiment Reasoning (VADER, Hutto and Gilbert, 2014) as a rules-based classifier. It uses a predefined dictionary and considers the context of the words, being `aware'' of the surrounding words and their impact on the sentiment of the target word. Sentiment scores are adjusted according to intensity modifiers such asvery"` or `extremely'', or punctuation and capitalization (`GREAT!!" is considered to be more intense than "great"), and negations are dealt with by flipping the sentiment score.

The `sentiment.ai` package (Wiseman et al., 2022) uses deep learning to perform accurate sentiment analysis on text which is context dependent. It uses transformer-based models, trained on large data sets, to identify the contexts in which sarcasm and ambiguous phrases appear. Its multi-language support is a plus. `sentiment.ai` seems to identify negative context more successfully than the lexicon packages, as the authors claim in their own tests, so check it on an external set first.[1]

1 https://github.com/BenWiseman/sentiment.ai

8.3.1 Sentiment over a Timeline

Let us work with an example to better understand the steps we need to take to perform sentiment analysis on a data set. Here we use the same data we analyzed in the previous chapters. Importing them into R and selecting the relevant columns and rows should be a breeze for you by now. We have chosen three brands, because comparison is crucial in marketing analysis.

8

```
library(dplyr)
library(lubridate)

# Prevent conversion of strings into factors
options(stringsAsFactors = FALSE)

# Read product reviews from the CSV file into a data frame
prodreviews <- read.csv("data/Product Reviews.csv")

# Select the desired columns
data <- prodreviews[, c("Content", "Rating",
                        "Brand", "Review_date")]

# Transform the character content of Review_date into date type
data$Review_date <- parse_date_time(
  data$Review_date,
  orders = c("mdy"),
  quiet  = FALSE         # Warning for every non-parsable element
)

# Select the relevant rows
data <- subset(data, Brand %in% c("Samsung", "Apple", "Amazon"))
```

After the data set has been loaded, we have to address an important detail: emojis and emoticons. Text can contain them, sometimes in abundance. They influence the sentiment of the reviews, and taking them into account can lead to better accuracy of the overall score (Shiha & Ayvaz, 2017) or (Gupta et al., 2020). There are also cases in which text can be "emojified," to better understand feelings about certain products (Hotz-Behofsits et al., 2025). Of the packages mentioned above, `vader` has a built-in lexicon which links emojis to sentiments. Methods have been proposed, though, which calculate sentiment analysis from emojis by using tweets and GitHub posts containing emojis to better classify text containing them (Chen et al., 2021). In R, there are several packages to deal with emojis, such as `textclean`, where functions like `replace_emoji()` or `replace_non_ascii()` transform emojis and emoticons into their descriptive text counterparts. It is good to use them both as they complement each other. Other such packages include `emoji` or `tidyEmoji`. We can also apply straightforward approaches, e.g., the manual identification of emojis and their transformation into text descriptions. Because our data set does not have emojis, the final result will not differ from the initial text. The following example is provided so that you can use it with your own data set when necessary.

Emoji normalization refers to converting emojis/emoticons into text tokens (e.g., "smiling face") prior to sentiment scoring. It improves recall for affect-rich, short texts and is achievable using functions such as `textclean::replace_emoji()`, `textclean::replace_emoticon()`, and `replace_non_ascii()` (for stripping if needed), or through models/dictionaries with built-in emoji valence.

```
library(stringr)
library(textclean)

# Replace the emojis in reviews with their explanation
data$Content <- replace_emoji(data$Content)

# Remove non-ASCII characters with suitable ASCII equivalent or
↪  removes them
data$Content <- replace_non_ascii(data$Content)
```

After this procedure, the text is ready for analysis. During the computations, we will use several sentiment analysis packages, but we will mostly focus on `sentiment.ai` in this chapter. This package seems to outperform `sentimentAnalysis` or `sentimentr` according to preliminary benchmarks reported by the package author. We have kept the other results for comparison.

```
library(sentimentr)
library(sentiment.ai)
library(SentimentAnalysis)
library(vader)
library(syuzhet)
library(data.table)

# init_sentiment.ai() is to be run once, at the beginning

# Stop early if the filtered data set is empty
if (nrow(data) == 0) {
  stop("No rows left after filtering")
}


# sentiment.ai
sentiment.ai.score <- sentiment_score(data$Content)

# From Sentiment Analysis
```

```
sentimentAnalysis.score <-
↪  analyzeSentiment(data$Content)$SentimentQDAP

# Assign a stable ID to each review
data$Review_id <- seq_len(nrow(data))

sentimentr.score <- sentiment_by(
  get_sentences(data$Content),
  element_id = data$Review_id
)$ave_sentiment
# Calculate and aggregate sentiment scores

# From VADER
vader.score <- vader_df(data$Content)$compound

# From syuzhet
syuzhet.score <- get_sentiment(data$Content)

# Compile results into a data table
comparison <- data.table(
  Review_id = 1:nrow(data),
  target = data$Content,
  sentiment.ai = sentiment.ai.score,
  sentimentAnalysis = sentimentAnalysis.score,
  sentimentr = sentimentr.score,
  vader = vader.score,
  syuzhet = syuzhet.score,
  Brand = data$Brand,
  Rating = data$Rating,
  R_date = data$Review_date
)
```

8

We have transformed the date to display data on a monthly basis and averaged `sentiment.ai` for each combination of `Month` and `Brand`. We have also renamed the "Content" column as "target" for easier integration with other packages. The plot of the graph is below.

```
library(ggplot2)
library(lubridate)

# Round 'R_date' down to the first day of its month, add it as a
↪  new column
comparison[, Month := floor_date(R_date, "month")]

# Average score for selected columns
monthly_aggregated <- comparison[, .(sentiment.ai =
↪  mean(sentiment.ai)), by = .(Month, Brand)]

# Plot the graph
```

```
ggplot(monthly_aggregated, aes(x = Month, y = sentiment.ai,
                               color = Brand, group = Brand)) +
  geom_smooth(method = "loess", se = FALSE, linewidth = 1.2) +
  geom_point(size = 3) + # Slightly larger points
  labs(x = "Month",
       y = "Average sentiment.ai score",
       color = "Brand"
      ) +
  theme_minimal() +
  theme(
    text = element_text(size = 12),
    axis.text.x = element_text(angle = 45, hjust = 1)
  )
```

The graph in ◘ Fig. 8.3 shows the monthly aggregated sentiment scores over a timeline using `sentiment.ai` for the three brands: Amazon (represented mainly by the Kindle Fire), Apple, and Samsung. The lines were smoothed using the LOESS method and indicate a general sentiment over time. The Amazon line indicates a positive trend, Apple's line apparently seems flat but increases constantly with slight variations, while Samsung's line is more volatile, indicating sentiment fluctuations. The Kindle Fire was released later than the iPad and most early Android tablets, on November 15, 2011, marketed before the Christmas holidays, showing it was well-received by customers over time. Apple seems to have stable and increasing customer satisfaction with its iPads, while Samsung's fluctuations in sentiment indicate mixed customer experiences, but the trend seems positive overall.

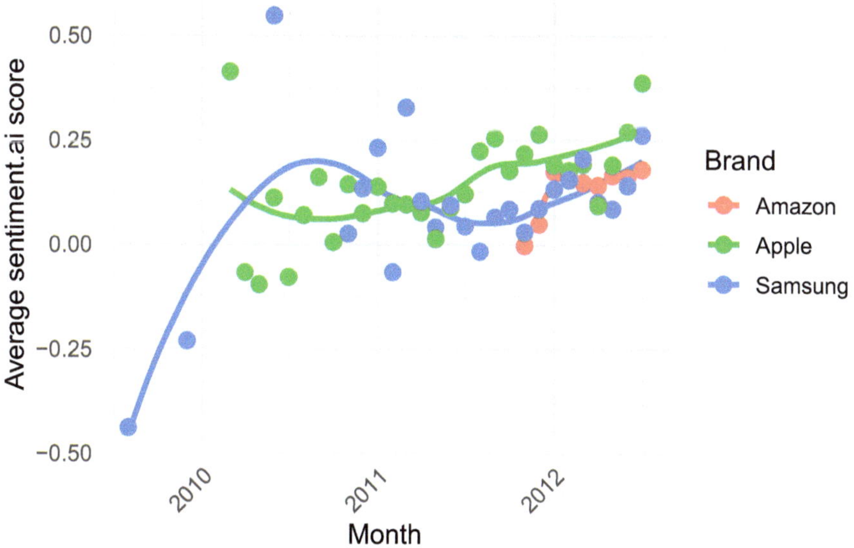

◘ **Fig. 8.3** Monthly aggregated `sentiment.ai` values over time for each brand. Authors' own figure

8

Fig. 8.4 Monthly aggregated `sentiment.ai` values for each brand. Authors' own figure

A different type of visualization is provided in Fig. 8.4 to show how sentiment toward the brands has evolved over time. It highlights differences in how customer perception is captured by the results of the `sentiment.ai` scores. This figure provides more detail to allow for a month-by-month comparison. Amazon has mostly positive sentiment scores, hinting at a generally favorable customer reception. Apple has a positive sentiment distribution, indicating steady customer satisfaction. Samsung has fluctuations in sentiment scores, but the overall sentiment, nevertheless, seems generally favorable.

```
ggplot(monthly_aggregated, aes(x = Month, y = sentiment.ai,
                                fill = Brand)) +
  geom_col(show.legend = FALSE) + # Use columns for visualization
  labs(
    x = "Month",
    y = "Average sentiment.ai score",
    fill = "Brand"
  ) +
  theme_minimal() +
  theme(
    text = element_text(size = 12),
    axis.text.x = element_text(angle = 45, hjust = 1)) +
  facet_wrap(~ Brand, ncol = 1, scales = "free_y")
```

8.3.2 Sentiment Word Networks

Now, let us gain a better understanding of Amazon's positive and negative feedback through the use of bigrams and word networks. Before we dive into the details, to recap, bigrams are pairs of consecutive words that represent common word associations when used in a particular context. Word networks are the relationships between words presented as graphs. The nodes correspond to words, and the edges indicate their co-occurrence. Both make it easier to identify key themes or structures in textual data. To illustrate this process, we have selected the Amazon values from the Brand column and separated them into strongly positive and negative groups, where the score is either greater than 0.7 or less than −0.7. Then we have preprocessed the information and set up the data set to create visualizations.

```
library(dplyr)
library(tm)
library(SnowballC)
library(wordcloud)
library(slam)
library(RWeka)
library(tidyr)
library(igraph)
library(ggraph)

# Filter Amazon reviews and split into positive and negative
kindle_reviews <- comparison %>% filter(Brand == "Amazon")
pos_reviews <- kindle_reviews %>% filter(sentiment.ai > 0.7)
neg_reviews <- kindle_reviews %>% filter(sentiment.ai < -0.7)

# Text preprocessing function
preprocess <- function(text) {
  text %>% tolower() %>%
    removeWords(stopwords("english")) %>%
    removePunctuation(ucp = TRUE) %>%
    stripWhitespace() %>%
    removeNumbers()
}

# Preprocess text and transform into a corpus
corpus_pos <- VCorpus(VectorSource(lapply(pos_reviews$target,
↪  preprocess)))
corpus_neg <- VCorpus(VectorSource(lapply(neg_reviews$target,
↪  preprocess)))

# Bigram function
bigram_tokenizer <- function(x) NGramTokenizer(x,
                                               Weka_control(min =
                                               ↪  2, max = 2))

# Create matrices for both positive and negative reviews
process_bigrams <- function(corpus) {
```

```
  tdm <- TermDocumentMatrix(corpus,
                                      control = list(tokenize =
                                      ↪ bigram_tokenizer))
  removeSparseTerms(tdm, 0.999) %>%
  as.matrix() %>%
  rowSums() %>%
  sort(decreasing = TRUE)
}

# Create data frames
v_pos_bigram <- process_bigrams(corpus_pos)
df_pos_bigram <- data.frame(
  word = names(v_pos_bigram),
  freq = as.integer(v_pos_bigram),
  row.names = NULL,
  stringsAsFactors = FALSE
)

v_neg_bigram <- process_bigrams(corpus_neg)
df_neg_bigram <- data.frame(
  word = names(v_neg_bigram),
  freq = as.integer(v_neg_bigram),
  row.names = NULL,
  stringsAsFactors = FALSE
)
```

So far, only preprocessing has been carried out. What we are about to do is to create a function to allow us to present the bigram word frequencies, both positive and negative, one on top of the other, so that we can compare them.

```
# Plot barplots
plot_word_data <- function(d, title) {
  par(mar = c(5, 4, 4, 2) + 0.1)  # Adjust margins
  barplot(d[1:30, ]$freq, las = 2, names.arg = d[1:30, ]$word,
          col = "lightblue", main = title, ylab = "Word
          ↪ frequencies",
          cex.names = 0.6)
}

# Plot the positive and negative reviews one under the other
par(mfrow = c(2, 1))
plot_word_data(df_pos_bigram, "Most frequent bigrams in positive
↪ reviews")
plot_word_data(df_neg_bigram, "Most frequent bigrams in negative
↪ reviews")
```

We can notice from the plots in Fig. 8.5 showing the 30 most frequent bigrams, positive and negative reviews contain the bigram "kindle fire," but, after that, they start to diverge. The positive reviews focus on the customers' satisfaction

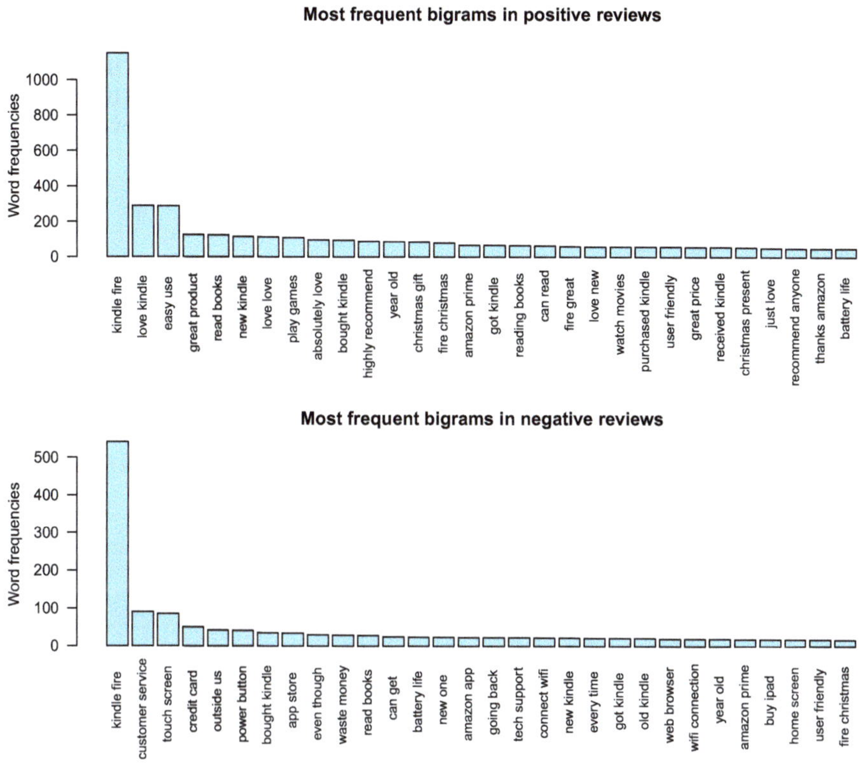

Fig. 8.5 Frequent bigrams. Authors' own figure

with the features of the product, such as ease of use, their emotional attachment to it, and its suitability as a gift. Negative reviews reveal customer service and technical problems, as well as dissatisfaction with the features or performance of the device. The comparison with iPad seems to be negative, perhaps, by showing that Apple devices are better.

```
# Hypothetical frequency sums based on visual inspection:
positive_total <- sum(df_pos_bigram$freq[1:30])
negative_total <- sum(df_neg_bigram$freq[1:30])

print(positive_total)
```

```
[1] 3677
```

```
print(negative_total)
```

```
[1] 1386
```

In the frequency count above, we can see that the most frequent bigrams show about a three-times higher positive count than the negative ones, but the situation changes for the total number of bigrams, which we are going to retrieve next.

```
# Sum the frequencies of positive/negative bigrams
positive_total <- sum(df_pos_bigram$freq)
negative_total <- sum(df_neg_bigram$freq)

print(paste("Total frequency of positive bigrams:",
↪  positive_total))
```

```
[1] "Total frequency of positive bigrams: 18693"
```



```
print(paste("Total frequency of negative bigrams:",
↪  negative_total))
```

```
[1] "Total frequency of negative bigrams: 12901"
```

A word network would provide further insights into their connections and frequency. Let us plot the positive terms to better understand the salient features which make customers happy with a brand, see ◘ Fig. 8.6. A function that can be used in a versatile way for both positive and negative reviews is a handy tool and is presented in the code below.

```
# Build and visualize word networks
visualize_word_network <- function(d, freq_threshold, title) {
  d_sep <- d %>%
    separate(word, c("word1", "word2"), sep = " ")

wordnet <- d_sep %>%
    filter(freq > freq_threshold) %>%
    graph_from_data_frame()

ggraph(wordnet, layout = "fr") +
    geom_edge_link(aes(color = freq, width = freq),
        arrow = grid::arrow(type = "closed", length = unit(0.15,
        ↪  "cm"))) +
    geom_node_point() +
    geom_node_text(aes(label = name), repel = TRUE, size = 3) +
    scale_edge_color_gradient(low = "lightblue", high = "blue") +
    scale_edge_width(range = c(0.5, 3)) +
    theme_void() +
```

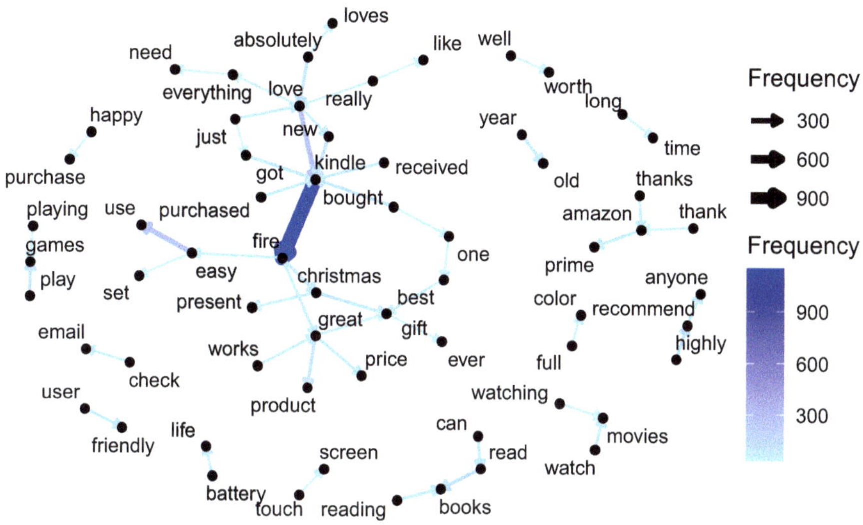

Fig. 8.6 Word network, positive reviews. Authors' own figure

```
    labs(title = title, edge_color = "Frequency", edge_width =
    ↪ "Frequency")
}

# Visualize the word network for positive reviews
visualize_word_network(df_pos_bigram, 30, "")
```

In the coding example above, and the graph which results from it, Kindle Fire, or simply Fire, is the main product. The central node is "kindle" and is strongly connected to "fire," indicating this is, unsurprisingly, the most frequent bigram in these reviews. This is as expected and is not new information. But "kindle" is associated with other positive terms, whose frequencies are emphasized by a thicker connecting line between them. Connections, such as "purchased kindle," "new kindle," "received kindle," or "bought kindle," show that many reviewers write about the buying experience. The user experience expressed by terms, such as "easy use" or "set easy," indicates the users find the item easy to operate and set up. Positive sentiments are expressed through "absolutely love" and "really like" and are strong selling points for the Amazon brand. Words like "great product" and "works great" indicate satisfaction with the product's performance. Mentions of gifts and holidays, such as "christmas gift," "best gift," and "present," indicate that the tablets sell close to celebrations. The multimedia elements of the tablet are expressed through bigrams such as "watch movies" or "play/playing games." A major selling point is expressed by "read(ing) books" and "can read." Positive brand association is seen in words like "thank(s) amazon," showing appreciation for the brand and the product. User friendliness, checking emails, product pricing,

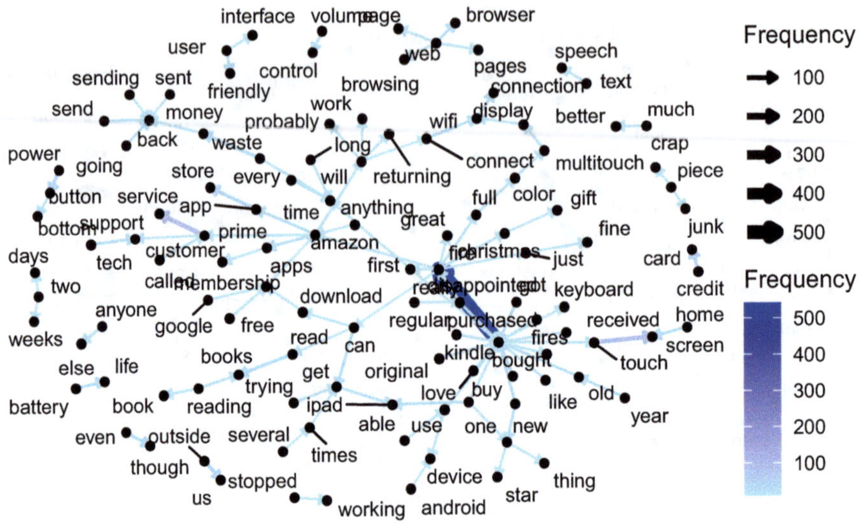

8

Fig. 8.7 Word network, negative reviews. Authors' own figure

and overall satisfaction are clear through bigrams such as "friendly user," "email check," "price product," or "one best." But let us analyze the negative reviews as well, see Fig. 8.7.

```
# Visualize the word network for negative reviews
visualize_word_network(df_neg_bigram, 10, "")
```

Obviously, the central term is, again, "kindle," combined with "fire," and is the central focus of many negative reviews too. This is strongly connected to "disappointed" and indicates a poor user experience. The purchasing experience is discussed too, through terms like "purchased kindle," "new kindle," "received kindle," and "bought kindle," although this time in a negative context. Major dissatisfaction can be seen for "customer service" or "customer support." Technical problems and malfunctioning are indicated by "power button," "stopped working," "tech support," "wifi connection," "connect wifi," "screen touch," "control volume," "battery life," "slow loading," or "freezing." Strong negative sentiments are expressed through harsh terms, such as "junk piece," "piece crap," or with elements of frustration, "waste money," "every time," and "long time." A painful moment for a company is when their products are compared unfavorably to competitors' products, for example, "buy ipad" and "got ipad," expressing dissatisfaction with Amazon. Other important terms, which bring to the fore other issues, include "credit card," "called support," "prime membership," or "outside us," showing payment problems or regional restrictions. Interestingly, the network of negative reviews is much denser than the network of positive reviews discussed above.

5574: *-.009*

OK, I've had my iPad for almost a month. I continue to suffer repeated WiFi problems. It's not my router, it works fine with my iMac and my iPod. It's time for Apple to admit there is a problem and get a software fix for this thing. It becomes useless to you since you won't be able to maintain a connection with the internet. WAIT TO BUY THIS UNTIL APPLE ADMITS AND FIXES THE PROBLEM!!! Other than that, it is very nice, but it really needs to work.

8367: *-.003*

For the money, you'd think the screen resolution would be acceptable, but it's not. The text is fuzzy and unpleasant to read, and, as you interact visually with this device, the screen is by far its most important feature. Otherwise, the device is excellent: fast, responsive, light-weight, etc. Unfortunately, the screen ruins this product. It looks like a knock-off.

Fig. 8.8 Sentence-based sentiment analysis. Authors' own figure

Detecting and managing negative feedback is extremely important, if it is ignored, it can severely damage the brand's reputation as companies need to retain their customer base and to, or try to, acquire new customers.

8.3.3 Detecting Negative Sections of Text

There are several ways to get a broader view of reviews and to detect exactly which sentences are negative, as can be seen in Fig. 8.8. A quick solution is given by the `sentiment.ai` package in conjunction with the `sentimentr` package.

```
library(magrittr)
library(purrr)
# Set seed for reproducibility
set.seed(42)

# Subdivision into sentences and score assignment to each of them
↪
# Filter data and sample one row per brand
output <- comparison %>%
  filter(Brand %in% c("Apple", "Samsung")) %>%
  filter(sentiment.ai < -0.6) %>%
  group_by(Brand) %>%
  slice_sample(n = 1) %>%
  ungroup() %>%
  # Subdivide reviews into sentences
  mutate(review = map(target, get_sentences)) %>%
  unnest(review)

# Calculate sentiment scores by review
sentiment_output <- sentiment_by(output$review, output$Review_id)

# Highlight sentiment results
highlight(sentiment_output)
```

We have selected the rows using the `sentiment.ai` score because the algorithm performs better at review level. We chose a higher negative intensity (−0.6), which means that we are focusing on reviews with an overall negative sentiment. A threshold of −0.6 is a practical and empirical (rather than absolute) value, chosen by us to maintain a balance between the most negative reviews, but at the same time ensuring we keep enough data for analysis. `sentimentr` performs at the sentence level, and by first using the `sentiment.ai` package at document level, we can select the strongly negative reviews, then, as the second step, we can use `sentimentr` to identify the sentences which drive that negativity. This example shows that by pinpointing the negative results overall, we might gain more precise results when we act at sentence level. Both reviews are randomly selected, but we can control the randomness with the `set.seed()` function for reasons of reproducibility. The first review is of an Apple product, and the second is a Samsung.

8.3.4 Sentiment Score and Ratings

8

It is common to encode an opinion on a product or service as a numerical value, typically a "star" value between 1 and 5, with 1 being the most negative and 5 the most positive. This is a quick snapshot of the overall satisfaction given by a customer, and it is a categorical variable (Al-Natour & Turetken, 2020). Although the 1-to-5 scale is formally ordinal, the perceived distance between levels is unequal because of the subjective opinion of each reviewer, and, as such, the "distance" between 1 and 2 stars is not the same as the distance between 4 and 5, e.g., Agresti (2010), p. 4–5 (discusses the non-equal spacing assumption for ordinal categories). In fact, in real-world settings, the majority of customers typically give overly favorable ratings, leading on aggregate to the so-called J-shaped distributions. Such distributions are extremely skewed, with a mass at the positive end of the rating scale (e.g., Moe et al., 2017). Similarly, the emotions expressed in words can travel on a different path to that of a rating. The sentiment score tries to reveal an emotional content that star ratings alone may not capture. Combining these two, however, we might acquire a more comprehensive understanding of customer feedback. Is a sentiment score directly correlated to the rating? The idea is to compare these two metrics to see if meaningful differences emerge. Let us find out if so with a scatterplot.

```
# Boxplot to visualize the relationship between sentiment.ai
↪  scores and Rating
ggplot(comparison, aes(x = factor(Rating), y = sentiment.ai)) +
  geom_boxplot() +
  labs(
    x = "Star rating",
    y = "`sentiment.ai` Score"
  ) +
  theme_minimal()
```

In ◘ Fig. 8.9, each box represents the distribution of sentiment scores for a star rating. The horizontal line within each box is the median sentiment score, and the

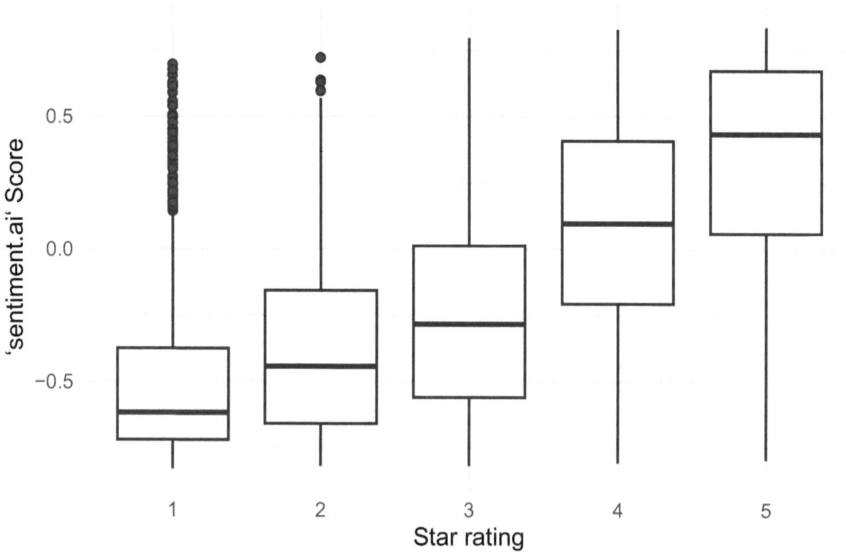

Fig. 8.9 Distribution of sentiment scores by star rating. Authors' own figure

upper and lower edges indicate the quartiles. Any dots outside the whiskers show the outliers. It is easy to see that there are reviews with higher sentiment scores with lower star ratings, showing that the emotional content may not align strictly with the numerical rating. But, in general, higher sentiment scores generally correspond to higher ratings, and the opposite for lower values. Is the correlation between these two values strong?

```
# Calculate the correlation between sentiment.ai and Rating
correlation <- cor(comparison$sentiment.ai, comparison$Rating, use
↪  = "complete.obs")
cat("Correlation between sentiment.ai and Rating:", correlation,
↪  "\n")
```

```
Correlation between sentiment.ai and Rating: 0.6251258
```

The results indicate a moderate to strong correlation, meaning that the sentiment score can be a good predictor of ratings. Let us check visually if these correlations match.

```
set.seed(42) # For reproducibility

# Examples of reviews with high sentiment.ai and high rating
high_sentiment_high_rating <- comparison %>%
```

Review_id	Target	sentiment.ai	Rating
10895	I am wanting to get a Kindle Fire for my grandson who is six years old. I want it to play games, video, and music. Would this be a good gift for a six year old? The price is very close to a dsi, and maybe mom could use it to read books also. What do you think?	0.7649378	5
16858	I bought this for my technology challenged wife. It connected to our WI-FI quickly and stays connected. She has had no problem using many apps on it. Highly recommended for anyone to buy!	0.7667760	5
9926	I think this is a GREAT deal for the value! LOVE IT Sure it is not perfect - a bit heavy.... however a GREAT item for my daughter who is 9! She LOVES IT!!!!	0.5799702	5

8

```
  filter(sentiment.ai > 0.5, Rating == 5) %>%
  slice_sample(n = 3)
cat("High sentiment, high rating reviews:\n")
```

```
High sentiment, high rating reviews:
```

```
# Display values in a nicely formatted table
kable(high_sentiment_high_rating[, .(Review_id, target,
↪  sentiment.ai, Rating)],
     format="markdown") %>%
  kable_styling(full_width = FALSE) %>%
  column_spec(1, width = "4em") %>%
  column_spec(2, width = "25em") %>%
  column_spec(3, width = "5em")
```

The table shows that whenever the sentiment score is high, the rating also corresponds. This should also be similar for the negative reviews.

```
set.seed(42) # For reproducibility

# Examples of reviews with low sentiment.ai and low rating
low_sentiment_low_rating <- comparison %>%
  filter(sentiment.ai < -0.5, Rating == 1) %>%
  slice_sample(n = 3)
cat("Low Sentiment, Low Rating Reviews:\n")
```

```
Low Sentiment, Low Rating Reviews:
```

```
kable(low_sentiment_low_rating[, .(Review_id, target,
↪  sentiment.ai, Rating)],
      format="markdown") %>%
  kable_styling(full_width = FALSE) %>%
  column_spec(1, width = "4em") %>%
  column_spec(2, width = "25em") %>%
  column_spec(3, width = "5em")
```

This example shows that there is also a correspondence with the negative reviews. But at this point, can we find reviews with a high sentiment score and a low rating?

```
set.seed(42)
# Examples of reviews with high sentiment.ai and low rating
high_sentiment_low_rating <- comparison %>%
  filter(sentiment.ai > 0.5, Rating == 1) %>%
  slice_sample(n = 3)
cat("High sentiment, low rating reviews:\n")
```

```
High sentiment, low rating reviews:
```

```
kable(high_sentiment_low_rating[, .(Review_id, target,
↪  sentiment.ai, Rating)],
      format="markdown") %>%
  kable_styling(full_width = FALSE) %>%
  column_spec(1, width = "4em") %>%
  column_spec(2, width = "25em") %>%
  column_spec(3, width = "5em")
```

Why does this happen? Valdivia et al. (2017) have observed that users sometimes write negative sentences but give positive ratings, and vice versa. Their suggestion is to avoid setting the user rate as a label for sentiment, meaning that if a rating is 1, it does not mean it is bad; and if it is 5, it does not mean it is good. It is much better to check the negative opinions using sentiment analysis first and, after that, compare them to the rating. However, the ratings may be influenced by other factors, such as J-shaped distributions and the underreporting of those with negative attitudes (Hydock et al., 2020), asymmetric social ratings (Muchnik et al., 2013), or higher attrition rates among customers with moderate brand experiences (Brandes et al., 2022). While some researchers propose avoiding the strict use of user ratings as sentiment labels, multiple structural and behavioral biases could also explain why

Review_	Target	sentiment.ai	Rating
9320	I am so disappointed with this tablet! Clearly, Amazon is deleting all the negative reviews on here because there is no way in hell this thing deserves 4 stars! Even Consumer Reports rated it really low! I wish my husband would have looked into this more thoroughly before purchasing it! The Kindle Fire is constantly freezing up, and I have to force quit, it will not respond when I touch on a link or photo until about the 4th time or unless I enlarge the page first, it will not allow me to scroll down a page, it will not pull down a menu bar fully, it will not pull up a full photo—only a partial section of the photo. If you are intending to use this for more than reading books, I highly recommend purchasing something else! Forget online magazines, blogs, Facebook, Pinterest and even online newspapers, online stores, etc...the Kindle cannot offer satisfactory performance on any of these! It is extremely poor at looking anything up on the Web! It is bad, bad, BAD!	−0.7189090	1
5375	I did not purchase my Ipad from Amazon. I thought I add a review. I am not too computer savvy, the reason I purchased an IPad is for simple Internet use and watching shows and movies and going through my emails so far I can barely order on Amazon or open my emails. It does not support flash so not everything opens. Also I have a hard time copying and pasting. It does not copy, and if it does, it is 50/50 chance of it working. My kid has a tablet kindle, and it does a lot more than the IPad. I heard there are ways of fixing problem by purchasing Apps, etc. I am still unhappy and I want my money back. My laptop is a better bargain.	−0.6908740	1
19,266	I was little disappointed, just because of these cons: -Poor battery time, using Wi-Fi, and programs randomly take 1 and 1/2 days to recharge during the day (my father's Iconia takes 3 days of use). -A lot of games have slow response, like it is an old hardware. -Samsung does not allow to move APPs to external SD card, and 4gb finishes very quick with GPS maps and APPs, mine is already full in 2 days: (-Touch screen is not as precise as Ipad at all. -USB host does not read hi power devices like external hard drive, only pendrive or memory cards. -Get hot on continuous use. -No flash LED -A lot of incompatible Apps for Android 4 (that is google fault) but the Pros: -Good Wi-Fi signal. -Good GPS signal. -Light and thin. Samsung took off a lot of quality to make it a low price.	−0.6647744	1

Review_id	Target	sentiment.ai	Rating
188	The special use I have become addicted to on Kindle is text to speech. I love listening to books on the drive back and forth to work, but unfortunately Kindle Fire absolutely cannot be used in this way—NO text to speech. I am sure its other features are great, but text to speech was a real core use for me and my iPad fine for everything else.	0.5069298	1
16333	This Kindle is great for surfing the "web"! I use my Kindle to browse my HUGE collection of child porn. Fantastic product, it is very easy to keep balanced next to me, while I finish "pleasuring myself." I WORK AT AMAZON!	0.6773046	1
21588	PURCHASED KINDLE FIRE FOR SON FOR BIRTHDAY AND HE USES IT EVERY DAY. PURCHASED ANOTHER BRAND FIRST AND SENT BACK AFTER ONLY TWO DAYS. AMAZON MADE BIRTHDAY SHOPPING EASY FOR ME...PURCHASED THE KINDLE FOR DAUGHTER-IN-LAW AND SHE LOVES IT.	0.5401485	1

some highly negative reviews receive high ratings (and the opposite). We will not give an example of low `sentiment.ai` and high ratings, but will leave this for you to do on your own. Hint: Modify the previous code using `filter(sentiment.ai < −0.5, Rating == 5)`.

8.3.5 The Classification of Emotions

The measuring of emotions relies on many elements. We may see expressions of subjective feeling in people's posture, gestures, and facial expressions, or sometimes as a physiological response or an overt (or covert) action. In product reviews, we are typically dealing with behavior which occurs after the purchase has taken place. It seems that "frustration, anger, disappointment, alienation, disgust, anxiety, alarm, guilt, shame, joy, happiness, hope, pride, jubilation, excitement, relief, amusement, and pleasure" are the varying reactions that customers experience in both negative or positive circumstances (Bagozzi et al., 1999).

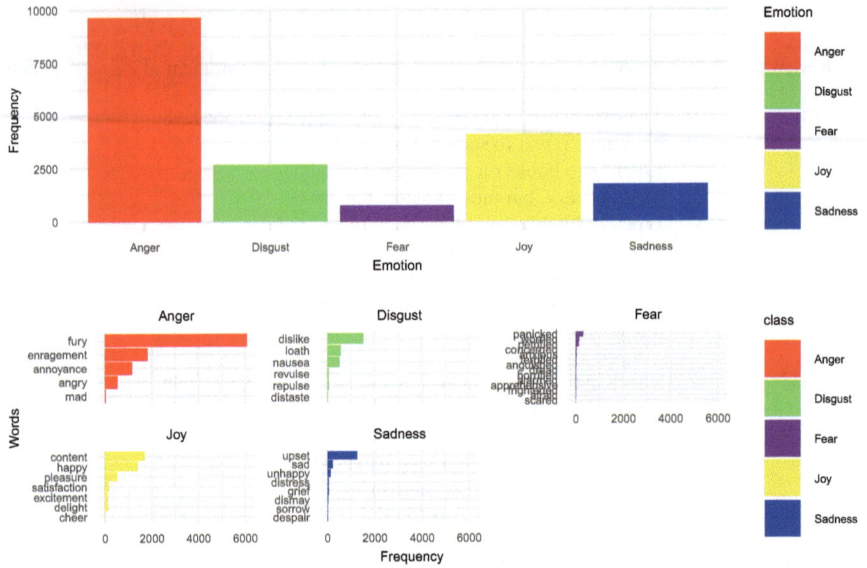

Fig. 8.10 (Top) Frequency of each emotion. (Bottom) Word distribution in phrases by the class of emotion. Authors' own figure

Let us consider five main emotions, joy, sadness, anger, fear, and disgust. Each of these can be defined by a set of words that are, in general, associated with that feeling. The 2015 cartoon movie by Pixar, *Inside Out*, depicts these emotions using colors. However, we could potentially replace these colors with emojis to represent each emotion, as highlighted by the approach taken by Hotz-Behofsits et al. (2025). Taking the first approach, let us link the colors used in the movie with the literature on color and emotion largely relating to Western Europe and North America. Joy is yellow and is characterized by words such as happy, cheer, content, excitement, pleasure, delight, or satisfaction (Tissari, 2008). Sadness is blue, characterized by words like sad, unhappy, distress, upset, sorrow, grief, despair, or dismay (Wierzbicka, 1992). Anger is red and characterized by anger, fury, rage, madness, annoyance (Chen et al., 2015). Fear is purple, and it is characterized by words like afraid, scared, frightened, petrified, horrified, terrified, dread, alarmed, panicked, anguished, anxious, worried, concerned, and apprehensive (Wierzbicka, 1990), which is an interestingly long list. Disgust is green and is characterized by the following: disgust, repulsion, nausea, distaste, dislike, loathing, or revulsion (Mizin et al., 2023). This is not a complete list, but these words are sufficient for our attempt to classify comments by emotions relating to a brand and product, for example, Amazon's Kindle, see Fig. 8.10.

```
library(sentiment.ai)
library(tidyverse)
```

```
# Create word vectors for each emotion
joy <- c("happy", "cheer", "content", "excitement",
         "pleasure", "delight", "satisfaction")
sadness <- c("sad", "unhappy", "distress", "upset",
             "sorrow", "grief", "despair", "dismay")
anger <- c("angry", "fury", "rage", "mad", "annoyance")
fear <- c("afraid", "scared", "frightened",
          "petrified", "horrified", "terrified",
          "dread", "alarmed", "panicked", "anguished",
          "anxious", "worried", "concerned", "apprehensive")
disgust <- c("disgust", "repulse", "nausea", "distaste",
             "dislike", "loath", "revulse")

# List of words that express emotion
emotions <- list(Joy=joy, Sadness=sadness, Anger=anger, Fear=fear,
↪  Disgust=disgust)

# Select the Kindle reviews
kindle_reviews <- comparison %>% filter(Brand == "Amazon")
em_words <- sentiment_match(x = kindle_reviews$target, phrases =
↪  emotions)
```

After completing the preprocessing, we can try to understand the frequency of the prevalence of each emotion and by which words they are characterized.

```
# Check the frequency of each emotion
emotion_freq <- em_words %>%
  count(class) %>%
  arrange(desc(n))

# Define colors for each emotion
color_map <- c('Joy' = 'yellow', 'Sadness' = 'blue', 'Anger' =
↪  'red', 'Fear' = 'purple', 'Disgust' = 'green')

# Plot the frequency of each emotion with specified colors
p1 <- ggplot(emotion_freq, aes(x = class, y = n, fill = class)) +
  geom_bar(stat = "identity") +
  scale_fill_manual(values = color_map) +
  labs(x = 'Emotion',
       y = 'Frequency',
       fill = 'Emotion'
     ) +
  theme_minimal() +
  theme(
    text = element_text(size = 6),
    plot.title = element_text(hjust = 0.5) # Center the plot title
  )
```

```
library(tidytext)

# Tokenize the phrases into words and count the frequency of each
↪ word by emotion class
word_freq <- em_words %>%
  unnest_tokens(word, phrase) %>%
  count(class, word, sort = TRUE) %>%
  filter(n > 1) %>%
  ungroup()

# Plot the word distribution for each emotion class
p2 <- ggplot(word_freq, aes(x = reorder(word, n), y = n, fill =
↪ class)) +
  geom_bar(stat = "identity") +
  facet_wrap(~ class, scales = "free_y") +
  scale_fill_manual(values = color_map) +
  labs(x = 'Words',
       y = 'Frequency'
     ) +
  coord_flip() +
  theme_minimal() +
  theme(
    text = element_text(size = 6),
    plot.title = element_text(hjust = 0.5), # Center the plot
    ↪ title
    strip.text = element_text(size = 6)
  )

# Combine the plots using gridExtra
library(gridExtra)
grid.arrange(p1, p2, ncol = 1)
```

Looking at the frequency distribution across the emotions in our data set, we can see that anger emerges as the most frequent, with about 10,000 occurrences—roughly twice the count for joy—while fear is the least represented (around 2500). Joy is still quite common, and sadness occurs at a level similar to fear. In the breakdown by emotion, we observe that, for anger, “fury” is the most frequent word, followed by “enragement,” “annoyance,” “angry,” and “mad.” Words defining the other emotions appear in descending order in a similar way.

8.4 The Change of Topics and Sentiments over Time

Understanding topic-sentiment evolution over a period of time enables marketers to track consumer sentiment about certain aspects of a product. This helps detect signals of discontent, not necessarily for a product overall, but also for a specific topic and with a temporal duration. Current topic models can reveal topic-sentiment pairs or how important a topic is over time, but the dynamic interaction between topics and sentiments over time is under-researched (Dermouche et al., 2014). In this section, we introduce such a tool because of its potential usefulness and further enrichment of the research. This can be done by using a mechanism to compare brands.

> *Topic-sentiment timeline* is a time series which tracks aggregate sentiment by topic and brand (e.g., monthly averages), to reveal drift, spikes, and brand gaps at the aspect level. It is generally built by combining topic probabilities (e.g., LDA/seeded LDA) with sentence/document sentiment and aggregating those by period.

We have taken our data set and selected the “Brand” and “Review_date” columns to the “Content.” After preprocessing, we carried out topic discovery, see ► Chap. 7.

```
library(quanteda)
library(sentimentr)
library(seededlda)
library(ggplot2)
library(dplyr)

corpus <- corpus(data$Content, docvars = data[, c("Brand",
↪  "Review_date")])

# Preprocess the text data
tokens <- tokens(corpus, remove_punct = TRUE)
tokens <- tokens_remove(tokens, stopwords("en"))
dfm <- dfm(tokens)

set.seed(42)
# Fit a seeded LDA model using seededlda package
lda_model <- seededlda::textmodel_lda(dfm, k = 5, verbose = FALSE)

# Extract the topic probabilities for each document
topic_probs <- as.data.frame(lda_model$theta)

# Add the date and brand to the topic probabilities
topic_probs$date <- docvars(corpus, "Review_date")
topic_probs$brand <- docvars(corpus, "Brand")

# Give columns a stable name
topic_probs <- topic_probs %>%
  rename(
    doc_date  = date,
    doc_brand = brand
  )
```

At this point, we can focus on the sentiment analysis. We used the `sentimentr` package and combined the topic probabilities with the sentiment score.

```
# Conduct sentiment analysis using sentimentr
sentiments <- sentiment(data$Content)
sentiments <- sentiments %>%
  group_by(element_id) %>%
  summarise(sentiment = mean(sentiment))

# Combine topic probabilities with sentiment
topic_sentiment <- bind_cols(topic_probs,
 sentiment = sentiments$sentiment,
 date = topic_probs$date, brand = topic_probs$brand)
```

The next step is to add the temporal data along with aggregating data on a monthly basis. For demonstration purposes, we have selected only two topics; in the exercise section, we have proposed a series of tasks for you to complete.

8

```
# Aggregate data on a monthly basis
library(lubridate)
library(dplyr)

# Rename columns, names previously generated in automatic manner
topic_sentiment <- topic_sentiment %>%
  rename(
    doc_date  = `date...6`,
    doc_brand = `brand...7`
  )

# Aggregate data on a monthly basis
topic_sentiment_monthly <- topic_sentiment %>%
  mutate(month = floor_date(doc_date, "month")) %>%
  group_by(month, doc_brand) %>%
  summarise(
    across(starts_with("topic"),
           ~ mean(.x * sentiment, na.rm = TRUE)),
    .groups = "drop"
  )


# Reshape data to long format for faceting
topic_sentiment_long <- topic_sentiment_monthly %>%
  pivot_longer(starts_with("topic"),
               names_to  = "topic",
               values_to = "sentiment_score")
```

```
# Plot the sentiment of topics over time, colored by brand,
↪ faceted by topic
ggplot(topic_sentiment_long,
       aes(month, sentiment_score, fill = doc_brand)) +
  geom_area(position = "stack", alpha = .6) +
  scale_fill_manual(values = c(Apple = "blue",
                               Samsung = "red",
                               Amazon = "green")) +
  labs(x = "Date", y = "Sentiment score", fill = "Brand") +
  facet_grid(rows = vars(topic), scales = "free_y") +
  theme_minimal() +
  theme(strip.text = element_text(face = "bold"))
```

In the visualization of the changes in the topic across time (see ◘ Fig. 8.11), we can see that the sentiment score associated with Topic 1 gradually increases over time. Amazon shows a rise in sentiment toward the end of the timeline because the product reaches the market during that period. Apple and Samsung show a relatively stable sentiment line, but with some fluctuations, showing lower levels of sentiment than for Apple and Amazon. The sentiment scores for Topic 2 show more variation over time compared to Topic 1. Amazon has a more pronounced fluctuation pattern, whereas Apple sees a steady increase, and Samsung has a consistent sentiment score with noticeable dips. The stacked area shows the cumulative sentiment for each brand over time, indicating which brand dominates the sentiment for each topic at a given point in time. Apple seems to have the

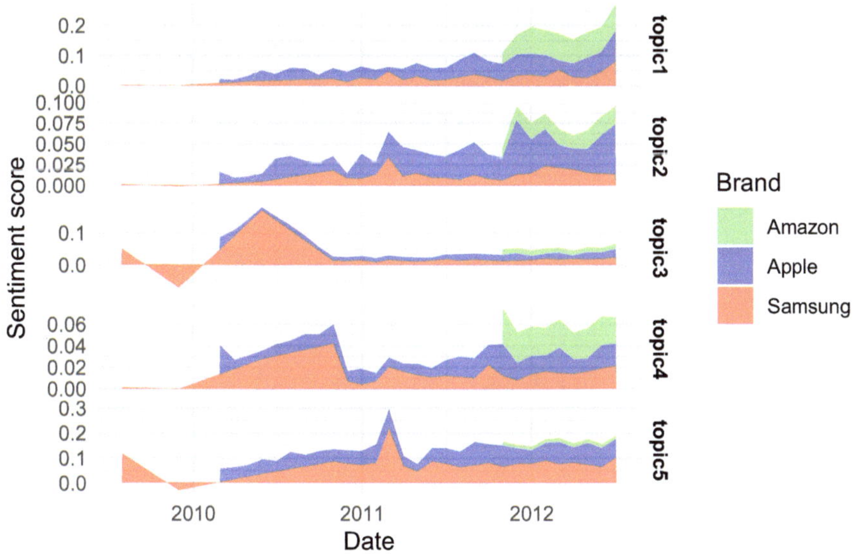

◘ **Fig. 8.11** Sentiment of topics over time by brand. Authors' own figure

most stable and positive sentiment across both topics, while Amazon and Samsung display more variability.

8.5 Vulgar Words in Negative Reviews

Profanity is the use of vulgar words that are considered socially unacceptable, especially in formal contexts. These terms are often an expression of extreme emotional arousal (Stephens & Zile, 2017)and, in turn, will elicit emotions in the reader, who might consider reviews including such words to be more credible (Rassin & Heijden, 2005). Interestingly enough, such language is positively related to honesty (Feldman et al., 2017). This information is not an incentive for you to swear, or swear more. If you ever review this book and leave comments, we will appreciate your honesty anyway, so there is no need to use profanity. There are several effects of the use of vulgar words in online reviews, for example, never receiving an answer back from the management of a hotel (Dan, 2023), a product-line owners, or customer service. Profanity has an effect on the credibility or the usefulness of the review, and this has been researched (Hair & Ozcan, 2018). Let us take two brands and check the negative reviews to see which brand accumulates more vulgar words.

```
# Filter and sample the reviews
sampled_reviews <- comparison %>%
  filter(Brand %in% c("Apple", "Samsung")) %>%
  filter(sentiment.ai < -0.5) %>%
  group_by(Brand) %>%
  ungroup()

# Split sentences and unnest
sampled_reviews <- sampled_reviews %>%
  mutate(review_sentences = map(target, get_sentences)) %>%
  unnest(review_sentences) %>%
  ungroup()

# Apply profanity_by
profanity_result <- profanity_by(sampled_reviews$review_sentences,
↪    sampled_reviews$Review_id)

# Filter for reviews that contain profanity
profanity_reviews <- profanity_result %>%
  filter(profanity_count > 0)

# Compare profanity counts by brand
profanity_comparison <- profanity_reviews %>%
  left_join(sampled_reviews, by = "Review_id") %>%
  group_by(Brand) %>%
  summarise(total_profanity_count = sum(profanity_count))
```

```
# Display the comparison results
profanity_comparison
```

```
# A tibble: 2 x 2
  Brand   total_profanity_count
  <chr>                   <int>
1 Apple                       6
2 Samsung                     9
```

It is your duty to understand better which brand collects more unacceptable but apparently honest words, and to understand why this is happening. In giving you an example of such a review, we do not take any responsibility for the text because these words are not ours, but in a real-world scenario you will encounter them online. Using a profanity count, we have filtered out at least one such word.

```
# Display an example review containing profanity
example_review <- profanity_reviews %>%
  left_join(sampled_reviews, by = "Review_id") %>%
  filter(profanity_count > 0) %>%
  select(Brand, review_sentences, profanity_count) %>%
  arrange(profanity_count) %>%
  slice(1)

# Display the results as a table
kable(example_review, format = "markdown")  %>%
  kable_styling(full_width = FALSE) %>%
  column_spec(1, width = "4em") %>%
  column_spec(2, width = "25em") %>%
  column_spec(3, width = "5em")
```

You may obtain different results regarding the polarity of a sentence or review depending on the package used, some of which miss the target completely. Nevertheless, `sentiment.ai` and `sentimentr` seem to deliver reliable results.

Exercise 1. Select several reviews and compare the sentiment scores obtained using different packages. What can you observe?

Exercise 2. Use sentiment over a timeline, at sentence level.

Exercise 3. Calculate how many reviews show a correct correlation between polarity scores and ratings, that is, where sentiment polarity aligns with the star rating. How many such coherent reviews are there in the data set?

Brand	review_sentences	profanity_count
Apple	Spent 15 minutes in the store playing on this thing, trying to figure out why the hell I would want to buy this. , I found myself awkwardly going through the "features" trying to find something to distinguish this product as something worth buying. , It goes on the Internet? , Wow. , I have got at least three different devices that do that. , It has a book? , So what? , I have a Nook that does that. , Even if I did not, I would sooner just buy a paperback than drop $600. , I knew this product was useless when I handled it in the store, come to find out it is more useless than I thought. , Can't print? , It would be bad enough if it were no different from a laptop. , Come to find out, it does LESS than most laptops and netbooks, but for more money. , Oh, and THIS IS NOT PORTABLE. , It is heavy. , I shortly tired of holding it and put it down. , This thing does not even do much more than my IPOD. , At least you can throw the IPOD in a purse. , Even your laptop can go in your backpack without too many worries since the screen is enclosed. , Not the case with this item that has a fragile, glass screen with no protection. , This is a device for those tools who go to Starbucks to be seen writing their manuscript and have to ice their boners whenever Steve Jobs announces a new scam **cough** sorry, I meant "product." A more discerning buyer will not purchase something so frivolous.	1

8

Exercise 4. Use topic modeling, with seeded words, at sentence level, to extract a sentiment score over a timeline. Compare two brands of your choice using this information.

Exercise 5. Create a new category of emotion, for example, "blame." Find some related keywords and carry out an emotion classification, trying to understand how this concept is perceived.

Conclusions

The chapter began with an introduction to sentiment analysis, discussing the difference between fact and opinion in extracting information from reviews, and outlining the methods used to perform it. We introduced several packages for sentiment analysis in R and then explored and compared their results. Sentiment trends over time were tackled to identify shifts in public opinion due to specific events. Emojis are part of modern communication, so we have provided an overview of these. Bigram pairs of consecutive words were analyzed to improve the extraction of

(continued)

information from word network graphs. We demonstrated the process of correlating sentiment scores with user ratings, understanding the relationship between them, and providing insights into customer feedback. Topic modeling, sentiment analysis, brands, and time were considered together to enrich the tools at our disposal when it comes to multifaceted comparison. Sentiment is more nuanced when it is expressed as emotion, so extracting the former makes our understanding of a text richer. Finally, we addressed the delicate topic of profanity in reviews and how to handle this information effectively. This chapter has provided a detailed walk-through of sentiment analysis from a number of perspectives, allowing the marketing analyst to extract information which can be used to inform future actions.

Discussion

Lexicon vs. ML vs. Transformers: Which approach would you use for a multilingual product review stream, and why? Compare interpretability, speed/cost, domain adaptation, and the data requirements.

Emoji strategy: You have a corpus which resembles tweets and is emoji-heavy. Would you either normalize the emojis to text, keep them and use emoji-aware models (e.g., VADER/transformers), or both? Describe your evaluation plan.

Negation and intensity: Design tests to ensure that sensible scores are given for not good, hardly great, and GREAT!! in your pipeline (lexicon or ML). Which metrics and error analyses would you use?

ABSA plan: Develop aspect-level insights regarding battery, screen, and price. What are the advantages of a lightweight ABSA approach (seeded topics + sentiment) over a supervised ABSA model? Specify the training signals and validation.

Topic-sentiment timeline: Choose either monthly or weekly aggregation; justify the smoothing you use; develop alerts for sudden drops in a key topic (e.g., battery life) for each brand.

Ratings vs. sentiment: Correlate text sentiment with 1–5 star ratings. What issues will you face when dealing with nonlinearity, sarcasm, and cold-start items? Propose calibration (e.g., isotonic regression) and thresholds for "mismatch" detection.

Profanity signals vs. policy: Profanity may increase the perception of honesty but reduce usefulness/credibility. Propose a moderation and analytics policy: count and redact, but also retain as an explanatory variable in the models; define the rules for reporting.

Classification of emotion: When would tracking anger/joy/fear/sadness outperform polarity? Suggest two marketing cases and the features to be monitored.

Take Home Message

- Sentiment is found in multiple granularities (document → sentence → phrase → aspect); choose the level by the decision you need.
- Four families of methods are important: lexicon, ML, hybrid, and advanced (transfer/transformers/ABSA); match them to the volume of data, domain drift, and interpretability.
- In R, practical stacks include `syuzhet`, `vader`, `sentimentr`, and `SentimentAnalysis`; each handles valence shifters differently.
- Emojis and emoticons can change polarity materially; either normalize them or use models which are emoji-aware to avoid bias.
- Combining topics with sentiment over time reveals brand- and aspect-level shifts you miss when dealing with global averages.
- Classes of emotion, such as anger, joy, fear, sadness, etc., provide better signals than polarity in campaigns and customer experience triage.
- Treat profanity as a feature which can be measured: Redact it in UI, and keep it for modeling; it is often connected with strong negative sentiment

References

Abdulla, N. A., Ahmed, N. A., Shehab, M. A., & Al-Ayyoub, M. (2013). Arabic sentiment analysis: Lexicon-based and corpus-based. *2013 IEEE Jordan Conference on Applied Electrical Engineering and Computing Technologies (AEECT)*, 1–6.

Agresti, A. (2010). *Analysis of ordinal categorical data*. John Wiley & Sons.

Al-Natour, S., & Turetken, O. (2020). A comparative assessment of sentiment analysis and star ratings for consumer reviews. *International Journal of Information Management*, *54*, 102132.

Alslaity, A., & Orji, R. (2024). Machine learning techniques for emotion detection and sentiment analysis: Current state, challenges, and future directions. *Behaviour & Information Technology*, *43*(1), 139–164. https://doi.org/10.1080/0144929X.2022.2156387

Atwal, G., Bryson, D., & Kaiser, M. (2022). The chopsticks debacle: How brand hate flattened Dolce & Gabbana in China. *Journal of Business Strategy*, *43*(1), 37–43.

Aung, K. Z., & Myo, N. N. (2017). Sentiment analysis of students' comment using lexicon based approach. *2017 IEEE/ACIS 16th International Conference on Computer and Information Science (ICIS)*, 149–154.

Bagozzi, R. P., Gopinath, M., & Nyer, P. U. (1999). The role of emotions in marketing. *Journal of the Academy of Marketing Science*, *27*(2), 184–206.

Baid, P., Gupta, A., & Chaplot, N. (2017). Sentiment analysis of movie reviews using machine learning techniques. *International Journal of Computer Applications*, *179*(7), 45–49.

Bakliwal, A., Foster, J., Puil, J. van der, O'Brien, R., Tounsi, L., & Hughes, M. (2013). *Sentiment analysis of political tweets: Towards an accurate classifier*.

Berger, J., Humphreys, A., Ludwig, S., Moe, W. W., Netzer, O., & Schweidel, D. A. (2020). Uniting the tribes: Using text for marketing insight. *Journal of Marketing*, *84*(1), 1–25. https://doi.org/10.1177/0022242919873106

Bollegala, D., Mu, T., & Goulermas, J. Y. (2015). Cross-domain sentiment classification using sentiment sensitive embeddings. *IEEE Transactions on Knowledge and Data Engineering*, *28*(2), 398–410.

Brandes, L., Godes, D., & Mayzlin, D. (2022). Extremity bias in online reviews: The role of attrition. *Journal of Marketing Research*, *59*(4), 675–695.

Büschken, J., & Allenby, G. M. (2016). Sentence-based text analysis for customer reviews. *Marketing Science*, *35*(6), 953–975. https://doi.org/10.1287/mksc.2016.0993

Cambria, E., Poria, S., Bisio, F., Bajpai, R., & Chaturvedi, I. (2015). The CLSA model: A novel framework for concept-level sentiment analysis. *Computational Linguistics and Intelligent Text Processing: 16th International Conference, CICLing 2015, Cairo, Egypt, April 14–20, 2015, Proceedings, Part II 16*, 3–22.

Chen, W.-F., Chen, M.-H., & Ku, L.-W. (2015). Embarrassed or awkward? Ranking emotion synonyms for ESL learners' appropriate wording. *Proceedings of the Tenth Workshop on Innovative Use of NLP for Building Educational Applications*, 144–153.

Chen, Z., Cao, Y., Yao, H., Lu, X., Peng, X., Mei, H., & Liu, X. (2021). Emoji-powered sentiment and emotion detection from software developers' communication data. *ACM Transactions on Software Engineering and Methodology (TOSEM)*, *30*(2), 1–48.

Dan, D. (2023). *Exploring the impact of negative words used in online feedback in hotel industry: A sentiment analysis, n-gram, and text network analysis approach.*

Denecke, K., & Deng, Y. (2015). Sentiment analysis in medical settings: New opportunities and challenges. *Artificial Intelligence in Medicine*, *64*(1), 17–27.

Dermouche, M., Velcin, J., Khouas, L., & Loudcher, S. (2014). A joint model for topic-sentiment evolution over time. *2014 IEEE International Conference on Data Mining*, 773–778.

Dhaoui, C., Webster, C. M., & Tan, L. P. (2017). Social media sentiment analysis: Lexicon versus machine learning. *Journal of Consumer Marketing*, *34*(6), 480–488. https://doi.org/10.1108/JCM-03-2017-2141

Fang, X., & Zhan, J. (2015). Sentiment analysis using product review data. *Journal of Big Data*, *2*, 1–14.

Feldman, G., Lian, H., Kosinski, M., & Stillwell, D. (2017). Frankly, we do give a damn: The relationship between profanity and honesty. *Social Psychological and Personality Science*, *8*(7), 816–826.

Frankel, R., Jennings, J., & Lee, J. (2022). Disclosure sentiment: Machine learning vs. Dictionary methods. *Management Science*, *68*(7), 5514–5532.

Gupta, S., Singh, A., & Ranjan, J. (2020). Sentiment analysis: Usage of text and emoji for expressing sentiments. *Advances in Data and Information Sciences: Proceedings of ICDIS 2019*, 477–486.

Hair, M., & Ozcan, T. (2018). How reviewers' use of profanity affects perceived usefulness of online reviews. *Marketing Letters*, *29*, 151–163.

Han, H., Zhang, J., Yang, J., Shen, Y., & Zhang, Y. (2018). Generate domain-specific sentiment lexicon for review sentiment analysis. *Multimedia Tools and Applications*, *77*, 21265–21280.

Hartmann, J., Huppertz, J., Schamp, C., & Heitmann, M. (2019). Comparing automated text classification methods. *International Journal of Research in Marketing*, *36*(1), 20–38. https://doi.org/10.1016/j.ijresmar.2018.09.009

Hatzivassiloglou, V., & Wiebe, J. (2000). Effects of adjective orientation and gradability on sentence subjectivity. *COLING 2000 Volume 1: The 18th International Conference on Computational Linguistics*.

Hotz-Behofsits, C., Wlömert, N., & Nabout, N. A. (2025). EXPRESS: Natural affect DEtection (NADE): Using emojis to infer emotions from text. *Journal of Marketing*, 00222429251315088.

Hu, M., & Liu, B. (2004). Mining and summarizing customer reviews. *Proceedings of the Tenth ACM SIGKDD International Conference on Knowledge Discovery and Data Mining*, 168–177. https://doi.org/10.1145/1014052.1014073

Hutto, C., & Gilbert, E. (2014). Vader: A parsimonious rule-based model for sentiment analysis of social media text. *Proceedings of the International AAAI Conference on Web and Social Media*, *8*, 216–225.

Hydock, C., Chen, Z., & Carlson, K. (2020). Why unhappy customers are unlikely to share their opinions with brands. *Journal of Marketing*, *84*(6), 95–112.

Jockers, M. L. (2015). *Syuzhet: Extract sentiment and plot arcs from text.* https://github.com/mjockers/syuzhet

Khoo, C. S., & Johnkhan, S. B. (2018). Lexicon-based sentiment analysis: Comparative evaluation of six sentiment lexicons. *Journal of Information Science*, *44*(4), 491–511.

Kumar, K. S., Desai, J., & Majumdar, J. (2016). Opinion mining and sentiment analysis on online customer review. *2016 IEEE International Conference on Computational Intelligence and Computing Research (ICCIC)*, 1–4.

Lee, T. Y., & Bradlow, E. T. (2011). Automated marketing research using online customer reviews. *Journal of Marketing Research*, *48*(5), 881–894. https://doi.org/10.1509/jmkr.48.5.881

Liu, B. et al. (2010). Sentiment analysis and subjectivity. *Handbook of Natural Language Processing, 2*(2010), 627–666.

Lu, B., Ott, M., Cardie, C., & Tsou, B. K. (2011). Multi-aspect sentiment analysis with topic models. *2011 IEEE 11th International Conference on Data Mining Workshops*, 81–88.

Mizin, K., Slavova, L., Letiucha, L., & Petrov, O. (2023). Emotion concept disgust and its german counterparts: Equivalence determination based on language corpora data. *Forum for Linguistic Studies, 5*, 72–90.

Moe, W. W., Netzer, O., & Schweidel, D. A. (2017). Social media analytics. *Handbook of Marketing Decision Models*, 483–504.

Mohammad, S., & Turney, P. (2010). Emotions evoked by common words and phrases: Using Mechanical Turk to create an emotion lexicon. *Proceedings of the NAACL HLT 2010 Workshop on Computational Approaches to Analysis and Generation of Emotion in Text*, 26–34.

Muchnik, L., Aral, S., & Taylor, S. J. (2013). Social influence bias: A randomized experiment. *Science, 341*(6146), 647–651.

Olsson, J. S., Oard, D. W., & Hajič, J. (2005). Cross-language text classification. *Proceedings of the 28th Annual International ACM SIGIR Conference on Research and Development in Information Retrieval*, 645–646.

Pozzi, F. A., Fersini, E., Messina, E., & Liu, B. (2016). *Sentiment analysis in social networks.*

Proellochs, N., & Feuerriegel, S. (2023). *SentimentAnalysis: Dictionary-based sentiment analysis*. https://CRAN.R-project.org/package=SentimentAnalysis

Rassin, E., & Heijden, S. V. D. (2005). Appearing credible? Swearing helps! *Psychology, Crime & Law, 11*(2), 177–182.

8

Rinker, T. W. (2021). *sentimentr: Calculate text polarity sentiment*. https://github.com/trinker/sentimentr

Rinker, T., Rinker, M. T., & LazyData, T. (2018). *Package "qdapDictionaries"*.

Rittman, R., Wacholder, N., Kantor, P., Ng, K. B., Strzalkowski, T., & Sun, Y. (2004). Adjectives as indicators of subjectivity in documents. *Proceedings of the American Society for Information Science and Technology, 41*(1), 349–359.

Roehrick, K. (2020). *Vader: Valence aware dictionary and sEntiment reasoner (VADER)*. https://CRAN.R-project.org/package=vader

Rohini, V., Thomas, M., & Latha, C. (2016). Domain based sentiment analysis in regional language-kannada using machine learning algorithm. *2016 IEEE International Conference on Recent Trends in Electronics, Information & Communication Technology (RTEICT)*, 503–507.

Rosso, P., & Cagnina, L. C. (2017). Deception detection and opinion spam. *A Practical Guide to Sentiment Analysis*, 155–171.

Saad, F. (2014). Baseline evaluation: An empirical study of the performance of machine learning algorithms in short snippet sentiment analysis. *Proceedings of the 14th International Conference on Knowledge Technologies and Data-Driven Business*, 1–8.

Schouten, K., & Frasincar, F. (2015). Survey on aspect-level sentiment analysis. *IEEE Transactions on Knowledge and Data Engineering, 28*(3), 813–830.

Shiha, M., & Ayvaz, S. (2017). The effects of emoji in sentiment analysis. *International Journal of Electrical and Computer Engineering (IJCEE), 9*(1), 360–369.

Stephens, R., & Zile, A. (2017). Does emotional arousal influence swearing fluency? *Journal of Psycholinguistic Research, 46*, 983–995. https://doi.org/10.1353/crt.2005.0015

Taboada, M., Brooke, J., Tofiloski, M., Voll, K., & Stede, M. (2011). Lexicon-based methods for sentiment analysis. *Computational Linguistics, 37*(2), 267–307.

Tirunillai, S., & Tellis, G. J. (2012). Does chatter really matter? Dynamics of user-generated content and stock performance. *Marketing Science, 31*(2), 198–215. https://doi.org/10.1287/mksc.1110.0682

Tissari, H. (2008). Happiness and joy in corpus contexts: A cognitive semantic analysis. *Happiness: Cognition, Experience, Language*, 144–174.

Valdivia, A., Luzón, M. V., & Herrera, F. (2017). Sentiment analysis in tripadvisor. *IEEE Intelligent Systems, 32*(4), 72–77.

Wang, X., Zhang, C., Ji, Y., Sun, L., Wu, L., & Bao, Z. (2013). A depression detection model based on sentiment analysis in micro-blog social network. *Trends and Applications in Knowledge Discovery and Data Mining: PAKDD 2013 International Workshops: DMApps, DANTH, QIMIE, BDM, CDA, CloudSD, Gold Coast, QLD, Australia, April 14–17, 2013, Revised Selected Papers 17*, 201–213.

Wankhade, M., Rao, A. C. S., & Kulkarni, C. (2022). A survey on sentiment analysis methods, applications, and challenges. *Artificial Intelligence Review*, *55*(7), 5731–5780.
Wierzbicka, A. (1990). The semantics of emotions: Fear and its relatives in English. *Australian Journal of Linguistics*, *10*, 359–375.
Wierzbicka, A. (1992). Defining emotion concepts. *Cognitive Science*, *16*(4), 539–581.
Wiseman, B., Nydick, S., & Wisner, T. (2022). *Sentiment.ai: Simple sentiment analysis using deep learning*. https://CRAN.R-project.org/package=sentiment.ai

Named Entity Recognition and Extractive Summarization

D. Dan, T. Reutterer, *Text Analytics in Marketing*, Classroom Companion: Business,
https://doi.org/10.1007/978-3-032-08086-8_9

Keywords
NER · spacyr · POS tagging · Dependency parsing · BILUO tagging scheme · Coreference resolution · Extractive summarization · TextRank/LexRank

This chapter provides an introduction to named entity recognition (NER) and extractive summarization, and their combination in marketing text analytics. It discusses NER methods, such as rule-based, statistical, and the newer neural models. It presents a brief survey of R tooling, with further related packages for users. Hands-on sections use real comments made about brands about specific products to explore what users could do with NER data, including extracting frequently encountered entities, conducting a simple analysis of the use of adjectives, and comparing how adjectives are used differently over time to draw simple conclusions about campaign effects. A dependency parse tree visualization is created to show how adjectives are connected with product features. Lastly, a simplified Fichtner's collaboration metric is proposed to allow for heuristics which consider differences in language complexity across brands. For summarization, emphasis is placed on extractive summarization methods. By the end of this chapter, readers will be proficient at building NER pipelines, be able to make appropriate and viable interpretations based on NER-informed insights, quantify and summarize identifiable stylistic trends, and make extractive summarizations which address a comparable "who/what/where/when" structure representing consumer opinion.

Learning Objectives

- Understanding what named entity recognition is.
- Understanding standard named entity recognition workflow.
- Learning how to apply named entity recognition in R.
- Learning how to extract information using `spacyr`.
- Understanding and selecting parts-of-speech tagging.
- Analyzing parts of speech over a timeline.
- Measuring language complexity.
- Tackling summarization.

Named entity recognition (NER) is used in NLP to find important information in documents. Its goal is to identify and classify meaningful text elements and their relationships to each other. Named entities (NEs) are important for a specific purpose or topic, determining their type and boundary. Although NEs do not have a direct and precise definition, due in part to their variety, they can be defined from a more practical point of view. They are elements which describe categories, such as people, organizations, locations, dates, times, percentages, and monetary amounts, among others. For example, a person can be identified by a name or an alias, and a location could be a city, village, or forest. These two categories, person and location, might be related by the place of birth of someone identified by their name. NER is a branch of NLP and helps us understand text questions such as "who?", "what?", "where?", and "when?", through simple principles (Nouvel et al., 2016).

> *Named entity recognition (NER)* is an NLP task which locates and classifies spans of text which refers to real-world objects of interest (e.g., organizations, people, locations, dates, or monetary values). It assigns predefined entity types and boundaries to tokens/spans so systems can answer "who/what/where/when" and link them to other information. The named entity (NE) is the token span in the text that denotes such an object (e.g., "Amazon," "New York," "€29.99").

As we have already demonstrated in the previous chapter when tracking the evolution of brand sentiment over time, in marketing, this information can be used to monitor several aspects of a product or brand. A company might want to know the opinion of their customers ("who"), what they think about their products, or brands ("what"), in which region or country they are located ("where"), and at which point in time they bought the product ("when"). They might also want to check on competitors for their development of technologies, national or international marketing strategies, or the pain points of a brand's customer perceptions. Some reviewing platforms, ranging in their focus from general topics (e.g., Yelp) to more specialized areas, such as travel (e.g., TripAdvisor) or movie review platforms (e.g., IMDb), aim to collect information on products and link it to consumer feedback (Popescu & Etzioni, 2007). If well extracted, NEs can be considered the building blocks of a summary, giving insights into the information contained in documents (Hassel, 2003).

An important application of NER is the possibility to anonymize the personal data contained in a document; this is very important as data privacy is paramount. Personal information can be hidden while the related data and the possibility of interpreting them can be used for statistical purposes or the development of segment-specific marketing campaigns.

9.1 How Does NER Work?

There are several ways of using NER, such as through rule-based systems, statistical models, and neural network models. Rule-based systems use predefined lists of entities, for example, gazetteers,[1] and regular expressions, like the ones we presented in ► Chap. 2. This is relatively simple to set up, but it is not very scalable or flexible if you have large heterogeneous sets of data. Statistical methods and machine learning

1 A gazetteer is akin to a geographical dictionary or directory.

algorithms use methods, like those we discussed for classification in ▶ Chap. 6. Some other frequently used approaches include hidden Markov models (HMM; Morwal et al., 2012), conditional random fields (CRF; Netzer et al., 2012; Sun et al., 2006), and maximum entropy (ME) methods (Chieu & Ng, 2003). These are more accurate than the rule-based systems, but the data used for training must be sufficiently large. The most accurate methods are the neural network models. They use techniques such as recurrent neural networks (RNN; Li et al., 2015), convolutional neural networks (CNN; Zhu et al., 2019), and transformers (Arkhipov et al., 2019). The computational power required by such models is high, and they also need large annotated data sets. Even then, however, results are not always perfect, and the process of identifying and classifying can be faulty, especially with entities that are ambiguous or context dependent. For example, Amazon may refer to the rainforest (an LOC) or the company (an ORG). Disambiguation is a complex task, but most recent transformer technologies understand context well and have made this more and more precise. It is necessary to mention that variability can cause misclassification, for example, in cases where an entity is referred to in different ways, like CR7 or Cristiano Ronaldo: This task is called coreference resolution, sometimes called named entity resolution, and is extremely useful in text analytics.

Coreference resolution is the process of linking multiple mentions of the same entity within or across documents (e.g., "Cristiano Ronaldo," "CR7," "he"). This greatly improves entity-level analytics (counts, sentiment, timelines) by avoiding fragmentation or double counting.

In an NER task, raw text must undergo several transformations, from preprocessing to the final NER output. Here, we will explain a generic NER method. Preprocessing helps transform the text into a more suitable format for the subsequent NER procedures. It starts by segmenting the text into sentences, which are represented by lists of strings. This is followed by tokenization, which helps break down text to the desired level of detail and becomes a list of strings. Next is the parts-of-speech (POS) tagging, which identifies which parts of speech specific words belong to: Tokens can be nouns, verbs, adjectives, and so on and are very useful for entity recognition. In modern contexts, tokens can be transformed into word embeddings; we will discuss this in ▶ Chap. 10. Next comes the entity detection, which helps classify the tokens into categories using one of the models discussed above. During this step, the model identifies the boundaries of the entity and its type. Then, relation detection comes into action, with the final result being in the form of text tuples associated with entities and relationships. See ◘ Fig. 9.1, inspired by Bird et al. (2009), and Dias et al. (2020), for a visual representation of the process.

The landscape of linguistic annotations is made more complex by the use of various formats, two of them being more common than others: the CoNLL-U format (Conference on Natural Language Learning-Universal Dependencies) (cf. Project, 2022; Schuster and Manning, 2016), originally created for the CoNLL 2006

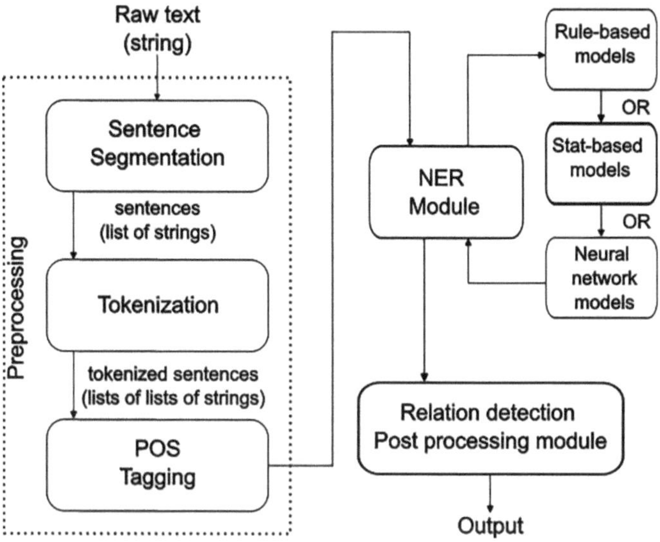

Fig. 9.1 Named entity recognition task. Authors' own figure

and 2007 shared tasks and later standardized by the Universal Dependencies (UD) project, and the text interchange format (TIF; Mullen et al., 2018). The former represents a highly standardized and widespread format for dependency structures across various languages. Its form is a plain text file containing several fields for each token, and it becomes useful when universal dependencies are needed. The latter, used in R especially, offers a flexible structure for text package objects, such as objects from corpora and tokens. All R packages which support this standard will be able to interact between them nicely; two R packages are `spacyr` and `quanteda`.

The choice of model depends on several factors, for example, the dimension of the data set, the presence of labeled data, the computational capacity available, or the degree of precision and accuracy needed from the results.

9.2 NER Using R: Package Overview

There are several packages which can be used in R. Each package might use a different model to annotate the text. One of them is `nametagger`, another is `OpenNLP`, which is based on the Apache OpenNLP library. Related to the latter is `entity`, which is a wrapper for `NLP` and `OpenNLP`. Another is `crfsuite`, providing an interface with CRF. Yet, another one is `udpipe`, a package developed by the Belgium Network of Open Source Analytical Consultants (BNOSAC). Packages like `nametagger`, `crfsuite`, or `udpipe` use CoNLL-U models [2], while `OpenNLP` has its own annotator. Last but not least, an important package, `spacyr` (Benoit & Matsuo, 2023), is used in R through an interface with the

2 CoNLL-U format: https://universaldependencies.org/format.html

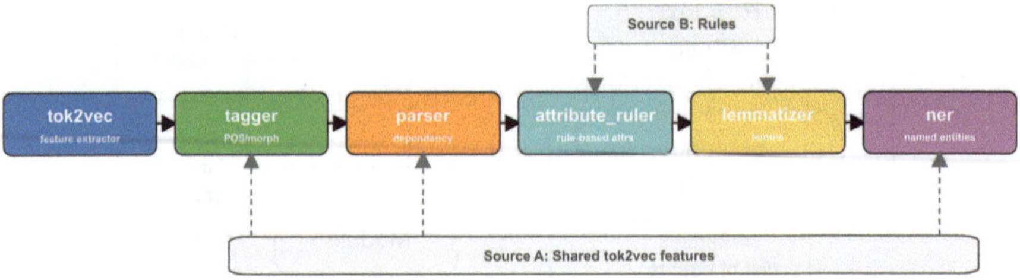

Fig. 9.2 spaCy pipeline components. Authors' own figure (based on the spaCy v3 pipeline description)

Python `spaCy` library (Vasiliev, 2020). `spaCy` uses neural network models and tries to predict entities based on them. The models are trained using large data sets. Depending on the need, they are optimized for speed, `sm` (small, vector-free, and fastest), for a balance between speed and accuracy, `md` (medium, includes a compact word-vector table), and for higher accuracy but with more computational power, `lg` (large, full word-vector table, and highest accuracy). These models exist for several languages, such as English, German, French, and many others. A pipeline for how `spaCy` carries out annotations is provided in Fig. 9.2 (the same pipeline runs under the hood when `spacyr` calls `spaCy`). The first component, "tok2vec," transforms tokens into embedded vectors (there is more about this in ▶ Chap. 10), which represent semantic meaning in a numerical space. These vectors are used by both the "tagger," which assigns POS tags, and the "parser," which analyzes the grammatical structure of the sentence. The "attribute_ruler" applies rules to elements such as lemma and POS and helps the "lemmatizer" standardize words as their root form. The last component, "ner," identifies named entities. It might loop back, however, to "tok2vec" for better detection.

The entities (or categories) for NER that `spaCy` extracts are basic; some names are intuitive, while others might need an explanation. The examples below are not exhaustive.

- PERSON: People, including fictional, aliases, former names
- NORP (nationalities, or religious or political): Nationalities or religious or political groups
- FAC (Facility): Buildings, airports, highways, bridges, hospitals
- ORG: Companies, agencies, institutions, NGOs
- GPE (geopolitical entity): Countries, states, cities, politically bounded regions
- LOC: Non-GPE locations, mountain ranges, bodies of water, deserts, rural areas
- PRODUCT: Objects, vehicles, foods (not services)
- EVENT: Named hurricanes, battles, wars, sports events, political events, cultural events, scientific events, economic events
- WORK_OF_ART: Titles of books, songs, paintings
- LAW: Named documents made into laws
- LANGUAGE: Any named language

spaCy includes some extended categories, too:
- DATE: Absolute or relative dates or periods
- TIME: Times smaller than a day
- PERCENT: Percentage, including "%"
- MONEY: Monetary values, including units
- QUANTITY: Measurements, e.g., of weight or distance
- ORDINAL: "first", "second", etc.
- CARDINAL: Numerals, such as 1, 10, 100, three, seventeen

The previous categories might have a letter assigned after them, for example, DATE_B. In spacyr, the BILUO tag is appended as a suffix to the entity type (e.g., PERSON_B, DATE_U). This is because it follows the BILUO tagging scheme, which stands for:

- B: Beginning of a multi-token entity (if the entity has only one token, use "U" instead)
- I: Inside of an entity (continuation of an entity started with B)
- L: Last token of an entity
- U: Unit entity (a single-token entity)
- O: Outside of any entity

This is used when the entity spans multiple tokens, and the current token is the first, inside, the last, etc., token in that sequence.

The BILUO scheme is a convention for entity spans for per-token labeling: begin, inside, last are used for multi-token entities; unit for single-token entities; and, outside for nonentity tokens. It lets models define precise boundaries for entities and is the suffix you see in, e.g., PERSON_B, ORG_I, DATE_U.

9.3 NER Information Extraction Using spacyr

In this subsection, we illustrate the functionalities of the NER process by using the R package spacyr, along with the sentiment data set we are already familiar with from ▶ Chap. 8. We will extract the most frequent entities for two brands and compare their counts. Then we will focus on the negative reviews and check how often specific entities are mentioned. Adjectives are often related to emotions, and checking them gives us more insights into how brands are perceived. However, adjectives can be related to other words, so we will also explore the part-of-speech (POS) dependencies. Tracking adjectives over time is a very useful way to measure the levels of satisfaction or dissatisfaction with products. Language complexity is another metric which can be calculated, is potentially important for understanding and comparing how people express their opinions about specific brands, and also gives a hint to managers on how to respond and match the users' styles.

9.3.1 Identifying and Describing Entities

After loading the `spacyr` library, the package introduces a function called `spacy_initialize()` to open the connection between R and Python, and which detects if the library exists and, if so, initializes it. Frequently, the cohabitation of R and Python can be problematic due to the environments Python might exist in and the versions or way it was installed on your operating system. For this data set, we suggest installing the model `en_core_web_lg`.

We will use the `comparison data set` from ▶ Chap. 8, which is a reduced version of the initial data set of product reviews. It contains the sentiment scores already assigned to each document, and we will select those which have a `sentiment.ai` score < -0.7, an empirical chosen threshold, so we can focus on the most negative reviews to identify the problems with the brands. We have also dropped some fields which we will not need, such as `sentimentAnalysis`, `vader`, `sentimentr`, or `syuzhet`, and selected two brands. In the example below, we chose Samsung and Apple.

9

```
library(spacyr)
library(dplyr)
library(lubridate)

# Initialize spaCy with a large English model
spacy_initialize(model = "en_core_web_lg")

# Clean and filter data, then add row numbers as Review_id
data <- comparison %>%
  select(-sentimentAnalysis, -sentimentr, -vader, -syuzhet) %>%
  filter(sentiment.ai < -0.7, Brand %in% c("Samsung", "Apple")) %>%
  mutate(Review_id = row_number())
```

Next we use the `spacy_parse()` function in the text column to perform some initial linguistic analysis. The parsed text is summarized as a table using the `parsedtxt` variable, which contains the text identifier (the number of the review), the sentence's position in the text, the token's position in the sentence, the actual word and its base (root) form, the grammatical category (e.g., noun, verb, adjective), and the NER labels as classifications for organizations, products, and so on.

```
# Parse text to extract syntactic dependencies
parsedtxt <- spacy_parse(data$target)
head(parsedtxt)
```

By carrying out this operation, we have lost some information from the original data set, but if we want to have a correspondence between each document, we can still merge this new data frame with an enhanced version of the original data set. Because it is helpful for the subsequent processing to separate the text into sentences, we transform each review's identification in the `data` frame by adding "text" to the numerical value of the "doc_id" field. After performing this operation, we save the data set to a new variable called `sent\_df`. We then merge this with the original data set to include the Brand column. Finally, we combine this data set with the `parsedtxt` data frame to create a new structure ready for analysis.

```
library(dplyr)

# Create doc_id, remove Review_id
data <- data %>%
  mutate(doc_id = paste0("text", as.character(Review_id))) %>%
  select(-Review_id)

# Tokenize text into sentences and assign sentence IDs
sent_df<- spacy_tokenize(data$target, what = "sentence",
                         output = "data.frame",
                         doc_id = data$doc_id) %>%
  rename(sentence = token) %>%
  group_by(doc_id) %>%
  mutate(sentence_id = row_number()) %>%
  ungroup()


# Merge back with original data to include the Brand and R_date
sent_df <- sent_df %>%
  left_join(data %>% select(doc_id, Brand, R_date), by = "doc_id"
  ↪ )

sentence_data <- parsedtxt %>%
  left_join(sent_df , by = c("doc_id", "sentence_id"))
```

The following code filters out invalid entity values, identifies unique `doc_id` and `entity` pairs, groups by brand and entity, counts the frequency of each entity for each brand, sorts by brand by the ascending number of appearances, and then selects the top ten most frequent entities per brand. A plot visualizes the frequency difference of the entities for each brand; see ◘ Fig. 9.3. For the meaning of the entities, check the beginning of this chapter.

```
library(ggplot2)

# Count top 10 unique entities per brand
entity_counts <- sentence_data %>%
```

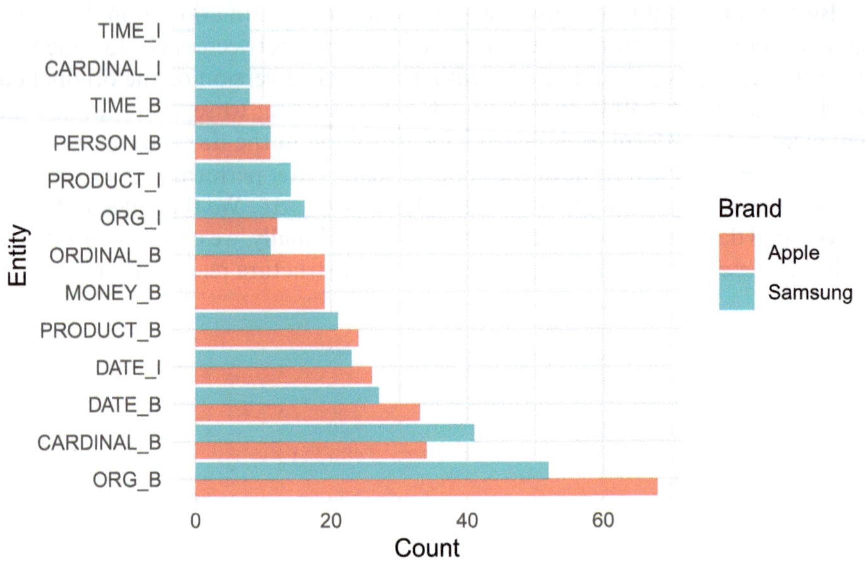

Fig. 9.3 Most frequent entities for each brand. Authors' own figure

9

```
  filter(entity != "") %>%
  distinct(doc_id, entity, .keep_all = TRUE) %>%
  group_by(Brand, entity) %>%
  summarize(count = n()) %>%
  arrange(Brand, desc(count)) %>%
  group_by(Brand) %>%
  slice_max(count, n = 10)

# Plot top entities for each brand
ggplot(entity_counts, aes(x = reorder(entity, -count),
                          y = count, fill = Brand)) +
  geom_bar(stat = "identity", position = "dodge") +
  labs(x = "Entity",
       y = "Count",
       fill = "Brand") +
  theme_minimal() +
  coord_flip()
```

Now, we want to find which ORG or PRODUCT entities are present in the negative reviews and how often. First, we filter for specific entities, such as "PRODUCT_B," "ORG_B," "ORG_I," and then we capitalize the tokens for both ORG and PRODUCT to ensure uniformity in the results. Then we group the tokens by brand, count the occurrences, filter tokens with more than five occurrences, and sort by descending counts. In the plot of the most frequent entities for each of the two brands, we can see (Fig. 9.4) how often competitors are mentioned in these reviews. For example, in the Samsung or Galaxy or Android reviews, there is

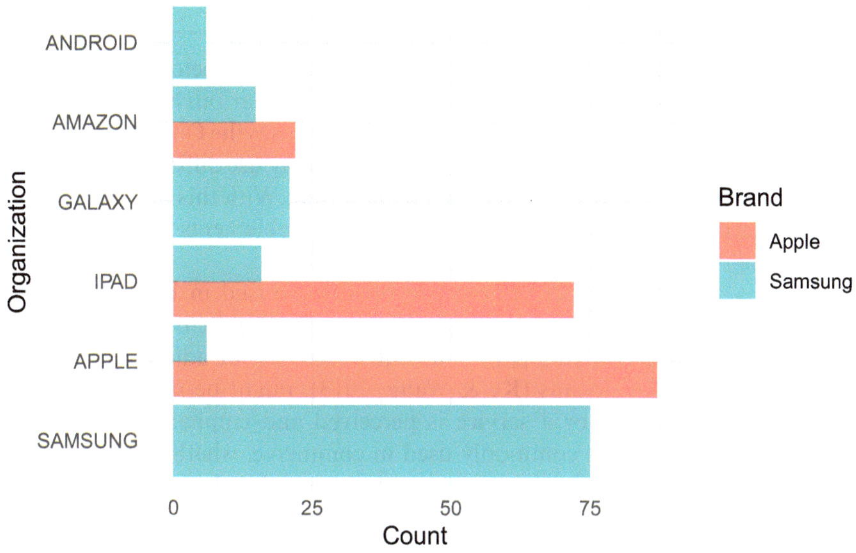

Fig. 9.4 Most frequent ORG/PROD entities subdivided by brand. Authors' own figure

no mention of an iPad or Apple product, while for Apple, Samsung is mentioned. Amazon is mentioned for both brands because it is the vendor.

```
# Filter and capitalize specific entities
op_entities <- sentence_data %>%
  filter(entity %in% c("PRODUCT_B", "ORG_B", "ORG_I")) %>%
  mutate(token = ifelse(startsWith(entity, "ORG") |
    startsWith(entity, "PRODUCT"), toupper(token), token))

# Count occurrences, filter, and sort
op_counts <- op_entities %>%
  group_by(token, Brand) %>%
  summarize(count = n()) %>%
  filter(count > 5) %>%
  arrange(desc(count))

# Plot most frequent entities by brand
ggplot(op_counts, aes(x = reorder(token, -count), y = count, fill
↪  = Brand)) +
  geom_bar(stat = "identity", position = "dodge") +
  labs(x = "Organization",
       y = "Count",
       fill = "Brand") +
  theme_minimal() +
  coord_flip()
```

9.3.2 Extracting Adjectives

The pos field identifies which category a word, or its lemma, belongs to, and uses a tag set that is generally well understood and useful across various applications. For a more detailed treatment, especially in English, spaCy uses the OntoNotes 5 version of the Penn Treebank tag set, while other languages may use different Treebanks. [3]. More details can be found in spaCy's documentation. With this understanding of the text structure, we can now proceed to extract specific elements from the analyzed content.

Emotions and sensory perceptions are often expressed in language through adjectives, and it is useful to understand this because they help us differentiate a brand and to detect underlying pain points. Repeated use of adjectives in reviews, or their appearance in slogans (Ke & Wang, 2013), might be persuasive (Ebaid, 2018) for how a product or a service is perceived and emphasizes strengths or weaknesses. Adjectives are commonly used in commerce, whether they appear in a simple basic form, or as comparatives or superlatives (Hakkarainen, 2016). They can elicit emotions and help people remember a specific attribute of a brand (Berger et al., 2021; Rocklage & Fazio, 2020)). We have selected the adjectives (ADJ) part of the reviews, grouped them by adjective token and brand, counted the occurrences, filtered adjectives with more than one occurrence, and then sorted by descending counts. After this, we have listed the 20 most frequent adjectives and the brands they are related to.

```
library(tidyr)

# Filter adjectives from sentence data and lowercase token
adj_entities <- sentence_data %>%
  filter(pos == "ADJ") %>%
  mutate(token = tolower(token))

# Count occurrences of adjectives by brand
adj_counts <- adj_entities %>%
  group_by(token, Brand) %>%
  summarize(count = n(), .groups = "drop")  # Count occurrences
  ↪  per brand

# Create columns for Apple and Samsung brands and counts
adj_counts_wide <- adj_counts %>%
  pivot_wider(names_from = Brand,
              values_from = count,
              values_fill = list(count = 0)) %>%
  rename(`Count Apple`   = Apple,
         `Count Samsung` = Samsung) %>%
  arrange(desc(`Count Apple` + `Count Samsung`))
```

3 spaCy's POS Tagging Documentation: https://spacy.io/docs/usage/pos-tagging#pos-tagging-english

```
# Display the top 20 most frequent adjectives
top_20_adj <- adj_counts_wide %>%
  slice_max(order_by = (`Count Apple` + `Count Samsung`), n = 20)

# Print results
print(top_20_adj)
```

```
# A tibble: 20 x 3
   token          `Count Apple` `Count Samsung`
   <chr>                  <int>           <int>
 1 other                     17              14
 2 new                       23               7
 3 same                       7              17
 4 bad                        4              16
 5 disappointed              11               8
 6 good                       8              11
 7 few                        6              12
 8 first                    11              6
 9 great                      6              11
10 more                      10               7
11 able                       4              10
12 many                       7               6
13 annoying                   1               9
14 long                       8               2
15 much                       2               8
16 sure                       5               4
17 unable                     6               3
18 dead                       5               3
19 most                       2               6
20 slow                       1               7
```

Basic adjectives describe a quality in a simple form without making any comparison. Comparative adjectives often end in "-er" and might appear together with degree adverbs such as "more" or "less." One such example is "better" (the comparative of "good") or "much better" (where much acts as a degree adverb modifying the comparative adjective "better"). Superlative adjectives go to the extreme; they often end in "-est" and are used with words like "most," "least," such as "best" or "least useful." In our data set, of the 20 adjectives, two are comparative, "better" and "bigger"; degree adverbs, so "more" and "much" are tagged as adverbs (ADV) in `spacyr` and are therefore treated separately, while the others are basic. As an exercise, we have left you the task of viewing all the adjectives and categorizing them.

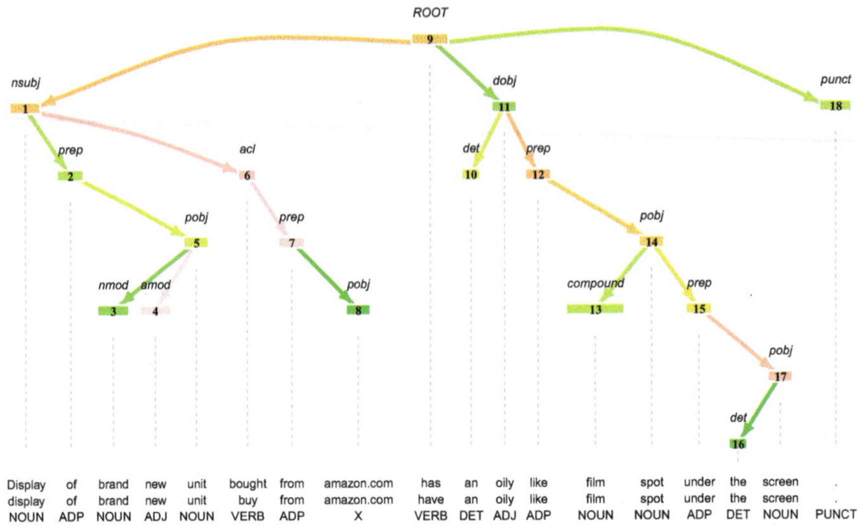

Fig. 9.5 POS dependencies. Authors' own figure

9

9.3.3 Dependencies and POS Highlighting

It is interesting and useful to obtain additional information from the text and better understand how parts of speech contribute to meaning. `spacyr`, in conjunction with the package `rsyntax`, helps us plot a tree of POS, highlighting the dependencies between words. If you want another example, you can substitute "text1" and assign a document of your choice to "doc_id"; see **Fig. 9.5** to visualize a syntactic-dependency parse tree and understand the grammatical structure of a sentence. The words are related to one another and this is indicated by the branches. The arrows point from a head word to a dependent word. The numbers correspond to the word order in a sentence to keep track of the order of appearance. The ROOT of the tree is the main verb, representing the central action, while other words are linked through different dependency relations. There are several labels in the image, such as "nsubj," "dobj," and "punct," which come from the universal dependency (UD) annotation scheme. For example, "nsubj" represents a nominal subject (who or what performs an action), "dobj" represents a direct object (the person or object that is the recipient of the action of a verb), "punct" is a punctuation mark. For a more complete list and definition of the labels, see De Marneffe et al. (2021). This type of analysis is also suitable for chatbots, search engines, or grammar correction tools.

```
library(rsyntax)

# Parse the text considering the dependencies
parsedtxt <- spacy_parse(data$target, dependency = TRUE)
```

```
# Plot the dependency tree for a specific document
plot_tree(
  as_tokenindex(parsedtxt),
  doc_id = "text1",
  token,
  lemma,
  pos,
  viewer_size = c(110, 150),
  textsize = 1,
  spacing = 2,
  viewer_mode = FALSE
)
```

It is useful to visualize some of the POS elements, especially those you are interested in. In the next example, we will select the first text in the data set and highlight the adjectives and nouns that refer to a number of specific entities. Although printed using shades of gray, we have encoded the entities in blue, the adjectives in red, and the nouns in green. Nouns are excellent candidates for product features (Kauffmann et al., 2019) and will allow you to capture the link between the adjectives and the nouns immediately. For the entities we are trying to understand more about, see the color-annotated text after the code.

```
library(dplyr)
library(htmltools)

# Filter for a specific document
doc_id_nr <- "text1"
parsed_data <- parsedtxt %>% filter(doc_id == doc_id_nr)

# Create a function to highlight annotations in text
highlight_annotations <- function(text, parsed_data) {
  tokens <- parsed_data$token
  entities <- parsed_data$entity
  pos_tags <- parsed_data$pos

  # Initialize an empty string to store the highlighted text
  highlighted_text <- ""

  for (i in seq_along(tokens)) {
    token <- tokens[i]
    entity <- entities[i]
    pos_tag <- pos_tags[i]

    # Highlight based on entity and POS tag
    if (entity != "") {
      highlighted_text <- paste0(highlighted_text,
                                 "<span style='color: blue;'>", token,
                                 ↪  "</span>")
```

```
    } else if (pos_tag == "ADJ") {
      highlighted_text <- paste0(highlighted_text,
                        "<span style='color: red;'>", token,
                        ↪  "</span>")
    } else if (pos_tag == "NOUN") {
      highlighted_text <- paste0(highlighted_text,
                        "<span style='color: green;'>", token,
                        ↪  "</span>")
    } else {
      highlighted_text <- paste0(highlighted_text, token)
    }

    # Add a space after each token
    highlighted_text <- paste0(highlighted_text, " ")
  }

  return(highlighted_text)
}

# Apply the function to the parsed text
highlighted_text <- highlight_annotations(text, parsed_data)

# Display inline
browsable(HTML(highlighted_text))
```



```
Display of brand new unit bought from amazon.com has
an oily like film spot under the screen. It seems to be
a manufacturing defect, according to Internet research
lots of users do experience the same problem with their
units. Waiting for Samsung to fix that problem or recall
of the affected units, cause most customers still have
this screen problem, even after they have had their units
exchanged. Btw that problem on my tab is visible even
when the unit is cold - so I do not think that it is
necessarily heat related. Otherwise, it is really a great
Tab - but sorry Samsung - for 600 $ I would like to own a
unit without a flaw. Hope that there will be soon a
solution or a worldwide generous recall / replacement
offer to satisfy Galaxy users & fans.
```

Explore this review and run the code again to visualize another review by simply substituting "text1" with another value, such as "text2," "text10," or "text42." You can create several combinations by extracting not only the adjectives and nouns but also adverbs. Adverbs can be classified as being of time, frequency, location, manner, degree, or as conjunctive adverbs. In sentiment analysis, the adverbs of degree, such as "extremely," "absolutely," "really," and so on, are the most relevant ones. These adverbs have a further classification, as found in Benamara et al. (2007), and a few examples of each class are given below:

- Adverbs of affirmation: certainly, definitely, absolutely, surely, indeed, undoubtedly, clearly, obviously

- Adverbs of doubt: possibly, maybe, apparently, likely, conceivably, arguably, supposedly, uncertainly
- Strong intensifying adverbs: extremely, incredibly, absolutely, totally, completely, remarkably, exceptionally, amazingly, terribly, deeply
- Weak intensifying adverbs: somewhat, fairly, slightly, moderately, rather, mildly, partly, relatively
- Negation and minimizers are those that negate or diminish sentiments: never, nowhere, nothing, hardly, barely, rarely, little, infrequently

Adverbs, ADV, can be extracted in a similar manner to adjectives, and the detection of both adjectives and adverbs in text (Roy et al., 2015) can be used to shape targeted marketing messages.

9.3.4 Tracking Adjective Usage over Time

Marketers are interested in assessing the performance of their efforts by analyzing the prevalence of adjectives in consumer reviews before, during, and after marketing campaigns or product launches. A successful campaign might be reflected in an increase in the use of positive adjectives and a decrease in negative ones. We next demonstrate the tracking over time of the frequency of negative reviews for a brand, together with those containing a competitor. If the information is extracted properly from the data set, such tracking can also be helpful in acquiring seasonal insights and supporting crisis management. The following code filters the `comparison` data set to include only adjectives related to two brands (Apple and Samsung). Then it groups and counts the adjectives by date and brand, creates a line chart to display the adjective usage over time, and adds a smoothing curve to show the trends.

```
# Filter for adjectives and the two brands
adjective_data <- sentence_data %>%
  filter(pos == "ADJ" & Brand %in% c("Apple", "Samsung"))

# Group by date and brand, then count the number of adjectives
adjective_counts <- adjective_data %>%
  group_by(R_date, Brand) %>%
  summarize(count = n()) %>%
  ungroup()

# Plotting the data with both lines and smoothing
ggplot(adjective_counts, aes(x = R_date, y = count, color = Brand,
↪  linetype = Brand)) +
  geom_line() +
  geom_smooth(method = "loess", span = 0.3, se = FALSE) +
  labs(x = "Date", y = "Number of Adjectives") +
  theme_minimal() +
  theme(axis.text.x = element_text(angle = 45, hjust = 1)) +
  guides(color = guide_legend(override.aes = list(size = 1)))
```

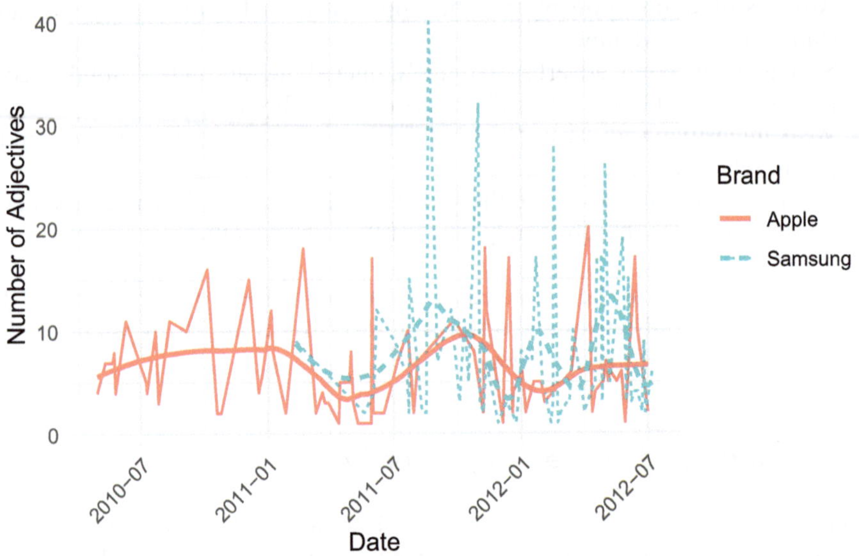

Fig. 9.6 Number of adjectives over time for Apple and Samsung. Authors' own figure

9

The graph in Fig. 9.6 plots the frequency of adjectives associated with two brands, Apple and Samsung. The trend for Apple shows fluctuations, with a general increase in the use of adjectives from 2010 to around mid-2012. A smooth trend line can also be seen. Samsung showed more variability between mid-2011 and late 2012. There is a general increase in variability over time, with peaks becoming more extreme. This might indicate more varied public and media reactions through a spike in adjective usage. Because the counts are raw and not adjusted for the number of reviews per month, some spikes may simply reflect changes in review volume rather than true shifts in language use. Consumers expressed negative feelings about Apple's products through the steady use of adjectives. Given that customers express their anger differently for the two brands, marketers can use this information to shape their communication strategies. The language used can be targeted at different segments of the population. It is possible to modify the previous code to add more brands, use a different smoothing method (for example, a linear model, `lm`) or use a stacked bar chart instead: replace `geom_line()` with `geom_bar(stat = "identity", position = "stack")`.

9.3.5 Language Complexity

Sometimes researchers are interested in studying the syntactic complexity in relation to the language proficiency shown in texts, and the overall (or "objective") proficiency in a target language (Ortega, 2003). When conducting these measurements, it is important to compare them against a benchmark or another unit, for example, unit A compared to unit B on a specific index can provide insights into accuracy and applicability (Szmrecsanyi, 2004). There are several metrics used to calculate syntactic complexity, and they are mainly used in linguistics, language acquisition, and computational linguistics. In this section, we demonstrate the use of a simple metric, which is based on the measurement of the density of verbs called Fichtner's C, (see Fichtner, 1980, and further explained in this document Samples et al., 2024), which is defined (in simplified form) as:

$$\text{Fichtner's C} = \frac{\text{Number of finite verb clauses}}{\text{Number of Sentences}} \times \frac{\text{Number of Words}}{\text{Number of Sentences}}$$

Note Fichtner (1980) actually counts finite verb clauses (i.e., tensed verbs heading independent or dependent clauses), but are approximated here by verb tokens. Our implementation treats every token tagged VERB as one clause, so the resulting index is an approximation of the original measure.

Using syntactic complexity in marketing allows for a detailed comparison of the language used to describe different brands. By analyzing metrics like Fichtner's C, marketers can gain insights into how brands are perceived and what level of complexity is used to describe them, thus tailoring their communication styles to specific audiences. The code below computes the index for Fichtner's C and compares the linguistic complexity between the brands on a table.

```
# Load necessary libraries
library(dplyr)
library(ggplot2)

# Calculate linguistic complexity for each document and brand
syn_com <- sentence_data %>%
  group_by(doc_id, Brand) %>%
  summarize(verb_num = sum(pos == "VERB"),
            sent_num = n_distinct(sentence_id),
            word_num = n()) %>%
  mutate(F_C = (verb_num / sent_num) * (word_num / sent_num)) %>%
  ungroup()

# Compare linguistic complexity between the two brands
brand_comparison <- syn_com %>%
  group_by(Brand) %>%
  summarize(avg_F_C = mean(F_C, na.rm = TRUE),
            sd_F_C = sd(F_C, na.rm = TRUE),
            median_F_C = median(F_C, na.rm = TRUE),
            n = n())

# Display the result
print(brand_comparison)
```

```
# A tibble: 2 x 5
```

```
  Brand    avg_F_C sd_F_C median_F_C     n
  <chr>      <dbl>  <dbl>      <dbl> <int>
1 Apple       55.2   89.0       37.7    87
2 Samsung     42.8   44.1       26.5    71
```

From the table, we can see that reviews containing Apple exhibit, on average, higher linguistic complexity, with a greater than average Fichtner's C index (`avg_F_C`) and a greater variability than Samsung, as shown by the higher standard deviation (`sd_F_C`). This could imply that content about Apple ranges from very simple to very complex, possibly depending on the type of document or context. In contrast, documents about Samsung are more consistent in terms of linguistic complexity, as indicated by the lower standard deviation (`sd_F_C`). This suggests that reviews about Samsung maintain a more uniform style across its documents. Both brands have median values (`median_F_C`) values lower than their respective averages (`avg_F_C`), indicating a right-skewed distribution. This means that most reviews have moderate levels of complexity, but there are some documents with very high complexity which raise the average. Notice that differences in reviews (in this case across brands) can also reflect the heterogeneity in language used by the clientele and not necessarily attributable to the brand as such. To visualize this, we can also plot the linguistic complexity measures.

9

```
# Plot the density of linguistic complexity for the two brands
ggplot(syn_com, aes(x = F_C, fill = Brand)) +
  geom_density(alpha = 0.5) +
  labs(x = "Linguistic Complexity (F_C)",
       y = "Density") +
  theme_minimal() +
  scale_fill_manual(values = c("Apple" = "blue", "Samsung" =
  ↪   "red")) +
  theme(legend.title = element_blank())
```

The visualization in ◘ Fig. 9.7 confirms our previous discussion. At the lower end of the linguistic complexity scale, both brands show a peak, and this shows that a larger proportion of their documents has low linguistic complexity. Apple reviews have a higher peak density compared to Samsung, which only indicates more mass near the mode; complexity depends on the peak's position along the F_C axis. The brands have long tails which reach higher levels of linguistic complexity, with Samsung having a more pronounced tail. This indicates that some documents have higher levels of complexity. Across the negative reviews, customers refer to Apple with more consistent linguistic complexity, so its documents are more homogenous. Customers who write about Samsung in a negative context use a slightly more varied writing style. Nevertheless, both brands, when they are described in negative terms, have a low level of linguistic complexity, indicating a precise focus and clear, straightforward communication.

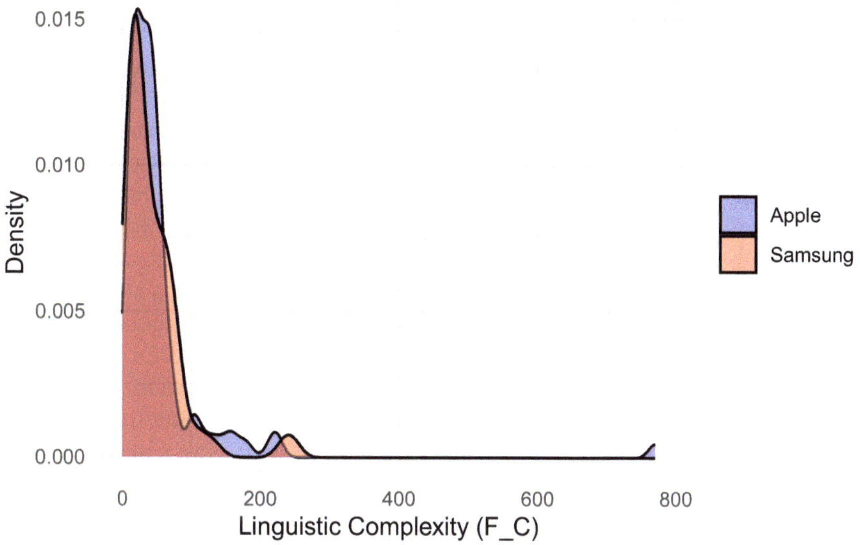

Fig. 9.7 Comparison of linguistic complexity for Apple and Samsung. Authors' own figure

9.3.6 Practical Tips

Several advanced techniques can be employed to enhance an NER task. An example is the use of consolidation functions to merge multi-word entities into a single token, or the concatenation of words into noun phrases, also called noun chunks. `spaCy` can use language models which are not limited to English, but also include German, Spanish, Portuguese, French, Italian, and Dutch, among others. `spacyr` can be integrated with other R text analysis packages, for example, `quanteda`, or `tidytext`, thus simplifying text manipulation and analysis tasks.

Additionally, as we have seen in ► Chap. 2, regular expressions can be helpful when extracting preposition-noun combinations from the corpus, and checking the most frequent noun for each preposition or other parts of speech. A clear understanding of the annotations and the meanings of the tags at different levels, as well as the tag sets present in various languages, is essential because these could influence your approach to NER and text analysis in general.

Using Python in the background of an R session can be very memory-intensive. Once your analysis is done, it is strongly recommended to use the `spacy_finalize()` function which terminates Python and frees up the memory it was using.

```
# Clean up and release spaCy resources
spacy_finalize()
```

9.4 Summarization

The word summary relates to something which is brief and concise. The word comes from the Latin word `summa`, which means "totality, gist." One will find summaries everywhere, such as a summary of a book, in the workplace, in the minutes of meetings, in news articles, and in customer reviews. Because we focus on the latter, we have to understand that this allows for an aggregated view of opinions, delivering something similar to "the wisdom of the crowd." Many texts are too long to read, and we often have too little time, and so the comment "too long, did not read." The abbreviation for this is TL;DR (again a shorter version of something), which is commonly used in online discussions, social media, etc., indicating content that is lengthy and that a summary is provided for whoever does not have time to read the whole text. TL;DR can be used as a label for the summary itself, or as a comment to indicate that the text is too long. Summaries are also useful for information retention and enhance the ability to learn something (Reder & Anderson, 1980), implying that they convey information in a very abridged form, creating a shortened version that retains only the essential information and main points. But how much can one summarize? In NLP, summarization can, generally, be achieved by using three approaches: extractive (Moratanch & Chitrakala, 2017), abstractive (Gupta & Gupta, 2019), or hybrid (El-Kassas et al., 2021). The first approach uses a selection (and extraction) of key sentences, or phrases, from the original text that act as a summary. This selection is typically based on statistical features such as importance scores, term frequency, or position. Abstractive summarization is a generative process that uses the rephrasing or paraphrasing of words which might not exist in the original text. This last approach involves understanding the context of a text and producing an abridged version that captures the gist of the original. The hybrid method is a combination of the first two. Below we will focus on extractive summarization because it can be accomplished relatively quickly, although it might be computationally intensive. It also fits nicely with the NER elements we have discussed so far.

> *Extractive summarization* is the selection and ranking of existing sentences/phrases (e.g., with graph-based centrality algorithms such as LexRank/TextRank) to produce concise synopses.
>
> *Abstractive summarization* generates new sentences that capture the gist of the material (often using neural models), and may include words not in the original. Hybrid methods combine both types. In this chapter, the emphasis is on the extractive methods which are practical in R.

9.4.1 Summarization in R

There are a few packages that help with the task of summarization in R, either directly or indirectly. One is `lexRankr`, another is LSAfun, and yet another one is textrank. The simplest one to work with is lexRankr. The implementation of the algorithm in R uses a stochastic graph-based method to assess the importance of a unit of text, such as a sentence, in a corpus (Erkan & Radev, 2004). The basic idea is that if the algorithm finds sentences which are similar to other sentences, it means that they are important. In this graph-base approach, sentences are nodes, and edges represent the similarity between sentences. To illustrate, let us take the "data" data frame and apply the algorithm.

```
library(lexRankr)
library(dplyr)
library(tidytext)

# Tokenize text data into sentences
tokenized_data <- data %>%
  unnest_sentences(sentence, target)

# Apply LexRank to rank sentences based on importance
ranked_sentences <- bind_lexrank(tokenized_data, sentence,
                                 doc_id, level = "sentences")


# Filter and get top 3 sentences for Apple
top_apple <- ranked_sentences %>%
  filter(Brand == "Apple") %>%
  arrange(desc(lexrank)) %>%
  slice(1:3)

# Filter and get top 3 sentences for Samsung
top_samsung <- ranked_sentences %>%
  filter(Brand == "Samsung") %>%
  arrange(desc(lexrank)) %>%
  slice(1:3)

# Display the results, for Apple
print(top_apple$sentence)

# Display the results, for Samsung
print(top_samsung$sentence)
```

```
[1] "the ipad in ?"
[2] "But it is not an iPad2."
[3] "No more apple products for us after this."

[1] "Its slower than ipad."
[2] "I did a lot of research on this tablet before
buying and saw nothing about this problem."
[3] "I will never buy a samsung product again!"
```

Considering that the data set was selected from negative reviews, the customers who talk about the Apple products express themselves in negative terms but not in a vehement way. The customers who talk about the Samsung tablets, however, seem to prefer Apple products.

To illustrate the use of another package to summarize text, let us take a look at `LSAfun`, which uses latent semantic analysis (Gong & Liu, 2001). The basic idea is to decompose the text into sentences and then choose a few `k`-candidate sentences to form the summary. Let us imagine a simple example, where we extract two sentences from the negative reviews data set, and try to understand the customers' reviews for both Apple and Samsung products from two sentences each. The function that performs this task is called `genericSummary()` and has several arguments. The first is the set of documents to analyze. The second is the number of sentences it needs to extract. And the third, called `split`, is a character vector which allows you to choose which symbols indicate the end of a sentence. `min` indicates the minimum number of words a sentence should contain. Here we will use only the first two arguments.

9

```
#install.packages("LSAfun")
library(LSAfun)
library(dplyr)
library(tidytext)

# We can recycle the sent_df data frame because it contains all
↪  the elements we need.

apple_data <- sent_df %>%
  filter(Brand == "Apple")

samsung_data <- sent_df %>%
  filter(Brand == "Samsung")

# Summarize to 2 sentences
summary_apple <- genericSummary(apple_data$sentence, k = 2)
summary_samsung <- genericSummary(samsung_data$sentence, k = 2)

# Display the results, for Apple
print(summary_apple)

# Display the results, for Samsung
print(summary_samsung)
```

```
[1] "I don't know why this P.O.S. has trouble with so
 ↪  many sites but here are some
examples of things I've run into (and these are
 ↪  condensed): 1) just now while on
Tripadvisor.com, I was trying to access the second page
 ↪  on the list of 'Local
```

```
Attractions' and it froze while loading, showing the
 ↪  message \"Updating your results\"
2) I am unable to scroll down on certain drop-down boxes
 ↪  on websites 3) occasionally
while doing a Google search I am unable to modify my
 ↪  search terms and it just defaults
back to my original search no matter how I attempt to
 ↪  enter it"
[2] "when i looked at the box, the original serial number
 ↪  was scratched off the barcode
label, telling me that the vendor had sent another
 ↪  (broken) device instead of the one that
was originally in the box"

[1] "Im very disappointed of the touch screen
 ↪  sensitivity, nothing compared with the
ipod touch i had, there are sometimes that i have to
 ↪  touch more than 4 or 5 times to get
a response It is a big problem when i try to logouton
 ↪  facebook always is the same i have
to zoom out the screen to make big buttons and not only
 ↪  in facebook, in all web pages is
the same, i tried many web browsers and the tablet is
 ↪  always calibrated but always i have
problems with the screen i think this is a software
 ↪  problem, because there is a program to
test the sensitivity and it seems that the screens
 ↪  response ok, I hope they will fix this soon
because this is very annoying, I like other companies
 ↪  than apple make tablets because
I was tired of itunes and all that, that is why i tried
 ↪  other brand."
[2] "Of course it shouldn't be hard to change this to my
 ↪  preferred language
(English UK) but it was sort of annoying to see that and
 ↪  have to correct it."
```

With this approach, we can see that the documents extracted are much longer, but are they really representative of the two brands?

Another graph-based ranking method, TextRank (Mihalcea & Tarau, 2004; Wijffels, 2020), can extract sentences or keywords. The nodes are words, and an edge is added when two words co-occur within a sliding window of `k` tokens (default $k = 4$ in `textrank_keywords()`); the edge weight reflects how often that co-occurrence happens. This structure is passed on to the PageRank algorithm (Xing & Ghorbani, 2004); implemented in Google's search engine, (Brin & Page, 1998), and named after one of its founders, Larry Page) to find the most important sentences which will form the summary of the text. In other words, the summary is made out of the most important sentences. A summary can also be created by using keywords. These represent documents and distill their content, expressing concepts, themes, or topics in just a few words, making the process of information indexing, searching, and retrieval easier. In the TextRank algorithm, a word network is built in a similar way to those that you have already encountered in ▶ Chap. 8, ▶ Sect. 8.3.2, for example. The link between words becomes important when two words frequently follow one another. In this case, PageRank is used as well, and the top third of the keywords is considered important. Finding which words are relevant can be done through the POS tagging we have seen in the NER part of this chapter using `spacyr`. Let us set this up and extract the important keywords. We have created a table that contains the sentences, lemmas, and parts of speech. We can look at the newly created data frame which contains all the information we need by selecting the fields "sentence_id," "lemma," and "upos."


```
# Add a unique identifier to each sentence and select relevant
↪  columns
sent_df_all <- sentence_data %>%
  mutate(textrank_id = paste(doc_id, sentence_id, sep = "_")) %>%
  select(textrank_id, doc_id, sentence_id, sentence, token, lemma,
  ↪  pos, Brand)

# Filter the data for sentences related to Apple
sent_df_apple <- sent_df_all %>%
  filter(Brand == "Apple")

# Filter the data for sentences related to Samsung
sent_df_smsng <- sent_df_all %>%
  filter(Brand == "Samsung")

# Display the first 10 rows of selected columns for Samsung
↪  sentences
head(sent_df_smsng[, c("sentence_id", "lemma", "pos")], 10)
```

```
   sentence_id      lemma   pos
1            1    display  NOUN
2            1         of   ADP
3            1      brand  NOUN
4            1        new   ADJ
5            1       unit  NOUN
6            1        buy  VERB
7            1       from   ADP
8            1 amazon.com PROPN
9            1       have  VERB
10           1         an   DET
```

Now, we can extract the most important keywords for both brands. For this example, we will choose nouns and adjectives and subset the data sets for multi-word frequencies. For space reasons, we have chosen different frequencies for the brands, but it is possible to play around and select a frequency threshold of > 0.

```
library(textrank)  # Load library

# Extract keywords for Apple (nouns/adjectives)
tr_kw_a <- textrank_keywords(sent_df_apple$lemma,
                             relevant = sent_df_apple$pos %in%
                             ↪  c("NOUN", "ADJ"))
# Filter: multi-word, freq >= 2
subset(tr_kw_a$keywords, ngram > 1 & freq >= 2)
```

```
               keyword ngram freq
33              e---mail     3    9
34                --mail     2    9
49      customer-service     2    5
57               new-one     2    4
72      first-generation     2    3
74              usb-port     2    3
77            list-price     2    3
80           apple-store     2    3
83         apple-product     2    3
93         serial-number     2    3
95          tech-support     2    3
97              web-site     2    3
104             year-old     2    2
105            many-site     2    2
107           long-story     2    2
109             next-day     2    2
110      wifi-connection     2    2
111            long-time     2    2
112            first-one     2    2
114           wifi-issue     2    2
116           same-thing     2    2
118        free-shipping     2    2
123     software-problem     2    2
124          credit-card     2    2
125    electronic-device     2    2
128         day-warranty     2    2
```

```
# Extract keywords for Samsung (nouns/adjectives)
tr_kw_s <- textrank_keywords(sent_df_smsng$lemma,
```

```
                         relevant = sent_df_smsng$pos %in%
                         ↪  c("NOUN", "ADJ"))
# Filter: multi-word, freq >= 4
subset(tr_kw_s$keywords, ngram > 1 & freq >= 4)
```

```
         keyword ngram freq
62 same-problem      2    4
65 model-number      2    4
66 touch-screen      2    4
67      web-page     2    4
80     same-loop     2    4
```

We set different cut-offs (`freq >= 2` for Apple, `>= 4` for Samsung) only to keep the tables brief—not because the corpora differ. For symmetry, use the same cut-off for both brands or call `slice_max(..., n = 10)` to take the top n keywords.

We can do the same procedure for sentences, but this time for both brands, applying the `textrank()` function to them. We can also plot the ranking of one of the brands to see this visually, as in ◘ Fig. 9.8. The ranking procedure might take a long time for larger data sets, but there are dimensionality reduction algorithms which are useful in such cases, for example, Minhash (Broder et al., 1998).

```
# Extract unique sentences for Apple and Samsung
sentences_apple <- unique(sent_df_apple[, c("textrank_id",
↪  "sentence")])
sentences_smsng <- unique(sent_df_smsng[, c("textrank_id",
↪  "sentence")])
```

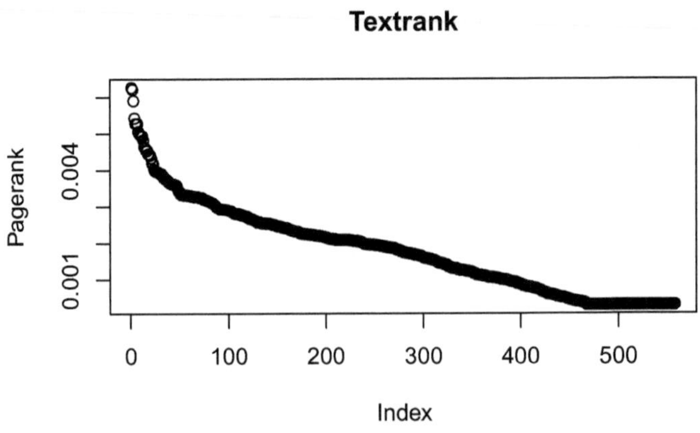

◘ **Fig. 9.8** TextRank sentence scores (Apple). Authors' own figure

```
# Filter terms by POS tags for noun and adjective, select relevant
↪ columns
term_apple <- sent_df_apple[sent_df_apple$pos %in% c("NOUN",
↪ "ADJ"),
                            c("textrank_id", "lemma")]
term_smsng <- sent_df_smsng[sent_df_smsng$pos %in% c("NOUN",
↪ "ADJ"),
                            c("textrank_id", "lemma")]

# Apply textrank to find relevant sentences
tr_apple <- textrank_sentences(data = sentences_apple, terminology
↪ = term_apple)
tr_smsng <- textrank_sentences(data = sentences_smsng, terminology
↪ = term_smsng)

# Plot pagerank for Apple's textrank results
plot(sort(tr_apple$pagerank$vector, decreasing = TRUE), type =
↪ "b",
     ylab = "Pagerank")
```

We have extracted the top three sentences for Apple, although we could have extracted as many as we wanted. They appear in ranking order.

```
# Top 3 sentences for Apple
sum_apple <- summary(tr_apple, n = 3, keep.sentence.order = TRUE)
print(sum_apple)
```

```
[1] "Got the product and had problems with it right
↪ away."
[2] "Just after I ordered and received this product,
↪ Apple released their newest IPad II."
[3] "Nor can I review all the items I purchased to use
↪ with the product."
```

Here we have extracted the top three sentences for Samsung.

```
# Top 3 sentences for Samsung
sum_smsng <- summary(tr_smsng, n = 3, keep.sentence.order = TRUE)
print(sum_smsng)
```

```
[1] "Problem solved with the tablet."
[2] "At first the tablet works just fine."
[3] "Love this tablet."
```

Interestingly, sentences with `textrank` are shorter than in the results obtained using the previous package. We can see that a comparison with other brands is made very often, especially in negative reviews. As an exercise, plot `pagerank` for Samsung's `textrank` results.

9.4.2 A Note

Abstractive summarization is a more complex form compared to extractive summarization. It involves generating new sentences that convey the main ideas of the original text. In R, abstractive summarization is not straightforward due to the lack of direct support for complex neural network models within R itself. However, you can use R to interface with other tools or libraries which support abstractive summarization, such as Python libraries via reticulate or external application programming interfaces (APIs). But in the next chapter, we will discuss more advanced tools for carrying out text analysis, and these will allow us to generate text, too.

Exercise 1. Select all the entities which refer to a person's name. Are they related to the data set?

Exercise 2. Visualize a series of nouns for two brands over a timeline.

Exercise 3. Create a model of linguistic complexity over a timeline.

Exercise 4. Read `spacyr`'s documentation and use a consolidation function to merge multi-word entities.

Exercise 5. Plot the relative importance of sentences in the `tr_smsng` variable.

Conclusion

The chapter began with an introduction to named entity recognition, its definition, and why this method is useful in marketing. We discussed several packages used for NER, with `spacyr` being our package of choice for performing analysis. The package is discussed in detail, and its types of annotation are also presented. We have focused on the extraction of entities, along with other parts of speech. We discussed the information extraction based on specific POS, such as adjectives whose frequency is also presented as a timeline on a brand-comparison plot. Continuing with visual representation, we used this to examine parts-of-speech dependencies, as well as entity, nouns, and highlighting adjectives. A special mention was given to the text complexity, which can offer insights into how customers express their frustration in negative reviews. Summarization is related to NER, especially via the keywords which

(continued)

are parts of speech. We also introduced three R packages which perform extractive summarization. This chapter has provided an overview of NER and summarization and complements the methods of text analysis discussed in previous chapters.

Discussion

Ambiguous entities: Is "Amazon" a river or a company? Design a disambiguation checklist of neighboring words, category priors, page/domain context, capitalization, and dependency cues and discuss the failure modes in reviews.

Anonymization and compliance: Given personally identifiable information in reviews, outline a masking policy using NER types (PERSON, GPE, ORG, DATE) to discuss how to audit recall/precision to align with GDPR requirements.

Trade-offs in the choice of package: spacyr vs. udpipe vs. OpenNLP—when would you use each for NER in R? Compare accuracy, speed, language coverage, install complexity, and features (POS/dependencies).

Adj/dependency insights: Propose a pipeline which extracts the adjectives attached to product/brand nouns using dependencies to track brand perception over time; define the validation metrics (inter-brand contrast, stability).

Summarization strategy: Contrast the use of LexRank/TextRank vs. LSA-based methods for thousands of reviews: how do you tune at sentence level, similarity threshold, n-sentences, and evaluate coverage and redundancy?

Take Home Message

- NER turns unstructured text into "who/what/where/when" facts using entity types and boundaries.
- Multiple routes exist in R (e.g., `spacyr`, `udpipe`, `OpenNLP`); `spacyr` combines `spaCy` with POS, dependencies, and NER, forming a single pipeline.
- BILUO tagging encodes entity span boundaries at token level, enabling clean extraction and counts.
- The combination of POS/dependency parsing with NER (e.g., focusing on adjectives tied to brands) provides granular insights into marketing (pain points, positioning).
- For large review sets, extractive summarization (e.g., LexRank/TextRank) is practical and complements NER by revealing characteristic sentences quickly.

References

Arkhipov, M., Trofimova, M., Kuratov, Y., & Sorokin, A. (2019). Tuning multilingual transformers for language-specific named entity recognition. *Proceedings of the 7th Workshop on Balto-Slavic Natural Language Processing*, 89–93.

Benamara, F., Cesarano, C., Picariello, A., Recupero, D. R., & Subrahmanian, V. S. (2007). Sentiment analysis: Adjectives and adverbs are better than adjectives alone. *ICWSM*, *7*, 203–206.

Benoit, K., & Matsuo, A. (2023). *Spacyr: Wrapper to the 'spaCy' NLP library*. https://CRAN.R-project.org/package=spacyr

Berger, J., Kim, Y. D., & Meyer, R. (2021). What makes content engaging? How emotional dynamics shape success. *Journal of Consumer Research*, *48*(2), 235–250.

Bird, S., Klein, E., & Loper, E. (2009). *Natural language processing with python: Analyzing text with the natural language toolkit*. O'Reilly Media, Inc.

Brin, S., & Page, L. (1998). The anatomy of a large-scale hypertextual web search engine. *Computer Networks and ISDN Systems*, *30*(1-7), 107–117.

Broder, A. Z., Charikar, M., Frieze, A. M., & Mitzenmacher, M. (1998). Min-wise independent permutations. *Proceedings of the Thirtieth Annual ACM Symposium on Theory of Computing*, 327–336.

Chieu, H. L., & Ng, H. T. (2003). Named entity recognition with a maximum entropy approach. *Proceedings of the Seventh Conference on Natural Language Learning at HLT-NAACL 2003*, 160–163.

De Marneffe, M.-C., Manning, C. D., Nivre, J., & Zeman, D. (2021). Universal dependencies. *Computational Linguistics*, *47*(2), 255–308.

Dias, M., Boné, J., Ferreira, J. C., Ribeiro, R., & Maia, R. (2020). Named entity recognition for sensitive data discovery in portuguese. *Applied Sciences*, *10*(7), 2303.

Ebaid, H. A. (2018). Adjectives as persuasive tools: The case of product naming. *Open Journal of Modern Linguistics*, *8*(6), 262–293.

El-Kassas, W. S., Salama, C. R., Rafea, A. A., & Mohamed, H. K. (2021). Automatic text summarization: A comprehensive survey. *Expert Systems with Applications*, *165*, 113679.

Erkan, G., & Radev, D. R. (2004). LexRank: Graph-based lexical centrality as salience in text summarization. *Journal of Artificial Intelligence Research*, *22*, 457–479.

Fichtner, E. G. (1980). Measuring syntactic complexity: The quantification of one factor in linguistic difficulty. *Die Unterrichtspraxis/Teaching German*, *13*(1), 67–75.

9

Gong, Y., & Liu, X. (2001). Generic text summarization using relevance measure and latent semantic analysis. *Proceedings of the 24th Annual International ACM SIGIR Conference on Research and Development in Information Retrieval*, 19–25.

Gupta, S., & Gupta, S. K. (2019). Abstractive summarization: An overview of the state of the art. *Expert Systems with Applications*, *121*, 49–65.

Hakkarainen, M. P. (2016). *They sell it how?: A study on adjective use in english and finnish ford adverts* [Master's thesis]. Itä-Suomen yliopisto.

Hassel, M. (2003). Exploitation of named entities in automatic text summarization for swedish. *NODALIDA'03–14th Nordic Conference on Computational Linguistics, Reykjavik, Iceland, May 30–31 2003*, 9.

Kauffmann, E., Peral, J., Gil, D., Ferrández, A., Sellers, R., & Mora, H. (2019). Managing marketing decision-making with sentiment analysis: An evaluation of the main product features using text data mining. *Sustainability*, *11*(15), 4235.

Ke, Q., & Wang, W. (2013). The adjective frequency in advertising english slogans. *Theory & Practice in Language Studies (TPLS)*, *3*(2).

Li, L., Jin, L., Jiang, Z., Song, D., & Huang, D. (2015). Biomedical named entity recognition based on extended recurrent neural networks. *2015 IEEE International Conference on Bioinformatics and Biomedicine (BIBM)*, 649–652.

Mihalcea, R., & Tarau, P. (2004). TextRank: Bringing order into text. *Proceedings of the 2004 Conference on Empirical Methods in Natural Language Processing*, 404–411.

Moratanch, N., & Chitrakala, S. (2017). A survey on extractive text summarization. *2017 International Conference on Computer, Communication and Signal Processing (ICCCSP)*, 1–6.

Morwal, S., Jahan, N., & Chopra, D. (2012). Named entity recognition using hidden markov model (HMM). *International Journal on Natural Language Computing (IJNLC)*, *1*.

Mullen, L. A., Benoit, K., Keyes, O., Selivanov, D., & Arnold, J. (2018). Fast, consistent tokenization of natural language text. *Journal of Open Source Software*, *3*(23), 655.

Netzer, O., Feldman, R., Goldenberg, J., & Fresko, M. (2012). Mine your own business: Market-structure surveillance through text mining. *Marketing Science*, *31*(3), 521–543.

Nouvel, D., Ehrmann, M., & Rosset, S. (2016). *Named entities for computational linguistics*. John Wiley & Sons.

Ortega, L. (2003). Syntactic complexity measures and their relationship to L2 proficiency: A research synthesis of college-level L2 writing. *Applied Linguistics*, *24*(4), 492–518.

Popescu, A.-M., & Etzioni, O. (2007). Extracting product features and opinions from reviews. In *Natural language processing and text mining* (pp. 9–28). Springer.

Project, U. D. (2022). *CoNLL-u format: A format for universal dependencies*. https://universaldependencies.org/format.html

Reder, L. M., & Anderson, J. R. (1980). A comparison of texts and their summaries: Memorial consequences. *Journal of Verbal Learning and Verbal Behavior*, *19*(2), 121–134.

Rocklage, M. D., & Fazio, R. H. (2020). The enhancing versus backfiring effects of positive emotion in consumer reviews. *Journal of Marketing Research*, *57*(2), 332–352.

Roy, R. S., Padmakumar, A., Jeganathan, G. P., & Kumaraguru, P. (2015). Automated linguistic personalization of targeted marketing messages mining user-generated text on social media. *Computational Linguistics and Intelligent Text Processing: 16th International Conference, CICLing 2015, Cairo, Egypt, April 14-20, 2015, Proceedings, Part II*, 203–224.

Samples, T. R., Ireland, K., & Kraczon, C. (2024). TL;DR: The law and linguistics of social platform terms-of-use. *Berkeley Technology Law Journal*, *39*(1), 47–108.

Schuster, S., & Manning, C. D. (2016). Enhanced english universal dependencies: An improved representation for natural language understanding tasks. *Proceedings of the Tenth International Conference on Language Resources and Evaluation (LREC'16)*, 2371–2378.

Sun, C., Guan, Y., Wang, X., & Lin, L. (2006). Biomedical named entities recognition using conditional random fields model. *International Conference on Fuzzy Systems and Knowledge Discovery*, 1279–1288.

Szmrecsanyi, B. (2004). On operationalizing syntactic complexity. *Le Poids Des Mots: Proceedings of the 7th International Conference on Textual Data Statistical Analysis*, *2*, 1032–1039.

Vasiliev, Y. (2020). *Natural language processing with python and spaCy: A practical introduction*. No Starch Press.

Wijffels, J. (2020). *Textrank: Summarize text by ranking sentences and finding keywords*. https://CRAN.R-project.org/package=textrank

Xing, W., & Ghorbani, A. (2004). Weighted PageRank algorithm. *Proceedings of the Second Annual Conference on Communication Networks and Services Research*, 305–314.

Zhu, Y., Wang, G., & Karlsson, B. F. (2019). CAN-NER: Convolutional attention network for chinese named entity recognition. *arXiv Preprint arXiv:1904.02141*.

References

Ortega, L. (2003). Syntactic complexity measures and their relationship to L2 proficiency: A research synthesis of college-level L2 writing. *Applied Linguistics, 24*(4), 492–518.

Popescu, A.-M., & Etzioni, O. (2007). Extracting product features and opinions from reviews. In *Natural language processing and text mining* (pp. 9–28). Springer.

[illegible]

Rocklage, M. D., & Fazio, R. H. (2020). The enhancing versus backfiring effects of positive emotion in consumer reviews. [illegible]

[illegible]

[illegible]

[illegible]

[illegible]

[illegible]

[illegible]

[illegible]

Word Embeddings and Transformers for Marketing Text Analytics

D. Dan, T. Reutterer, *Text Analytics in Marketing*, Classroom Companion: Business,
https://doi.org/10.1007/978-3-032-08086-8_10

Keywords
Word embeddings · word2vec · CBOW · Skip-gram · Negative sampling · Cosine similarity · GloVe · FastText · Transformers · Self-attention

This chapter details the procedures for extracting information contained in embeddings within marketing text analytics. It establishes the notion of embedding space, including word embeddings and word vectors and demonstrates how similarities and analogies are calculated (cosine similarity). It also covers word2vec, through the continuous bag-of-words (CBOW) and skip-gram models, along with sliding windows, negative sampling, backpropagation, and hyperparameters for effective training. The chapter describes transformer architecture, positional encoding, self-attention, encoder-decoder stacks, and their applications for language as well as sequential marketing data. It contains applied examples in R, including training a model on product reviews to determine brand associations (i.e., Apple, Samsung), neighborhood visualizations in UMAP and clustering, and vector arithmetic to see how we interpret products. Abstractive summarization and question answering for tablet reviews are presented as an example of transformers, underlining how unstructured feedback can provide insights at scale. Finally, the chapter explains how to interpret the outputs of the model, warns against mimicking large models statistically, and concludes with exercises.

Learning Objectives

- Understanding the concept of word embedding.
- Seeing how word vectorization is used.
- Tackling the concept of similarity using vectors.
- Understanding `word2vec` and its training model.
- Dealing with the concept of transformers.
- Understanding the concept of context and different embedding values.
- Using word embedding to extract information.
- Using transformers for text abstractive summarization.
- Setting up questions and answers using transformers.

10.1 Introduction to Word Embeddings

The history of human language is tied to the evolution of our species (Johansson, 2013; Luef, 2018), and it is constantly changing (Milroy, 1995). Our language encodes emotions, experiences, cultural significance, and context very effectively. There seems to be a very tight relationship between language and thinking, and they affect each other in several ways, such as in the perception of time, space, or even colors (Boroditsky, 2001; Winawer et al., 2007). The words we hear, read, or write can be transformed into vectors of numbers which capture information not only about the word itself but also about its context and its links to other related words. Word embedding is a concept that has been part of academic and industrial AI discourse for quite some time. The name does not ring a bell immediately, perhaps because it originates in mathematics: An embedding is a function that maps elements from one space onto another (Haroske & Triebel, 2011). The concept has been extended to NLP, where words, as the main components of the human language, are mapped onto a mathematical concept represented by a continuous vector space (Mikolov et al., 2013), becoming embedded there. Word embedding has been used in research on finance, where it is used to generate financial lexicons (Das et al., 2022), historical corpora (Wevers & Koolen, 2020), agriculture (Guo et al., 2021), and music (Kumar et al., 2018), to name just a few areas where it is of increasing interest.

Word embedding maps words (or sub-words) onto points in a continuous vector space, where the geometric proximity shows the semantic and syntactic closeness gleaned from data (e.g., co-occurrence statistics). Embeddings enable the use of algebra for language (nearest neighbors, analogies) and underlie tasks such as retrieval, clustering, and classification.

Word embedding has seen a growing number of applications in marketing. For example, Timoshenko and Hauser (2019) use word embeddings and a machine learning classifier to identify customer needs from user-generated content. Toubia et al. (2021) use embedding to quantify the semantic progression of a successful (marketing) narrative. More recently, embedding has been used to evaluate and predict the performance of email campaigns and recommended targeting policies for new promotions, e.g., (Ellickson et al., 2024) as well as to extract relevant contextual product characteristics and other information from unstructured text and image data, using this information to estimate demand or to derive product recommendations (Compiani et al., 2023; Sisodia et al., 2024).

Word embedding can be trained on large text corpora and allows for fast access to semantic relationships and similarities between, for example, specific products and brand names (e.g., "Kindle Fire" and "Amazon") and also to their characteristics expressed in words such as "tablet," "e-book reader," "gift," or "customer service." While word embedding focuses on the process of mapping words onto a vector space, a word vector is a directly related concept and refers to how a word is mapped onto a numerical sequence.

10.2 What Is a Word Vector?

In the following simple example, we focus on words which are related to emotions, and we represent them through two components: polarity and intensity. Their numerical values are encoded in a very subjective way. Polarity, which can be negative or positive, is expressed as a range between -1 (negative) and 1 (positive). Similarly, intensity can also be given values over a defined range, such as (0,1). When there is no emotional quality present in a word, the value is 0, while for intense emotion, the value is 1. The subjective emotional quality of a word like "joy" can be positive and intense, and it can be represented by two subjective numbers: [0.9, 0.7]. On the x-axis, the polarity = 0.9, while on the y-axis, intensity = 0.7. See ■ Table 10.1 for a more complete emotional data set. In a two-dimensional space, such as a scatterplot, and indeed in three-, four- or n-dimensional space, there is a correspondence between points and vectors that start at an origin and have several components, for each dimension, one component.

While points and vectors are not strictly the same, points can represent vectors in a vector space (see ■ Fig. 10.1). The word "joy," expressed by the coordinates [0.9, 0.7], describes a vector and also marks its endpoint. The set of all these vectors forms a space, in our case an emotional vector space. In real life, emotions such as anxiety and fear are often perceived as being very similar, and this can be reflected mathematically by their proximity on a two-dimensional plane.

The distance from the origin to a point is called magnitude, but vectors can also provide direction, so they can capture orientation as well. While it is not possible to apply mathematics to words directly, doing so using numerical transformations of

■ **Table 10.1** Emotional vector space. Table compiled by the authors

Word	Polarity	Intensity
Joy	0.9	0.7
Happiness	0.8	0.6
Contentment	0.6	0.3
Excitement	0.7	0.9
Anger	−0.5	0.8
Rage	−0.9	1.0
Sadness	−0.7	0.6
Grief	−0.8	0.85
Fear	−0.6	0.7
Anxiety	−0.7	0.8
Calmness	0.3	0.2
Boredom	−0.1	0.1

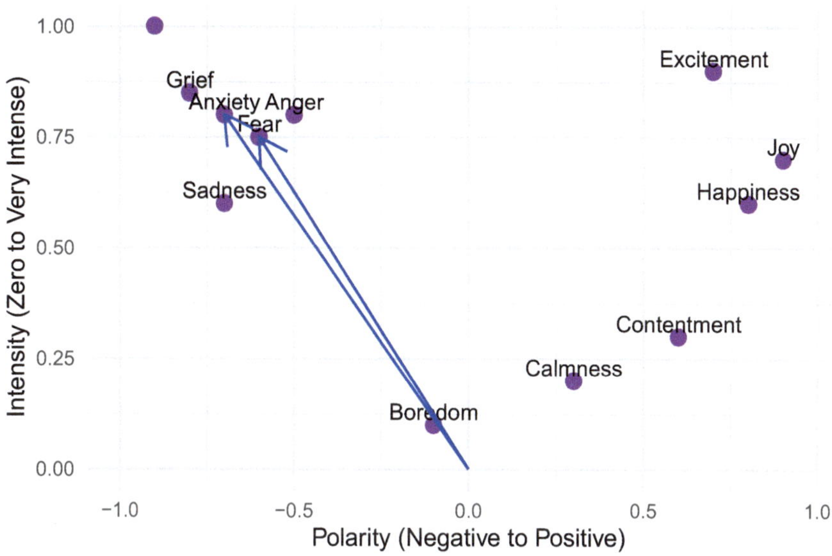

Fig. 10.1 Words expressing emotions: polarity vs. intensity. Authors' own figure

these words is feasible, resulting in values represented on a surface (or in a space). The similarity of these values is equivalent to the similarity in meaning of the words, which can be calculated through a measure called cosine similarity.

10.3 Cosine Similarity

Cosine similarity is a popular metric for evaluating the similarity between two vectorized entities, such as vector representations of words or, more generally speaking, text. This is accomplished by computing the cosine value of the angle between the entities, with a value of 1 (i.e., $\cos(0) = 1$), indicating that the vectors are identical. If the vectors oppose each other, they form a 180-degree angle (π rad) where $\cos(\pi) = -1$, indicating that they are opposite. If the vectors are perpendicular, the angle is 90 degrees, which can be expressed as $\frac{\pi}{2}$, and $\cos\left(\frac{\pi}{2}\right) = 0$, indicating they are unrelated. In case you are rusty on this topic, a refresher on trigonometry can be useful here, especially the unit (trigonometric) circle.

To better illustrate this with an example, let us consider two words, "fear" and "anxiety," along with their vector representations: fear ([-0.6,0.7]) and anxiety ([-0.7, 0.8]). Let us denote the angle between these two vectors by θ. The cosine similarity between the vectors **F** and **A** is given by the formula:

$$\cos\theta = \frac{\mathbf{F} \cdot \mathbf{A}}{\|\mathbf{F}\| \, \|\mathbf{A}\|}$$

Table 10.2 Emotion characteristics table. Table compiled by the authors

Word	Polarity	Intensity	Arousal	Valence	Dominance
Joy	0.9	0.7	0.8	0.9	0.7
Happiness	0.8	0.6	0.7	0.85	0.7
Contentment	0.6	0.3	0.4	0.75	0.5
Excitement	0.7	0.9	0.9	0.85	0.8
Anger	−0.5	0.75	0.8	0.15	0.4
Rage	−0.9	0.95	0.95	0.1	0.3
Sadness	−0.7	0.6	0.5	0.35	0.4
Grief	−0.8	0.85	0.7	0.2	0.3
Fear	**−0.6**	**0.7**	**0.9**	**0.3**	**0.4**
Anxiety	**−0.7**	**0.8**	**0.9**	**0.3**	**0.4**
Calmness	0.3	0.2	0.3	0.65	0.5
Boredom	−0.1	0.1	0.2	0.5	0.35

Bold indicates the emotion(s) with the most similar profile (i.e., closest values across the listed dimensions).

10

The numerator represents the dot product of the vectors: $\mathbf{F}\cdot\mathbf{A} = (-0.6)(-0.7)+(0.7)(0.8)$, while the denominator is the product of the magnitudes of the vectors: $\|\mathbf{F}\|\,\|\mathbf{A}\| = \sqrt{(-0.6)^2+(0.7)^2}\,\sqrt{(-0.7)^2+(0.8)^2}$.

Plugging these values into the formula, we obtain a cosine similarity value of approximately 0.999948. This high degree of similarity (close to 1) shows that these emotional expressions are perceived as being very similar, both in everyday understanding and in their numerical representation. A cosine similarity close to 1 indicates that there is a very small angle between these two vectors.

Instead of using two features, we can generalize this into many; see Table 10.2. We started with a basic example in two dimensions using polarity and intensity, and we have extended the example by adding three more dimensions to capture better the spectrum of the emotional characteristics of the words. In addition, arousal deals with the state of alertness or the energy of an emotion, the valence represents how pleasant or unpleasant an emotion is, and dominance shows how much control or influence an emotion exerts. While visualizing in more than two (or three) dimensions is tricky, this is not very demanding computationally. If we take a look at only the numbers, they may seem meaningless at first glance, but they are crucial in computational linguistics, as we can carry out several operations using these vectors and land in a region, i.e., reach a point in the vector space where the combination of features and words will show major densities and the positions of the vectors in nearby locations. In Table 10.2, we highlight in bold the most closely related emotions. Let us take a closer look at the row elements that are similar in the vector space; are they similar in meaning too?

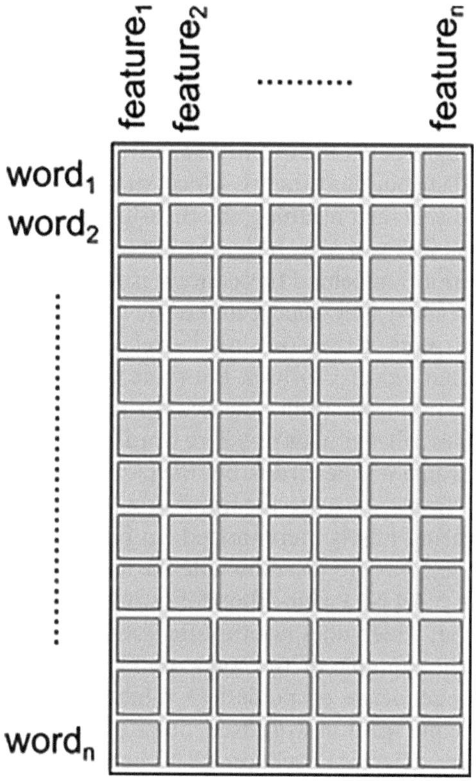

Fig. 10.2 Embeddings matrix. Authors' own figure

Notice that the two emotions, anxiety and fear, are expressed as vectors. If you take the numbers in the corresponding positions, they are very similar. We can also notice a fundamental insight: Similarity in numbers equals similarity in significance. Because we have vectors, we can calculate analogies, following the classic example, king – man + woman = queen (Mikolov et al., 2013). We can, therefore, check: if anxiety stands next to fear, joy stands next to what? If you do the computations, you obtain a vector that is very close to happiness. This is the way word embedding can be used to identify analogies. In Fig. 10.2, we can see how the word embedding takes the form of a matrix (the pictures that are not otherwise stated as the authors' are inspired by Alammar and Grootendorst (2024)). The features, such as polarity, intensity, arousal, valence, and dominance from Table 10.2, and others, appear vertically in the matrix, while words from the vocabulary, such as joy, happiness, and many more, are seen in the rows.

Now let us try to understand how these numbers are generated. An intuitive lead is given by the fact that, in a large corpus, similar words appear in similar contexts through their co-occurrence and generate similar vectors, i.e., similar embedding. Word embedding is used to assist or to improve tasks you have already seen, such as sentiment analysis, topic modeling, classification, and even translation, by using the semantic information of words encoded in the vectors. A popular algorithm to establish word embedding that tries to capture semantic similarities between words is `word2vec`, (Mikolov et al., 2013).

10.4 Creating Word Embedding

The work of linguists such as Ferdinand de Saussure (1857–1913), or anthropologists who made strong contributions to linguistics, such as Franz Boas (1858–1942), highlighted the importance of context in understanding language. In 1957, in his distributional theory which studies how the distribution of words in a text can reveal their meaning, the British linguist John Rupert Firth coined the phrase "[y]ou shall know a word by the company it keeps" (see Evert et al., 2008). The simple intuition behind this concept is that the meaning of the words is determined by the context they appear in, i.e., by the other words surrounding them. Some semantic aspects of the words can be defined by homonymy or polysemy. Homonymy means that words can look the same but have unrelated meanings. Terms like "mean" can "mean" (pun intended) or signify unpleasant, primitive, or average. Polysemy describes situations where words can have related meanings, as in the sentence "the frame was beautiful, but the painter was framed": The first occurrence of the word "frame" refers to the frame of a painting, while the second one refers to the painter being falsely incriminated. In both homonymy and polysemy, context analysis is necessary to disambiguate the target words.

An NLP algorithm, following Firth's theories and focusing on words in context but which does not capture polysemy or homonymy directly is word2vec. As with the example of the contextualized emotional vector space, it represents words as a sequence of numerical values in a more generic vector space. Note that the same word in word2vec, despite having a different context, cannot be represented by different sequences of numbers. There are two main procedures performed by word2vec: continuous bag-of-words (CBOW) and skip-gram. The first one predicts what a target word will be based on the surrounding words, and the second tries to predict the surrounding words based on a target word. We will explain how this is accomplished. Before doing so, however, we need you to familiarize yourself with some more basic concepts.

The words in a corpus will be transformed into embedded numbers created through the training of a neural network. Like all the tasks in artificial intelligence, the purpose of this operation is predictive. Let us consider ◘ Fig. 10.3 and understand how word2vec is implemented conceptually.

Initially, we have the vocabulary, and each word in the vocabulary is represented as a one-hot vector. This representation, similar to ◘ Fig. 4.2, considers all the words as vectors of the size of the vocabulary. When we select a specific word, that word will have a one corresponding to the index of the word, and all the other ones are zero. It is like focusing on the existence of that word; see ◘ Table 10.3. This way, we map each word to a position vector. The words do not necessarily have to be in alphabetical order; they can also be in order of appearance. If a word is repeated, it takes the index of the first occurrence.

Now having represented the vocabulary, we can take a single input word, for example "summer," as the center word, which has been fed into the neural network. This is the skip-gram approach; see ◘ Fig. 10.4. Panel A holds the vocabulary (with, for example, a size V of 1,000 words). Panel B holds x, the one-hot vector

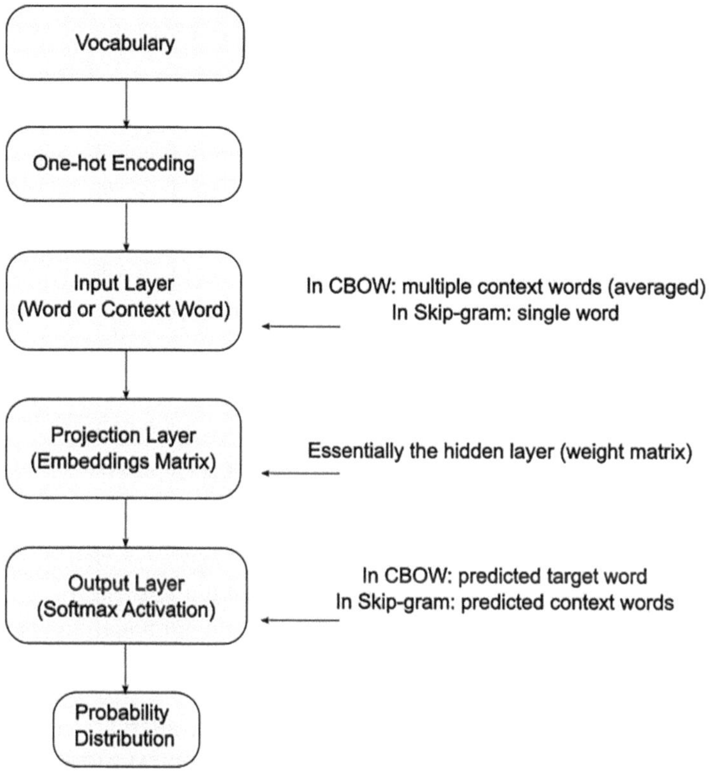

Fig. 10.3 The word2vec operation scheme. Authors' elaborated figure

for "summer," at index 2 (shape $V \times 1$). Panel C holds the input/embedding matrix E with one row per vocabulary word (shape $V \times d$), where d is the dimension of the word vectors (embedding size; for example, 300). Multiplying $E^{\top} x$ selects the row of E corresponding to `summer'' and returns it as a column vector of length $d$, so $h = E^{\top} x$ is the embedding ofsummer''`. The hidden layer is therefore a lookup table, i.e., the word-vector representation of the word "summer." This vector is then sent to the output layer, which is a classifier. The projection layer, where the embedding matrix resides, is the learned mapping that transforms the one-hot vector into a continuous vector (i.e., embedding). The softmax function converts the output into a probability distribution over the vocabulary. Panel D shows the result, a vector $\mathbf{p}$ of length V containing the probabilities of which words are close to the input word. C is the output (context) matrix with one row per vocabulary word (shape $V \times d$, also called output embeddings). When we compute $\mathbf{z} = C\mathbf{h}$, the i-th score is the dot product $z_i = c_i^{\top}\mathbf{h}$ between the output vector for word i and the center-word embedding $\mathbf{h}$. Softmax then turns these scores into probabilities over all words. The figure shows higher probabilities for "The" and "sale," the true neighbors for "summer." For background on skip-gram and CBOW, (see Mikolov et al., 2013).

Table 10.3 One-hot encoding of a sentence. Table compiled by the authors

Word	Index	One-hot vector
The	1	[1, 0, 0, 0, 0, 0, 0, 0, 0, 0, 0, 0, 0]
summer	2	[0, 1, 0, 0, 0, 0, 0, 0, 0, 0, 0, 0, 0]
sale	3	[0, 0, 1, 0, 0, 0, 0, 0, 0, 0, 0, 0, 0]
campaign	4	[0, 0, 0, 1, 0, 0, 0, 0, 0, 0, 0, 0, 0]
went	5	[0, 0, 0, 0, 1, 0, 0, 0, 0, 0, 0, 0, 0]
viral	6	[0, 0, 0, 0, 0, 1, 0, 0, 0, 0, 0, 0, 0]
on	7	[0, 0, 0, 0, 0, 0, 1, 0, 0, 0, 0, 0, 0]
social	8	[0, 0, 0, 0, 0, 0, 0, 1, 0, 0, 0, 0, 0]
media	9	[0, 0, 0, 0, 0, 0, 0, 0, 1, 0, 0, 0, 0]
and	10	[0, 0, 0, 0, 0, 0, 0, 0, 0, 1, 0, 0, 0]
increased	11	[0, 0, 0, 0, 0, 0, 0, 0, 0, 0, 1, 0, 0]
brand	12	[0, 0, 0, 0, 0, 0, 0, 0, 0, 0, 0, 1, 0]
awareness	13	[0, 0, 0, 0, 0, 0, 0, 0, 0, 0, 0, 0, 1]

Here we presented only the skip-gram model, but alternatively the CBOW approach can be used too, where you can take multiple context words and use them as input, often by averaging their one-hot vectors (see Wang et al., 2017).

CBOW (continuous bag-of-words) is a predictive algorithm that targets a word depending on its surrounding words in context (it is fast and useful for frequent words).

A skip-gram predicts the context words using a target word (this works better for rare words and is often paired with negative sampling). Both of these learn word embeddings that place semantically related words in close proximity.

As a real-world example, when you are writing, your favorite instant-messaging app uses an algorithm that tries to guess what your next word will be, based on what you have already typed. Let us assume that you want to send the sentence we presented in Table 10.3 to your business partner: "The summer sale campaign went viral on social media and increased brand awareness." Which words would a trained model, such as one created with word2vec, predict for you to type after "increased"? Would it be sales, traffic, engagement, or something else? Figure 10.5 represents a stylized version of an embedding, where the trained language model represents the weights of the neural network, which would propose a series of "next words" using a specific probability.

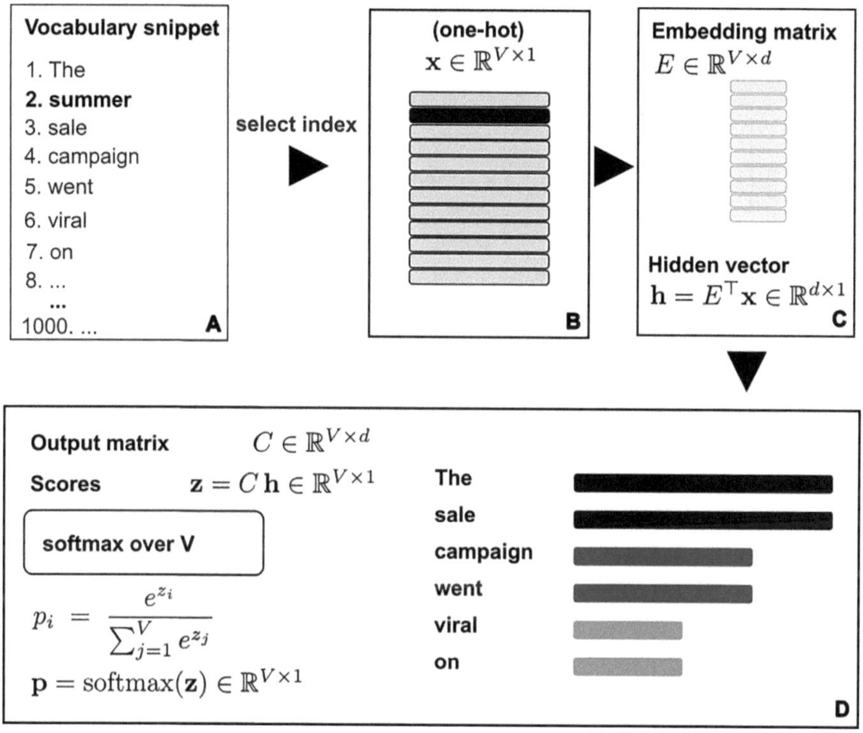

Fig. 10.4 Skip-gram architecture: maximize probability of true context words ("The," "sale") given the center word "summer." Authors' own figure

The two words in the input, "and" and "increased," are the tokens we want the model to process (see the left-hand side of Fig. 10.5) and are mapped onto their corresponding embedding, which is the output of a trained word2vec model. This embedding is shown in the embedding matrix, where each row corresponds to a word in the vocabulary, such as "aback," "abandon," "able," and "about,", and each column corresponds to one feature of the embedding vector. The neural network computes a score for each word in the vocabulary, which is then converted into a probability distribution using a function such as softmax. For example, given the input words provided, the model assigns probabilities to candidates for the next word, such as "sales" (with a probability of 0.36), "brand" (0.38), and others, based on how well they fit the patterns it has learned. If the model has learned through training that a phrase like "and increased sales" is common, the probability of seeing "sales" after "and increased" is high. Next, we will see how these models can be trained.

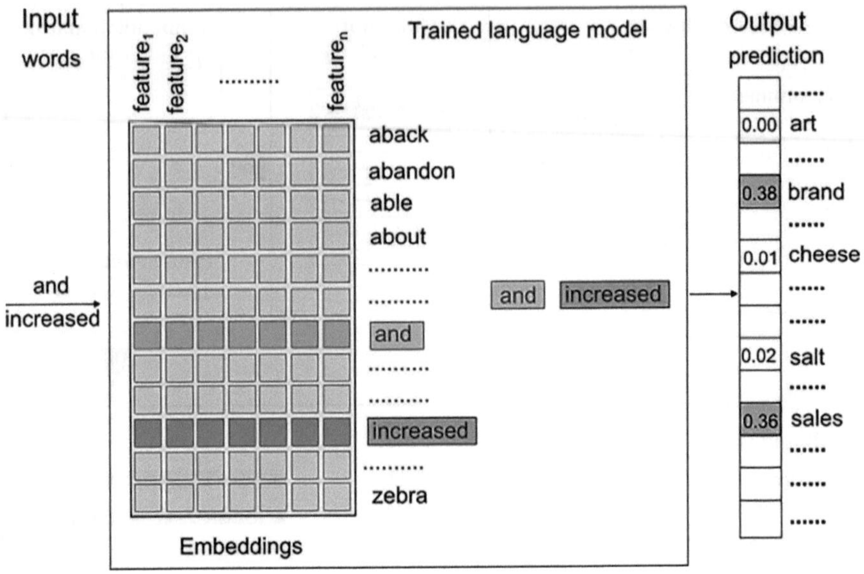

Fig. 10.5 A trained model for guessing the next word. Authors' own figure

10.5 Algorithms in Language Model Training

For training word embedding, we first need to provide the training algorithm with the context of the surrounding individual words. This is accomplished by defining the concept of a sliding window. Moving the window over the text generates several context-target pairs. They capture the local contexts of words by building structured examples, helping the model to learn which words appear together frequently, and identifying meaningful relationships inside the corpus. The window represents a certain number of words before (and after) a target word and can generate a data set to train a model. There can be any number of words, but some capture information better than others. This information assesses which words are near other words. Statistically speaking, if a word appears in a specific context, other words related to that context will be there too. Let us start with a simple example, with a window of two words, for the sentence we have already used: "The summer sale campaign went viral on social media and increased brand awareness."

In Fig. 10.6, two tables can be seen. Each row shows how the sliding window, which is made of two words, advances. The word after that is the target word. Visually, the two-word window slides to the right, capturing just a part of the sentence. A data set is built in the table to the left to save all the information captured from the sliding window. Each pair of words used as an input will have a single word associated with it as an output of the data set we have generated.

To take this a step further and to morph the window differently, we can select two words before and two words after a target word, and use the basic idea of CBOW (Jang et al., 2019). So, given an even number of words as an input defined

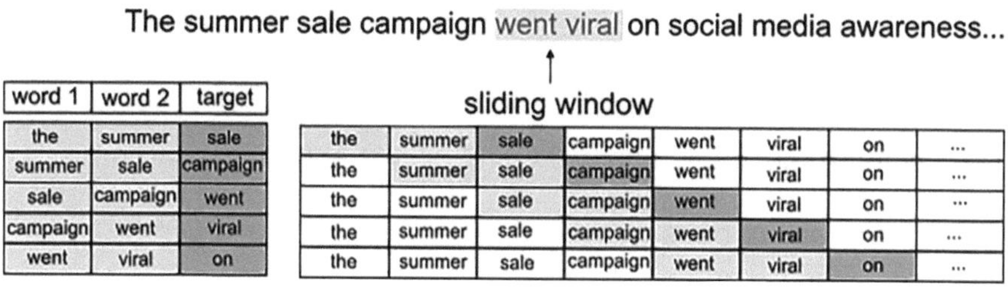

Fig. 10.6 The sliding window concept. Authors' own figure

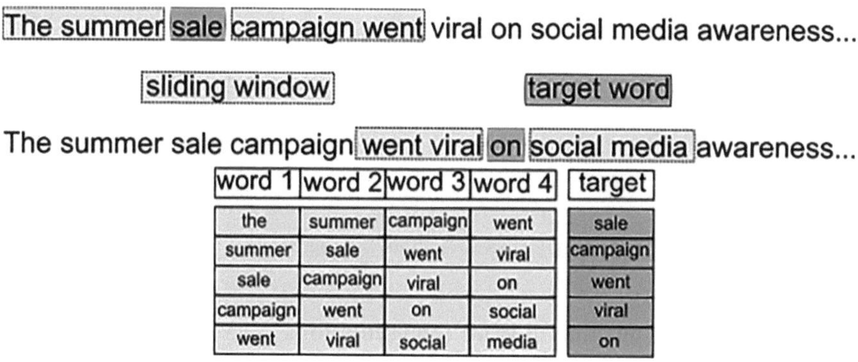

Fig. 10.7 CBOW approach. Authors' own figure

by a specific window size (for example, two), the output is the word in the middle. Note that in this approach, the target word is not part of the input, but it is the word that is omitted and then predicted based on the surrounding context.

In Fig. 10.7, the sliding window technique is applied to a sentence using CBOW. Each line in the table is a subset of the sentence, showing how the window captures different segments as it moves from left to right. Here we are trying to predict a target word based on the surrounding context words, two after and two before it (i.e., a context size = 2 on each side, total window = 4). The two shades of gray represent the sliding window words (the input in light gray) and the target word (the output in dark gray).

A complementary approach is to have an input word and guess what the two words before and the two words after it would be. This is demonstrated in Fig. 10.8, which adds further information and shows how the training process for the word-embedding model is carried out. For example, by applying the sliding-window approach above (i.e., using one input and two candidate target words before and after the input), the input word "sale" is associated with "the," "summer," "campaign," and "went," and the training data set continues with the next input word and its related words. At the very beginning of the process, the initial model contains no information provided by random embedding, meaning that the model is untrained at the outset. If you have the word "sale," which word would be a neighbor? In an untrained model, the prediction would be random, and, likely, it

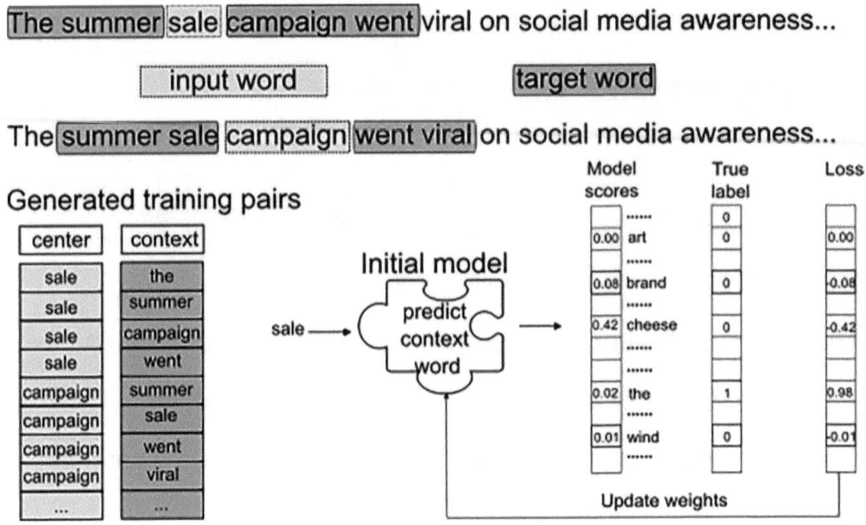

■ **Fig. 10.8** Word-embedding training process. Authors' own figure

could not learn any meaningful word representations (yet); its predictions would be totally inaccurate.

In ■ Fig. 10.8, the "Model scores" column shows the probabilities the model assigns to each word in the vocabulary as a possible neighboring word for "sale." The "True label" column shows an example of the correct neighboring word as a so-called one-hot encoded vector (in this case, "the"), which means applying a value of 1 to the correct word and a zero to all the others. The "Loss" column represents the difference between the actual target and the value from the untrained model. This error value is used to update the model's parameters through backpropagation and retraining (Goh, 1995; Rumelhart et al., 2013). Backpropagation is a fundamental method used to train neural networks. The error value (the difference) is "sent" backward through the network to adjust the weights. The operation is performed several times until the network learns to give more accurate predictions.

After we had done the same process to cover all the samples in the data set, we finished one epoch of training. The process is repeated for several epochs until the model becomes stable and yields significant results, or until a certain planned number of epochs have been performed. Eventually, we will have acquired a trained model, and we can extract the word-embedding matrix from it, which is our main goal.

10.6 Optimizing Embedding

In calculating how to predict the next word, the most computationally expensive part is the projection of the output vocabulary. To improve this task, first, we need to generate high-quality embedding; then, we need to use this embedding to train

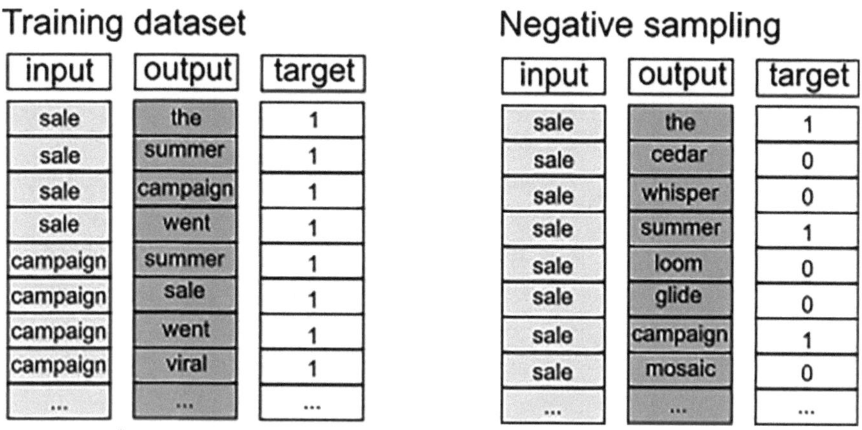

Fig. 10.9 Skip-gram with negative sampling. Authors' own figure

a language model (to carry out next-word prediction). At this point, we assume that we have a fully trained embedding, and we can now switch from the training phase to prediction. Now, instead of predicting a neighboring word directly, the model calculates a score for a given input-output word pair to indicate if they are neighbors or not (1 or 0). This switch effectively changes the model from a regular neural network for next-word prediction into a logistic-regression model, which is simpler and faster to compute. The structure of our data set changes slightly through the addition of a new column assessing the presence of two neighboring words. We do not now have to look to guess the next word anymore, or if the words are neighbors or not. This operation can be done very quickly, but with one caveat: If all the examples are positive, meaning that each target value is 1, we have a model that will always return 1, meaning it has perfect accuracy, which is a clear case of overfitting. To overcome this, negative samples of words which are not neighbors are sampled at random from the vocabulary, and a target value of 0 is assigned to those word pairs. This concept was introduced by Gutmann and Hyvärinen (2010) and is shown in Fig. 10.9.

> *Negative sampling* is a trick for training word embeddings which, instead of updating all the output classes (via softmax), updates only the model parameters for a small set of noise (negative) word pairs (labeled 0) and for the true pair (labeled 1). It reduces computation dramatically and improves the learning stability of skip-gram models.

Before the training process starts, we have to check which words are involved and how many words are in the vocabulary of the corpus. Let us combine the skip-gram and negative-sampling methodologies and show how word2vec uses them during the training process. At the start of the training phase, it creates the input matrices (embedding) and output matrices (context); see Fig. 10.10. Note that

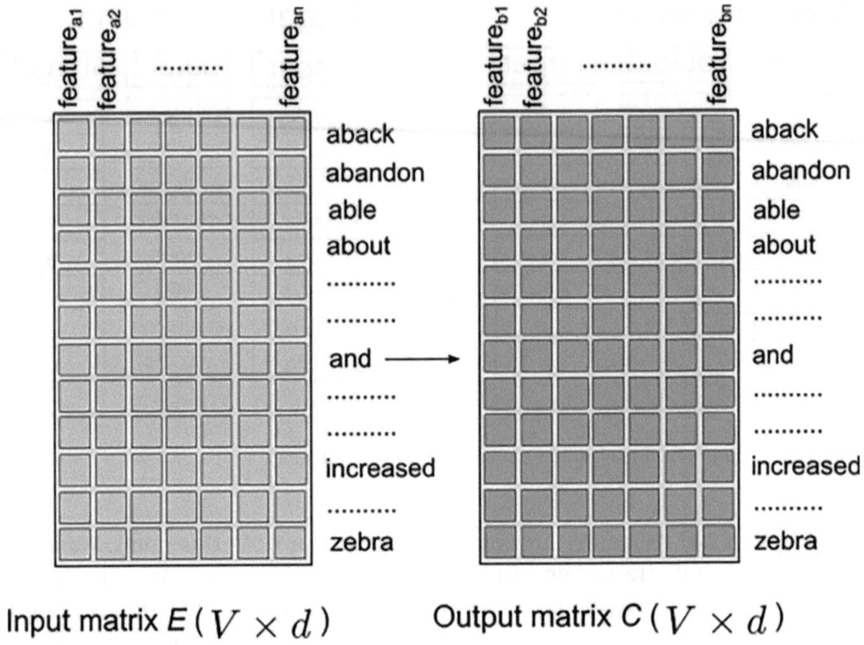

Fig. 10.10 Embedding and context matrices. Authors' own figure

10

these matrices are exactly the same size, containing the same vocabulary and the same number of features. What differs between them is that the values of the features will be different, and after the conclusion of the training process, there will be two distinct matrices, but of the same size.

As in any training process, the matrices are initially populated with random values. Both have a unique embedding vector for each word in the vocabulary, meaning that a word in the embedding matrix will have different values in the context matrix. Each word is represented as a row. The second dimension of the matrices holds the number of features, a concept similar to the emotional space where we had just two: valence and intensity. While 300 is a commonly employed value, the number of features can range from 50 to 500, or any number you find suitable. It is important to note that they do not have any predetermined label assigned to them. Figure 10.11 shows how the algorithm updates the model's parameters. A series of computational steps are performed to improve the embedding of the words, i.e., the correspondence between the words and their context.

The training mechanism of the two matrices, embedding and context, follows the standard procedure of training a neural network using backpropagation mentioned in the previous section. This entails a forward pass, a loss or error function calculation, a backward pass (called backpropagation), and a parameter update. At the beginning, during the first forward pass, the values in the matrices, also called

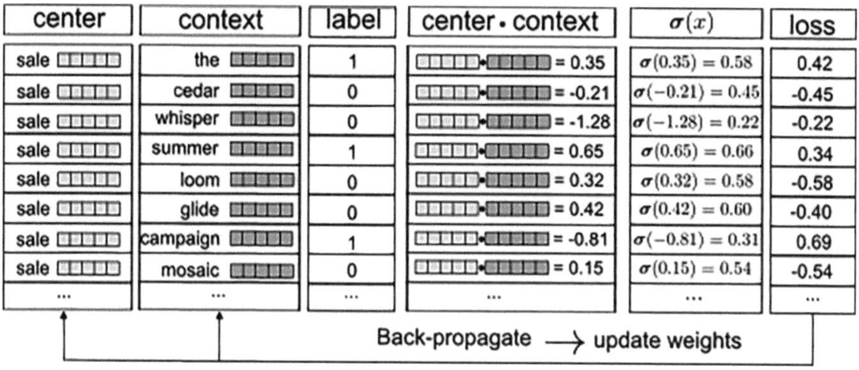

Fig. 10.11 The word2vec training process. Authors' own figure

weights or parameters, are populated with randomly assigned values to facilitate effective learning. If we look at Fig. 10.11 again, the dot product of input (center) and output (context), center · context, is calculated using random values. The result is passed on to the sigmoid function $S()$ and yields a value between 0 and 1, which, in turn, is compared to the value in the *label** column to compute the error, hence, carrying out the loss function. This is an extremely important value because the model parameters are iteratively updated based on this to make the error value as close as possible to 0. The updating procedure is done through backpropagation (Rumelhart et al., 1986) from the output layer to the input, updating the parameters through an optimization algorithm called gradient descent.

10.6.1 Details of the training process

Training a neural network, as we are doing here, can involve optimizing the process using hyperparameters. This term is a combination of two words: "hyper," from Greek, meaning "above" or "beyond," and parameter, which was initially composed of two words, "para," meaning "beside," and "metron," meaning "measure." So, a hyperparameter is a variable which operates before training begins at a higher level and can influence the final model. One such parameter is the window size, which can have a strong impact on the outcome. A small window learns specific and tight relationships between words, such as "milk" and "shake." A larger window learns broader relationships, such as "milk" and "animal." Another parameter is the dimensionality of the word vector (the columns in Fig. 10.2). A higher dimension captures subtle relationships between words, but it can lead to overfitting and increased computational costs. A lower dimension is faster but might not capture all the nuances of the relationships between words.

At this point, we are calculating the gradient of the error of the embedding vectors. This involves computing the partial derivatives of the loss function for each element of the embedding and context vectors. This step is essential to update the parameters, both for embedding and context matrices. The generic updating formula can be expressed as:

$$\theta = \theta - \eta \cdot \nabla_{\theta} J(\theta)$$

where θ is the parameter being updated, η is the learning rate, and $\nabla_{\theta} J(\theta)$ is the gradient of the cost function $J(\theta)$ for the parameters θ.

Both the embedding and context matrices follow the same steps. Each word's vector is updated by slowly moving in the direction that reduces the error. This involves subtracting a constant fraction, identified by η, of the gradient of the loss from the current vector with respect to the embedding vector.

Let us denote the embedding vector of the input word as v and the context vector of the output word as u, and the error calculated as E. The updates can be expressed mathematically as:

$$v = v - \eta \cdot \frac{\partial E}{\partial v}$$

$$u = u - \eta \cdot \frac{\partial E}{\partial u}$$

These equations represent gradient descent updates for the parameters v and u, where η is the learning rate, and $\frac{\partial E}{\partial v}$ and $\frac{\partial E}{\partial u}$ are the gradients of the error function E with respect to v and u.

10

The partial derivatives of the error function E with respect to the variables v and u, $\frac{\partial E}{\partial v}$ and $\frac{\partial E}{\partial u}$, depend on the specific form of the error function used. It often involves the sigmoid function of the dot product of v and u, compared against the actual target (1 or 0 in our case). This process is repeated for each training example, gradually modifying the values of the embedding by minimizing the overall error in predicting the context words given the input words. Here we denote the error for a single training example by E, while $J(\theta)$ is the loss aggregated over the whole data set (typically the sum or average of all individual E values). In the context of word2vec and similar models, we often use the terms interchangeably for a single example. The loss function J for the entire data set would be the sum (or average) of the individual errors E for each training example.

Let us focus on a practical and simple example to understand exactly what happens. Following how the procedure was described in Fig. 10.11, we can define our error function as:

$$E = t - \sigma(v \cdot u)$$

where $\sigma()$ is the sigmoid function, and t is the target (0 or 1).

Calculating the partial derivatives, knowing that the derivative of the sigmoid function is $\sigma'(x) = \sigma(x)\,(1 - \sigma(x))$ and the derivative of a constant value, such as t, results in $t' = 0$.

$$\frac{\partial E}{\partial v} = -\sigma(v \cdot u)(1 - \sigma(v \cdot u)) \cdot u$$

$$\frac{\partial E}{\partial u} = -\sigma(v \cdot u)(1 - \sigma(v \cdot u)) \cdot v$$

We have to update the vectors to:

$$v_{\text{new}} = v_{\text{old}} - \eta \cdot (-\sigma(v_{\text{old}} \cdot u_{\text{old}})(1 - \sigma(v_{\text{old}} \cdot u_{\text{old}})) \cdot u_{\text{old}})$$

$$u_{\text{new}} = u_{\text{old}} - \eta \cdot (-\sigma(v_{\text{old}} \cdot u_{\text{old}})(1 - \sigma(v_{\text{old}} \cdot u_{\text{old}})) \cdot v_{\text{old}})$$

We can use a numerical example to understand the whole process better.

$$v = [0.5, 0.3]$$

$$u = [0.1, 0.2]$$

$$t = 1 \quad \text{(positive example)}$$

$$\eta = 0.1 \quad \text{(learning rate)}$$

Calculate:

$$v \cdot u = 0.5 \cdot 0.1 + 0.3 \cdot 0.2 = 0.11$$

$$\sigma(0.11) \approx 0.5275$$

Error:

$$E = 1 - 0.5275 = 0.4725$$

Gradient for (v):

$$-\sigma(0.11) \cdot (1 - \sigma(0.11)) \cdot [0.1, 0.2] \approx [-0.0249, -0.0498]$$

Update (v):

$$v_{\text{new}} \approx [0.5, 0.3] - 0.1 \cdot [-0.0249, -0.0498] \approx [0.50249, 0.30498]$$

You can see that the new values of the vector are close to the original ones, but by performing this task several times, the values will be adjusted to obtain an optimal error function.

10.7 Other Types of Embedding and Models

There are other popular algorithms for representing the vector space, such as Global Vectors (GloVe; Pennington et al., 2014), developed at Stanford, and FastText (Bojanowski et al., 2017), developed by Facebook (now Meta). As with word2vec, the aim is to capture meaning in the text using an unsupervised algorithm. GloVe is based on the concept of the co-occurrence matrix, which is built for an entire corpus, summarizing how often word pairs occur together. The main idea is that ratios of co-occurrence probabilities contain useful information. Words like "coffee" and "cappuccino" would have similar vector representations, as they frequently appear together (co-occur) in certain contexts: social meetings, breakfasts, in bars, etc. While word2vec focuses on context using sliding windows, GloVe uses a co-occurrence matrix for the entire corpus. FastText, instead, builds on word2vec, incorporating sub-word information to improve their vector representation, meaning that words are broken down into character n-grams. This improves the probability of including underrepresented words which are out-of-vocabulary. Such examples can be words which do not appear in the training session but appear in a corpus and should be analyzed. So, if a new word appears, it is broken down into familiar sub-words (or n-grams). FastText performs well at capturing how morphological details are defined. Languages with many words can benefit the most from using this algorithm. For example, German is a good fit because it has many compound words and inflectional changes, and it is morphologically rich.

There is an increasing number of other methods that are designed to learn word embeddings. For example, Doc2Vec (Le & Mikolov, 2014) associates a unique vector with each document or paragraph, focusing on larger portions of text rather than single words. Sent2Vec (Pagliardini et al., 2017) builds sentence-level representations from unigrams and bigrams. Embedding from language models (ELMo; Peters et al., 2018) focuses on the context of the sentence to generate word vectors using stacked bidirectional long short-term memory (LSTMs), while bidirectional encoder representations from transformers while bidirectional encoder representations from transformers (BERT; Devlin, 2018) uses the transformer architecture to generate context-aware embeddings, or Generative Pre-trained Transformers (GPT; Radford et al., 2018), another transformer-based architecture, which became extremely popular, starting with version GPT-3 in 2020 (Brown, 2020) . Transformers represent a further development of word vectors as they allow for the capturing of context, or generating text that fits nicely into a specific context. Below we present a brief discussion of the building blocks of this architecture.

10.7.1 Transformers

A transformer is an important type of neural network. It uses word embedding to learn context and implicit meaning by detecting relationships between words in sentences. Transformers are the main architectural framework for the unsupervised learning models underlying BERT or GPT. The link to word embedding discussed in the previous section is that the input tokens, which are words or sub-words, are transformed into arrays of numbers, but with a twist. Unlike in word2vec, transformers add a position encoding to the vectors to ensure that the model captures the position of each word in a sentence. This dual information is passed on to the transformer model. They rely on a self-attention mechanism (introduced by Vaswani et al., 2017) to process input sequences in parallel. The transformer architecture includes an encoder, which processes the input sequence, and sometimes, but not always, a decoder which generates the output sequence. In addition, there are multi-head self-attention layers, which run in parallel and focus on different elements of the input. After establishing an attention layer, it applies feedforward layers and then uses positional encoding. There are three types of transformer: (i) encoder-only, which are designed to understand text (e.g., BERT); (ii) decoder-only, which are designed to generate text (e.g., GPT); and (iii) encoder-decoder sequences, which are useful for translating languages and for any sequence-to-sequence task such as text summarization. This section drew on the basic explanation of transformers by Alammar and Grootendorst (2024).

> *A transformer* is a type of neural architecture which processes token sequences through self-attention (weighing relationships between tokens) and positional encoding (injecting order). It includes encoder-only variants (e.g., BERT, for understanding), those which are decoder-only (e.g., GPT, for generation) and encoder-decoder versions (for sequence-to-sequence tasks, e.g., translation/summarization).

To illustrate and to better understand the transformer concept, ◘ Fig. 10.12 presents an encoder-decoder architecture. The diagram shows how language translation can be processed. The phrase "to be happy" is sent to an encoder made up of six layers, each representing a state of processing. The output from the decoder leads to the correct translation, in this case the German "glücklich sein."

A more detailed representation of the encoder and decoder layers sheds more light on their internal working (see ◘ Fig. 10.13). The encoder consists of a feed-forward neural network which processes data through a series of transformations, and a self-attention mechanism to evaluate the importance of different sections of the input, which aims to capture dependencies and relationships. The decoder has its own feed-forward neural network, used to produce the output, an encoder-decoder attention element, which allows the decoder to focus on the important parts of the input sequence, and a self-attention mechanism for considering the previous output when generating the next token.

As an example, let us now focus on the encoder and add more detail by zooming in on one layer; see ◘ Fig. 10.14. Let us take the vectorized sequence (token embeddings, analogous to word vectors such as word2vec) for the words "To," "be," and "happy," each denoted in turn as x_1, x_2, x_3. When applying the self-attention mechanism, we obtain contextualized embeddings which capture context. For example, "to" is influenced by "be" and "happy," and the mechanism can weight other words by relevance (including position information). Also, some distinct features of the words may be emphasized, and semantic relationships between

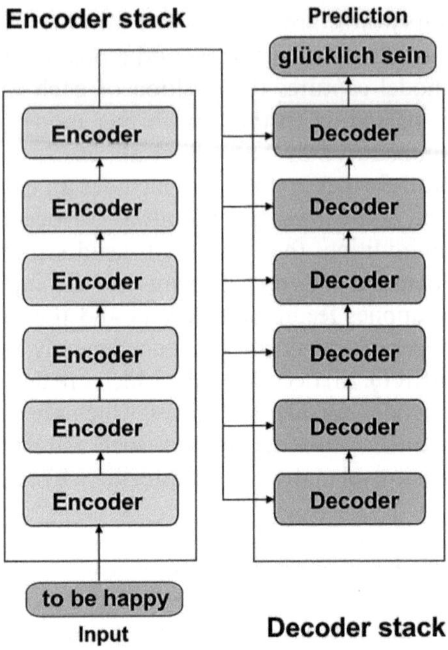

Fig. 10.12 Transformer, encoder, and decoder. Based on "Transformer, stacked layers and sublayers" (Wikimedia Commons, CC BY 4.0); see Credits for details

10

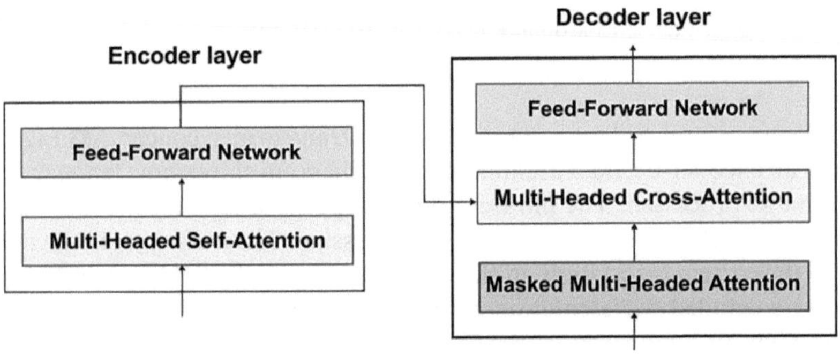

Fig. 10.13 Transformer, encoder, and decoder detail. Based on "Transformer, stacked layers and sublayers" (Wikimedia Commons, CC BY 4.0); see Credits for details

words may be highlighted. The resulting embeddings, shown by y_1, y_2, y_3, are more refined and context-aware representation. The transformation of y_1, y_2, y_3 into z_1, z_2, z_3 within the encoder layer is achieved by applying a position-wise feed-forward network (applied to each position independently) to process the attention output further and extract and refine features from the y vectors (for more detailed information, see Vaswani et al., 2017). Including multiple layers is important so that each of them can refine the vector representation for greater precision.

After processing all the layers, the final output of the encoder stack will contain a context-aware representation of the input sequence and serves as the bridge between the encoder and decoder. The main idea is that while a word can be translated accurately without such context-rich information, doing the same for a

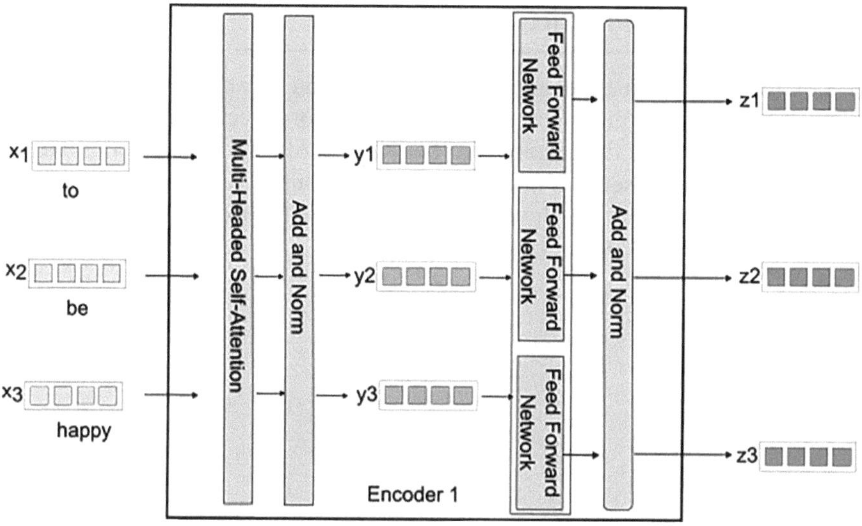

Fig. 10.14 A detailed view of an encoder in a stack. Authors' own figure

phrase would result in much greater precision if the context were included. The result of the encoding of the phrase "to be happy" is a set of contextualized representations for each word in the sentence. While as an input we have "to be happy" (3 tokens), the output contains three vectors, one for each word, typically of the dimension $d_{model} = 512$ or $d_{model} = 768$, as in many standard applications of the algorithm.

The vector for "to" becomes $\vec{v}_{to} = [v_{to,1}, v_{to,2}, \ldots, v_{to,d_{model}}]$, the vector for "be" becomes $\vec{v}_{be} = [v_{be,1}, v_{be,2}, \ldots, v_{be,d_{model}}]$, and the vector for "happy" becomes $\vec{v}_{happy} = [v_{happy,1}, v_{happy,2}, \ldots, v_{happy,d_{model}}]$.

In other words, each of the vectors $\vec{v}_{to}, \vec{v}_{be}, \vec{v}_{happy}$ contains information not only about the word itself but also about its context inside the sentence. Using this layered approach, the self-attention mechanism provides a result which captures the interactions between words, and the feed-forward layers in the encoder refine these contextual representations. The numerical representation expressed as a vector for the word "to" contains information about its relationship to "be" and "happy," the one for "be" contains information about its relationship to "to" and "happy," and the one for "happy" contains information about its relationship to "to" and "be." These final output vectors capture semantic and syntactic information about each word in the context of the whole sentence. Transformers can be used to carry out several tasks, such as classification, translation, or even language generation. But they also have the potential to be employed for other (predictive or generative) tasks involving sequential information other than language, such as for creating histories of customer-firm interactions (e.g., Kim et al., 2025) or market basket data (Gabel & Ringel, 2024).

In the next section, we will focus on the more basic word2vec application, before going on to use transformers.

10.8 Word2vec in Practice

Perhaps the best way to understand how word embedding works is to use a practical example. One of the most common tasks that word2vec is used for is to find analogies which prove the relationship between words. To illustrate this, we have used our book's data set and have selected the "Content" and "Brand" columns. The purpose is to check which words of interest are embedded in similar vectors which capture similar contexts.

```
library(data.table)
library(lubridate)
library(word2vec)

# Read the data set into a data.table
prodreviews <- fread("data/Product Reviews.csv",
                     select = c("Content", "Brand"))
```

The `word2vec()` function has transformed and embedded the words using the CBOW method. We have selected a dimension of 200, a sliding window of 5 words, and limited the number of iterations to 30.


```
# Train word2vec model
model <- word2vec(x = tolower(prodreviews$Content), type = "cbow",
↪   dim = 200, window=5, iter = 30)
```

As a basic operation, we can search for terms such as "apple" and "samsung," and find which words are similar (i.e., close to the focal brand name) in the word-vector space.

```
# Find similar words to apple
result_a <- predict(model, c("apple"), type = "nearest", top_n =
↪   5)
print(result_a)
```

```
$apple
  term1   term2 similarity rank
1 apple  apples  0.7145024    1
2 apple     ios  0.7050035    2
3 apple samsung  0.6755056    3
4 apple     rim  0.6742749    4
5 apple      hp  0.6641442    5
```

The closest words to "apple" include comparisons to Samsung, Research in Motion (RIM), Hewlett Packard (HP), and a reference to its operating system, iOS.

```
# Find similar words to samsung
result_s <- predict(model, c("samsung"), type = "nearest", top_n
↪    = 5)
print(result_s)
```

```
$samsung
    term1    term2 similarity rank
1 samsung     asus  0.7393969    1
2 samsung     acer  0.7289189    2
3 samsung motorola  0.7063525    3
4 samsung    nexus  0.7028567    4
5 samsung    vizio  0.7005945    5
```

The closest words to "samsung" are linked to a series of other brands that, perhaps, are perceived as being similar or to which it is often compared. Note that even without data cleaning and preprocessing, this is an easy and straightforward way to detect co-occurrences of competing brands and brand associations in texts.

We can also visualize how words are placed next to or far from each other. We can structure the analysis by creating a corpus, preprocessing it, and creating a document-term matrix. For convenience, we have selected 50 words (otherwise, if we employ all of them, the image would look too crowded and it would be impossible to see them). The idea here is to choose just a few words and then visualize them.

```
library(tm)
library(magrittr)

# Select the Content column
reviews <- prodreviews$Content

# Preprocess the corpus
corpus <- Corpus(VectorSource(reviews)) %>%
  tm_map(content_transformer(tolower)) %>%
  tm_map(removePunctuation) %>%
  tm_map(removeNumbers) %>%
  tm_map(removeWords, stopwords("en")) %>%
  tm_map(stripWhitespace)

# Extract the words from the document-term matrix
words <- colnames(as.matrix(DocumentTermMatrix(corpus)))

# Remove duplicates and empty strings
```

```
word_list <- unique(words[words != ""])
# Select the first 50 words
word_list <- head(word_list, 50)

# Check embeddings and remove the empty values, if any
embedding <- predict(model, word_list, type = "embedding")
embedding <- na.omit(embedding)
```

We have used the same CBOW model as above, but the result type now is "embedding," not "nearest." In this case, the 50 words selected would be represented as a series of numerical values. To visualize the terms, we can use a dimensionality reduction technique which compresses the high-dimensional spaces into two or three dimensions. In the present case, we can use uniform manifold approximation and projection (UMAP), implemented in the umap package and visualized with the `plotly` library. Several algorithms perform a similar task, such as t-distributed Stochastic Neighbor Embedding (t-SNE; Van der Maaten & Hinton, 2008).

```
library(ggrepel)
library(plotly)
library(umap)

# Visualize embeddings using UMAP
visualization <- umap(embedding, n_neighbors = 15)

# Transform into a data frame
df <- data.frame(word = rownames(embedding),
                 x = visualization$layout[, 1],
                 y = visualization$layout[, 2],
                 stringsAsFactors = FALSE)

# Plot embeddings using Plotly
plot_ly(df, x = ~x, y = ~y, type = "scatter", mode = 'text', text
↪ = ~word) #%>%
```

```
  #layout(title = "CBOW Embeddings Visualization")
```

The plot displayed in ◘ Fig. 10.15 shows the distribution of the words based on their embedding vectors, but transformed into a two-dimensional space. The closer the words are positioned to each other, the more related (or similar) they are. If we take a closer look, we can see that terms like "hulu," "netflix," as well as "ebooks" and "games," appear close to each other. This might indicate that a tablet can serve several purposes, for watching movies, playing games, and reading ebooks. These words appear as a group, implying that they are frequently used in similar contexts.

Fig. 10.15 CBOW embeddings visualization. Authors' own figure

Words that are placed far apart, contextually, have less in common. This word "mapping" can be used for several purposes in marketing. One is for competitive analysis carried out for two or more brands, and another is for recommendation systems, by discovering which products are frequently mentioned together in online reviews. Yet, another could be in personalized marketing campaigns. Last but not least, selecting relevant words for SEO or ads could give a company an advantage over its competition by using the most appropriate keywords (see Reisenbichler et al., 2022).

To analyze how close these words are to each other, we can use a hierarchical clustering method and calculate the cosine distance between the word "vectors" using the `proxy` library.

```
library(proxy)

# Use the proxy package to compute the cosine distance
embedding_cos <- dist(embedding, method = "cosine")
```

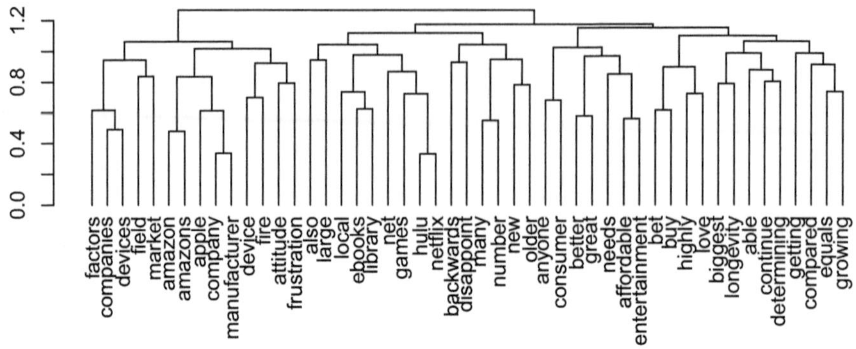

Fig. 10.16 Cluster dendrogram of embedded words. Authors' own figure

```
# Perform hierarchical clustering, plot the dendrogram
plot(as.dendrogram(hclust(embedding_cos)), horiz = FALSE, cex =
↪  0.2)
```

As shown in Fig. 10.16, we can see from looking at the dendrogram that words like "hulu" and "netflix" appear to be closely related, as is "games." Obviously, the same device can be used to watch the two streaming services as well as to play games.

10

One of the most common things we can do with vectors is to perform arithmetical operations. What vectors might we create if we take the embedding for "kindle" and move away from it by subtracting "good," and thus reducing its positive association? The result given by adding "bad" would lean toward terms that are not favorable. We could think of it in this way: "If (the word) kindle is associated with good, what words associate kindle with bad?" This example demonstrates how we can process word vectors arithmetically, and the outcome shows how useful this operation can be.

```
# Get the vectors for specific words: 'amazon', 'apple', 'good',
↪  'bad', 'screen'
kindle <- predict(model, newdata = "kindle", type = "embedding")
good <- predict(model, newdata = "good", type = "embedding")
bad <- predict(model, newdata = "bad", type = "embedding")

# Perform vector arithmetic for the word kindle
result_kindle <- kindle - good + bad

# Find the top 10 words closest to the result vector for kindle
similar_kindle <- predict(model, newdata = result_kindle, type =
↪  "nearest", top_n = 10)
print(similar_kindle)
```

```
$kindle
        term similarity rank
1     kindle  0.9984323    1
2     kindel  0.7714513    2
3    kindles  0.7541807    3
4      kidle  0.7478809    4
5     kinkle  0.7471732    5
6      kndle  0.7398569    6
7     kindal  0.7393759    7
8     kendle  0.7232242    8
9      kinle  0.7011244    9
10         k  0.6855328   10
```

This unexpected result comes from the series of words which are a mistyping of the word “kindle” and shows that careful preprocessing is essential for meaningful text analysis.

Let us perform further operations: We can add positive characteristics, such as “good,” “fast,” and “cheap” and remove words like “bad,” “slow,” and “expensive.” In doing so, we can try to shift toward more positive qualities (the one we have added) and move away from negative ones (the ones we have subtracted). After this, we can check which words are embedded close to both “kindle” and “ipad.”

```
# Get the vectors for the kindle and ipad
kindle <- predict(model, newdata = "kindle", type = "embedding")
ipad <- predict(model, newdata = "ipad", type = "embedding")

# Get the vectors for good, bad, fast, slow, cheap and expensive
good <- predict(model, newdata = "good", type = "embedding")
bad <- predict(model, newdata = "bad", type = "embedding")
fast <- predict(model, newdata = "fast", type = "embedding")
slow <- predict(model, newdata = "slow", type = "embedding")
cheap <- predict(model, newdata = "cheap", type = "embedding")
expensive <- predict(model, newdata = "expensive", type =
↪  "embedding")

# Perform vector arithmetic for the kindle word
result_kindle <- kindle + good + fast + cheap - bad - slow -
↪  expensive

# Perform vector arithmetic for the ipad word
result_ipad <- ipad + good + fast + expensive - bad - slow - cheap

# Find the top 10 words closest to each result vector
similar_kindle <- predict(model, newdata = result_kindle, type =
↪  "nearest", top_n = 10)
similar_ipad <- predict(model, newdata = result_ipad, type =
↪  "nearest", top_n = 10)
```

```
# Print the results for kindle
print(similar_kindle)
```

```
$kindle
          term similarity rank
1       kindle  0.9957064    1
2         fast  0.8844871    2
3        quick  0.8438365    3
4        sleek  0.8350880    4
5  wonderfully  0.8345558    5
6         good  0.8332866    6
7       kindel  0.8235799    7
8       simple  0.8204671    8
9      solidly  0.8192567    9
10        well  0.8092886   10
```

The words which show the positive qualities of Amazon's Kindle are related to the response time of the machine (fast, quick), that it is sleek, perhaps that it does some task extremely well, that its use is straightforward, and the tablet looks solid, among others.


```
# Print the results for ipad
print(similar_ipad)
```

```
$ipad
         term similarity rank
1  economical  0.9407232    1
2     ereader  0.9154697    2
3         pad  0.9062951    3
4   expensive  0.8988186    4
5        imac  0.8940031    5
6      iphone  0.8841532    6
7     itouch  0.8775398    7
8     elegant  0.8763888    8
9       fluid  0.8541148    9
10  efficient  0.8540065   10
```

The positive words related to Apple's iPad show a degree of ambivalence, since it seems to be perceived as economical by some, but expensive by others. Also, the iPad is associated with an e-reader and that it is integrated into Apple's ecosystem (e.g., "imac," "iphone," "itouch"). Other positive associations include "efficient" and "elegant," and perhaps that images are "fluid" on the screen.

Marketers can use such information in several ways. For example, for Kindle, Amazon could emphasize the simplicity, yet solidity of the tablet, as well as its quick response to commands. Apple's marketing could focus on its design and its integration with other Apple devices, emphasizing that the iPad is not just a tablet but an efficient tool.

10.9 Transformers in Action

In this section, we will illustrate the use of transformers through the R package `text` (Kjell et al., 2023). This package provides an interface with trained deep learning models which allow several NLP tasks to use the power of transformers and Python via R. Several tasks can be carried out using transformers, for example, topic modeling, named-entity recognition, sentiment analysis, and many more. These have already been explored in previous chapters using more classical approaches. In this section, we will focus on two tasks, one is text summarization, developing what we discussed in ▶ Chap. 9 further, and the second is related to searching for information (i.e., questions and answers).

10.9.1 Text summarization

Summarization is important in marketing (Hartmann & Netzer, 2023) because it helps marketing analysts condense large volumes of customer feedback into shorter, concise insights, which can be used to inform further action. It is useful for understanding customer sentiment or identifying trends at scale. In the next example, we summarize a series of randomly selected customer reviews. We have set a seed for reproducibility, filtered the data set for the Amazon brand, and randomly selected 100 reviews to speed up the computational process. These reviews are then linked into a single string to produce a single document. Then, we applied the `textSum()` function, and by using a trained deep learning model (`t5-small`), we have summarized the text. The summary is abstractive and is generated as a string that is between 5 and 100 tokens long. The result is stored in the `ts` variable, which can be printed using the `cat()` function.

```
library(text)

# Install text required python packages in a conda environment
↪   (with defaults).
# textrpp_initialize(save_profile = TRUE) saves the profile
textrpp_install()
textrpp_initialize()

# Select the Amazon brand
amazon_reviews <- prodreviews[prodreviews$Brand == "Amazon", ]
```

```
# Set seed for reproducibility
set.seed(123)

# Sample 1000 indices from the available reviews
sampled_ind <- sample(1:nrow(amazon_reviews), size = 100, replace
↪ = FALSE)

# Extract the content of the sampled reviews
sampled_reviews <- amazon_reviews$Content[sampled_ind]

# Concatenate the text into one big string
big_review <- paste(sampled_reviews, collapse = " ")

# Perform the summarization operation, use the t5-small model
ts <- textSum(big_review, min_length = 5L, max_length = 100L,
↪ model = "t5-small", device = "gpu", tokenizer_parallelism =
↪ TRUE, logging_level = "warning", return_text = TRUE,
↪ return_tensors = FALSE, clean_up_tokenization_spaces = FALSE,
↪ set_seed = 42L )
```

10

```
# View the results
cat(ts[[1,1]])
```

```
the Kindle Fire is a great device for reading and
↪ watching movies . it's a good way to
get a Kindle, but it isn't as good as the ipad . if
↪ you're a fan of the e-book, you'll be able
to use it for a lot of time.
```

You can see the good and bad points of the device immediately. It is also possible to select different data, for example, by choosing another brand or making a comparison between them. The more data you have, the more precise the summaries will be.

10.9.2 Information search, questions and answering using transformers (Q&A)

Searching for information and customer feedback plays a central role in modern marketing. Transformers have revolutionized this by providing accurate, context-aware retrieval systems, allowing brands to analyze vast amounts of consumer queries and intent with high precision. Also, transformer-powered chatbots have had an impact on customer interactions by automating the question-and-answer process (Smith & Albaum, 2010). Q&As give direct insights into customer experiences and pain points. In contrast to surveys, Q&As provide real-time feedback, providing unexpected insights, a more conversational approach to dynamic exchanges, and scalability. Q&As will not replace surveys, especially when there is the need for structured information on aspects of a product with a corresponding statistical analysis. Nevertheless, there is a growing body of literature exploring the ability of transformer-based language models to mimic consumer research (for an overview, see Arora et al., 2025; Sarstedt et al., 2024). Despite the enthusiasm for "silicon sampling," there is recent research which has also identified its limitations (e.g., Goli & Singh, 2024; Stromberg et al., 2025).

To illustrate this, here is a list of questions that we would like to see answered.

```
# List of questions to be answered
questions <- c(
"How is the Kindle screen?",
"How is the Amazon customer service?",
"How much memory does the Kindle Fire have?",
"Where is the Kindle tablet camera?",
"Does the brand Amazon offer good value for the money?"
)
```

We have stored the questions in a vector, then iterated each question by applying the `textQA()` function, dedicated to asking questions. There are several models that can be used; you can try substituting the one proposed here with different ones; check the `text` package specifications for this. Also, the answers can vary depending on the exact prompt used to question the language model (see Liu et al., 2023, on prompting and the prompt engineering of language models).

```
# Initialize a list to store the answers
answers <- vector("list", length(questions))

# Iterate over each question and apply the textQA function
for (i in seq_along(questions)) {
  answers[[i]] <- textQA(
    question = questions[i],
    context = big_review,
    model = "deepset/roberta-base-squad2",
    device = "cpu",
    tokenizer_parallelism = FALSE,
    logging_level = "warning",
    top_k = 10L,
    doc_stride = 128L,
```

```
    max_answer_len = 20L,
    max_seq_len = 384L,
    max_question_len = 64L,
    handle_impossible_answer = FALSE,
    set_seed = 202208L
  )
}
```

```
# Print the answers
for (i in seq_along(questions)) {
  cat("Question:", questions[i], "\nAnswer:",
  ↪ paste(unlist(answers[[i]][4]), collapse = ", "), "\n\n")
}
```

10

```
Question: How is the Kindle screen?
Answer: back-lit, great, great, back-lit, perfectly lit
 ↪ and easy to navigate
or read, 10.1, glare, great, great screen display, sharp
 ↪ and videos
are very crisp

Question: How is the Amazon customer service?
Answer: great, great, you honestly have a customer for
 ↪ life, great as always,
great as always, loyal, expedited shipping, honestly have
 ↪ a customer for life,
monopolizing these, expedited shipping

Question: How much memory does the Kindle Fire have?
Answer: 8 GB, 8gig, 8gig, 8 GB memory, 7 inch, ten, No
 ↪ extra memory slot,
7-inch, 7"", No extra memory slot? what for? use the
 ↪ cloud

Question: Where is the Kindle tablet camera?
Answer: front & back, GPS, front & back camera, there
 ↪ isn't a camera,
kindle fire, sd slot, smartphone, It's almost an IPad,
 ↪ I-pad, laptop
```

```
Question: Does the brand Amazon offer good value for the
↪   money?
Answer: this technology could be so affordable, its well
↪   worth the price,
you can't go wrong with this at all, Amazon has a winner,
↪   the Kindle Fire
is perfect for funtionability and price, it is so worth
↪   the money,
well worth the money!!!, Kindle is a bargain, Amazon has
↪   a winner!,
it's much cheaper
```

The answers seem to provide useful information about the characteristics of the Kindle Fire, or about the Amazon brand in general. The precision of the answer allows for further questions or further analysis. You could also select a different product and ask the same questions for a comparative analysis.

Throughout this book, we have come across the many standard and modern approaches for tackling text analysis in marketing. The ever-changing technological support in terms of packages equips the marketing analyst with powerful tools for analyzing and discovering latent messages in user-generated content by transforming huge volumes of text into manageable parcels of information.

As an end note, the models presented in this chapter find text, or generate text, by repeating (like a parrot) patterns found in the training data, but truly understanding or reasoning about language is still a human quality. Machines can produce output based on statistical probabilities (the word stochastic is used in these cases), but do not (yet) have a comprehension of its meaning (Bender et al., 2021).

Exercise 1. Practice using other vectors, such as “kindle” - “good” + “ipad,” and find out things about ipad.

Exercise 2. Instead of CBOW, use the skip-gram method to train a word-embedding data set.

Exercise 3. Use the function `textNER()` from the `text` package for named entity recognition tasks.

Exercise 4. Use the function `textTopics()` from the `text` package to extract topics.

Exercise 5. Select a positive and negative subset from the main data set, and summarize each of them and compare the results.

Conclusion

The chapter began with an introduction to word embedding and the word2vec algorithm. It presented a walk-through of the transformation of a corpus into a vector representation of the words. The first example started with a two-dimensional array which showed the way to construct a manageable structure. From this point on, multidimensional vectors were easier to understand. Word2vec was analyzed in detail, and both continuous bag-of-words and skip-gram were mentioned as techniques, as well as negative sampling. A simple practical example was offered for a better understanding of the training mechanism for neural networks. An example of backpropagation showed how training reaches the optimal values of embedding. The next step was the explanation of transformers, an AI algorithm which has received a lot of attention. There was also a succinct explanation of the use of encoders, encoders-decoders, and decoders. Examples of word embedding were given to show their applications in marketing, tackling analogies, clustering, and also for vector operations. The chapter ended with the presentation of two operations using transformers via the `text` package. The first dealt with summarization and the second with the implementation of a Q&A mechanism.

Discussion

Vector analogies and bias: Using the embedding pipeline in ▶ Chap. 10, test the classic analogies (e.g., tablet − amazon + apple →?). Outline the detection and mitigation of social bias in nearest neighbors (e.g., vocabulary curation, debiasing, human review).

Hyperparameters that matter: Propose defaults and trade-offs for vector dimension, window size, subsampling, min_count, epochs, and learning rate. How will you judge stability (repeat runs, neighbor overlap @k)?

Nearest-neighbor lexicon building: Create a list of brand synonyms from embeddings by using cosine similarity thresholds and manual vetting. Specify the evaluation of precision@k, marketing relevance checks, and intruder-term tests.

Out-of-vocabulary and morphology: For a corpus which contains many out-of-vocabulary or morphologically rich tokens (e.g., German compounds), make an argument for FastText over plain word2vec showing the expected gains and caveats.

Transformers for summarization Q&A: Using this chapter's transformer demos, state their constraints (latency, context window), hallucination risk, and evaluation (factuality spot-checks for Q&A).

Compliance and privacy: For embeddings which encode sensitive entities, describe the personally identifiable information scrubbing to be used before training and a retention policy for the derivative vectors used in marketing analytics.

Take Home Message

- Embeddings map words onto vectors in a continuous space using proximity ≈ to identify semantic closeness.
- Cosine similarity is the preferred metric for comparing vectors in NLP tasks.
- Word2vec learns embeddings using CBOW or skip-gram, often employing negative sampling to speed up training.
- Hyperparameters (window, dimensions, epochs, learning rate) shape quality and computation time significantly.
- Word2vec, GloVe (global co-occurrence), and FastText (sub-words) often improve coverage, especially for languages which are morphologically rich.
- Transformers use positional encoding and self-attention; select encoder/decoder variants by task (understanding vs. generation vs. seq2seq).
- For marketing, these tools are particularly useful: Clustering themes, building brand lexicons, retrieval, and briefing-style summaries. Remember that models match stochastic patterns and are not "machines which understand."

References

Alammar, J., & Grootendorst, M. (2024). *Hands-on large language models: Language understanding and generation*. O'Reilly Media, Inc.

Arora, N., Chakraborty, I., & Nishimura, Y. (2025). AI–human hybrids for marketing research: Leveraging large language models (LLMs) as collaborators. *Journal of Marketing*, *89*(2), 43–70.

Bender, E. M., Gebru, T., McMillan-Major, A., & Shmitchell, S. (2021). On the dangers of stochastic parrots: Can language models be too big? *Proceedings of the 2021 ACM Conference on Fairness, Accountability, and Transparency*, 610–623.

Bojanowski, P., Grave, E., Joulin, A., & Mikolov, T. (2017). Enriching word vectors with subword information. *Transactions of the Association for Computational Linguistics*, *5*, 135–146.

Boroditsky, L. (2001). Does language shape thought?: Mandarin and english speakers' conceptions of time. *Cognitive Psychology*, *43*(1), 1–22.

Brown, T. B. (2020). Language models are few-shot learners. *arXiv Preprint arXiv:2005.14165*.

Compiani, G., Morozov, I., & Seiler, S. (2023). Demand Estimation with Text and Image Data (September 28, 2023). Chicago Booth Research Paper No., *Available at SSRN*: https://ssrn.com/abstract=4588941orhttp://dx.doi.org/10.2139/ssrn.4588941

Das, S. R., Donini, M., Zafar, M. B., He, J., & Kenthapadi, K. (2022). FinLex: An effective use of word embeddings for financial lexicon generation. *The Journal of Finance and Data Science*, *8*, 1–11.

Devlin, J. (2018). Bert: Pre-training of deep bidirectional transformers for language understanding. *arXiv Preprint arXiv:1810.04805*. https://doi.org/10.5771/9783845276564-1266

Ellickson, P. B., Kar, W., Reeder III, J. C., & Zeng, G. (2024). Using contextual embeddings to predict the effectiveness of novel heterogeneous treatments. *Available at SSRN 4845956*.

Evert, S. et al. (2008). Corpora and collocations. *Corpus Linguistics. An International Handbook*, *2*, 1212–1248.

Gabel, S., & Ringel, D. (2024). The market basket transformer: A new foundation model for retail. *Available at SSRN 4335141*.

Goh, A. T. (1995). Back-propagation neural networks for modeling complex systems. *Artificial Intelligence in Engineering*, *9*(3), 143–151.

Goli, A., & Singh, A. (2024). Frontiers: Can large language models capture human preferences? *Marketing Science*, *43*(4), 709–722.

Guo, X., Hao, X., Tang, Z., Diao, L., Bai, Z., Lu, S., & Li, L. (2021). ACE-ADP: Adversarial contextual embeddings based named entity recognition for agricultural diseases and pests. *Agriculture*, *11*(10), 912.

Gutmann, M., & Hyvärinen, A. (2010). Noise-contrastive estimation: A new estimation principle for unnormalized statistical models. *Proceedings of the Thirteenth International Conference on Artificial Intelligence and Statistics*, 297–304.

Haroske, D. D., & Triebel, H. (2011). Embeddings of function spaces: A criterion in terms of differences. *Complex Variables and Elliptic Equations*, *56*(10-11), 931–944.

Hartmann, J., & Netzer, O. (2023). Natural language processing in marketing. In *Artificial intelligence in marketing* (Vol. 20, pp. 191–215). Emerald Publishing Limited.

Jang, B., Kim, I., & Kim, J. W. (2019). Word2vec convolutional neural networks for classification of news articles and tweets. *PloS One*, *14*(8), e0220976.

Johansson, S. (2013). The talking neanderthals: What do fossils, genetics and archeology say? *Biolinguistics*, *7*, 035–074.

Kim, K., McCarthy, D., & Lee, D. (2025). Generative multi-task learning for customer base analysis: Evidence from 1,001 companies. *Symposium on Artificial Intelligence in Marketing*.

Kjell, O., Giorgi, S., & Schwartz, H. A. (2023). The text-package: An r-package for analyzing and visualizing human language using natural language processing and deep learning. *Psychological Methods*. https://doi.org/10.1037/met0000542

Kumar, A., Rajpal, A., & Rathore, D. (2018). Genre classification using word embeddings and deep learning. *2018 International Conference on Advances in Computing, Communications and Informatics (ICACCI)*, 2142–2146.

Le, Q., & Mikolov, T. (2014). Distributed representations of sentences and documents. *International Conference on Machine Learning*, 1188–1196.

Liu, P., Yuan, W., Fu, J., Jiang, Z., Hayashi, H., & Neubig, G. (2023). Pre-train, prompt, and predict: A systematic survey of prompting methods in natural language processing. *ACM Computing Surveys*, *55*(9), 1–35.

Luef, E. M. (2018). *The talking species: Perspectives on the evolutionary, neuronal and cultural foundations of language*.

McCormick, C. (2016). Word2vec tutorial-the skip-gram model. *Apr-2016.[Online]. Available*: http://Mccormickml.Com/2016/04/19/Word2vectutorial-the-Skip-Gram-Model.

McCormick, T., Chen, K., Corrado, G., & Dean, J. (2013). Efficient estimation of word representations in vector space. *arXiv Preprint arXiv:1301.3781*.

Mikolov, T., Yih, W., & Zweig, G. (2013). Linguistic regularities in continuous space word representations. *Proceedings of the 2013 Conference of the North American Chapter of the Association for Computational Linguistics: Human Language Technologies*, 746–751.

Milroy, J. (1995). William labov, principles of linguistic change. Volume i: Internal factors (language in society 20). Oxford: Blackwell, 1994. Pp. Xix+ 641. *Journal of Linguistics*, *31*(2), 435–439.

Pagliardini, M., Gupta, P., & Jaggi, M. (2017). Unsupervised learning of sentence embeddings using compositional n-gram features. *arXiv Preprint arXiv:1703.02507*.

Pennington, J., Socher, R., & Manning, C. D. (2014). Glove: Global vectors for word representation. *Proceedings of the 2014 Conference on Empirical Methods in Natural Language Processing (EMNLP)*, 1532–1543.

Peters, M. E., Neumann, M., Iyyer, M., Gardner, M., Clark, C., Lee, K., & Zettlemoyer, L. (2018). Deep contextualized word representations. In M. Walker, H. Ji, & A. Stent (Eds.), *Proceedings of the 2018 conference of the north American chapter of the association for computational linguistics: Human language technologies, volume 1 (long papers)* (pp. 2227–2237). Association for Computational Linguistics. https://doi.org/10.18653/v1/N18-1202

Radford, A., Narasimhan, K., Salimans, T., & Sutskever, I. (2018). *Improving language understanding by generative pre-training*. OpenAI technical report. https://cdn.openai.com/research-covers/language-unsupervised/language_understanding_paper.pdf

Reisenbichler, M., Reutterer, T., Schweidel, D. A., & Dan, D. (2022). Frontiers: Supporting content marketing with natural language generation. *Marketing Science*, *41*(3), 441–452.

Rumelhart, D. E., Durbin, R., Golden, R., & Chauvin, Y. (2013). Backpropagation: The basic theory. In *Backpropagation* (pp. 1–34). Psychology Press.

Rumelhart, D. E., Hinton, G. E., & Williams, R. J. (1986). Learning representations by back-propagating errors. *Nature*, *323*(6088), 533–536.

Sarstedt, M., Adler, S. J., Rau, L., & Schmitt, B. (2024). Using large language models to generate silicon samples in consumer and marketing research: Challenges, opportunities, and guidelines. *Psychology & Marketing*, *41*(6), 1254–1270.
Sisodia, A., Burnap, A., & Kumar, V. (2024). Generative interpretable visual design: Using disentanglement for visual conjoint analysis. *Journal of Marketing Research*, 00222437241276736.
Smith, S. M., & Albaum, G. S. (2010). An introduction to marketing research. *Accessed September*, *5*, 2017.
Stromberg, M., Moe, W. W., Reutterer, T., & Schweidel, D. A. (2025). Blind spots in broad strokes: Caveats for the use of LLMs in marketing research. *Available at SSRN*.
Timoshenko, A., & Hauser, J. R. (2019). Identifying customer needs from user-generated content. *Marketing Science*, *38*(1), 1–20.
Toubia, O., Berger, J., & Eliashberg, J. (2021). How quantifying the shape of stories predicts their success. *Proceedings of the National Academy of Sciences*, *118*(26), e2011695118.
Van der Maaten, L., & Hinton, G. (2008). Visualizing data using t-SNE. *Journal of Machine Learning Research*, *9*(11), 2579–2605.
Vaswani, A., Shazeer, N., Parmar, N., Uszkoreit, J., Jones, L., Gomez, A. N., Kaiser, Ł., & Polosukhin, I. (2017). Attention is all you need. In *Proceedings of the 31st International Conference on Neural Information Processing Systems* (pp. 6000–6010). Curran Associates, Inc.
Wang, Q., Xu, J., Chen, H., & He, B. (2017). Two improved continuous bag-of-word models. *2017 International Joint Conference on Neural Networks (IJCNN)*, 2851–2856.
Wevers, M., & Koolen, M. (2020). Digital begriffsgeschichte: Tracing semantic change using word embeddings. *Historical Methods: A Journal of Quantitative and Interdisciplinary History*, *53*(4), 226–243.
Winawer, J., Witthoft, N., Frank, M. C., Wu, L., Wade, A. R., & Boroditsky, L. (2007). Russian blues reveal effects of language on color discrimination. *Proceedings of the National Academy of Sciences*, *104*(19), 7780–7785.

Credits

Chapter 3

Figures 3.5 and 3.6 are courtesy of webscraper.io.

Chapter 6

Figure 6.10 Neural networks. Based on "Derived Neuron schema with no labels.svg" by Dhp1080 (SVG adaptation by Actam), via Wikimedia Commons, CC BY-SA 3.0. Changes: redrawn with a new layout; added a multi-neuron network, labels, and equations; typography and colors adjusted. This adapted figure is licensed by the authors under CC BY-SA 3.0. Source: https://commons.wikimedia.org/wiki/File:Derived_Neuron_schema_with_no_labels.svg—License: https://creativecommons.org/licenses/by-sa/3.0/

Chapter 7

Figure 7.2. Latent Dirichlet allocation (plate notation with layered explanation). Adapted from "Smoothed LDA.png" by Slxu.public, Wikimedia Commons, CC BY-SA 3.0 (commercial reuse permitted). Changes: redrawn; added left-hand layered explanation (I–V); expanded θ and z structures; added word histograms; relabeled/relayed out connections. The adapted figure by the authors is licensed under CC BY-SA 3.0. Source and license links as above.

Figure 7.4. Analysis workflow and `stm` package features. Reproduced from Roberts, M. E., Stewart, B. M., & Tingley, D. (2019). stm: An R Package for Structural Topic Models. Journal of Statistical Software, 91(2), 1–40, Figure 2. Creative Commons Attribution 3.0 (CC BY 3.0). Source: https://doi.org/10.18637/jss.v091.i02—License: https://creativecommons.org/licenses/by/3.0/ (No changes were made.)

Chapter 10

Figure 10.12. Transformer encoder and decoder. Adapted from "`Transformer,_stacked_layers_and_sublayers.png`" by dvgodoy, Wikimedia Commons, CC BY 4.0 (2021). Changes: redrawn in grayscale; labels, arrows, and layout modified. This adapted figure by the authors is licensed under CC BY 4.0. Source: `https://commons.wikimedia.org/wiki/File:Transformer,_stacked_layers_and_sublayers.png`—License: https://creativecommons.org/licenses/by/4.0/

Figure 10.13. Transformer encoder and decoder detail. Adapted from "`Transformer,_stacked_layers_and_sublayers.png`" by dvgodoy, Wikimedia Commons, CC BY 4.0 (2021). Changes: redrawn in grayscale; labels, arrows, and layout modified. This adapted figure by the authors is licensed under CC BY 4.0. Source: `https://commons.wikimedia.org/wiki/File:Transformer,_stacked_layers_and_sublayers.png`—License: https://creativecommons.org/licenses/by/4.0/

Use of AI

Portions of code formatting were assisted by OpenAI's ChatGPT-3; all code was subsequently reviewed and tested by the authors.

MIX
Papier aus verantwortungsvollen Quellen
Paper from responsible sources
FSC® C105338
www.fsc.org

If you have any concerns about our products, you can contact us on
ProductSafety@springernature.com

In case Publisher is established outside the EU, the EU authorized representative is:
Springer Nature Customer Service Center GmbH
Europaplatz 3, 69115 Heidelberg, Germany

Printed by Libri Plureos GmbH
in Hamburg, Germany